MILITARY ORDER OF

Editors: Ben H. Willingham

75th
Anniversary
Edition

MILITARY ORDER OF THE STARS AND BARS

75th Anniversary Edition - 2013

Table of Content

Preface and Acknowledgements

This anniversary book is the work of many people. The former leaders of the Order have proved invaluable insight into their respective administrations and many members have sent in biographies of their ancestors. Our Commander General has been maintaining the files on our ancestors and has proved their service to insure any and all errors have been eradicated. It was the database of ancestors that set the stage for our theme, "Seventy-five years of heritage." When you study the war, you cannot help but wonder how our ancestors found the motivation to carry on for four long years without adequate food, clothing, shelter, ammunition and almost any other necessity of life. They surely believed in their cause; they had to know it was right and just. We, their descendants, need to honor and remember their sacrifice and service by making sure the truth is known and told at every possible venue. The political forces in this country driven by the liberal left are doing all possible to eradicate our history and heritage; they want us to believe our ancestors were monsters whereas in fact, they were the ones who created this wonderful country and made the United States truly UNITED. Now is the time for our voices to be heard. Stand up and support our heritage, support your ancestors in this time of need for if you don't, they and what they died for will soon be forgotten.

A special thanks to the Museum of Southern History in Jacksonville, FL for the research on articles for this book. Thanks to the numerous contributors of articles for this work. Our editor, Jeff Sizemore, deserves our thanks for his tireless work in arranging the articles and text into a useable manuscript. We owe our Commander General, Toni Turk, thanks for having the vision to push this Anniversary Book project to completion.

Ben H. Willingham
Historian General
Chairman, Anniversary Book Committee
February 28, 2013

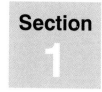

Greetings and Biographies

Messages from the General Executive & Staff Officers

On behalf of the General Executive Officers of the Military Order of the Stars and Bars, it is with great pleasure that this 75th Anniversary Book is now a reality. As you will read in chapter 1 of this Anniversary Book, each of your officers has taken the time to greet you the member.

Message from the Commander General

Gentlemen of the Order,

The 75th Anniversary Book is the first anniversary book produced since the 65th Anniversary Book in 2003 – during the administration of Jeffery Wayne Massey 2002-2004. During the interim, a watershed event was the separation of the Order from the Sons of Confederate Veterans in 2006 and its re-emergence as a wholly independent heritage group – a return to the status that it had for the first fifteen years of its existence. The Pre-SCV period included the first three administrations. The SCV period occupied the next twenty-seven administrations. Mine is the fourth administration since the SCV split. Details of the first twenty-nine administrations were covered in earlier anniversary books. The administrations completed since 2003 are:

- 2004-2006   Daniel Wilbur Jones
- 2006-2008   Philip Herbert Law
- 2008-2010   Dr. Charles Anthony Hodges
- 2010-2012   Max Lee Waldrop, Jr.

Over 7700 men have joined the Order in the past seventy-five years. Twenty percent of that number is currently active; one third is deceased; and nearly half are inactive. A goal has been set for our 75th anniversary year to increase the active membership to 2000 by the end of 2013. We can do that through reactivating just ten percent of those who have previously stood in our ranks. As a first step we have direct-mailed nearly 3500 former members of the Order with an invitation to return. As a second effort we have furnished our Society leadership with the contact information for those former members residing within their boundaries with encouragement for chapter and society fellowship efforts.

In the first eight months of my term as Commander General the following events have transpired:

- The completion of the computerization of the membership records of the Order – a six year undertaking;
- The beginning of the digitization of the records of the Order by Family Search in Independence, Missouri;
- The GEC's passage of one-man/one-vote for our annual conventions;
- The re-engrossing of the Order's Bylaws;
- The inauguration of the Colorado Society;
- The establishment of the "Sesquicentennial News" which appears daily at www.statsandbarsblog.org
- The production of the 75th Anniversary Book.

This year marks the Sesquicentennial of the high-water mark of the Confederacy. We honor those who served in positions of command in the Confederacy by keeping the memories of their service alive. That message is coordinated through our publications and our website. At the individual level we honor our relatives whose Confederate service has been vetted. A listing of nearly 5200 qualifying leaders of the Confederacy is enumerated in the concluding pages of this anniversary book. I extend my personal appreciation to every Compatriot of the Order for the individual effort to honor our dead

Thanks,

Toni Turk
Commander General

Message from the Lt. Commander General

Happy Birthday!

What a milestone! It has been 75 years since our founding back in 1938. One has to wonder who might read this book 50 years, or even 75 years from now. I expect that the Order will be thriving at that time, but we cannot take that for granted. We need to take steps today to protect that future vision.

One of my first assignments as Lt. Commander General was to become the Chairman of our Membership Committee. This is a very challenging assignment because of the changing demographics of our society. Consider that we are an aging population. The last of the baby-boomers was born in 1964. This last group of "boomers" will be 50 years old next year. Beyond that point the percentage of younger Americans will get smaller and smaller for the foreseeable future.

Many of the organizations that our fathers loved are now threatened with falling membership, or even extinction. That is a probable outcome for those organizations that remain complacent. To offset that threat we need to aggressively recruit new members and build a solid membership base for the future.

Our greatest potential for new members is thru other heritage groups. These groups contain members who have already demonstrated their appreciation and love for their heritage. These individuals are tailor made for our organization. We just need to identify these folks and reach out to them.

We are currently engaged in a mailing to approximately 2,000 individuals who we believe are qualified for MOS&B membership. Of course, we won't get all of them as new members but we should have a success rate of at least 5-10%. As we proceed with the mailing we will also list all of these individuals according to their state of residence. This will allow Membership Expeditors to conduct a secondary recruitment at the state level.

We need to identify Membership Expeditors in every State. These individuals should make the initial contact with every prospective member. They also need to help that person get thru the application process. All too often prospective members get bogged down and discouraged by this process. Our Expeditors should help them fill out the application and assist them in getting service records, census records, and inexpensive birth and death certificate copies online.

Over 8,000 individuals have joined the Order since its founding in 1938. Over 3,000 of these former members are still alive and have simply drifted away from us. They stopped paying their dues and became inactive on our rolls. We intend to have a conversation with each and every one of these individuals as well.

Again, we are interested in identifying Membership Expeditors in every State. If you are interested in this position we would like to hear from you. Now is the time for all of us to stand shoulder-to-shoulder in defense of our heritage. Together we can make a difference by expanding our membership. Please join me in this vital effort. Deo Vindice.

Sincerely,

Wm. Howard Jones
Lt. Commander General

Message from the Adjutant General

The Military Order of the Stars and Bars has 1,509 active members as of October of 2012, although the membership continues to face declining numbers. This is 148 members less than in June of 2009 and forty less than July of 2011. The current median member age has also increased by one year to 65. Our youngest member is 13 and our oldest 100.

The MOS&B is the only Confederate heritage society that is actually founded by Confederate officers. On August 30, 1938, in Columbia, South Carolina a group of surviving Confederate officers felt a duty to recognize, acknowledge and preserve the contribution of the Confederate leadership and thus formed the "Order of the Stars & Bars." The realization that the memory of their sacrifice to a worthy cause was about to be lost through the passing of their comrades and the written distortions of the history books, these dedicated men established our distinguished organization. As the ranks diminished it was placed upon the sons and grandsons of the organization to perverse their memory so as death and sacrifice was not futile. We have just transcended through another Presidential election, which is 152 years after the election that ignited a war and the culture of misunderstanding this period of history has been greatly augmented through time. We must educate the masses and recruit to preserve our heritage. Thirty-five of our compatriots have made a full commitment to our cause by becoming life members over the past year, although our new members have decreased by eighteen in the same span to 84.

We now have MOS&B members in 42 states, to include the District of Columbia and seven states with memberships of 100 or more with Texas having the furthermost of 224. We also have compatriots in seven foreign countries, although our active chapters have declined to 82, two less than in 2011. Our listserv has continued to improve over the last four years from 785 in 2009 to 912 in 2012; this is 61% of our membership. Overall, the numbers are declining slightly and the median age of 65 is of great concern for the longevity of our organization. There is presently a vigorous effort to invite over 3,500 inactive members back to the Order and LCG Howard Jones is recruiting SCV members who have the same commitment to their heritage. The goal is to achieve 2,000 new members in 2013. Although, this is a temporary solution to the aging Order as we are confronted with seeking recruitment for the next generation of great-grandsons to fill our ranks.
In conclusion: It is with immense honor that I serve the descendants of the Confederate Officers Corps and I look forward to working with you to strengthen our Southern heritage for our ancestral brethren.

William L. Caynor Sr.
Adjutant General

Message from the Communication General

The MOS&B is noted for its use of the communications media available to it. From early use of e-mail contacts and teleconferencing to use of the full internet services available today our organization continues to take advantage of all intra-organization communications methods.

The upgraded and outstanding web site provides quick and easy access to all our programs, goals, staff, etc. for both MOS&B members and interested non-members.

The on-line store offers a professional site for members to shop and buy our merchandise, thus contributing to the income of the Order and assisting in funding such programs as the Scholarships and the Literary Awards.
The Officer's Call newsletter is published eleven times a year, three copies of which are printed and eight are issued electronically. In November of each year the Confederate War Journal magazine is printed and sent to all current members.

To ensure almost instantaneous two-way communications between Leadership and members the Headquarters "listserv" provides a method to reach all members who have a recorded e-mail address. In addition the addresses of all staff members are available on the web site and any member can contact any one of them as they need to.

As Communications General I have the privilege of reviewing virtually all forms of the Order's correspondence and I am proud to say that the MOS&B is abreast of and using all the most modern techniques to the advantage of all our members.

Respectfully submitted,

Gary M. Loudermilk, DCS
Communications General

Message from the Quartermaster General

The following events have occurred during my tenure as the Quartermaster General of the MOS&B:

- Transitioning from traditional mail order shopping to a digital PayPal on-line store.
- Sales in excess of $2000 at our 2012 San Antonio Convention.
- Reducing actual inventory and having suppliers directly ship items to our customers.
- Adding new purchase options on certain items.
- Adding new items to the store.
- Liquidation of non-selling inventory.

I'd like to thank everyone for their assistance and support!

Robert W. Turk
Quartermaster General

Message from the Chaplain General

This year, the Military Order of the Stars and Bars, continues to celebrate the sesquicentennial and our rebirth in 1938. In this celebration of our history is the recognition and honoring of our spiritual roots of our beloved southland. The Chaplaincy Corp of the Confederate Army was deeply incorporated with a standard of one chaplain per regiment or every ten companies. The Confederate

Chaplain was typically from the professional clergy and drawn throughout the South. Most of them had been pastors of thriving churches across the southland. Almost all of our MOS&B chapters also have appointed Chaplains who serve our Compatriots. I am exceedingly proud to be the Chaplain General of the Military Order of the Stars and Bars, appointed by our Commander General Toni Turk. I am following in the chaplaincy linage of not only previous chaplain generals, and this is also our way of honoring the chaplains who served our compatriots in the Confederate army in the war against northern aggression.

As was stated previously, the standard was to have one chaplain per regiment or every ten companies of troops. The Chaplains of the Confederate Army were evangelical chaplains spreading the Word of God to all servicemen who would listen, but also just as fervent for the southern cause of independence. Often, these patriotic chaplains took up the arms of the fallen and fought beside their men. Such a man was the Reverend Isaac Taylor Tichenor, who was a renowned sharpshooter also as he was adept with the Sword of the Spirit (the Word of God). Reverend Tickenor was just an example of one minister of the Gospel whose fervency in the heat and fog of battle overtook him. Most of these Confederate Chaplains returned to the communities from whence they came and continued their ministries in the pulpits of churches across the southland. One result over a period of many decades after the war was that the evangelical churches became more deeply rooted in their culture of being a distinct part of the United States. Thus we today recognize this as our southern gospel in not only our music, but also our more fundamental theology and proclamation. We embrace as part of us, all the various Christian Faiths, from our Pentecostal brothers to our Catholic brothers. All this is very much embedded into our present day chaplaincy corps. We in the south have imbedded in our souls a belief in God and Country.

I am thankful for the privilege of carrying on this distinctly southern chaplaincy tradition as the Chaplain General in our beloved Military Order of the Stars and Bars. A question I ask myself and maybe you do also is: knowing that our purpose for southern independence was right, why did God allow our defeat? I lean toward the understanding of how our God acts in history in that this had to be God's providential way for us as a people of the United States of America, and celebrating our way of life as Southerners.

Raymond Holder

Chaplain General

Biographies of the General Executive Officers

The biographies herein give a brief description and accomplishments of the General Executive Officers of the Military Order of the Stars and Bars. These individuals have contributed their time and resources well beyond what they have modesty described herein. We commend them for their service to the Order and to their communities.

Toni Turk – Commander General (2012-2014)

My great-great-grandfather, James Wesley Merritt, enlisted February 28, 1861, at Rome, Georgia, as a private in Co. C, 1st Georgia Regulars. His unit was dispatched to the Army of Northern Virginia, where he participated in the Seven Days Battle from June 25 to July 1, 1862. He received medical attention at Chimborazo Hospital in Richmond. On August 26, 1862, he was transferred to the 1st Battalion Virginia Mounted Rifles. In December his new unit was designated the 34th Battalion Virginia Cavalry. He was elected as a 2nd Lieutenant with Company D and served with this unit until it disbanded in Lynchburg, Virginia, in April 1865 – having been active in the Shenandoah Valley, following their return from the Battle of Gettysburg. After his unit laid down its arms a detachment of Union soldiers had him hold his left hand against a tree and shot a Minié ball through it, maiming him for life, with the statement that it was in payment for his serving as the officer of his detachment, which had raised arms against the Union. His two brothers were also lieutenants – one serving with the Forrest Escort and the other with the 65th Georgia Infantry. In December 1865 James Merritt and his new bride left Georgia to escape Reconstruction and headed for Texas. When they left, his family told him that if ever ran into trouble to tell people that his uncle was Orrin Beck of Tippah County, Mississippi, and his cousin was General Nathan Bedford Forrest. It was my privilege to hear these stories from his granddaughter, who had heard them directly from her grandfather.

Career: I graduated with a Master's degree in Southern History from Midwestern University in Wichita Falls, Texas. This was followed with postgraduate work in a number of universities, and finally a doctorate from BYU. I served as a Russian linguist with the US Army Security Agency during the Berlin Wall and Cuban Missile Crises and then as an aerial photography interpreter with the Defense Intelligence Agency during the Vietnam War. My professional career spanned forty-two years in education. I am currently the Mayor of Blanding, Utah – a position that I have held for the past eight years.

I joined the MOS&B in June 1969 as member number 654, and became a charter member of both the Texas Chapter and the Texas Society. My National service began in 2008 when I was selected to serve as Adjutant General under Past Commander General Anthony Hodges. I was honored to continue service in that role under Past Commander General Max Waldrop, who also tasked me with the assignment of Genealogist General. I am an Emeritus Accredited Genealogist for the Southern States, having first been accredited in 1970. My selection to serve as the Commander General from 2012 to 2014 is a signal honor. I have recruited a team of highly motivated and accomplished men to serve with me. I am absolutely confident that your new leadership team will serve our Order well. I am committed to be a synergistic and working Commander General. With your support together we can ensure the longevity of the Military Order of the Stars and Bars.

William Howard Jones – Lt. Commander General (2012-2014)

Howard Jones is a Marine Corps veteran and a graduate of the University of Oregon. He recently retired from the business world after 48 years as an entrepreneur in the battery industry. He is looking forward to serving both our Commander General and the members of the Order in his new position.

Howard has distinguished himself as a member of the Order and through his participation in various heritage groups. He is the founder and the current Commander of the California Society. He is also as an ATM Executive Councilor and a member of the GEC.

For twelve years Howard served as a Commissioner on San Mateo County's Local Agency Formation Commission. He is a three-time former President of the Peninsula Civil War Round Table. He is also a former President of the Silicon Valley Chapter, Sons of the American Revolution.

Howard's primary concern is the preservation of our heritage. Current demographics create considerable challenges for all heritage organizations. He is determined to do whatever is needed to assure that our ancestors – and the cause that they fought for – are remembered for future generations. In this regard, Howard frequently speaks to other heritage organizations on the subject.

Howard and his wife, Cathy, will celebrate their 50th wedding anniversary next year. They have two daughters and three granddaughters. Howard brings a wealth of experience and enthusiasm to the Order. He looks forward to the challenges ahead.

William L. Caynor – Adjutant General (2012-2014)

William Caynor is an Army & Air Force veteran and holds three degrees from separate institutions to include a BA in History from the University of Alaska. He is presently an Operations Manager for an electric utility in Steamboat Springs, Colorado and is anxious to serve the new Commander General and the Order.

William has dedicated his life to preserving the remembrance of our gallant southern heritage by researching and writing the stories that few entertain through the history books. He is currently authoring his third book on the subject and has written numerous articles. He has been a member of the Order since 2005, serving first as a Chapter Adjutant and then as a National Aide-de-Camp, Historian General and is presently the Provisional Commander of the Colorado Society of MOS&B.

William is also a devout member of the Son of Confederate Veterans and the Sons of the American Revolution and is descended from more than twenty-five ancestors who served during the Second War for Independence.

William is a believer in educating the masses of the true reasoning's for the war and our ancestors' sacrifices illustrated through their dedication in a noble cause. In order for this to be successful, social organizations such as the MOS&B must thrive to preserve the recorded memories. Without this, history and these reminiscences will be lost through time. We must find ways for retention and attraction of the Order to multiply the membership and educate the public for the preservation and survival of our heritage.

William and his wife, Dawn, have been married for twenty-eight years and have two children. He brings a wealth of knowledge and experience to the Order as well as professionally and is honored and eager to serve as a representative of the Order and of his southern ancestry.

Sigmund Joseph Reckline, Jr., PhD – Chief of Staff

Sigmund is a native of Baltimore, Maryland. He was an electronic warfare systems specialist honorably discharged from the U.S. Air Force as a Cold War veteran. Ever since, he has pursued a career as a consultant to the commercial nuclear industry. He has worked on many world-class, time-driven projects over the years in project management and engineering specializing in instrumentation & controls and electrical.

Sigmund has earned a Doctor of Philosophy in Leadership for Higher Education from Capella University, a Doctor of Philosophy in Business from Madison University, a Master of Business Administration from the University of Notre Dame, a Bachelor of Science from Siena Heights University, and a Bachelor of Arts from West Virginia University. Much of his graduate educational pursuits have been focused on Leadership, Organizational Behavior, and Strategy.

He served as President of the South Potomac Forest Property Owners' Association and as a member of the Board of Directors for Power One Federal Credit Union. He is a published author and former President of Global Transitions Publishing Company. He has been honored as a Distinguished Professor by Mu Nu Chapter of Phi Theta Kappa International Honor Society and is a member of Alpha Sigma Lambda National Honor Society. He is also a member of the Royal Order of Scotland.

In his spare time, he has been an adjunct instructor for several colleges and universities. He was instrumental in developing the Bachelor of Applied Science in Nuclear Technology degree program for Siena Heights University. He also worked at improving academic success for Clemson University in 2006 through 2008 academic years.

Sigmund is active in several hereditary societies. He is a devout but ecumenical Christian. He is the Herald of the Priory of Saint Matthew in San Antonio, Texas (Sovereign Military Order of the Temple of Jerusalem) and has been recommended for Deputy Grand Herald of the Grand Priory USA.

His primary focus with the Military Order of the Stars and Bars is to help the other Officers and the organization become even more successful. He sees current trends robbing younger generations of their identities by spinning hereditary societies as something "elitist" and negative. He feels we cannot preserve our heritage and honor what our ancestors believed in and fought for if we cannot convince our youths that they are beneficiaries of that legacy. He has three grown sons and three grandchildren. He lives with his wife and daughter.

Charles Thomas Boardman – Judge Advocate General

Tom is a Vietnam veteran and was a Captain in the Marine Corps. He holds a Bachelor of Arts in U.S. History from the University of California at Irvine and a Juris Doctorate from Northwestern School of Law. He has been a sole practitioner in Portland Oregon for twenty nine years.

He is the lead attorney in Webber vs. First Student et al., in the U.S. District Court for Oregon, representing a school bus driver, the father of four small children, fired solely for refusing to remove a Confederate battle flag from his private vehicle.

Tom has identified over 180 blood relatives who served the Confederacy. His qualifying ancestor is Captain Byrd S. Newman, Company "I", 51st Tennessee Infantry. In addition to Captain Newman, Tom is related to Lieutenant Generals A.P. Hill, James T. Longstreet, Richard Taylor and Leonidas Polk, Major General James Johnston Pettigrew, Brigadier General States Rights Gist, Lieutenant Colonels John Pelham, and Walter Taylor. Notable Confederate civilians include Sarah Knox Taylor, first wife of President Jefferson Davis, and noted Secessionists David V. Stokely, William Henry Gist and Henry Stuart Foote.

He is also a member of the Sons of the American Revolution, the Descendants of Point Lookout, the Sons of Confederate Veterans, the Sons of Union Veterans of the Civil War and holds life memberships in the Disabled American Veterans, and the Military Order of the Purple Heart.

Conway Bagwell Moncure – Treasurer General

Conway is a Certified Public Accountant who practiced public accounting in Virginia and North Carolina for over 30 years before he retired, and was also a securities dealer and investment advisor for a national securities brokerage firm.

As a graduate of Virginia Tech, with a major in accounting, his professional background includes being an adjunct professor of accounting for Wake Technical and Southside Virginia Community Colleges. He is a 32nd degree Mason and has held positions with The Grand Lodge of Virginia.

Conway's military service in the army includes being the Chief Subsistence Officer at Aberdeen Proving Ground and Edgewood Arsenal, Captain and a Reserve Company Commander at Ft. Lee, Virginia.

He is currently an employee and volunteer for The Museum of the Confederacy in Richmond, VA, and gives guided tours of the White House of the Confederacy. His membership in Confederate causes includes being a life member of the SCV, General Longstreet Camp, and the MOS&B General George Pickett Chapter, of which he is the current commander.

He is a member of the White House Association in Montgomery, Al., and has received the UDC National Defense Medal and the Confederate Memorial Chapel Medal.

Conway's great grandfather was 2nd Lt. Eustace Conway Moncure, Co. B, 9th Virginia Calvary, and was a scout for General Robert E. Lee in the Great War. He is proud to be associated with the Order and has pledged to use his talents to enhance and enlarge its presence.

Listing of Past Commanders-in-Chiefs and Commander Generals

Past Commanders-in-Chief: Residences:

1.	1938-1945	Homer Atkinson	(1848-1945)	Virginia
2.	1945-1948	Dr. Capt. George Bolling Lee	(1872-1948)	New York
3.	1948-1953	Lt. Walter Scott Hancock	(1869-1959)	Missouri
4.	1953-1954	Dr. Maj. William Remshart Dancy	(1877-1960)	Georgia
5.	1954-1957	Donald Bain Todd	(1876-1958)	Tennessee
6.	1957-1959	James Kyle Senter	(1912-1996)	Tennessee
7.	1959-1961	Alvis Ildefonse Downs, Jr.	(1921-2012)	Tennessee
8.	1961-1963	Frank Everett Larue, Jr	(1933-2002)	Texas
9.	1963-1964	Col. John Amasa May	(1908-1976)	South Carolina
10.	1964-1966	Tom White Crigler, Jr.	(1897-1986)	Mississippi
11.	1966-1968	Stanley Wayne Van Zandt	(1926-1984)	Arkansas
12.	1968-1970	Dr. James MacDonald Edwards	(1930-2001)	Georgia
13.	1970-1972	H Paul Porter	(1912-1983)	Virginia
14.	1972-1974	Dr. Laurence Michael Oden	(1918-2000)	Mississippi
15.	1974-1976	Dennis Wayne Rainoshek	(1935-)	Texas
16.	1976-1978	Col. Lindsey Patterson Henderson, Jr.	(1922-2001)	Georgia
17.	1978-1980	Dr. Ralph William Widener, Jr.	(1922-2011)	Texas
18.	1980-1982	John E. Hunter	(1923-1999)	Texas
19.	1982-1984	Ronald Turner Clemmons	(1947-)	Tennessee
20.	1984-1986	Mark Lea (Beau) Cantrell	(1951-)	Oklahoma
21.	1986-1988	John L Echols, Sr.	(1941-)	Mississippi
22.	1988-1990	Edward Overton Cailleteau	(1945-)	Louisiana
23.	1990-1992	Robert Lewis Hawkins, III	(1951-)	Tennessee
24.	1992-1994	Charles Herbert Smith	(1934-)	Oklahoma
25.	1994-1996	Perry James Outlaw	(1941-)	Alabama

Past Commander Generals:

26.	1996-1998	James Troy Massey	(1955-)	Arkansas
27.	1998-2000	Josiah Bynum (Joe) Gay, III	(1929-2012)	Virginia
28.	2000-2002	Albert Dean Jones, Jr.	(1946-)	North Carolina
29.	2002-2004	Jeffery Wayne Massey	(1962-)	Oklahoma North
30.	2004-2006	Daniel Wilbur Jones	(1928-)	Carolina
31.	2006-2008	Philip Herbert Law	(1948-)	Alabama
32.	2008-2010	Dr. Charles Anthony Hodges	(1954-)	Tennessee
33.	2010-2012	Max Lee Waldrop, Jr.	(1954-)	Tennessee

Edward Overton Cailleteau – Past Commander-In-Chief (1988-1990)

Edward Overton Cailleteau was born on December 15, 1945 in Baton Rouge, Louisiana. He is the son of the late Dr. and Mrs. Edward Grant Cailleteau and grandson of the late Dr. and Mrs. Ralph C. Cailleteau and the late U.S. Senator and Mrs. John Holmes Overton, all of Alexandria, Louisiana.

He was educated in the public schools of East Baton Rouge Parish with the exception of one year at Jefferson Military College, Washington, MS. He graduated from Louisiana State University with a B.S. degree in 1970. He majored in History.

In 1974 he married the former Virginia Riggs of Mobile, a member of UDC on the Record of her great-grandfather, Reuben Riggs, Co. A, 1st Maryland Cavalry. Reuben Riggs' cousin, Joshua Warfield Riggs, was a member of Co. B, 43rd Virginia Partisan Rangers, under the command of Col. John Singleton Mosby. They have one daughter, Virginia Kathleen, a member of the UDC and formerly a member of the CofC.

Cailleteau joined SCV and MOS&B in 1979. Originally a member of Headquarters Camp 584 and the General Society, MOS&B, he assisted in the organization of the Louisiana Society, MOS&B and affiliated with the Francis T. Nicholls Camp No. 1362 in Baton Rouge. Cailleteau was instrumental in the organization of SCV Camps in New Orleans, Lafayette and Monroe, and MOS&B Chapters in New Orleans, Baton Rouge and Lafayette. He transferred his SCV membership to the Colonel Charles D. Dreux Camp No. 110 in New Orleans in 1986. He is a member of the Maj. Gen. Earl Van Dorn Chapter, MOS&B, also in New Orleans.

In MOS&B, Cailleteau was Commander-in-Chief (1988-90); Commander of the Trans-Mississippi Department (1985-86); Chief of Staff (1984-86); Parliamentarian (1986-88); Commander, Louisiana Society (1980-83); and Adjutant, Louisiana Society (1979-80 and 1989-present).

In SCV, Cailleteau has served as Commander, Army of the Trans-Mississippi Department (1986-88); Commander, Louisiana Division (1984-86); and Adjutant, Louisiana Division (1986-88). He has served as Parliamentarian of the SCV under five Commanders-in-Chief and, as acting Parliamentarian under two Commanders-in-Chief. Cailleteau was put in the Chair by the-then CIC, SCV William D. Hogan and presided over the General Convention in Columbus, GA in 1991 when the motion was made, discussed and voted on to purchase Elm Springs at Columbia, TN to serve as the Permanent Headquarters.

Cailleteau established the Louisiana *True Delta* Division newsletter and edited same from 1984 to 1986 and again from 1995 to 2001.

Cailleteau is a member of Society of the Cincinnati in the State of Virginia, Sons of the American Revolution, Sons of the Revolution, Society of Colonial Wars, Society of the War of 1812, Society of the Founders of the City of New Orleans, Society of the Sons and Daughters of the Pilgrims, Royal Society of St. George, First Families of Tennessee and Founders of Old Mobile Society.

Robert L. Hawkins, III – Past Commander-In-Chief (1990-1992)

Robert L. Hawkins, III, was born in Randolph County, Missouri on April 7, 1951. He was educated at Westminster College, Central Missouri State University, and the University of Missouri - School of Law. He is a member of the M. M. Parson SCV Camp # 718 and the Marmaduke MOS&B Chapter; as well as, being a life member of both. Along with being MOS&B Commander-In-Chief, he was also the SCV Commander-in-Chief (1992-1994). He is also a member of the Society of the

Southern Cross, Forrest Cavalry Corps, Morgan's Men's Association, and the Confederate Historical Association of Belgium.

Robert L. Hawkins, III, is also the recipient of the following awards: O'Connor Missouri Silver Star (1995), Robert E. Lee Chalice (1993), Jefferson Davis Chalice (1994), George Graham Vest Oratorical (1995), John Randolph of Roanoke Oratorical (1995). He directed the funerals of W. C. Quantill (1992) and Jesse James (1995).

Charles Herbert Smith – Past Commander-In-Chief (1992-1994)

Charles Herbert Smith was born October 12, 1934 in Sebetha, KS. He grew up in central Oklahoma where his grandfather had homesteaded in 1889. He graduated from Oklahoma State University, 1958, with a bachelor of fine arts. He was head of the Graphics Department for the FAA and retired in October 1988. He formed and currently operates his own company, CSA Graphic Communicators, Yukon, OK. His military service was with the 13th Cavalry, 1st Armored Division, United States Army.

He married Carolyn Holliman in 1967. He has two children, Charles Michael Burton and Michelle Elizabeth Susan. He enjoys firearms, hunting, re-enactment and speaking.

Smith became a charter member of the Brigadier General Stand Watie Camp #1303 in February 1970 and was later elected to two terms as Oklahoma Division Commander (1989 & 1990). Other offices include Commander, Trans-Mississippi Dept.; SCV Chief of Staff; and Commander-In-Chief. In 1978, he organized the Brigadier General Douglas H. Cooper MOS&B Chapter and was elected their first Chapter Commander. He was elected Lieutenant Commander-In-Chief and Commander-In-Chief. His MOS&B awards include the Robert E. Lee Chalice, Gold Award, Distinguished Service Medal and Meritorious Service Medal.

He established the *Rebel Yell,* monthly newsletter for Camp 1303. It is currently the oldest camp newsletter in the SCV. As Department Commander, he assisted Col. Joseph B. Mitchell in re-writing the SCV Constitution and again later for the MOS&B. As Commander-In-Chief, he led an aggressive campaign to establish a national headquarters and directed re-establishment of the *Confederate Veteran* publication for the membership. He designed the General Staff Medal for SCV.

Perry J. Outlaw – Past Commander-In-Chief (1994-1996)

Perry James Outlaw was born August 19, 1941 in Jackson, Alabama. He received his BS degree in 1963 and his MA in 1965 from Auburn University. He joined the Raphael Semmes Camp II SCV, Mobile, Alabama in 1972 and joined the Franklin Buchanan MOS&B Chapter # 2297, Mobile, Alabama in 1983.

The offices he had held include: Chapter-Editor, Adjutant, Commander; Society – Editor, Adjutant, Lt. Commander, Commander; Army – Lt. Commander, Commander; and National – Lt. Commander-In-Chief, and Commander-In-Chief. His MOS&B Awards include the Distinguished Commander Status, AOT Gold Star Award (1994), and the Robert E. Lee Chalice (1996).

Through his leadership and the assistance of many individuals, the following for the Order were accomplished during his administration. Refer to the list of accomplishments by Commander Outlaw on page 9 of the MOS&B 60th Anniversary Book that was published in 1998.

Perry J. Outlaw is married to Harriet B. Outlaw and they have six children along with many grandchildren. He has been a teacher, coach, and school administrator and retired in 1992 with 29 years of service. He has also retired from the Alabama National Guard with 21 years of service. He is also a member of the United Methodist Church.

James Troy Massey – Past Commander General (1996-1998)

A native of Searcy County, Arkansas, he was born in 1955 in Harrison, Arkansas. He has resided in Harrison since 1977 with his wife, Beverly. Their daughter, Whitney, is a graduate of the University of Arkansas, and resides in Fayetteville with her husband, Bo, and son, Wyatt Troy. Graduating from Arkansas Tech University in Russellville, Arkansas in 1977 with a Bachelor of Science Degree in Parks and Recreation Administration, he deviated from his college degree and veered into the insurance industry. He retired as a Senior Claims Representative for Arkansas Farm Bureau Insurance Company with thirty-four years of service in December 2011. He organized the General Patrick R Cleburne, Arkansas Society, MOS&B, in 1983 and served as its first commander. Later he served as Commander-General of the national organization in 1998-2000. There have been several offices he has served through the years and numerous awards received, the highest being the Lee Chalice. In 2004 he organized the United Sons of Confederate Soldiers Association-Arkansas for those who did not have a Confederate officer or government official. Volunteerism is of high importance as he has served as Past Governor of the Missouri-Arkansas Kiwanis District and Past Board Chairman of the North Arkansas College trustees. Historically, he is a Past President of the Arkansas Society, Sons of the American Revolution, receiving the Patriot medal and Past President of the Boone County Historical Society. He is a life member of the Scottish Rite, York Rite bodies and two Masonic lodges. He presently serves as Secretary/Treasurer of the Ozark Shrine Club in Harrison. Razorback football and baseball; St. Louis Cardinals baseball; and Dallas Cowboy football rank as his favorite sporting events. With the addition of a new grandson in 2012, he has added being with his grandson as another enjoyable hobby.

While as Commander-General he laid out his goals of better communication with the membership. He asked Dan Jones and eventual Commander-General, to research and publish the 60th Anniversary Edition of the MOS&B. Commander Jones did an excellent job in his research and final product. Commander Massey wanted the societies to work on five projects. The first was to research and submit their "Top 100 Books of the Confederacy." This effort was completed and published with good results. The second challenge was to research each Confederate flag in their society whether of their state or other Confederate states. This completed project was submitted to the Museum of the Confederacy as part of their legacy in maintaining and preserving hundreds of Confederate flags. They completed their book on all of the Confederate flags in their possession and our MOS&B flag project added to their vast arsenal of knowledge on all known Confederate flags. Thirdly, each society was asked to contact all of their Real Sons and interview them on video or audio. The interview consisted of asking them questions about their Confederate father and also of their own personal history. It was a huge success and very involved for those participating and gathering this precious information. Those videos were turned over to MOS&B HQ in Elm Springs and never located when the MOS&B inventory was transferred after the dissolution. Fourthly, he envisioned a MOS&B Tour of a battlefield site and historic area. Collin Pulley was chosen to lead in this endeavor. The HQ was Virginia but Harper's Ferry and Sharpsburg were visited on tour buses during the daytime. In the evening several great speakers on the WBTS in that area spoke of the battles and campaigns. Everyone had a great time. He remembers all the cigars that Commander Dan Jones and he smoked during those tours and after dinner in the evening. The fifth project was a MOS&B Commemorative coin celebrating 65 years of the Order and used as a fund raiser.

He traveled to many states for several events. Each society was unique and very courteous in greeting the CG. There are untold memories and new friends that were made on those journeys. One event that he remembered fondly was at Gettysburg for their 135th anniversary, was inducting into the MOS&B, two descendants of Generals Pickett and Longstreet. The Longstreet Monument was dedicated that weekend and the reason that his descendant grandson, Mr. Patterson, was present. On Saturday, he had the honor of inducting George Pickett V. They lined up at the Virginia Monument to begin the induction. Present in this contingent was Virginia MOSB members and later CG Albert Jones and his lady, Denise, plus Ed Bearrs. Ed asked if we would be interested in going to the exact location where General Pickett gave the order for the Virginians to come out of the tree line onto the field for the charge. They all followed Ed to the location, in his opinion, of the order. So on the spot or nearby, Pickett was inducted into the MOS&B where his Gr-Gr-Gr-Gr Grandfather gave the order to move out and form the line of battle.

Commander Massey had the pleasure of going to conventions and events in Indian Territory, Missouri, Louisiana, Texas, Florida, North Carolina, Virginia, Alabama, Mississippi, Georgia and Tennessee. His fundraising chairman was Lt. Commander Joe Gay, who did a fantastic job in selling MOS&B items. They would laugh through the years of Joe's story that he sold MOS&B merchandise out of the back of his car at funerals. He was a great salesman. These are just a few of my memories of a great experience of two years as MOSB Commander-General. On a historical note, the title of Commander-General was bestowed upon my office in 1998. It was voiced by PCIC Lindsey Henderson during the business session that he wanted the Commander-General title to be re-instated instead of Commander-in-Chief, to differentiate us from our sister organization. It passed with Lindsey's influence.

Josiah Bynum (Joe) Gay, III – Past Commander General (1998-2000)

Josiah Bynum Gay, III, 82, a lifelong resident of Franklin and a true Southern Gentleman, passed away on July 16, 2012. Mr. Gay was a son of the late Josiah B. Gay, Jr. and Lois Hartman Gay and was a member of Emmanuel Episcopal Church. He was an Eagle Scout and a Navy veteran and was educated at Virginia Polytechnic Institute and Richmond Professional Institute. After retiring from Union Camp Corp., Joe established Franklin Lumber Sales.

As Commander-General of the Military Order of the Stars and Bars, Joe created the Jackson Medal to recognize those who were caretakers of Confederate grave sites. He was also a Past Commander of the George Pickett MOS&B Chapter and the Virginia Society of the MOS&B. He was instrumental in the formation of the Urquhart-Gillette Camp of the Sons of Confederate Veterans and was a Past Commander. He was also active in the Scottish Rite of Freemasonry, Nobles of the Mystic Shrine and the Sons of the American Revolution. He was a member of the Southampton Historical Society, the Henry Lee Society, the Stuart-Mosby Society, the Order of the Southern Cross, and the National Gavel Society.

Left to cherish his memory are his wife of 54 years, Anne Franklin Gay, one daughter, Ferreby G. Sinclair and her husband Steve and their daughter Ansley of San Gabriel, CA, and one son, Ashby Lee Gay of Richmond, VA. The memorial service was held at 2 p.m., Thursday, July 19, 2012 at Emmanuel Episcopal Church with the Rev. Edmund Pickup officiating.

Albert Dean Jones, Jr. – Past Commander General (2000-2002)

Albert Dean Jones, Jr. was born July 11, 1946 in Henderson, NC, and was raised in Oxford, NC. He attended East Carolina University and served in the US Marine Corps as a sergeant with a tour in Vietnam. After finishing Hardbarger Business College, he married Denise Owens. Together, they raised a son, Brian and a daughter, Kelly, while owning and managing a horse business.

Most of his career was spent in the construction business with a sideline of buying and selling US militaria; with emphasis on Marine Corps insignia.

After joining the Col. Henry King Burgwyn SCV Camp 1485 and the Capt. James I. Waddell MOS&B Chapter in 1992, he began serving both the SCV and MOS&B in the capacity of MOS&B adjutant and NCSCV Division as parliamentarian.

In 1995, after serving as NC Society Chief of Staff, he was elected NC Society Commander and served four years. After revamping the NC Society, he was elected ANV Committeeman in 1996; Lt. Commander General in 1998; and served as Commander-General in the years of 2000-2002.

Many new programs were started during his tenure, but the complete revamping of the scholarship program and the MOS&B endowment fund were his favorite programs.

His MOS&B awards include the Robert E. Lee Chalice, the Gold Star Award, the Distinguished Service Award, and the Meritorious Service Award. He also holds the title of Distinguished Commander. His SCV awards include the Distinguished Service Medal, Meritorious Service Medal and various other awards. He was awarded the Military Service medals for both MOS&B and SCV for his service in Vietnam from 1968-1969.

He is proud to be a Kentucky Colonel and a member of the Order of the Southern Cross and a member of the Sons of the American Revolution.

In service to his town and county, he has served on the board of directors for the Washington County Historical Society. He was vice-chairman of the Town of Plymouth Board of Adjustments, President of the Plymouth Downtown Development Association, along with membership in the Small Town Economic Project for the town of Plymouth.

Jeffery Wayne Massey – Past Commander General (2002-2004)

Jeff Massey was born October 15, 1962, at Marshall, Arkansas. He graduated in 1981 from Marshall High School. He graduated with Honors from the University of Arkansas in 1985 and the University of Oklahoma School of Law in 1990. He interned for the Oklahoma Department of Securities, and was the first recipient of the Carl Albert Executive Internship from the State of Oklahoma. After law school, worked for ODS as an Enforcement Attorney. Jeff's office was across the street from the Murrah Federal Building which was destroyed in the Oklahoma City Bombing of April 19, 1995. For his rescue efforts during the bombing, Jeff was awarded the Sons of the American Revolution *Medal of Heroism, the SCV's J. Edgar Hoover Law and Order Award, and the MOS&B's Law and Order Medal.*

Following the bombing, Jeff opened his own private law practice in Oklahoma City. He is a member of various Oklahoma Bar Association committees and is the General Counsel for the Oklahoma Rifle Association. He is a graduate of the Oklahoma College of Trial Advocacy and serves as a guest lecturer at the University Of Oklahoma College Of Law. He has taught Business Law, Contracts, English Legal History, Bankruptcy, and has served as an instructor for the AIPLS. He is a member of the Federal CJA Trial panels for the Western, Eastern and Northern Districts of the Federal Courts in Oklahoma. He is licensed to practice law in both Arkansas and Oklahoma.

Jeff and his children (Nicholas & Shelby) belong to the Waterloo Road Baptist Church. Jeff is the Sunday School Director, former Chairman of Deacons, serves on various committees and teaches Men's Bible Studies. Jeff is active in the Oklahoma City Civil War Roundtable, the Sons of the American Revolution and is compiling information on a future book.

Jeff was a Charter Member of the General Jo Shelby Camp #1414[SCV] and the Abner-Cone-Langston-Shaver-Wright Chapter [later the Captain James Tyrie Wright Chapter]. He served as 2nd Lieutenant Commander, 1st Lieutenant Commander and Chapter Commander. Jeff has also uniquely served as Commander of the Arkansas Society, MOS&B (1988-1990) and subsequently the Indian Territory Society (2010-Current). He also served with the Oklahoma State History Military Exhibits Committee during the construction of the Oklahoma History Center. He was instrumental along with ML Cantrell, Charles Smith and Dr. James Caster in ensuring that the Confederate Room and First National and Cherokee Braves Confederate Flags remained at the Oklahoma History Center.

Jeff is the longest serving Judge Advocate in the History of the Order and has served on the National MOS&B Staff since 1992. It was in that year that MOS&B Commander-in-Chief Charles Smith posted Jeff to the position of Deputy Judge Advocate General. In 1994, Jeff CIC Perry Outlaw appointed Massey as the Judge Advocate General. Interestingly, SCV CIC Norman Dasinger appointed Massey as JAG of the SCV during the same years. Jeff would also serve as JAG for the administrations of Troy Massey, Joe Gay, Dan Jones, Phil Law and recently PCG Max Waldrop. JAG Massey and the Constitution Committee undertook extensive drafting of the MOS&B Constitution for compliance with state, federal and corporate compliance issues.

Jeff served on the Investments Committee due to his degree in economics and history with the Oklahoma Department of Securities. He served with Col. JEB Stuart IV from 1992 through 2012, during which the value of the assets of the Order increased by X5. also served on the Investments Committee. Jeff managed the mutual fund portfolios and investment diversification.

In 2000, Massey was elected Lt. Commander General and then Commander General in 2002. During his administration the Order redoubled its efforts to reconstitute the membership rolls of previous members. Special emphasis was made on increasing the Scholarship Awards and national partnerships with other historical organizations. Massey attended MOS&B/SCV conventions in Missouri, Arkansas, Texas, Louisiana, Mississippi, Alabama, Tennessee, Georgia, Florida, North Carolina, South Carolina, Maryland and Virginia. He was the Keynote Speaker at the Alabama, Arkansas, Florida, Texas, and Oklahoma Conventions. In Virginia, he was the Jeff Davis Memorial Day Speaker at Hollywood Cemetery. He also spoke at Beauvoir during Confederate Memorial Day, staying at the famed "Hayes Cottage" before its destruction in Hurricane Katrina.

Massey also authorized the *Jefferson F. Davis Southern Heritage Award* for outstanding individuals who provided a pro-Southern action, portrayal, benefit, authorship, and production. Recipients included director Ron Maxwell and artist Mort Kunstler. Massey also developed the Confederate Legacy Endowment Fund for receiving life gifts to MOS&B. This fund was established for financial assistance for monument restoration, historical archives, and artifact acquisition.

The Books for Beauvoir Campaign was tasked with procuring over 1,000 books for the President Jefferson Davis Library at Beauvoir in Biloxi, Mississippi. The Genealogy Committee has undertaken an extensive automation of the application forms and procedures. The First Website (www.mosbihq.org) was established with 'online' forms, history, contact information and company store. His Administration also published the *65th Anniversary Book* which compiled and updated the membership rolls and history of the Order. Additionally the Order assisted in the restoration of Hilliard's Legion flag [Alabama]; restoration of the cemetery wall in Fayetteville [Arkansas]; the Jefferson Davis Memorial project in Richmond [Virginia]; donations to the Museum of Confederacy; the Gen. McCain Library; the Confederate Memorial Hall in Oklahoma City.

Massey also authorized the creation of the Confederate Officers General Staff Coin. These 'challenge-style' coins of the US Military honored CSA Generals' Forrest, SD Lee, Stand Watie, Robt E. Lee, and President Jeff Davis. Massey also The General Staff of 2002-2004 was especially adept under the leadership of Chief of Staff Curtis Hopper, K. Patrick Sohrwide, PCG Dan Jones, PCG Phil Law, PCG Dr. Anthony Hodges, Richard Knight, Esq., Dr. John Killian, Dr. Fred McNary, Rodney Williams, Russ Lenzini (webmaster); JEB Stuart IV, PCG Charles Smith, Brothers Troy, David and Sam Massey, PCG Albert Jones, PCG Joe Gay and PCG Mark Lea 'Beau' Cantrell.

Awards received include the Distinguished Commanders Status, the ATM Gold Star and the Robert E Lee Chalice and Jefferson Davis Chalice-SCV. Massey has received the Colonel John Pelham Distinguished Service Award, the Lt. Charles William Reed Meritorious Service Award, the Army of Trans Mississippi Distinguished Service Award, the Army of Trans Mississippi Meritorious Service Award. He has also received the General Thomas Hindman Award, the Patrick R. Cleburne Award, the General Stand Watie Award, the Order of the Grey Kepi and the Indian Territory Confederate Award.

Philip Herbert Law – Past Commander General (2006-2008)

Profession: He has a PhD, MBA, and BS in Business Administration and Organizational Management. His work experience consists of Medical Sales Management and Marketing (1982 – present) and a Professor of Marketing and Management (1992-present).

Confederate Ancestor: He joined MOS&B on September 13, 2000 under service of Major General Evander McIver Law (Law's Alabama Brigade, Army of Northern Virginia) who surrendered. Additional officer ancestors include Judge John Adney Law (Probate Judge Pike County, AL 1861-65), Colonel Junius Augustus Law, Alabama Artillery Brigade: Forts Morgan, Blakeley and Port of Mobile, Mobile, AL.

National Service: Commander General (2006-2008), Army of Tennessee Commander (2004-2006), Aide de Camp (2002-2004). Various leadership committees.

Alabama Society: Society Commander (2006-2008), Lt. Commander Alabama Society (2004-2006). Commander, Franklin Buchanan Chapter 58, Mobile, AL (2004-2013).

Order and Society Awards: Distinguished Commander Society (DCS), General Robert E. Lee Chalice, Gold Star Award-Army of Tennessee, and numerous Order and Society Awards from Commanders General 2002-2006 and Alabama Society Commanders (2002-2006).

Historic Interests and Affiliations: Civil War Preservation Trust (CWPT) – projects and initiatives. Alabama Historic Commission (AHC) – state wide projects and initiatives. Baldwin/Mobile Counties – historic preservation, restoration, and promotion of Fort Morgan, Fort Gaines, and Fort Blakeley Battlefields. Baldwin/Mobile Counties – historic waterway preservation, restoration, and promotion of artifacts, sites, and protected areas including the entrance to Mobile Bay, ironclads CSS Huntsville, CSS Tuscaloosa, and USS Tecumseh. Authentic Battlefield Re-enactments as CS Cavalry, infantry, navy, marines, and artillery, and general officer staff. Research into history of naval tactics observed and conducted by the CS Navy in the Mobile/Gulf Coast areas.

Dr. Charles Anthony Hodge – Past Commander General (2008-2010)

Born- October 2nd 1954; Lawrenceburg, Tennessee

Personal-Spouse, Dr. Jill P. Hodges (Orthodontist); Children: Rachel, 26, Attorney; Jeb, 23, graduate University of Alabama, August, 2012; Benton, 23, Senior, University of Alabama

Education- Attended University of Alabama; B.A. Biology and Chemistry, UT-Chattanooga, 1976; D.D.S. (Doctor of Dental Surgery), UT Center for the Health Sciences, Memphis, 1981

Professional- Private practice of General Dentistry for 32 years in Chattanooga (Red Bank); served in various offices/committees of the Chattanooga Area Dental Society

Historical - "life-long" interest in Civil War and family history inspired by family oral history passed down by elderly relatives in North Alabama and Middle Tennessee; began collecting Civil War artifacts as a 6 year old child with items from his collection being displayed at Chickamauga and Chattanooga National Military Park (and other National Park sites such as Chancellorsville and Gettysburg), the Atlanta History Center, the Carter House and Carnton Mansion in Franklin, Tennessee, the Museum of East Tennessee History in Knoxville, and numerous other sites.

He began to study Civil War period medicine while in dental school in the late 70's; as well as, began lecturing on this topic shortly after graduating dental school in 1981, delivering addresses at East Tennessee School of Medicine, Virginia Tech University, medical and dental societies, historical societies and clubs, and many National Military Parks/Battlefields. Assisted Dr. James I. "Bud" Robertson of Virginia Tech and Broadfoot Publishing Company in reprinting the *Medical and Surgical History of the War of the Rebellion* (reprinted under the title of *Medical and Surgical History of the Civil War).*

Member of numerous historical and genealogical organizations including: the "Color Bearers" of the Civil War Trust, the Sons of the Revolution, Military Order of the Stars and Bars, Company of Military Historians, and the Order of the Southern Cross. Long time board member of the East Tennessee Historical Society and Museum of East Tennessee History. Past President and current Stewardship Chairman of the Friends of Chickamauga and Chattanooga National Military Park.

Other hobbies include fly fishing, canoeing, shooting antique military weapons, and following Alabama Crimson Tide football.

Max Lee Waldrop, Jr. – Past Commander General (2010-2012)

Max is a proud graduate of the University of Mississippi with a Bachelor and Master of Business Administration Degrees. He has served as a Regular Army Infantry Officer with the 101st Airborne Division (1976-1980), retired from BellSouth Telecommunications as a Senior Executive (1980-2004), and worked in several other companies at the Director level in South Carolina (2003; 2006-2007) and Alabama (2003-2005).

He was called back to BellSouth to assist in the telecommunications restoration effort for New Orleans immediately after Hurricane Katrina for nine months (2005-2006). Returning home to Springfield, TN he accepted the position of Vice President and Chief Operating Officer of New Hope Construction, Inc., a non-profit company that builds and ships complete residential house packages to other non-profit community agencies throughout the nation (2007-2012). Max lives in Springfield, TN with his wife, Sheila, three daughters, and a granddaughter and is currently serving as the Facilities Manager for Grace Baptist Church.

Max joined the MOS&B in 2004 under his collateral ancestor William Carroll Waldrop who graduated from the University of Mississippi Law School in 1858. He and his father, LTC (Ret) Max Lee Waldrop, were both commissioned 2LT in the US Army (Infantry) out of Ole Miss (1953 and 1976). Of special note is that in 1861, Max's Great, Great Grandfather William Franklin Waldrop enlisted from Lafayette County with the 22nd MS Infantry Regiment, Company K and served as 3rd Sergeant. This makes three of the past five Waldrop generations to enlist in the military from Lafayette County, MS.

Max has been a Chapter Commander of the Brigadier General John Hunt Morgan Chapter # 17 in Huntsville, AL; a 2nd and 1st Lt. Commander for the Alabama Society, Editor of the Alabama State Society Newsletter The Yellowhammer; and has served the National MOS&B as the Chief of Staff 2006-2007), Adjutant General (2007-2008), Historian General (2006-2008), Lt Commander General

(2008-2010) and Commander General (2010-2012). Max has held membership in the SCV, the Civil War Trust (Color Bearer), the Sons of the American Revolution, the Company of Military Historians, the Order of the Southern Cross, the Clan McCord Society, and the Gideons. He has competitively raced in over 65 events as an Ultra runner nationally and internationally and surpassed standard at the 50 mile, 100 mile, and 24 hour events. He is also a US Patent holder.

Department Officers' Biographies

The biographies herein give a brief description and accomplishments of the Department Officers of the Military Order of the Stars and Bars. These individuals have contributed their time and resources well beyond what they have modesty described herein. We commend them for their service to the Order and to their communities.

Michael Cain Griffin, Sr. – ANV Councilor

Michael Cain Griffin ("Cain") lives in the Charleston, South Carolina area. He was fortunate to have lived many places in the U.S. while his Dad served in the U.S. Air Force.

He is currently the Commander of General Pierre Gustave Toutant Beauregard Chapter #300 of the Military Order of the Stars Bars (MOS&B) in Mt. Pleasant, SC. He is a recipient of the MOS&B's Major Pelham award. He is a life member of the MOS&B at the national and society level.

He was formerly a member of the General Maxcy Gregg MOS&B chapter in Columbia. S.C. before he transferred his membership to the Battle of Dingles Mill MOS&B chapter in Sumter, S.C. to help it retain viability. After that he was active in founding and is a charter member of the Beauregard MOS&B chapter.

He is married to the former Tammy Ann Steele of Summerville and they have three children.

He is a member and serves with the youth ministry of Northside Baptist Church in North Charleston, SC.

He graduated from the College of Charleston in 1980 with a Bachelor of Science in Business Administration. He is a licensed CPA in the state of South Carolina. He has been employed with Cape Romain Contractors, Inc., a marine contractor, since 1997.

He joined the MOS&B on the record of his great-great uncle, Major Nathan Snow Blount, commander of the 7th Florida Infantry Regiment. Nathan was a Florida pioneer who fought the Seminoles. He raised a company for Confederate service from Polk County, Florida called the South Florida Bulldogs which mustered into Confederate service as Company E of the 7th Florida Infantry and served in the Army of Tennessee. Nathan's grandfather was in the South Carolina Militia from the Beaufort district and served in the American Revolution under General Francis Marion. Nathan's great-great uncle was William Blount, Paymaster for North Carolina Continental troops, signer of the U.S. Constitution, Congressman from Tennessee and last Territorial Governor for Tennessee.

He enjoys playing the bugle for Confederate memorial services. He is past Commander of the General Ellison Capers Sons of Confederate Veterans (SCV) Camp #1212 in Moncks Corner, SC. He has also served as Lt. Commander and Quartermaster. He received the SCV Meritorious Service award twice.

John Northrop Williams – ANV Councilor

I was born and raised in Virginia. My father had a Construction Company, so I started working at age 12. After graduating from High School I went into the Army Security Agency, serving four years. Then I received the GI bill and went to college at Elon College in North Carolina. I moved in 1972 to Lubbock, Texas to get a Masters at Texas Tech University. I was forced out because of the birth of my son. After a few years I was divorced from my first wife, and moved back to Virginia.

After being advised by my father to never go into Construction, I went into Construction because of my love for the trades.

I started a small construction corporation, and worked 7 states around Washington, D.C. for many years. The economy continued to get bad, then good, then bad over the years, so I moved to Florida.

I was picked up as a Commercial Superintendent in West Palm, and built waste water treatment plants, a 10 story Hilton Hotel, and other high rise office buildings.

I was picked up by The Marriott, and moved to Atlanta as an owner's representative for Marriott. I built hotels around the southern US. I got bored of office politics and took a job as Superintendent with a large corporation out of Atlanta, and then the traveling really started. I worked from Texas to North Dakota to Maine and back to Florida and everywhere in- between. We built Large Box Commercial projects. The owner died and his sons took over and ran the business into the ground. I retired and never looked back. I have had a very interesting life, but my interest in history and the MOS&B has stirred something inside.

Bert Blackmon – AOT Councilor

Confederate Ancestors Biography: My First Cousin 4 times removed, Melville Beverage Cox, enlisted with his brother Thomas and many others from the Wilson District of Grayson County on May 29, 1861. There were enough enlistees to form their own Company and most of the members were related by blood or marriage. It was entitled, Company C of the 45th Virginia Infantry. Melville enlisted as a Sergeant but soon was commissioned a first Lieutenant. When his Captain was promoted, He was promoted to Captain and took over command of the Company. Thomas enlisted as a Corporal but finished the war as a first Lieutenant.

They spent most of the war fighting in what we now call West Virginia with a few forays into Maryland and down into the Shenandoah Valley. They were quite successful in keeping the Union Army from getting a grip on the lower portion of West Virginia.

On August 26, 1863, at the battle of White Sulfur Springs, Melville was shot through both legs with the same bullet. His men evacuated him to the rear and, when he could travel, he was sent home and placed on the invalid roll. That was his status until the close of the war. After some severe bouts with infections, his wounds healed but he had to walk with two canes for the rest of his life.

After the war Captain Mel (as he was known for the rest of his years) returned to his first love, farming. With his wounds making it difficult to walk, he could not be successful as a farmer so he worked for a time in a bank, then became licensed as an attorney. He also served for a time in the Virginia Legislature.

His wounds did not prevent him from fathering a family of eleven, all of whom became very successful. One of his children, Creed Fulton Cox, graduated from VMI and West Point. He served in the U.S. Army from the Spanish American war to World War two rising to the rank of General. Melville Beverage Cox passed from this life in 1906 on the 4th of July.

Career: I graduated from Troy State University in 1972 and went to work as a History Teacher, basketball and track coach and bus driver. I retired in 1996. I retired from the Alabama National Guard in 1998. I currently work part time in a local Hardware Store.

MOS&B Background: I have been a member of the MOS&B since 1999 and was one of the founding members of the St. John Richardson Liddell Chapter # 271 in Bay Minette Alabama. I have served three times as Commander of the Chapter and currently serve as the Chapter Genealogist. I have also served as the Alabama State Adjutant.

Staff Officers' Biographies

The biographies herein give a brief description and accomplishments of the Staff Officers and Committee Chairs of the Military Order of the Stars and Bars. These individuals have contributed their time and resources well beyond what they have modesty described herein. We commend them for their service to the Order and to their communities.

Rev. Raymond Holder – Chaplain General

Raymond Holder is a graduate of the University of Southern Mississippi, in the class of 1967, with a B.S degree and a 2003 graduate of New Orleans Baptist Seminary with a Master's of Divinity degree. Shortly after graduating from the seminary, he became an ordained minister and became a hospice chaplain after almost a year being a resident chaplain at Scott & White Hospital in Temple, Texas, completing clinical pastoral courses and is with Altus Hospice of Houston, serving the Houston area.

He is a past Commander of the Sons of Confederate Veterans Albert Sidney Camp #67 in Houston, Texas, the current chaplain of The Texas Chapter # 5 of the Military Order of the Stars & Bars of Houston, Texas. He is an active committee member of The Southern Heritage Ball, which is held annually at the River Oaks Country Club of Houston and is a member of the Order of the Southern Cross.

Raymond is concerned about the spiritual and cultural preservation of our Southern Heritage which he believes is under attack by the secular progressive forces of our country. He wants to be a helping spiritual servant to the MOS&B compatriots in any way that he can. Therefore, he welcomes all to this purpose.

Raymond looks forward to serving as the Chaplain General of MOS&B. He, in the last few years, has had much experience in meeting the spiritual and pastoral care needs of individuals and families with very diverse spiritual backgrounds. He welcomes all to talk with him.

Gary M. Loudermilk – Communications General & Scholarship Committee Chair

Gary Loudermilk interrupted his college career at Sam Houston State University in 1955 to spend four years in the U. S. Navy. He returned in 1959 to complete his undergraduate education and pursue postgraduate work, culminating with his Ph.D. in Adult Education Administration.

His work experience includes 30 years with a major communication company, twenty years of which were spent in the Education and Training Department. His final 10 years were spent in the headquarters of the company in Stamford Connecticut and Dallas Texas where he held the title of Director of Training Administration and Results. After taking early retirement from the company, he and his wife relocated to Comanche Texas where they owned and operated a small cattle ranch.

During their time in Comanche, Gary was involved in several civic organizations in Comanche including serving as Director and Board Member of Cross Timbers Health Clinics, Inc. and as Director and Secretary of the Board of the Comanche Housing Authority. He also served a term as a County Commissioner of Comanche County.

In 2001, reflecting his interest in his family heritage, Gary, his two sons and several cousins founded a new MOS&B Chapter, the Major John Loudermilk Chapter # 264, honoring Gary's great grandfather who was killed at the battle of New Hope Church. Gary has served in various chapter positions and served as Lt. Commander and Commander of the Texas Society.

He was elected an ATM Executive Councilor (2006-2008) and then ATM Commander (2008-2010). At the National Convention in Columbia SC in 2009 he volunteered to assume the additional duties of Quartermaster General and Communications General. He served as QM General for almost three years and continues in the Communications General position.

In addition to many other heritage organization awards, he has received the MOS&B Distinguished Commander Medal (DCS), the Award of Honorary Commander General (HCG), the Gold Star Award and the MOS&B's highest Award, the Robert E. Lee Chalice. The UDC has conferred their National Defense Medal on him.

Gary is a founding member of the Descendants of Confederate Veterans, (DCV) a Texas Heritage Organization in which his wife and daughter Theresa both belong. He and Dorothy, his wife of 55 years, are retired and reside in Brownwood Texas, enjoying their growing number of great grandchildren.

Ben H. Willingham – Historian General

Ben Willingham is a retired senior Naval Officer and a graduate of Georgia Tech and the Naval War College. After many years as a Naval Aviator, he retired from his second career in 2005 after spending several decades living in Zurich, Switzerland in the investment industry. Ben has previously served as Chief of Staff of the Order; as well as, in numerous Chapter and Society positions. He was chairman of the 2011 Sesquicentennial MOS&B convention. He is the editor of the MOS&B "Sesquicentennial News" published daily on the Society blog www.starsandbarsblog.org and he is the Commander of the Sons of the Confederacy in Jacksonville. He has proven 13 Confederate officer ancestors in his direct family but is most proud that there is not a single Union soldier present in his family genealogy. He has received the UDC Jefferson Davis medal for history and research.

He is active in numerous heritage groups and has been the President of the Museum of Southern History in Jacksonville, FL for the last ten years. The museum, under Ben's guidance conducts educational programs for schools as well and groups of interested people from various locations throughout northern Florida and southern Georgia.

Ben is dedicated to historical accuracy. He doesn't care if you like it, just learn the truth and deal with it. With this conviction foremost in mind, the museum has refused to accept public money so as to preserve its intellectual honesty. He has been a leader in the community insuring that our ancestors are not forgotten and that their principles are still alive. Ben and his wife, Erika, have two sons and a daughter living in Zurich. They live in Atlantic Beach, FL.

Robert William Turk – Quartermaster General

Robert William Turk is a United States Marine Corps Cold War veteran and a graduate of the University of Houston. He has been a public school teacher for the past 23 years in both Texas and Utah and currently teaches 5th grade in Blanding, Utah.

Robert and his wife, Valarie, were married on April 2, 1982. They have four daughters, three son-in-laws and eight grandchildren. Robert enjoys history and has been a Confederate re-enactor at various battles including Gettysburg.

Stephen Clay McGehee –
Webmaster General & Deputy Quartermaster General

Stephen first joined the Order in February 1992 under Lt. Colonel John Pelham. He had previously joined the SCV under his great grandfather, William Pelham McGehee. In 1995 he founded Adjutant Workshop, Inc., which develops software for political campaigns. This was based on his experience as a candidate for public office; he has been on the staff of several political campaigns since then. He is also vice-president of a non-profit corporation that provides financial and logistical support to missionaries in Sierra Leone, West Africa.

The Code of Confederate Flag Etiquette was compiled and edited by Stephen as a part of the Confederate Colonel project that he founded in 2007. This Code was adopted by the MOS&B in 2011. He has been a guest on radio talk shows on various Southern and Confederate topics. The culture of the Old South and the Southern gentleman and Southern lady are dear to his heart and he works hard to encourage, preserve, and promote them - they are what prompted the Confederate Colonel project. The name "Confederate Colonel" was inspired by being awarded the title of Kentucky Colonel in 2004.

He and his wife, Laura, live in Volusia County, Florida and have two sons and two grandsons. The entire family is very active in church ministry activities.

Stephen began serving as MOS&B Webmaster General in 2010 and is a recipient of the Colonel John Pelham Distinguished Service Award. In addition to building and maintaining the MOS&B web site and web store, he also built and maintains the Confederate Colonel blog, the Southern Agrarian blog, a church web site, a site for missionaries stationed in West Africa, a family web site, a WWII Navy veteran's web site, and several business web sites and web stores.

A Confederate flag flies from a 25' flag pole in the McGehee front yard every day of the year.

Jeffrey L. Sizemore –
Editor & Deputy Communications General

Jeffrey was born and raised in Jacksonville, Florida. He is a Senior Engineer whose experience in the electrical power industry started in Jacksonville, Florida and led him to Kissimmee, Florida to work for the Kissimmee Utility Authority in 1991. He is a graduate of the University of Miami (BSEE), Jacksonville University (BS), and Webster University (MBA).

He joined both the MOS&B & SCV under his paternal Great-Great Grandfather Ensign James Marion Sizemore of the 1107th Georgia Militia District, Chattahoochee County, Georgia. He also has another officer ancestor whose name is 3rd Lt. Jonas Daniel of Company C, Alabama 22nd Infantry. His ancestors have always lived in the South dated back to his American Revolutionary ancestors, John Lawson Irwin and Jared Irwin of Georgia.

After joining the MOS&B in 1995, he has served as the Colonel L. M. Park Chapter # 52 adjutant; as well as, the State Society as the editor of the MOS&B Florida Society newsletter, *The Stainless Banner.* Since 2009, he has served also as the editor of the MOS&B's *Officer's Call.*

He is also involved in the Sons of the American Revolution in which he serves as the Chapter President and Regional Vice President, FLSSAR. He also is served as an outpost commander for the Royal Ranger Outpost #35.

He and his wife, Joy, live in Kissimmee, Florida. Upon doing genealogy together, both have found ancestors dating back to the American Revolution period. Joy is also active in her UDC chapter and DAR chapter.

He is proud to be associated with the Order and will continually serve and use his talents to further the cause of the Military Order of the Stars and Bars.

Ed Stack – Awards Chairman

Confederate Ancestors: Ed is the GG Grandson of 1st Lieutenant Michael Edward Stack, Irish Regiment, Company 6, Louisiana Militia, and the GG Grandnephew of Private Thomas H. Cummings, Washington Artillery Battalion, Company 4, Louisiana Militia. Ed became a member of the MOS&B in 2008, and is the immediate Past Commander of Maj. Edgar Burroughs (Princess Anne Cavalry) Chapter 281, Virginia Society, MOS&B. Ed is also a member of the SCV, and is the Historian and Newsletter Editor for SCV Camp 9, the 13th Virginia Mechanized Cavalry (all of the Camp 9 members ride motorcycles).

Military Service: Ed enlisted in the U. S. Marine Corps in 1969, at age 17, and served on active and inactive duty until 1979. In 1980, Ed enlisted in the U. S. Navy, and retired from military service in 1992. While in the military, Ed attended off-duty college courses and earned his Bachelor's Degree in Criminology.

Civilian Life: Upon retirement from the military, at age 40, Ed was accepted into the 16th Virginia Beach Police Academy and served in the Uniformed Patrol Division, as a Master Police Officer, until his retirement in 2000. Ed decided to use his remaining G. I. Bill educational benefits, and returned to college the same year. In 2001, Ed earned his Associate of Applied Science Degree in Computer Electronics Technology. In 2002, Ed went to work for Blackwater USA, as a firearms instructor for Navy Programs. Ed deployed to Iraq in 2004, and performed duties as a Blackwater Security Contractor, in support of the Coalition Provisional Authority, in Al-Hillah. Ed stayed with Blackwater until 2005. In 2006, Ed trained and supervised a fifteen-man security detail aboard the SBX-1, a Missile Defense Agency project. From 2007 until present, Ed works as a Training Development Specialist at the Navy– Marine Corps Intelligence Training Center, and participates in a variety of training evolutions in support of the U. S. military, law enforcement, and foreign military/law enforcement entities, at Academi (formerly known as Blackwater, Xe, and U. S. Training Center).

Personal: Ed is married to Jessica, his wife of forty-two years, and resides in Virginia Beach, VA. Ed is a Life Member of the VFW, a member of the Fraternal Order of Police, and a member of the Knights of Columbus. Ed's hobbies include collecting domestic and international police insignia (Ed has a little over 4700 pieces in his collection), firearms, military postcards, United States stamps, and researching his family genealogy. Ed has two younger brothers, Robert Michael and Michael Joseph, both of whom are U. S. military veterans. Ed's father, Robert Walter, served in the Army during World War Two, and his grandfather, Robert Gustave, served in the Navy during World War One.

Organizational History and Structure

"We, the posterity of the Officer Corps and civil officials of the Confederacy, do pledge ourselves to commemorate and honor the service of leadership these men rendered in the cause of fundamental American principles of self-determination and states' rights and to perpetuate the true history of their deeds for the edification of ourselves, our society, and for generations yet unborn."

As you read the above pledge, we as members of the Military Order of the Stars and Bars are reminded of what our Confederate ancestors, both officers, and soldiers, fought for during the period from 1861 to 1865 most commonly referred in the south as the War Between the States. Veterans of all wars fought for the cause for which they risked their lives and none should be forgotten.

The Purpose of the

Military Order of the Stars and Bars

The original text was taken from earlier versions of the Anniversary Book and revised by Ben H. Willingham to reflect the current activities. Thanks are given to Mark Lea "Beau" Cantrell for his work on the original version.

Though not usually posed in the following terminology, the real question beneath inquiries concerning the need for the MOS&B is:

> "Why a separate organization for commemoration of the Confederate Officer Corps and the officials of the civilian Confederate Government?"

It is apparent that, though most of the questions regarding the MOS&B are prompted by a sincere wish to know, some questions proceed from a hostility founded upon lack of knowledge, misinformation and unwarranted resentment.

The Military Order of the Stars and Bars is distinguished from other heritage organizations in that the founders of the Order included actual Confederate Veterans, all of whom had served the Cause as commissioned officers of the Confederate Armed Forces. All of the Founding Members of the Order were members of the United Confederate Veterans. Establishing the Order forty-nine years after the founding of the UCV, the creator of the Order perceived a need which had not been addressed by other Confederate associations. It was actually believed by the Order's Founders that the unique contribution of the Confederate Officer Corps and civilian officials to the South had not been specifically addressed by either the UCV or any other Confederate heritage group. Even today, except for the full generals and brigadiers and an even smaller number of field and company-grade officers, almost all of the members of the Confederate Officer Corps are without memorials, biographies or commemorations. The attention given to the memory and history of the Confederate elected and appointed officials is even less.

The essential, basic unit of the Confederate Army was the company. Most companies were locally raised in a given county, usually by a local planter, politician, businessman, merchant or professional. In some instances battalions, regiments and even legions were organized largely through the efforts of just one man. Not only did these captains, majors, occasional colonels and generals recruit and organize the basic components of the armies of the South, in many instances these same officers either paid for directly, or raised, the monies needed to equip, uniform and supply the units.

The late, great Professor Bell Wiley established in his book, The Life of Johnny Reb, that the greatest single age group among Confederate soldiers was from eighteen to twenty-five years. Through the medium of his monumental book, Generals in Gray, Ezra Warner advised that the average age of full generals of the Confederacy was forty-eight years. Mr. Warner then described the average age of the respectively descending grades of general officers of the Confederacy until he reached the lowest grade, that of brigadier. Warner advised that the average age of Confederate brigadiers was thirty-six years. Generally, the age of Junior, Company and Field-grade Officers of the Confederate Army fall between the age of general officers and the age of the enlisted men of the Army. In considering the relative ages of different ranks the enlisted men tended to be relatively young, single, unproductive men, much like the enlisted ranks of most armies. In contrast, most of the Officer Corps left wives, children, farms, stores, shops, public offices and professional practices to serve the Cause of Southern Independence. A realization of these circumstances does not imply a diminution of the sacrifices of the Confederate enlisted men. It does imply a greater awareness of the significantly different sacrifices that were made by most of the members of the Officer Corps.

An examination of any of the unit histories which include muster rolls and disposition of personnel will show that the Confederate Officer Corps suffered a much higher percentage of casualties than did the enlisted personnel. A review of the Story of the Six Hundred will demonstrate the abhorrent conditions in which the Officer Corps was held while they were prisoners of war. It is common knowledge that the Officer Corps was more severely punished in terms of the deprivation of their civil liberties after the War than were the enlisted men of the Confederacy. Thus, the Confederate Officer Corps sacrificed more initially to create the armies of the South, they suffered more during the conduct of the War and, after the cessation of hostilities the former officers were more harshly treated.

Though the elected and appointed members of the Confederate Government were not usually exposed to service in the field, the moral courage required to publicly support and officially serve the Confederate Cause had to be great. The estates of most members of the Government were singled out for utter destruction by occupying Yankee armies. Many of the officials of the Government, the rare exceptions being those who were able to escape the country, were imprisoned for various amounts of time after the end of the War. This included President Davis and the entire Cabinet.

Despite these extraordinary experiences, these men have been largely ignored by posterity.

The members of the Military Order of the Stats and Bars bear an extra responsibility to their Confederate Heritage. Compatriots of the Order should not consider themselves to be better because of an accident of birth, an event over which no individual has ultimate control.

If you love the South, if you love and revere the sacrifices of your Confederate ancestors for the South, please help preserve the memory of a truly forgotten and ignored class of Southern heroes and martyrs, the Officer Corps of the Confederate Armed Forces and the elected and appointed officials of the Confederate Government. You can do this by becoming a member of the Military Order of the Stars and Bars or, if you are not descended from one who served the Cause as an officer or as an official of the Confederate Government, by supporting the Order and its projects and programs.

The Principles & Duty

The principles and duty of General Society of the MOS&B are to serve in literary, historical, benevolent, patriotic, educational and non-political function. It shall strive:

(a) To cultivate the ties of friendships, among descendants of those who shared the responsibilities of Southern leadership in the War Between the States;

(b) To provide leadership in the collecting and assembling of data, documents, and materials relating to the Confederacy; however, the organization should also preserve the history of the Colonial and Federal periods of our history since the antecedents to the War Between the States are to be found in these periods;

(c) To provide for future generations of the descendants of Confederate officers and civilian officials in the Executive and Legislative branches of government an organization to commemorate and honor the leadership of their forefathers;

(d) To consecrate in our hearts the flag of the Southern Confederacy, not as a political symbol, but as an emblem of a heroic epoch for which our forefathers fought and died;

(e) To maintain a united front against doctrines subversive to the fundamental principles set forth in the Bill of Rights which, as a part of the Federal Constitution, guarantees freedom of speech and the press, together with all other rights and privileges therein provided for the protection of political minorities and of individual citizens; and

(f) To encourage and support the true loyalty of the Constitution of the United States of America.

Early History

On June 10, 1889, in New Orleans, Louisiana, a group of proud surviving soldiers of the Confederate States of America organized an association called the United Confederate Veterans. Its goals were to protect and defend the honor and dignity of the memory of the Confederate soldier. As the ranks of the aged veterans of the UCV began to thin with the passage of time, a group of the surviving Confederate officers met in Columbia, South Carolina on August 30th, 1938 to discuss their concerns that the unique contributions made by the Confederate leadership were not properly chronicled in our nation's history books. They felt a particular duty fell to them as members of the Officers Corp.

This first meeting of what they named the "Order of the Stars & Bars" was convened with a great deal of enthusiasm by sixteen former Confederate officers (WBTS and UCV); as well as, an additional forty-seven male descendant of Confederate officers in attendance. These dedicated men were unanimous in voting to begin a new CSA veteran society that would hold annual meetings. The OSB was unique in that the organization was made up of veterans and their descendants with the understanding that as the original Confederate officers died that it was the sacred responsibility of their male offspring to continue to carry on the purposes of the Order.

Our first Commander-in-Chief was Homer Atkinson or Petersburg, Virginia, served the South as a Private in Company B, 39th Virginia Infantry. He was subsequently advanced to the rank of General during the period of the United Confederate Veterans. He served as the chief officer of the Order from the beginning until his death in 1945. In addition to commanding the new Order, he also served two terms as Commander- in-Chief of the United Confederate Veterans. Other successful leaders assumed the role of commander including Gen. Robert E. Lee's grandson Dr. George Bolling Lee. In later years of the Order, eligibility qualifications were broadened to allow collateral male descendants of Confederate commissioned officers as well as of any elected or appointed member of the Executive Branch of the Confederate Government. This brought additional members and new vigorous leadership to the Brotherhood.

The name of the Order was changed to "The Military Order of the Stars and Bars" at the 39th General Convention held in Memphis, Tennessee in 1976. The first National Flag of the Confederate States of America, the Stars and Bars, was accepted as the official insignia of the Order and the commanding officer would be called the Commander General of the Military Order of the Star and Bars.

Today the fraternal Military Order of the Stars & Bars, a non-profit 501(c) 3, non-political educational, historical, patriotic, and heritage group continues its dedication to the preservation of Southern history and remains the only heritage organization actually founded by Confederate veterans. A wide range of programs have been added to reorganize outstanding contributions in the fields of history, fine arts and journalism. College scholarships and monetary awards are offered to emphasize the need for truth in Confederate history. Prestigious literary prizes are awarded to authors and publishing houses. Monuments are being erected to the CSA soldiers. Journalists who practice ethical and fair reporting of local and Southern history are recognized. An emphasis is placed on American Patriotism and the honoring of all American veterans.

The Order works with other like-minded heritage and patriotic groups such as the United Daughters of the Confederacy, Order of the Southern Cross, the Museum of the Confederacy and the Sons of the American Revolution to promote a truthful history of Confederate States as well as general American history. We partner with Washington and Lee University in the preservation and interpretation of Lee Chapel.

The Order also emphasizes family tradition and encourages our membership to preserve their family's Confederate history for posterity. To that end, each MOS&B membership application with its genealogical records becomes a permanent historical record and files of deceased members are at the National MOS&B Archives in Oklahoma City, Oklahoma. All MOS&B Headquarters files are being digitized.
Members are leaders in the collecting of data, documents and relics that preserve the history and heritage of the Southland and the War Between the states, but also in the preserving of the history of America's Colonial, Revolutionary and Federal periods. The Order remains fervent in its Patriotism and support of the basic principles of the United States Constitution.

As in decades past, the Military Order of the Stars and Bars continues to cultivate the ties of friendship and create Brothers united in their common purposes. The friendship and fellowship of individuals united in a shared heritage and history remains of prime importance to the membership. Meetings and annual National Reunions are times of education and learning, but also opportunities for the good times shared by the Compatriots of the Order.

Founders of the Order

The *Military Order of the Stars and Bars* was formally established on August 30, 1938, in Columbia, SC. There were sixty-two charter members. Of this number fifteen were veterans of the War Between the States; eleven of whom saw service as officers. The remaining four achieved post-war advancements within the United Confederate Veterans.

Charter Members serving as officers during the WBTS were:

Name	Dates	Rank	Unit
Ashe, Samuel A'Court	(1848-1938)*	Captain	Confederate Troops - AAG
Bell, Holland Middleton	(1839-1943)	Captain	AL 41st Inf., Co. H
Bishop, Carter R.	(1850-1941)	Cadet	VMI, Co. C
Brock, Noah Monroe	(1836-1942)	2nd Lieutenant	VA 10th Cav., Co. B
Halsey, Stephen Peters	(1843-1939)	Major	VA 21st Cav., F&S
Hill, Wyatt Tucker	(1846-1938)	2nd Lieutenant	VA 3rd Inf. (Reserves), Co. A
Keyser, Peter James Jr.	(1847-1939)	2nd Lieutenant	VA 3rd Inf. (Reserves), Co. G
Lowry, James A.	(1845-1942)	3rd Lieutenant	NC 48th Inf., Co. A
Robinson, Benjamin McCain	(1845-1938)	1st Lieutenant	AL 63rd Inf., Co. G
Stewart, James M.	(1842-1939)	Major	SC 22nd Inf., Co. G
Wood, William Morison	(1846-1943)	Cadet	VMI, Co. A

*Posthumous Founder d. 8/29/1938

Charter Members serving as enlisted during the WBTS (advanced under UCV) were:

Atkinson, Homer	(1848-1945)	Private	VA 39th Inf., Co. B
Claytool, John Milton	(1846-1945)		TN 12th Cons Inf. Co. H
Dowdy, John Andrew Jackson	(1848-1943)	Private	TX 24th Cav., Co. C
Evans, William McKendree	(1847-1939)	Private	VA Richmond "Parker" L Arty
Gellette, Otto Richard	(1846-1944)	Corporal UCV	UCV

Non-WBTS- Veteran Charter Members of the Order were:

Name	Relation	Dates	Last Address
Bailey, James Milton	son	(1876-1954)	Penland, NC
Barton, COL Robert Thomas	son	(1891-1980)	Richmond, VA
Bond, LT James Sullivan	son	(1871-1963)	Savannah, GA
Burroughs, Oliver Berrien Jr.	grandson	(1889-1962)	Augusta, GA
Cheatham, MG Benjamin Franklin	son	(1867-1944)	Stratford, VA
Cunningham, COL Carlton Brown	grandson	(1896-1946)	Chicago, IL
Dancy, MAJ Dr. William Remshart	grandson	(1877-1960)	Savannah, GA
Deford, Samuel Davies Drewry	grandson	(1907-1988)	Richmond, VA
Dennis, MAJ Jere Clemens	son	(1861-1954)	Dadeville, AL
Earle, Dr. Baylis Haynsworth	son	(1870-1942)	Greenville, SC
Gardner, LT James	grandson	(1888-1950)	Augusta, GA
Green, Ernest Matthews	son	(1871-1949)	Raleigh, NC
Hancock, MAJ Walker Kirtland	grandson	(1901-1998)	Gloucester, MA
Hancock, LT Walter Scott	son	(1869-1959)	St. Louis, MO
Holman, Hubert Thomison	grandson	(1905-1994)	Fayetteville, TN
Holman, Wayne James Jr.	grandson	(1907-1985)	Plainfield, NJ
Hopkins, COL Walter Lee	grandson	(1889-1949)	Richmond, VA

Hopkins, MAJ Dr. William Benjamin	grandson	(1883-1952)	Tampa, FL
Hume, MG Edgar Erskine Sr.	son	(1889-1952)	Carlisle, PA
Hurt, Hon. Earl Evans	grandson	(1887-1971)	Dallas, TX
Johnson, Dr. James Vandergrift	grandson	(1889-1944)	Tacoma, WA
Jones, Jonathan Ashley	son	(1871-1956)	Atlanta, GA
Law, William Latta Jr.	grandson	(1896-	Richmond, VA
Lee, CAPT Dr. George Bolling	son	(1872-1948)	New York, NY
Lesley, Theodore L.	grandson	(1911-1978)	Tampa, FL
McCullough, LTC James D'Alvigny	son	(1877-1952)	Honea Path, SC
McDavid, Albert Calhoun Sr.	grandson	(1887-1964)	San Antonio, TX
McLean, COL James Douglas	grandson	(1894-1958)	Quantico, VA
Old, COL William Whitehurst Jr.	son	(1873-1956)	Norfolk, VA
Opie, BG Hierome Lindsay	grandson	(1880-1943)	Staunton, VA
Pickett, LT Charles	grandson	(1894-1965)	Fairfax, VA
Powe, Thomas Erasmus	son	(1872-1945)	Cheraw, SC
Ratliff, Clifton H	son	(1876-1953)	Redlands, CA
Simmons, Hon. Thomas	son	(1861-1950)	Fort Worth, TX
Slemp, COL Rep. Campbell Bascom	son	(1870-1943)	Knoxville, TN
Smith, William O.	grandson	(1905-	Dallas, TX
Squires, Rev. William Henry Tappey	son	(1875-1948)	Norfolk, VA
Stephens, Hon. Alexander William	son	(1874-1943)	Atlanta, GA
Tabor, COL Dr. George Reed	son	(1864-1947)	Tishomingo, OK
Tilghman, COL Harrison Samuel	son	(1885-1961)	Easton, MO
Wharton, Roger Daniel	son	(1890-	Manassas, VA
Wheeler, COL Joseph Jr.	son	(1872-1938)*	Wheeler, AL
Wherry, Douglas	son	(1870-1940)	Richmond, VA
Wickham, Henry Taylor	son	(1849-1943)	Richmond, VA
Wood, Clement Richardson#	grandson	(1888-1950)	Delanson, NY
Wooten, BG William Preston	son	(1873-1950)	Washington, DC
Wright, Howard Pearce	son	(1881-1966)	Jacksonville, FL

*Posthumous Founder d. 8/6/1938

#Suggested the name for the Order

The following Founders served as Commander-in-Chief of the Order:
1938-1945   Homer Atkinson
1945-1948   George Bolling Lee
1953-1954   William Remshart Dancy

History of the Order (2006-2008)

The two years that marked CG Hodge's administration may be described as years of "retrenchment" and "reform." All of our efforts were necessarily devoted to the Order's infrastructure, which unfortunately left us little time to focus on the Order's charitable, educational, and historic mission.

During CG Hodge's administration, the Order: (1) Restored its relationship with the IRS, under the threat of administrative penalties and the loss of tax-exemption; (2) Restored its status with the State of Tennessee, under the threat of administrative dissolution; (3) Staunched the flow of monies from a reduced treasury; (4) Initiated "reform" measures to give the grassroots a larger say in governance; and (5) emphasized the role of the Board of Directors in the discharge of its fiduciary duties and responsibilities.1

1. __The IRS__. On June 18, 2008, a Director acting at my request telephoned the IRS to gather information concerning the application process for a Group Organization exemption. During his conversation with the representative, the Director learned that the Order's "tax returns" (the Form 990) had not been filed for the five fiscal years ending July 31, 2007. *Until then,* we had no knowledge of the Order's failure to file tax returns.

Within weeks, the IRS notified the Order that it would be fined $30,000 for failure to file the tax returns. The IRS also notified the Order that it could be stripped of its tax-exempt status.

This sudden and dramatic intervention by the IRS dominated our attention *for a full year.*

When learning of the Order's delinquency, we immediately had all of the Order's financial records shipped to Columbia, Tennessee to the CPA firm that handled the Order's accounting work until 2003. I drove from Chattanooga to Columbia, Tennessee two different times to meet with the CPA firm. The Director who initially uncovered the delinquency met me there, and he visited the CPA firm a third time. We asked the CPA firm to take whatever steps were necessary to reconstruct the financial records and to file accurate Forms 990 as quickly as possible. The firm did so.

In the months that followed, the Order filed an appeal to the IRS, seeking "abatement" of the $30,000 fine. The Director who first learned of the situation spoke with the IRS on thirteen different occasions. Fortunately, the Order's appeal was eventually successful. The fine was abated and the Order was restored to good standing.

It still isn't entirely clear what happened (or didn't happen) during those five years, but our research uncovered some serious flaws in the Order's business model. In summary, a lack of continuity among the directors and officers, a wholesale reliance on unsupervised volunteers, poorly articulated assignments and directions, and a misunderstanding of individual responsibility were at the heart of the problem.

Accordingly, the failure to file the tax returns was the product of a faulty structure, where a systemic breakdown was likely to occur. The Order simply did not have the internal controls and safeguards in place to insure that the Order operated in an environment of strict compliance.

The cost of reconstructing the records and filing the tax returns was a heavy financial burden, especially in view of the severe losses the Order suffered in net asset value, due to the downturn in the financial markets. Accounting fees easily exceeded $10,000. But, the Order had only itself to blame. Had the Order been filing the tax returns on time, this expense would have been avoided.

---

[1] "Board," "Board of Directors" and "Directors in this discussion refer to the General Executive Council and its members.

---

2. The State of Tennessee. The Order is incorporated in Tennessee and to remain in good standing the Order must, at a minimum, file an Annual Report. In the years prior to our administration, some consideration was given to re-incorporating in another state, although this was not accomplished. Even so, while this was under consideration, the Order stopped filing annual documents with the State of Tennessee and, in due course, Tennessee Secretary of State notified the Order that its charter would be administratively dissolved. To avoid dissolution, the Order had to take immediate corrective action, which it did.

Even worse, had the Order re-incorporated in another state, the Order would have automatically lost its existing IRS tax-exemption. The Order would have had to reapply for a new tax-exemption, a process that could have taken six months or longer. [2]

The possibility that the Order might have re-incorporated in another state without fully appreciating the ramifications of such a move underscored the Order's lack of internal controls.

3. Financial Resources. The Order's financial resources began to severely decline in the three years prior to our administration. The decline can be blamed on the financial markets and on the cost of operating an office and paying an employee. Little could be done about the financial markets, although the Order did resort to an all-cash position in late 2008. But, it was the office operation that devoured so much of our administration's time, talent, and treasure. The office was hemorrhaging cash at a time when the Order could least afford such an expense. The very difficult decision to close the office and to move all operations "in-house" to unpaid volunteers was discussed for a full year. When the decision was finally made, the actual transfer of books and records to various locations was a serious undertaking. The office was a serious diversion of scarce resources, including time.

4. "Reform" Measures. Over the years, the Order's governing documents, namely, its Constitution and its Bylaws (separate documents), had become cumbersome and difficult to synchronize. Moreover, those documents had developed a "cut and paste" character consistent with documents that are frequently amended. It was our thought that these documents should be rewritten and republished, although it was beyond our capacity to do so in the two years allotted to us.

Still, we thought we could begin by taking measures to reform the Order's voting protocols, which had evolved into a tradition wholly disconnected from the governing documents. At the 2008 Annual Meeting, for example, there were as many registered "aide-de-camp" delegates as there were registered chapter delegates. These *appointed* "aides-de-camp" wielded power and influence far in excess of the chapters, which was an abuse obvious to everyone. Fortunately, amendments were adopted at the 2009 Annual Meeting that severely curtailed the authority of aides-de-camp to cast votes at annual meetings.

Since the adoption of that measure, "reform" efforts have continued, and this is one of the legacies of our administration of which we are very proud.

5. The GEC. At our first board meeting following my election, held in the fall of 2008, we distributed a printed guide to the directors, summarizing their responsibilities as directors and emphasizing their duty to ask for relevant information and to *report* relevant information. We elevated director "education" and "awareness," and that effort continues to this day. It is another legacy of our administration of which we are very proud.

2 The SCV re-incorporated in Texas without appreciating the tax consequences and, as a result, lost its tax-exemption. It then had to reapply with the IRS.

As stated out the outset, the necessary application of almost all of our resources to the Order's infrastructure severely limited our capacity to concentrate on our mission. However, the work that was done during the two years we were in office created a pathway for subsequent administrations to succeed.

Both the Order and CG Hodges extend a sincere "thank you" and express our deep appreciation to JAG Richard Knight and PCIC Albert Jones for their many hours and hard work in resolving these important matters.

Conventions from 1952 to 2014

Listed herein are the dates and the respective cities in which the Military Order of the Stars and Bars held their annual convention. As noted over the years listed the conventions varied by the time of year in which the convention was held and it wasn't settled to hold it during the summer till 1963.

Jackson, MS	June 3-6, 1952
Mobile, AL	June 9-11, 1953
Edgewater Park, MS	Sept 24-25, 1954
New Orleans, LA	Sept 29-Oct 1, 1955
Atlanta, GA	Sept 27-29, 1956
Richmond, VA	Nov 11-14, 1957
Jackson, MS	Oct 19-21, 1958
Memphis, TN	Oct 18-20, 1959
Montgomery, AL	Oct 23-25, 1960
New Orleans, LA	Oct 1-3, 1961
Jackson, MS	Oct 21-23, 1962
Lynchburg, VA	Aug 16-18, 1963
Atlanta, GA	Aug 14-16, 1964
Little Rock, AR	Aug 12-15, 1965
Charleston, SC	Aug 11-13, 1966
Biloxi, MS	Aug 17-19, 1967
Nashville, TN	Aug 14-16, 1968
New Orleans, LA	Aug 13-16, 1969
Houston, TX	Aug 6-8, 1970
Richmond, VA	Aug 12-14, 1971
Savannah, GA	Aug 3-5, 1972
St. Augustine, FL	Aug 8-11, 1973
Biloxi, MS	Aug 8-10, 1974
Alexandria, VA	Aug 14-16, 1975
Memphis, TN	Aug 12-14, 1976
Dallas, TX	Aug 18-20, 1977
Savannah, GA	Aug 17-19, 1978
Asheville, NC	Aug 8-12, 1979
New Orleans, LA	Aug 6-9, 1980
Richmond, VA	Aug 13-15, 1981
Oklahoma City, OK	Aug 12-14, 1982
Orlando, FL	Aug 4-6, 1983
Biloxi, MS	Aug 8-11, 1984
Raleigh, NC	Aug 8-10, 1985
Nashville, TN	Aug 6-10, 1986
Mobile, AL	Aug 5-8, 1987
Columbia, SC	Aug 3-6, 1988
Oklahoma City, OK	Aug 16-19, 1989

Fayetteville, AR	Aug 8-11, 1990
Columbus, GA	July 31-Aug 2, 1991
Wilmington, NC	Aug 5-8, 1992
Lexington, KY	Aug 8-11, 1993
Mobile, AL	Aug 4-6, 1994
Chattanooga, TN	July 27-29, 1995
Richmond, VA	Aug 1-3, 1996
Nashville, TN	July 30-Aug 2, 1997
St. Louis, MO	Aug 5-8, 1998
Mobile, AL	July 28-31, 1999
Charleston, SC	Aug 2-5, 2000
Lafayette, LA	July 31-Aug 4, 2001
Memphis, TN	July 30-Aug 4, 2002
Asheville, NC	July 30–Aug 2, 2003
Dalton, GA	July 28-31, 2004
Nashville, TN	July 20-23, 2005
Mobile, AL	July 20-22, 2006
Richmond, VA	June 21-23, 2007
Springdale, AR	May 15-17, 2008
Columbia, SC	June 12-14, 2009
Oklahoma City, OK	April 29-May 1, 2010
Jacksonville, FL	July 14-16, 2011
San Antonio, TX	June 7-9, 2012
Springdale, AR	May 30-June 1, 2013
Charleston, SC	July 10-12, 2014

As compiled by PCG Jeff W. Massey

Awards and Medals

Annual National Awards are presented once a year at the National Convention. Most are submitted by a member of the GEC, Departmental Commanders or Society Commanders. These individuals will be notified when nominations are due. Forms for submission will be furnished or made available on the National web site. All nominations for awards must be submitted with written documentation that lists specifics reasons for the nomination.

Chapter Commanders who wish to make nominations for National Convention Awards should work through their Society Commanders and use the Chapter forms available on the web site to submit to the Society. Nomination deadlines are important as certificates must be printed and medals prepared. All interested parties should familiarize themselves with the nomination forms and deadlines published on the National web site to insure participation in the awards process.

Work and activities performed while carrying out the duties of an elected or appointed office are not reasons for award nominations as such duties are the requirements of office. Likewise, the normal requirements expected for all members of the Military Order of Stars and Bars are not qualifications for Awards.

Robert E. Lee Chalice: The highest award presented by the GEC, the Lee Chalice is an engraved silver chalice which is presented annually to a member who has served the Military Order of the Stars & Bars with long and distinguished service. It is an Annual National award. All recipients must be past recipients of The Gold Star. It may be awarded only once to a member. The Chalice is accompanied by a gold medal suspended from a gold ribbon and a miniature. Nominations for the Robert E. Lee Chalice are solicited from voting members of the General Executive Council. Nominations must be accompanied with a written narrative on the nominee. The narrative should be at least fifty (50) words and not more than one hundred fifty (150) words. The list of nominees, with accompanying narratives, is distributed to the voting members of the General Executive Council. The individual receiving the largest number of votes will be declared the recipient. In case of a tie, another ballot with the two individuals receiving the largest number of votes in the initial balloting will be submitted to the General Executive Council to select the recipient. The recipient is named at the annual National Convention by the Commander General.

The Gold Star: This Annual National award is presented by voting members of the GEC to an outstanding member from each of the following departments: Army of Northern Virginia, Army of Tennessee, and Army of Trans-Mississippi. It is the Order's second highest award. Each recipient receives a gold medal as well as an appropriate certificate reflecting the Confederate hero for which it is named. The awards are presented at the National Convention.

Army of Northern Virginia *General Samuel Cooper Award*
Army of Tennessee
General Joseph E. Johnston Award
Army of Trans-Mississippi
General Albert Sidney Johnston Award

The Distinguished Commander Medal: This Annual National award is presented by the Commander General to senior members who have demonstrated long, dedicated service to the Military Order of the Stars & Bars. The Award is a gold medal inlaid with red enamel and suspended from a yellow gold ribbon. A certificate signed by the Commander General and a miniature medal is also given. Recipients are also authorized to indicate this distinguished status by using the letters "DCS" (*Distinguished Commander Status*) after their names on all official correspondence and records. It is generally presented by the Commander General at the National Convention.

Honorary Commander General: The General Society in convention assembled may elect Honorary Commander Generals from among those who have rendered distinguished and notable service to the Society, or to the state or nation. A Past Commander General cannot receive this award. The acceptance of this award prohibits the recipient from being elected Commander General.

The Confederate Legacy Citation of Honor: The Confederate Legacy Endowment is presented to MOS&B members who by their Sacrificial Giving have denoted their Special Confidence and Esteem in the Order. Recipients receive a certificate signed by the Commander General and Adjutant General and are entitled to wear the Confederate Legacy Drop. Complete details regarding membership are on the National web site.

The Col. John Pelham Legion of Merit Award: This is an Annual National award presented by the Commander General for exceptional work by an individual member on behalf of the *General Society.* Candidates must have demonstrated outstanding leadership skills and personify the leadership of the Confederate Officers Corp. The award is both a miniature gold medal suspended from a red ribbon for first time recipients and a certificate. Recommendations for this award should be made in writing to the Commander General.

Lt. Charles Read Meritorious Service Award: Presented and approved by the Commander General, this Annual National award is given in recognition to an individual member for work promoting the General Society at the *Chapter* level. Nominated members should have demonstrated the highest work ethic and proven themselves in promoting the Military Order of the Stars and Bars. First time recipients receive a miniature medal suspended from a light blue ribbon along with a certificate. Recommendations for this award should be made in writing to the Commander General.

The Maj. Gen. Patrick R. Cleburne Meritorious Service Award: The Commander General presents this Annual National certificate to members who have performed meritorious acts for furtherance of the National Military Order of the Stars and Bars.

The Commander General's Award: The Commander General awards this Annual National certificate to individuals who have rendered outstanding personal service to the Commander General in the performance of his duties.

The Varina Howell Davis Award: A gold miniature medal with the likeness of the First Lady of the Confederacy, this one time National award is presented by the Commander General to ladies who have demonstrated unusual support for the Military Order of the Stars & Bars and its goals. A certificate comes with the medal. Medals are numbered and International Headquarters must be advised of the recipient, date of presentation and the medal number. This information is maintained in a log at IHQ. This is the highest award the MOS&B gives to a lady for continued unusual support of the Order. Recommendations for this Award should be made in writing to the Commander General. Nominations should include a narrative of not less than fifty (50) and not more than two hundred fifty (250) words.

The Joseph Evan Davis Award: This Annual National award is a gold medal with the likeness of Joseph Evan Davis, son of President and Mrs. Jefferson Davis. It comes with a certificate. Recipients must be a member in good standing of the Children of the Confederacy or the Military Order of the Stars & Bars between the ages of 12 and 18 years of age. Presented and approved by the Commander General upon recommendation to him by a Military Order of the Stars & Bars member, this award requires a narrative of not less than fifty (50) and not more than two hundred fifty (250) words.

The Winnie Davis Award: This Annual National award is a beautiful certificate bearing the portrait of "The Daughter of the Confederacy" and is presented to ladies who have demonstrably supported the purpose and goals of the MOS&B. This award requires recommendations to be made in writing.

Judah P. Benjamin Award: A multicolored certificate signed by the Commander General, this award is presented in behalf of the Military Order of the Stars & Bars, to a non-member, either male or female, in the promotion and preservation of Southern Heritage and History. This is the highest award presented to a non-member.

The Rebel Club: Because recruiting of new members is vital to the Military Order of the Stars & Bars, the Rebel Club was created to recognize individual members who excel in the recruitment of new members. Certificates as well as miniature medals depicting the Great Seal of the Confederacy are presented by the National Society to individual members who have demonstrated successful membership recruiting for the Order in the past year. Those who sponsor 3-4 new members receive a certificate while a Bronze miniature medal is awarded for 5 new members, a Silver miniature for 7 and a Gold miniature for 10 or more. The Rebel Club is an Annual National award.

Law and Order Medal: The Law and Order Medal is an Annual National award presented by the Commander General to a law enforcement officer, local, state or federal, for conspicuous gallantry and dedication beyond the call of duty. The recipient is presented a full size medal.

General Thomas Jackson Medal: The Stonewall Jackson medal program is an Annual National award administered through PCG Josiah Gay, III and the Jackson Committee. Awards are presented to MOS&B members who have maintained a Confederate Officer's grave for a minimum of two years, placed a bronze marker and a Confederate Cross of Honor. All information is provided on the National web site.

Honorary Membership: The certificate bears the signature of the Commander General and is awarded following approval for honorary membership. Honorary membership may only be bestowed upon a gentleman who is ineligible for membership in the Military Order of the Stars & Bars. Honorary memberships carry all rights of participation, but do not have a vote. The person must be nominated by a voting member of the General Executive Council or the General Convention and must receive a majority of acceptance by this body. Currently, (1) all surviving sons of a Confederate veteran, regardless of rank, have been approved for honorary membership as well as (2) all surviving veterans of World War I.

Henry Timrod Southern Culture Award: This Annual National award is given for outstanding contributions by a current Military Order of Stars and Bars member towards the understanding, appreciation and explanation of our Southern Heritage and Way of Life. In addition, one non-member per year may be honored with this award. The award may be given for contributions in the form of fine art, literature, scholarly articles, cinema, art, theatre, poetry, architecture, etc. Submissions must demonstrate a positive reflection and contribution to Southern culture. Nominations should be made in writing to the Awards Chairman by April 1 of each year.

Colonel Walter H. Taylor Award: This Annual National award is presented to the Military Order of the Stars & Bars State Society that regularly publishes a newsletter judged to be the most outstanding in the Order. Points are awarded based on:

Format	15
Society and Nat'l News	30
Historical Content	20
Regular Publication Schedule	15
Overall Interest and Appeal	20
Total	100

To be considered for competition, three copies of each newsletter published must be submitted together to the Awards Chairman by April 1st of each year. Decisions of the judging are final. The publication schedule for competition purposes is National Convention- April 1 of the following year. Winners receive a certificate noting their achievement.

Captain John Morton Award: This Annual National award is presented to the Chapter publishing the newsletter selected as the outstanding Chapter publication in the Military Order of the Stars & Bars. To be considered for competition, three copies of each newsletter published must be submitted together to the Awards Chairman by the first of April of each year. Decision of the judging is final. Points are awarded based on:

Format	15
Society and Nat'l News	30
Historical Content	20
Regular Publication Schedule	15
Overall Interest and Appeal	20
Total	100

The publication schedule for competition purposes is National Convention to April 1 of the following year. Winners receive a certificate noting their achievement.

The J.E.B. Stuart Award: This Annual National award is presented to the *Society* whose scrapbook has been judged best in the Order. It should document the activities of the Society in the fulfillment of the goals and objectives of the Order. Scrapbooks are judged on attractiveness and uniqueness of appearance, documentation of current activities and meetings of the past year, theme and overall interest. Societies who wish to enter scrapbooks in the competition must send the scrapbook to the Awards Chairman no later than the first of April of each year. It is suggested that submissions be insured for shipping. Submitted scrapbooks will be available to be picked up after the competition at the National Convention and will not be mailed back if not picked up. Winners receive a certificate noting their achievement.

The T. J. Fakes Award: This Annual National award is presented to the *Chapter* whose scrapbook has been judged best in the Order. The award is presented at the National Convention. It should document the activities of the Chapter in the fulfillment of the goals and objectives of the Order. Scrapbooks are judged on attractiveness and uniqueness of appearance, documentation of current activities and meetings of the past year, theme and overall interest. Chapters who wish to enter scrapbooks in the competition must send the scrapbook to the Awards Chairman no later than first of April of each year. It is suggested they be insured for shipping. Submitted scrapbooks will be available to be picked up after the competition at the National Convention and will not be mailed back if not picked up. Winners receive a certificate noting their achievement.

Col. Walter Hopkins Distinguished Chapter Award: This award is presented by the Commander General to the Chapter that best exemplifies the purposes and principles of the Military Order of Stars and Bars as exhibited by its activities, services, membership and leadership. The completed *Chapter Annual Report* must be submitted with the nomination along with any other documentation.

The Lt. Gen. Simon Buckner Award: This certificate is presented as an Annual National award to those Chapters that can document the retention of the same number of paid members from the preceding calendar year or an increase in the number of paid members from the preceding calendar year. This is determined and submitted by State Society Commanders and/or Adjutants no later than the first of April prior to the National Convention. All information submitted must be approved by MOS&B IHQ.

War Service Medal: The WSM is presented to an active member of the Military Order of the Stars & Bars who has served honorably in combat for our nation. Service must have been in a combat zone for 30 consecutive or 60 non-consecutive days of duty or have drawn Hostile Fire or Imminent Danger pay. Please see the Veterans of Foreign Wars Eligibility requirements for full criteria that must be met. Applications must be approved by the MOS&B War Service Committee. Applications and costs are available on the National MOS&B web site.

Southern Cross of Military Service: This Medal is presented to an active member of the Military Order of Stars and Bars who has served honorably in our nation's military without participating in combat. Applicants must be approved by the MOS&B War Service Committee. Application and costs are available on the National MOS&B web site.

Real Grandson Medal: The Real Grandson Medal may be presented to a real documented linear grandson of a documented Confederate Veteran. Application must be made to the Real Grandson Committee using the approved application with submission cost that is available on the National web site.

Real Great Grandson Medal: The Real Great Grandson Medal may be presented to a real documented linear great grandson of a documented Confederate Veteran. Application must be made to the Real Great Grandson Committee using the approved application with submission cost that is available on the National web site.

Real Great Great Grandson Medal: The Real Great Great Grandson Medal may be presented to a real documented linear great great grandson of a documented Confederate Veteran. Application must be made to the Real Great Great Grandson Committee using the approved application with submission cost that is available on the National web site.

Eagle Scout Certificate: The Eagle Scout Certificate is presented on behalf of the Commander General to deserving Boy Scouts, MOS&B members or non-members, in recognition of achievement of the status of Eagle Scout. Application for the certificate may be made by Chapters, Societies or members of the GEC. Application information is available on the National web site.

Gen. Robert E. Lee Leadership Award: The Military Order of the Stars and Bars offers this certificate award to JROTC and ROTC cadets that most reflects the leadership values personified by General Robert E. Lee. Commanding Officers of Senior ROTC and Junior ROTC units are responsible for determining recipients of this award. Minimum qualification criteria follow.

1. Cadet is a college or high school junior;
2. Possess a minimum 3.0 Cumulative GPA;
3. Ranked in the top 5% of in his or her military class; and
4. Administration of awards is the responsibility of local MOSB Chapters.

Local MOS&B Chapters should, at their own expense and discretion, present a saber or other suitable accouterment to an award recipient. The MOS&B State Society may elect to manage this program for state chapters and may choose to identify and award a state level cadet recipient. The award for the state recipient must be differentiated from any chapter recipients. The local MOS&B Chapter will coordinate permission to present the award from the Commanding Officers of individual SROTC programs. The same will apply for coordinating permission from individual JROTC programs and its high school principals or area school superintendents. Wherever possible, awards should be presented by a member of the local MOSB Chapter. The Chapter or Society may provide at their expense an additional award to the recipient at either Chapter or Society level.

Membership Certificate: Every man accepted for membership in the Military Order of the Stars & Bars will be issued a multi-colored certificate of membership stating his name, membership date and number and the name and rank of his ancestor. This certificate is signed by the Commander General. Replacement and Supplementary Ancestor Certificates are available through IHQ.

Last Commission: Upon the death of a current member of the Order, Chapter Adjutants should complete the Last Commission form located on the web site and forward to IHQ. If possible, a copy of the obituary should accompany the form. IHQ will print a Last Commission certificate that the Chapter or Society Chaplain or other designated member may deliver to the family members. If personal delivery is not available, the Last Commission will be mailed to the next of kin.

Certificate of Appreciation: This certificate may be presented to any non-member, male or female, for their contributions to the protection of Southern Heritage and/or the advancement of the Military Order of the Stars & Bars.

MOS&B Scholarships: The Military Order of the Stars & Bars awards college scholarships of $1000 each. These Scholarships are appropriately named for Confederate Generals Robert E. Lee, Patrick R. Cleburne and Nathan Bedford Forrest. The number of Scholarships awarded is determined annually by the GEC. All applicants must be a genealogically proven descendent of a Confederate Officer or descendant of a member of the Confederate Executive or Legislative branches of government or descendent of a member of the Confederate States legislatures, judiciary or executive branches of state government. Three separate Letters of Recommendation attesting to the applicant's character, ability, dependability and integrity are required with the application package. At least one recommending letter must be from an educator. Letters from relatives are not acceptable. All applications must have a support letter from a Chapter or Society. All requirements being equal, preference is given to current MOS&B members and close relatives of current members. All current information, forms and deadlines may be secured on-line at the national MOS&B web site.

The Douglas Southall Freeman History Award: The award shall be made for the best published book of high merit in the field of Southern history beginning with the colonial period to the present time. The award shall be given only to works of high merit. If no work is submitted that meets the high standards of the Freeman History Award regulations, no award shall be given that year. The award shall be in the amount of $1,000 paid directly to the author. The winner also shall receive an engraved trophy denoting that he was the recipient of the award. All books to be considered for this year's award shall be submitted to the Freeman History Committee by the publisher. All entries must be accompanied by a letter from the publisher giving the official date of publication. All entries must be accompanied by a biographical sketch of the author. If the winning book goes to a second printing, it shall contain the acknowledgment that it was selected as the winner of the Freeman History Award plus stating the year it was awarded. The book shall also list the previous winners with additions as necessary. In response to the educational and historical charge set forth in the national Military Order of the Stars & Bars constitution, the Douglas Southall Freeman History Award was established. The award was named in honor of the premier historian of General Robert E. Lee and the Army of Northern Virginia.

The General Basil W. Duke Award: This annual award shall be given to encourage the re-issuance of out-of-print books that accurately present history of the War for Southern Independence. The Award shall be in the amount of $1,000 presented directly to the publisher of the reprinted volume. The publisher shall receive an engraved trophy denoting that he was the recipient of the award all books to be considered for this award shall be submitted to the Judging Committee by the first of April by the publisher. Invitation to participate in the competition is extended to any publisher who issues a book between May 1st of the previous year and April 1st of the current year, that has not been republished since the expiration of the original copyright. All entries must include a letter from the publisher stating the year the book was published originally, and the date the reprint was issued. The judges shall consider the quality, accuracy, style and value to Confederate historiography when selecting the winning book. Regimental histories, autobiographies, memoirs and biographies of noted Confederate leaders are among the types of books to be considered for this award. If the winning book goes to a second printing, it shall contain an acknowledgment that selected as the winner of the General Basil W. Duke Award, plus stating the year it was awarded.

The John Esten Cooke Fiction Award: The award shall be given annually to encourage writers of fiction to portray characters and events dealing with the War Between the States, Confederate heritage, or Southern history in a historically accurate fashion. The award shall be in the amount of $1,000 paid directly to the author. The winner shall receive an engraved trophy denoting that he/she was the recipient of the award. All books to be considered for this year's award shall be submitted to the John Esten Cooke Fiction Award Committee by the first of April. Invitation to participate in the contest is extended to any person who has written a book-length work of fiction published between May 1st, two years prior and April 1st of this year. All entries must be accompanied by a letter from the publisher stating the official date of publication. Each entry must be accompanied by a biographical sketch of the author. The judges will consider the effectiveness of research, accuracy of statement, and excellence of style in selecting the winner. All entries must be book length. If the winning book goes to a second printing, it shall contain the acknowledgment that it was selected as the winner of the Cooke Fiction Award along with stating the year the award was made.

Basic Organizational Structure

The membership of the Military Order of the Stars and Bars is composed of legitimate male descendants, lineal or collateral, of those who served as officers in the Confederate Army or Navy to the end of the War, or who died in prison or while in actual service were killed in battle, or who were honorably retired or discharged, and descendants of elected and appointed officials of the Executive or Legislative branch of the civil government.

The MOS&B National Constitution, Article V divides the General Society into three Departments, State Societies and Chapters. In addition, it prescribes the organization and duties of MOS&B Chapters. The Chapter is the basic unit of the Society. Chapters may be formed in states where State Societies already exist, in which case they become part of the State Society and remain assigned thereto. National Headquarters will also maintain the Jefferson Davis Chapter #1 for members who are not part of a State Society or a local Chapter.

Five National members are required to form a new Chapter. When fifteen MOS&B members residing in the State where a State Society has not been formed create one or more Chapters and then application may be made to form a new State Society to the General Executive Council (Art. V, Sect. 3). Such application should be made to:

The Commander General
IHQ, Military Order of the Stars and Bars
P.O. Box 1700
White House, Tennessee 37188-1700

The three Departments that State Societies are assigned to are; (1) Army of Northern Virginia, (2) Army of Tennessee Department and (3) Army of the Trans Mississippi.
The Army of Northern Virginia Department consists of the following State Societies: District of Columbia, Maryland, North Carolina, South Carolina, West Virginia, Virginia and all States east of the State of Ohio and north of the State of Virginia.
The Army of Tennessee Department consists of the following State Societies: Alabama, Georgia, Florida, Indiana, Kentucky, Mississippi, Tennessee and those States not included in the other two Departments' regions.
The Army of the Trans Mississippi Department consists of the following State Societies: Arkansas, Louisiana, Missouri, Oklahoma, Texas and States West of the Mississippi River.

A National Convention, or National Reunion, is held annually. Reunions are held in cities throughout the United States. Upcoming Reunions are planned for Jacksonville, Florida in 2011 and San Antonio, Texas in 2012. These National reunions are family events that allow members to gather in a fraternal body to conduct the business of the General Society as well as to attend educational sessions, visit historical sites and informally meet with new and old compatriots. The Reunion includes a prayer breakfast, Awards banquet, business sessions and concludes with a black tie or period dress Grand Ball.

Throughout the Order, the State Societies and local Chapters have regular meetings and conventions, hold Jefferson Davis Banquets, Lee-Jackson Banquets, sponsor historical War Between the States lectures and participate in patriotic memorial events. While heritage preservation and education are the primary function, the gathering of compatriots is always a social event enjoyed by those sharing a common Southern heritage.

Chapter Officers' Duties and Responsibilities

It is understood that every Chapter may not have every position listed here simply because of Chapter size. However, all Chapters are required as a minimum to have a Commander, Lieutenant Commander and Adjutant. As Chapters numbers and activities increase, more positions will be needed not only to carry out the goals and purpose of the Military Order of the Stars and Bars, but also to train new leadership for the future.

Chapter Commander: He has a unique responsibility to provide leadership, to encourage, assist, guide, maintain esprit de corps, and above all, to work to achieve harmony within the Chapter, State Society, National MOS&B as well as other organizations and groups with which the Chapter has a relationship. The Chapter Commander presides at all meetings or delegates his subordinates to preside. He appoints all committees with input from others that he feels necessary to help run the Chapter.

First Lieutenant Commander: This officer is second only to the Commander in responsibility. He presides in the absence of the Commander. Upon resignation or death of the Commander, the First Lieutenant Commander automatically becomes Chapter Commander. He also serves as the program chairman for the Chapter. In most Chapters it is assumed that he will succeed the Commander if he has proven himself equal to the task in the eyes of his fellow members.

Second Lieutenant Commander: This officer is third in responsibility and upon a vacancy in the position of First Lieutenant Commander succeeds to that post. He may serve as the publisher of the Chapter newsletter, direct activities of the editor, and coordinates the printing of Chapter publications such as a Chapter Handbook. He develops ideas and programs to raise funds for the Chapter treasury and for special purposes and projects which he may be assigned.

Adjutant: The Adjutant maintains all Chapter records, prepares Chapter rosters with the assistance of the Chapter Treasurer, prepares and submits all reports such as the Annual Chapter Report to the various Society, Department and National Headquarters. He records the minutes of all Chapter meetings, submits approved Applications for membership in the Chapter to the Society Genealogist, maintains current membership Applications, MOS&B information pamphlets, prospective members list, grave location forms, etc. He also conducts Chapter correspondence as required.

Treasurer: The Treasurer is responsible for the Chapter's financial records and reports. These responsibilities include the receiving of all monies paid to the Chapter, such as dues and dispersing them to the right channels, paying all bills incurred by the Chapter, keeping an account of all financial transactions of the Chapter, and handling all banking business for the Chapter. In many Chapters these treasury duties are combined with the Adjutant.

Chaplain: The Chaplain offers prayers at the opening of the Chapter Meeting and the MOS&B Benediction at the close of the meeting, serves at Memorial Services, Roll of Honor Services, graveside services, grave markings, and other occasions when it is appropriate, to ask for Divine Guidance.

Historian: The Historian is responsible for maintaining the Chapter scrapbook and acting as the recorder of Chapter history. He may be asked to submit the Chapter Scrapbook for the National Convention. The position may be combined with another officer in some Chapters.

Judge Advocate: The Judge Advocate is the Chapter legal advisor and acts as parliamentarian at official Chapter sessions. If an attorney is a Chapter Member then it would be useful for him to fill this role.

Genealogist: The Chapter Genealogist should be available to help any new potential member in filling out his Application for Membership or any current member doing the same with a Supplemental Ancestor. He should be familiar with local, state and national archives and libraries where genealogical research is found. He should be competent in using the Internet and be familiar with sources to help in genealogical research.

Color Sergeant: The Color Sergeant serves in Memorial Services, Roll of Honor, special programs and parades as the arranger and/or principal color bearer for the National and Confederate flags. He will lead the membership at Chapter meetings in the Pledges/Salutes of Allegiance to the National, State and Confederate flags. At all Chapter functions he acts as Sergeant at Arms with the responsibility to maintain order and decorum.

Quartermaster: The Quartermaster is responsible for the care and maintenance of the Chapter flags, supplies and equipment, and ensures its availability as necessary at Chapter meetings, Memorial Services, Roll of Honor, funerals, parades, and other functions in which the Chapter takes part.

Executive Council: The Executive Council is composed of all elected Chapter Officers as well as the Past Chapter Commanders for the previous four years. Working as a team under the commander's leadership, they shall be responsible for the overall long range direction of the Chapter and are deeply involved in planning the Chapter's programs and activities. Matters of major importance concerning the Chapter's future should be brought before this council before presentation to the Chapter.

Succession: Every officer has a unique and special responsibility to preserve and maintain custody of all Chapter records generated during his term of office or entrusted to his care. Upon his departure from office, he is required to turn over to his successor, in good order, all records in his possession. In the absence of an immediate successor, such records shall be turned over to the Adjutant until a new officer is selected as in the case of elected Chapter officers.

Department, State Societies and Chapter History

The General Society is divided into Departments, State Societies, and Chapters. There are three Departments: Army of Northern Virginia, Army of Tennessee, and Army of the Trans-Mississippi. State Societies are formed in states within the three Armies, and these Societies are then divided into local units called Chapters. The following background history of these Departments, States Societies, and Chapters have been compiled from individual submittals, past publications, website information to give our membership a broad background of the organization as a whole.

Army of Northern Virginia

The Department hereby known as the Army of Northern Virginia is comprised of six Societies upon which two are in-active at this time. The active State Societies in the Army of Northern Virginia Department are the Maryland Society, the North Carolina Society, the South Carolina Society, and the Virginia Society. Chapters that have been chartered under the Army of Northern Virginia that have no State Society are as follows: New York Chapter # 169 in New York City, NY; CSS Tallahassee Chapter # 209 in West Hartford, CT; and John C. Pemberton Chapter # 229 in Philadelphia, PA.

Maryland Society

The Maryland Society is comprised of three chapters which are the Colonel Richard Thomas "Zarvona" Chapter #54 in Waldrof, MD; The Maryland Line Chapter # 191 in Annapolis, MD; and the Captain Charles F. Linthicum Chapter # 216 in Darnestown, MD. The first chapter to charter in Maryland was The Maryland Line Chapter. By 1986, there were three chapters within the state.

Captain Charles F. Linthicum Chapter # 216

The charter for the Captain Charles F. Linthicum Chapter was granted on June 3, 1995. There were fifteen charter members when this chapter was established. A major project for the Chapter has been the upkeep and refurbishing of Confederate graves and markers in Bealsville Cemetery. The Chapter has also had various picnics and fund raisers at the Kennedy Farm in Sharpsburg, Maryland.

North Carolina Society

The North Carolina Society was organized on February 28, 1978. It was in 1987 that the NC Society started holding that Annual Confederate Memorial Weekend in Raleigh at the State Capitol with a parade. On January 19, 1990, the first annual Robert E. Lee Birthday Celebration was held at the State Capitol in Raleigh and was sponsored by the Captain James I. Waddell Chapter. The NC Society also sponsored a booth at the 125th Anniversary of the Battle of Bentonville Re-enactment.

At the NC Society Convention in May 1995, Albert Jones of Raleigh, NC was elected the new Society Commander. He began a reorganization of the Society beginning with a survey of the chapters. The NC Society also established a newsletter in the spring of 1996 entitled *Farthest to the Front*, which won the Colonel Walter H. Taylor Society Newsletter Award for 1996 and 1997. Their project of photographing the graves of all Confederate Generals with a North Carolina connection was gathered up and published in 1998 with this project being chaired by Byron Brady.

Other highlights of the NC Society were (1) Tarheel Chapters were the recipient of the Dr. James M. Edwards Distinguished Chapter Award for the Best Chapter in the Confederation in 1997 and 1998; (2) The General William D. McCain Award for the Society recruiting the most new members in the ANV was awarded to North Carolina in 1997 and 2007; (3) Home of the Capt. John Morton Newsletter Award for the Best Chapter newsletter in the Confederation from 1994 - 2001, 2006 and again in 2011; (4) Recipient of the Col. Walter H. Taylor Award for the Best Society Newsletter in 1997, 1999, 2000 and again in 2006 and (5) a Tarheel Chapter was the winner of the "Turner J. Fakes Award" for the Best Chapter Scrapbook in the Confederation in 2006, 2007, 2010 and again in 2011.

The chapters that had been chartered in the State of North Carolina as part of this Society are as follows:

Asheville Chapter # 7	Asheville, NC
Brigadier General Rufus Barringer Chapter # 18	Charlotte, NC
Brigadier General William R. Boggs Chapter # 19	Winston-Salem, NC
Capt. James I. Waddell Chapter #32	Raleigh, NC
Charlotte Chapter # 42	Charlotte, NC

Col. Charles Courtenay Tew Chapter # 47	Durham, NC
Garnett-Pettigrew Chapter # 67	Greensboro, NC
Lt. William C. Ferrell Chapter # 148	Wilson, NC
Lt. Wilson Bailey Chapter #149 & # 208	Raleigh, NC
Major General William Dorsey Pender Chapter # 151	Dunn, NC
Major Absolom Knox Simonton Chapter # 152	Statesville, NC
The Immortal 600 Chapter # 190	Louisburg, NC
Col. Robert F. Webb Chapter # 195	Raleigh, NC
1st Lt. Wiloughby Lynn Hockaday Chapter # 203	Sea Level, NC
Topsail Rifles / Beaufort Harbor Guards Chapter # 217	Sea Level, NC
General Robert D. Johnston Chapter # 247	Lincolnton, NC
Capt. Asbury T. Rogers Chapter # 266	Asheville, NC
CSS Ram Albermarle Chapter # 291	Plymouth, NC
Capt. Henry C. Grady Chapter # 296	Anson / Union / Mecklenburg Counties, NC
Lt. Thomas D. Lattimore Chapter # 304	Rutherfordton, NC

Brigadier General Rufus Barringer Chapter # 18
Charlotte, NC

The Brigadier General Rufus Barringer Chapter applied for a charter in 1986 under the auspices of Commander Arthur R. Claiborne. This chapter has participated in raising funds for charity, gone on field trips, and restored gravesites in the Charlotte, NC area. It has also participated in memorial ceremonies on Confederate Memorial Day at the Elmwood Cemetery.

Among the graves that have been restored by this chapter are Brigadier General Rufus Barringer and Brigadier General Thomas Drayton gravesites. They have also assisted in the placement of 118 Confederate Monuments in the Elmwood Cemetery. They also helped to erect a monument at the site of the North Carolina Military Institute in Charlotte.

Brigadier General William R. Boggs Chapter # 19
Winston-Salem, NC

The Brigadier General William R. Boggs Chapter was organized in the summer of 1986 in Winston-Salem and held their first meeting in August of that year. In 1990, the chapter began to sponsor an annual War Between the States and Antique Only Gun Show in March. In May of each year, the chapter participates in Confederate Memorial Services held in the Salem Cemetery. They also contribute funds to many Confederate related organizations as a result of the profit they make each year at their gun show.

Captain James Iredell Waddell Chapter # 32 – Raleigh, NC

In 1988, the Capt. James I. Waddell Chapter was chartered with 36 members and held their charter banquet April 8, 1989 at Ballentines in Cameron Village. The name of the chapter was chosen because he was born July 13, 1824 in nearby Pittsboro, just west of Raleigh. Capt. James Iredell Waddell was a distinguished Confederate naval hero and Captain of the CSS *Shenandoah*. He died on March 18, 1886 and is buried in Annapolis, Maryland.

Upon being charter, the chapter immediately began publishing *The Shenandoah* as their official newsletter. Byron Brady became their first editor. This newsletter has been awarded the Capt. John Morton Newsletter Recognition Award for the Best Chapter newsletter in the Confederate in 1994, 1995, and 1997 to 2001.

In 1989, the chapter began sponsoring an annual birthday celebration for General Robert E. Lee at the State Capitol. The ceremony is always held on January 19th. Every ceremony has had standing room only crowds and the Confederate First National Flag has flown over the Capitol during the ceremony.

In the summer of 1995, the chapter began an annual tradition called the Commander's Ice Cream Social which was held at the Fred Fletcher Park in Raleigh. In later years, corporate sponsors have been secured to help offset the cost.

The chapter is also the 1997 recipient of the Dr. James M. Edwards Distinguished Award for the best chapter in the confederation. They have also restored the grave of North Carolina General Lawrence O'Bryan Branch in the City Cemetery located in Raleigh, NC.

Garnett–Pettigrew Chapter # 67 – Greensboro, NC

The Garnett-Pettigrew Chapter was established in 1984. The chapter members decided to name the chapter for two generals of equal rank, one from Virginia and one from North Carolina. These men were General Richard Garnett of Virginia and General James J. Pettigrew of North Carolina.

Richard Brooke Garnett was promoted to the rank of Brigadier General in November 1851, and was killed at Gettysburg on July 3, 1863 during the Pettigrew-Pickett charge. James Johnston Pettigrew was promoted to Brigadier General on February 26, 1862. General Pettigrew survived the fighting at Gettysburg, but was wounded at Falling Waters in rear guard action during the withdrawal to Virginia. He died from wounds three days later.

The chapter has dedicated a state road marker commemorating Major General Stephen Dodson Ramseur. This marker is located in Milton, NC. They have also sponsored the Guilford Courthouse Battleground Chapter of the Tar Heel Junior Historians. The Junior Historians is a program of the NC Museum of History and is open to all students between the 4th and 12th grades.

The chapter has an on-going flag preservation project to collect donations at meetings and special events which are then forwarded to the Museum of the Confederacy in Richmond for their flag preservation efforts. Each December the chapter presents awards to chapter members they deem to have done the most to exemplify the dedication to the cause embodied by the actions of CSA Officers, our forefathers, imprisoned by Union forces at Fort Delaware on May 8, 1865.

The chapter newsletter, *The Garnett-Pettigrew Gray Line!* was the recipient of the "Captain John Morton Newsletter Award" for the years of 1996, 2006, and 2011. Then in 1998, the chapter was recognized as Best Chapter in the Confederation. They have also been the recipient of the "Turner J. Fakes Award" for the years of 2006, 2007, 2010, and 2011.

The Garnett-Pettigrew Chapter # 67 has adopted and maintained five Confederate Infantry Brigade markers including A. P. Hill Headquarters, Carter's Battery, 11th Mississippi Regiment and the state monuments of Tennessee, Mississippi, and Georgia at the Gettysburg National Military Park.

Lt. Wilson Bailey Chapter #149/#208 – Raleigh, NC

The Lt. Wilson Bailey Chapter was formed at the National SCV/MOS&B Convention held in Asheville, NC in 1979 and its charter was issued shortly thereafter. Lt. Wilson Bailey was wounded and died at the first battle of the Wilderness in 1862.

The chapter has placed a bronze plaque at the entrance to General Stephen Dodson Ramseur Drive in Royal, NC on October 20, 1997 in a formal ceremony that included many North Carolina re-enactors. This road was built and named by the commander's son-in-law and his wife, Billy and Linda Bailey Hux.

Major Absalom Knox Simonton Chapter #152 – Statesville, NC

The Major Absalom Knox Simonton Chapter was formed in August 2007 and is the North Carolina Society's newest chapter.

The Immortal 600 Chapter – Louisburg, NC

The namesake for the Immortal 600 Chapter was the 600 Confederate Officers who were placed in a position to shield Federal troops on Morris Island from Confederate artillery fire from Fort Sumter in South Carolina. This chapter organized and chartered in 1993.

Along with the Franklin Rifles SCV Camp #310, they sponsor an annual program in December to collect donations from its members, purchase Christmas fruit, and deliver it to eight Rest Homes and Special Care Homes in Franklin County.

Colonel Robert F. Webb Chapter #195 – Raleigh, NC

On July 1, 1969, the Colonel Robert F. Webb Chapter was organized. The chapter received its name from Robert F. Webb, the last Colonel of North Carolina's famed "Bloody Sixth" Regiment. Later the name was changed to Webb-Bailey Chapter on August 1, 1990. Then on September 22, 1993, the Webb-Bailey chapter voted unanimously to change its name back to the Colonel Robert F. Webb Chapter. The members made this change due to the fact that the Robert F. Webb chapter name had the distinction of being Wake County's oldest MOS&B chapter and they wanted to hold this title for historical accuracy. It was subsequently re-chartered on January 1, 1994.

The chapter has been involved in a number of significant historical and heritage preservation projects. For years, they cared for the Warren County grave of Anne Carter Lee, youngest daughter of General Robert E. Lee, until Anne's remains were moved to the Lee family crypt in Lexington, VA on September 27, 1994.

The Topsail Rifles/Beaufort Guards Chapter # 217
Sea Level, NC

The Topsail Rifles/Beaufort Guards Chapter was chartered on February 14, 1994 under the name of 1st Lt. Wiloughby Lynn Hockaday/Black River Tigers Chapter. The chapter changed their name to the current one in 1997.

General Robert D. Johnston Chapter #247 – Lincolnton, NC

The initial organizational meeting to establish the General Robert D. Johnston Chapter was held in June 1997. General Johnston was born and raised in Lincoln County and was a childhood classmate and close friend to General Robert F. Hoke and General Stephen D. Ramseur. General Johnston was a gallant leader who received five wounds in the service to the CSA.

A second organizational meeting was held in July 1997 in which there were discussions concerning the future chapter projects to be conducted and a possible trip to Winchester, VA for a Memorial Service for General Johnston. The first regularly scheduled meeting was held on September 27, 1997 at the Western Steer Restaurant in Lincolnton, NC.

Captain Asbury T. Rogers Chapter #266 – Asheville, NC

The Captain Asbury T. Rogers Chapter, MOS&B, was formed in October, 2001. The Chapter meets quarterly, on the third Tuesday in October, January, April and July. Because members reside throughout western North Carolina, locations for the meetings vary.
The Chapter currently is active in locating, identifying, cleaning, restoring and maintaining the grave sites of Confederate Officers in western North Carolina.

CS Ram Albemarle Chapter #291 – Plymouth, NC

On September 30, 2004, the CS Ram Albemarle Chapter was chartered in Plymouth. After almost two years of planning by Past Commander General Albert Jones, Jr. and Harry Thompson, the NC Society finally welcomed the Plymouth Chapter into the Society.

In keeping with the Chapter's habit of meeting in historical homes and buildings, the Charter Banquet was held in the Lathem House, one of the oldest and grandest homes in Plymouth. Commander General Dan Jones and NC Society Commander Bob Owens presented the Charter to PCG Jones. Then each Charter Member present signed the Charter.

The Chapter chartered with ten members and the potential for 25-30 additional members and should soon become one of our largest chapters.
The Charter Members are: PGC Jones; Harry Thompson; Chris Grimes; Bob Grimes; Peter Roscoe, Walter White, Edward Harding, Philip Morris and Richard VanDorn. Most were able to attend the Charter Banquet.

Special invited guests included: Commander General Dan Jones, NC Society Commander Bob Owens, Assistant Adjutant General George Valsame, and NC Society Chief of Staff Charles Hawks. All were treated to a fantastic "home cooked" meal by the owners of the Lathem House, Sue and Joe Pate, and later heard an interesting program on the chapter's namesake by chapter member Harry Thompson.

Capt. Henry C. Grady Chapter #296 – Anson/Union/Mecklenburg Counties, NC

The chapter is named for Henry C. Grady who enlisted in Monroe (Union County) in 1861 at the age of 17 into Company D, 37th NC Infantry. Voted in a Corporal in '61, he rapidly rose in rank. He was captured at Hanover Courthouse in '62, wounded at Chancellorsville in May '63. Grady was mortally wounded at age twenty. He is buried in the Spotsylvania Confederate Cemetery.

Anson, Union, and Mecklenburg Counties area produced crops to feed the troops, cotton to buy equipment and needed supplies, and many items to arm the troops. Among other industries, Charlotte had the Naval Shipyard. Wadesboro was one of six cotton depots in the state of North Carolina. Wadesboro was home to the Arnold & Cooley factories. Bayonets, dirks, daggers, and swords were made at their factory on West Wade Street. Their Jones Creek factory manufactured rifled muskets. This factory was powered by a sixty acre mill pond that was created especially for the factory in 1862.

Lt. Thomas D. Lattimore Chapter #304 – Rutherfordton, NC

The Lt. Thomas D. Lattimore Chapter of the MOS&B was formed by descendants and relations of the officer to honor his commitment to the Confederacy and his role as a historian and supporter of commemoration events following the war. Lt. Thomas D. Lattimore wrote the official history of the 34th N.C. Regiment for inclusion in Clark's History of the Civil War. After the war he served as the Clerk of Superior Court of Cleveland County, NC for 22 years. During that time he was the leader/ planner of many Confederate veterans reunion events in Shelby, NC, and throughout the state.

The Lt. Thomas D. Lattimore Chapter cares for his gravesite (as well as the grave of his wife Matilda) in the Sunset Cemetery in Shelby N.C. In addition to regular spring and fall cleaning days, the Chapter places wreaths on the couple's graves each Christmas season.

In addition, the chapter cares for the grave of Judge G. W. Logan, a member of the Confederate Congress. His grave is in the Rutherfordton City Cemetery, in Rutherford County, NC. The stone is badly damaged and is in need of repair. The Lt. Thomas D. Lattimore Chapter of the MOSB plans to raise money to repair the stone. In addition, the Chapter plans to place a holiday wreath on his grave each December.

On Saturday, June 2, 2012, members of the Lt. Thomas D. Lattimore Chapter #304 participated in the Town of Rutherfordton's 225th anniversary celebration.

The celebration included a walking tour through the town's historic district and visits to several antebellum homes and churches. More than 30 costumed docents and guides volunteered their services.

Lattimore Chapter Commander Robin Lattimore and his daughter Charlotte dressed in full antebellum attire to lead visitors through the town.

South Carolina Society

The Military Order of the Stars and Bars (MOS&B) was born in South Carolina on August 30, 1938. The 48th Annual Reunion of the United Confederate Veterans and the 43rd Annual Convention of the Sons of Confederate Veterans met at the Columbia Hotel in Columbia, South Carolina August 30 through September 2, 1938. On August 30, 1938 an organizational meeting was held at 3:00 PM and the Order of the Stars and Bars, as it was known then, was created. The initial membership was composed of 17 former commissioned officers of the Confederate States military and 47 male descendants of Confederate officers. Two South Carolinians, both descendants of Confederate officers, were among the original members of the MOS&B. These were Dr. Baylis H. Earle of Greenville and James d'Alvigny McCollough of Honea Path.

The name of the organization was changed to the Military Order of the Stars and Bars at the annual convention in Memphis, Tennessee effective August 15, 1976. As there are no former Confederate officers still living, membership in the MOS&B is restricted to male descendants of Confederate officers and elected officials. The survival of the MOS&B is due in large part to the late General William D. McCain of Mississippi. He served as Adjutant General of the MOS&B from 1954 to 1993. He also served as Adjutant in Chief of the Sons of Confederate Veterans from 1953 to 1993. The modern history South Carolina Society of the Military Order of the Stars and Bars began on October 1, 1984 when the General Maxcy Gregg Chapter was chartered. The charter members were

W. C. Smith, III, David Cooper, Ed Crosby, Dr. Jean LaBorde, Jr. Wesly Drawdy, George Martin, and Henry Durant. This was the only MOSB chapter in South Carolina at that time. It was closely related to the General Wade Hampton Camp, No. 273, Sons of Confederate Veterans and shared the same adjutant for several years.

As of July 1, 1999 the South Carolina Society of the MOS&B now has four active chapters with a total of 57 members. The Society officers for 1998-2000 are Wayne D. Roberts, Commander; William E. DuBose, Jr., Lieutenant Commander; P. Ronald Hamilton, Adjutant; and Michael G. Kelly, Genealogist. The General Maxcy Gregg Chapter, chartered in Columbia in 1984, has 25 members. Officers for the General Maxcy Gregg Chapter are R. Brett Bradshaw, Commander; Harrison Gasque, Lieutenant Commander; Roger O. Harley, Adjutant. The Battle of Dingles Mill Chapter was chartered in Sumter December 23, 1987 and has five members. Officers of the Battle of Dingles Mill Chapter are William E. DuBose, Commander; Benjamin P. McNeese, Jr., Lieutenant Commander; and John A. DuBose, Adjutant. The Major M. C. Butler Chapter chartered in Belvedere June 30, 1997, has nine members. Officers of the Major General M. C. Butler Chapter are R. Jason Goings, Commander and Perry Craig Morris, Adjutant. The Colonel James McCollough Chapter, chartered in Greenville June 30, 1997, has 18 members. Colonel James McCollough Chapter officers are Joseph L. Montgomery, Commander; Tom Tucker, Lieutenant Commander; and Kenneth Derrell Morgan, Adjutant.

The South Carolina Society of the Military Order of the Stars and Bars has been very active with projects over the past several years. In 1993 the Society undertook a series of weekend cleanup expeditions to restore the historic Capers-Guerry cemetery in Sumter. This cemetery was severely damaged by Hurricane Hugo. There has been continuing involvement of the Society in the defense of the Confederate flag atop the South Carolina State House. In 1994 The Society donated $2,000 received from National Headquarters for the defense of the flag. In 1995 a new monument was dedicated to Confederate Medal of Honor recipient Lieutenant Alexander McQueen. The Society contributed $500 to this project. Also in 1995, the Society donated copies of The Roll of the Dead to several public libraries across South Carolina.

In 1996 The South Carolina Society of the MOS&B began holding its annual Lee-Jackson banquet in January. This has become a special time for members, wives, and guests to gather and share mementos and stories of their ancestors and Confederate soldiers. The January 2001 Lee-Jackson banquet is scheduled at Oakley Park in Edgefield. This was the home of Confederate Brigadier General Martin Witherspoon Gary.

In 1997 the South Carolina Society of the MOS&B began annual battlefield tours. These tours have been led by Wayne D. Roberts, Society Commander 1993-1994 and 1998-2000. The first tour was at the Battle of Congaree Creek in Lexington County. In 1998 the tour focused on the Atlanta campaign with stops at the Battle of Kennesaw Mountain, the Battle of Kolbs Farm, Marietta, and Kennesaw (Big Shanty during the Great Locomotive Chase). The 1999 tour focused on the campaign for the Charleston and Savannah Railroad with visits to battlefields, earthworks, and sites including the Battle of Pocotaligo, the Battle of Tullifinny Crossroads, the Battle of Coosawhatchie, the Battle of Honey Hill, Stoney Creek Battery, Tomotley Battery, Bees Creek Battery, Pocotaligo Battery, Gardens Corner, Stoney Creek cemetery, Old Sheldon Church, and the Church of the Holy Trinity in old Grahamville. The 2000 tour focused on Sherman's march through South Carolina. Battlefields visited included Rivers Bridge, Broxton's Bridge, and Congaree Creek.

As an outgrowth of these battlefield tours, the Society has implemented a plan to place historical markers on South Carolina battlefields. The first historical marker will be on the battlefield at Pocotaligo and should be erected during the year 2000. Other historical markers have been discussed for the battlefields at Tullifinny Crossroads and Coosawhatchie.

The chapters that had been chartered in the State of North Carolina as part of this Society are as follows:

Battle of Dingles Mill Chapter #12	Sumter, SC
General Maxcy Gregg Chapter # 98	Columbia, SC
John C. Calhoun Chapter # 126	Aiken, SC
Richard Kirkland Chapter # 174	Camden, SC
Major General Matthew Calbraith Butler Chapter # 232	Belvedere, SC
Colonel James McCullough Chapter # 242	Greenville, SC
Brigadier General Gabriel and Col. George Rains Chapter # 294	Aiken, SC
Col. Stephen Jackson Chapter # 295	Florence, SC
General P. G. T. Beauregard Chapter # 300	Charleston, SC
Captain Stephen Dill Lee Chapter # 301	Charleston, SC

Virginia Society

The formation of the Virginia Society was first suggested by Past Commander-in-Chief H. Paul Porter in December 1974. Subsequent correspondences occurred over the next couple of year with individual chapters being encouraged to charter to grow the membership. Then in 1977, the Virginia Society became a reality.
The past commanders of the Virginia Society include:

1977-79 Flavius Burfoot Walker, Jr.
1979-81 Earl Foster Harvey
1981 Jack K. Wyatt
1981 Hon. Thomas M. Moncure, Jr.
1981-84 Charles R. Higginbotham, Jr.
1984-86 James Harrison Monroe
1986-88 Anthony Patrick Smith
1988-90 Catesby Penniman Jones
1990-92 Josiah Bynum Gay III
1992-94 Hon. G. William Hammer
1994-96 Collin Graham Pulley, Jr.
1996 -1998 Charles Dan McGuire
1998- 2000 Hon. Richard Bender Abell
2000-2002 John C. Stinson
2002-2004 A. Clarke Magruder, Sr.
2004-2006 Jerrell G. Keathley
2006-2008 Raymond Warren Gill, Jr.
2008-2010; William Evans Barr
2010-2012 Walter Allen Mock

Current Officers:
Henry Heyer Knauf, Commander 2012-2014
Robert Edward Lee Scouten, Lieutenant Commander
Joseph Judson Smith, III, Adjutant.

Since its founding, the Virginia Society has expanded rapidly to become one of the Order's largest societies with over 180 members in eight chapters. The Society publishes a membership Directory and two newsletters annually and has established an annual awards system modeled on the MOS&B national awards system to honor members and non-members who have made significant contributions to the Virginia Society or to the Order. The Virginia Society's web site, www.vamosb.org, is linked to the Order's national web site and lists all chapters by name, location, and points of contact. The Society makes donations annually to institutions or activities which honor and commemorate the history and sacrifices of the Confederacy's officer corps and its elected and appointed governmental officials, most recently to the Museum of the Confederacy, Richmond, and to Confederate Memorial Park, Pt. Point, Maryland. The Society also collaborates routinely with organizations such as the United Daughters of the Confederacy, Sons of Confederate Veterans and the Stuart-Mosby and Pickett societies. Collaboration with other military and historical organizations throughout the state enables Society officers to participate regularly in local, state and national heritage activities and ceremonies. We are determined to ensure the Virginia Society adjusts rapidly to the expanding challenges of the 21st Century.

The members of the Virginia Society, MOS&B, are dedicated to commemorating the valor and sacrifices of the Confederacy's officer corps and its elected and appointed officials and the true history of their deeds. The chapters that had been chartered in the Commonwealth of Virginia as part of this Society are as follows:

Colonel Elijah Viers White Chapter #48	Leesburg, VA
General Samuel Cooper Chapter #105	Alexandria, VA
George E. Pickett Chapter #115	Richmond, VA
James T. Jackson Chapter #123	Suffolk, VA
Samuel Ali Mann Chapter #179	Matoaca, VA
General Fitzhugh Lee Chapter #181	Hampton, VA
Hupp-Deyerle-McCausland Chapter #237	Roanoke, VA
Colonel Thomas H. Williamson Chapter #249	Chase City, VA
Slemp-Pridemore Chapter #151	Jonesville, VA
Skipwith Dance Denoon Chapter #260	Powhatan, VA
Colonel Walter H. Taylor Chapter #269	Norfolk, VA
Major General John Bankhead Magruder Chapter #258	Fredericksburg, VA
Lt. General Jubal Anderson Early Chapter #277	Hillsville, VA
Major Edgar Burroughs and Prince Ann Cavalry Chapter #281	Virginia Beach, VA
Cox-McFalls-Creech Chapter #287	Wise, VA
The Immortal 600 Chapter # 298	Swoope, VA

General Samuel Cooper Chapter #105 – Alexandria, VA

The General Samuel Cooper Chapter #105 is named General Samuel Cooper, the senior general officer of the Confederacy and resident of Alexandria. Among his other accomplishments as Adjutant and Inspector General of the CSA, General Cooper played a crucial part in safeguarding and handing down to history the great majority of Confederate military and personal records which exist today.

The chapter was founded on July 31, 1973 with 15 charter members. The chapter has been involved in heritage and community events since its founding. Each year at the historic Christ Church, a Confederate Memorial Service is held. An annual banquet marking the birthday of General Lee is sponsored by the chapter. They have also been active in the local Toy for Tots campaign during the Christmas season; as well as, participated in the restoration and conservation projects at the Manassas National Battlefield.

James T. Jackson Chapter #123 – Suffolk, VA

The James T. Jackson chapter was organized in mid-November 1993. It was chartered on December 1, 1993. The name James T. Jackson was selected to honor him and the "Jackson Grays" for defending the First National Flag. Mr. Jackson owned and operated The Marshall House in Alexandria, VA. In 1861, after Virginia had seceded, a Union force under the command of Colonel Elmer E. Ellsworth invaded Alexandria. Seeing the "Stars and Bars" atop the hotel, Colonel Ellsworth and some soldiers entered The Marshall House, went to the roof and on coming down with the First National Flag, Mr. Jackson confronted them. Then Mr. Jackson killed Colonel Ellsworth and was shot and bayoneted by Colonel Ellsworth's men. Thus, Mr. Jackson a civilian became one of the first casualties of the War for Southern Independence.

Hupp-Deyerle-McCausland Chapter #237 – Roanoke, VA

The Hupp-Deyerle-McCausland chapter was chartered on March 11, 1996, and was named for Abraham Hupp, Colonel Andrew Deyerle, and General John McCausland.

Major General John Bankhead Magruder Chapter #258 – Fredericksburg, VA

On December 1999, members started the process of setting up the chapter that would become known as the Major General John Bankhead Magruder Chapter #258. Some credit must go to Compatriot and life time member Roy Baker Snapp, who brought it to the attention of A. Clarke Magruder, Virginia Society of MOS&B, that there is a abundance of compatriots that have joined Matthew Fontaine Maury Camp #1722, Fredericksburg, Virginia, with ancestry, that were Officers of the Confederacy.

Then March 8, 2000, A. Clarke Magruder, Adjutant, Virginia Society and Richard Abell, Commander of the Army of Northern Virginia, contacted Commander Richard A. Miller, Sr. requesting time to discuss forming a New Chapter in Fredericksburg, Virginia. After the meeting, the two Generals discussed the naming of the New Chapter. Jan V. Harvey proposed the name of Lieutenant General Thomas Jonathan "Stonewall" Jackson. Charles A. Embrey, Sr. suggested the dual name of Major General John Bankhead Magruder. Some time went by and applications were filed for membership into the Military Order of the Stars and Bars by Charles A. Embrey, Sr., John M. Embrey, Jr., Charles A. Embrey Jr., Jack E. Buttgen, Louis Buttgen, Jr., John T. Donnelly Jr., and Louis Buttgen III.

After the August 9th meeting of the Matthew Fontaine Maury Camp, Sons of Confederate Veterans, at the Salem Church Library, fellow compatriots nominated and elected the 3 officers needed to form a New Charter. Raymond W. Gill, Jr. was elected as Commander, Jan V. Harvey, elected as Adjutant, and Charles A. Embrey Sr. elected as Lieutenant Commander with a New Chapter bearing the name with full agreement, Compatriot Jan V. Harvey conceded to Major General John Bankhead Magruder by stating "I am out numbered by 7 MacGregor's who are of the same ancestry as John B. Magruder". We elected John M. Embrey Jr., as Chaplain, Jack E. Buttgen, as Treasurer, Louis Buttgen III, as Sergeant-At-Arms, Charles A. Embrey Jr., as Assistant Chaplain and John T. Donnelly Jr., as Webmaster/Historian.

November 8, 2000, New members of the MOS&B. who were sworn in by Lieutenant Commander, A. Clarke Magruder, Virginia Society MOS&B. were Charles A. Embrey, Sr., Charles A. Embrey, Jr., John M. Embrey, Jr., Jack E. Buttgen, Louis Buttgen, Jr., Louis Buttgen III, John T. Donnelly, Jr. and Jan V. Harvey.

Richard Abell Commander of the Army of Northern Virginia MOS&B. swore in the officers, Charles A. Embrey Sr. as Lieutenant Commander and Jan V. Harvey as Adjutant of the New Chapter after which, Commander John Stinson, Virginia Society MOS&B presented the New Charter to Adjutant Jan V. Harvey and Lieutenant Commander Charles A. Embrey, Sr. They accepted the Charter on behalf of Commander Raymond W. Gill, Jr. who was unable to attend that meeting.

December 4, 2000, Raymond W. Gill Jr. was first sworn in to the MOS&B. by A. Clarke Magruder Sr. Adjutant Virginia Society of the MOS&B, then Richard Abell Commander of the Army of Northern Virginia MOS&B, swore him in as Commander of the New Major General John Bankhead Magruder Chapter # 258. This took place at the General Samuel Cooper # 105 Chapter's Annual Christmas Dinner in Alexandria, Virginia. Some Compatriots of the New Chapter that witnessed this proud occasion were Lt. Commander Charles A. Embrey Sr., Assistant Chaplain Charles A. Embrey Jr., Treasurer Jack E. Buttgen, and Compatriot Louis Buttgen Jr.

Major Edgar Burroughs and Prince Anne Cavalry Chapter #281 – Virginia Beach, VA

In 2003 several members of SCV Princess Anne Camp 1993 (now Camp 484), decided there was a need to form a new MOS&B chapter in Virginia Beach. Membership in the SCV camp had grown from its inception a year earlier to over 50 members. Several had ancestors who were officers. So the stage was set to proceed with a charter application. After consideration the prospective members chose a name that reflected the historical makeup of the area and also honored local ancestors. Princess Anne County was chosen as part of the name. Likewise, the 15th Virginia Cavalry, which was composed of several Princess Anne County companies, was incorporated as well.

The members also searched for someone who was recognized as a local hero and a standout among the officers who served the Confederacy, as well as Princess Anne County and its surrounding areas. Major Edgar E. Burroughs served with the 15th Virginia Cavalry until 1862 when he resigned his commission due to poor health. In June of 1863, through Major Oscar F. Baxter, Jr., MD, he was authorized by the Secretary of War to organize a company of partisan rangers to harass the Union forces around Princess Anne county and in the Norfolk area. Known as the Burroughs' Battalion, Partisan Rangers, they were very successful throughout Princess Anne County, Currituck County, North Carolina, and along the Atlantic seaboard of both states.

The charter was presented on March 29, 2004, by Virginia Society Commander Clarke Magruder. Past Commander Kenneth Harris, a charter member, is a direct descendant of Major Burroughs and was instrumental in establishing the Chapter. We continue to grow and hope that you will consider honoring your Confederate officer ancestor by joining us.

Meeting are held with the Princess Anne Camp #484, Sons of Confederate Veterans, on the last Monday of each month (except for December) at 6:30 pm at Gus & George's Spaghetti & Steakhouse, 4312 Virginia Beach Boulevard, Virginia Beach, VA 23452-1238.

Army of Tennessee

The Department hereby known as the Army of Tennessee is comprised of eight Societies. The State Societies in the Army of Tennessee Department are the Alabama Society, the Florida Society, the Georgia Society, the Indiana Society, the Illinois Society, the Mississippi Society, the Ohio Society, and the Tennessee Society.

Chapters that have been chartered under the Army of Tennessee that have no State Society are as follows:

General Basil W. Duke Chapter # 71	Georgetown, KY
General George Baird Hodge Chapter #85	Covington, KY
George W. Johnson Chapter #118	Louisville, KY
Lt. Colonel John Parker Bowman Chapter # 139	Redford, MI
Colonel Albert P. Thompson #250	Paducah, KY

Alabama Society

The Military Order of the Stars and Bars was chartered in the State of Alabama on July 21st, 1984. First known as the Maj. Graham Davis Society, the name was constitutionally changed to The Alabama Society in 2008 by the Society membership. The first Commander was S. Gayden Latture followed Tommy Allison, Alan Dismukes, Phillip Law and Robert Mc Lendon. Current 2012-2014 officers are Dr. Richard Rhone, Commander; Rev. John Killian, First Lt. Commander; Dr. Richard Price, Second Lt. Commander and Walter Dockery, Society Adjutant.

As with the national membership, the Society has faced a decline in membership, but still remains active at both the State and Chapter level. Our members are involved in numerous heritage groups including the Society of the Order of the Southern Cross, Society of the War of 1812, Sons of the American Revolution and Sons of Confederate Veterans. Our newsletter *The Yellowhammer* is published quarterly. The Alabama Society, its Chapters and its membership actively participated in the placing of the Alabama Confederate Monument at Altoona Pass, the Tannehill Confederate Ironworks Monument as well as numerous CSA grave markings, dedications, cemetery restoration projects and presentations at educational and heritage events. Under the direction of the Brig. Gen. John Kelly Chapter, the Confederate Monument at Tannehill State Park was recently cleaned and re-painted, and overhanging trees trimmed. The State Society placed new Confederate Flags at the monument. The Gen. St. John Liddell Chapter helped erect the Civil War Monument in Baldwin County. The Gen. Josiah Gorgas Chapter erected the Nathan Bedford Forrest Monument in Gainesville as well as the Gen. Robert Rodes Monument in Tuscaloosa and the Confederates Veterans Memorial at Bryce Hospital in Tuscaloosa.

Annual meetings are held in April on the University of Alabama following the annual John C. Calhoun Sanders Lecture Series honoring the University Corp of Cadets. At this lecture, the Gorgas Chapter presents the Robert E. lee Leadership Sabers to the Outstanding ROTC cadets. Members of the Society have served in numerous State and National offices in the various heritage groups such as the OSC, War of 1812 and SCV as well as MOS&B.

The chapters that had been chartered in the State of Alabama as part of this Society are as follows:

President Jefferson Davis Chapter #1	Daphne, AL
Brigadier General John Hunt Morgan Chapter #17	Huntsville, AL
Catesby A.P.R. Jones Chapter #41	Selma, AL
Colonel Stephen F. Hale Chapter #57	Athens, AL
ADM Franklin Buchanan Chapter #58	Mobile, AL
Deshler-O'Neal Chapter #60	Tuscumbia, AL
General E. P. Alexander Chapter #78	Alexander City, AL
Brigadier General John Herbert Kelly Chapter #90	Birmingham, AL
General John T. Morgan Chapter # 93	Rainbow City, AL
Pelham-Forney Chapter #172	Jacksonville, AL
William Wirt Allen Chapter #199	Montgomery, AL
Nicola Marschall Chapter #204	Auburn, AL
Alexander Hamilton Stephens Chapter #227	Bryant, AL
Colonel Samuel S. Ives Chapter #255	Lexington, AL
Brigadier General St. John Richardson Liddell Chapter #271	Bay Minette, AL
Major General Edward Cary Walthall Chapter #274	Talladega, AL
General Josiah Gorgas Chapter #299	Tuscaloosa, AL

Catesby A. P. Roger Jones Chapter #41 – Selma, AL

The Catesby A. P. Roger Jones Chapter was chartered October 15, 1995 at Cahaba, Alabama during the annual Military Order of the Stars and Bars fall muster. The chapter was named in honor of Catesby A. P. Roger Jones who was the Commander of the Selma Naval Ordinance Works which was captured by Wilson's Raiders in April 1865. Descendants of Commander Jones still reside in Selma and also occupy his home.

Deshler – O'Neal Chapter #60 – Tuscumbia, AL

The Deshler-O'Neal Chapter was founded in December 1983 and was named for General James Deshler and General Edward A. O'Neal.

Brigadier General E. P. Alexander Chapter #78 – Alexander City, AL

The General E. P. Alexander Chapter was chartered on November 15, 1991 with twelve charter members. The Chapter's namesake, General E. P. Alexander, was chosen by the chapter because of his prominence in the Army of Northern Virginia; as well as, the fact that Alexander City, AL was named for the General. When the railroad was being planned from Birmingham, AL to Columbus, GA, a delegation of the representatives of Youngville, AL met General Alexander in Opelika, AL with a petition to have the railroad run through their town. This became a reality and in the 1870s the town changed its name to Alexander City in honor of the General.

Brigadier General John Herbert Kelly Chapter #90 – Birmingham, AL

When this chapter was charter, it was determined to name the chapter after Brigadier General John Herbert Kelly. From studying some about him, we know that adversity entered into this Carrollton, Alabama native's life early with the loss of both parents.

Orphaned before the age of 7 years old, he came under the nurture and guidance of a grandmother, Mrs. J. R. Hawthorn. Influential and persuasive relatives secured him a cadetship at the United States Military Academy at West Point, New York. At the age of 17, he entered the military institute as a member of the Class of 1861 on July 1, 1857 and would become associated with fellow plebes by the names of Judson Kilpatrick, John Pelham, Emory Upton and George Armstrong Custer. The secession crisis of late 1860 canceled his plans to join his fellow cadets in the approaching graduation ceremonies. In accord with the state of South Carolina seceding from the United States, he tendered his resignation from the academy on December 29, 1860 and offered his services to the new Confederacy. Commissioned a 2nd Lieutenant of artillery in the Confederate Army, he was subsequently promoted to Captain on October 5, 1861 and was assigned the responsibilities of Assistant Adjutant General on the staff of General William Joseph Hardee. He was commissioned a Major on September 23, 1861 with the organization of the 14th Arkansas Infantry at Pocahontas, Arkansas. He entered the April, 1862 battle of Shiloh at the helm of the 9th Arkansas Infantry and would boldly lead the regiment forward through an enfilade fire to capture a Union battery. For his gallantry, he was decorated with a promotion to Colonel on May 5, 1862 and was placed in command of the 8th Arkansas Infantry. He led the 8th Arkansas through the campaigns of Perryville, Kentucky and Murfreesboro, Tennessee, where he received a wound to his arm. At the September, 1863 Battle of Chickamauga, he was a direct subordinate to Brigadier General William Preston who later recorded in his official report that "During the struggle for the heights, Colonel Kelly had his horse shot under him, and displayed great courage and skill." Thereafter, his superiors successfully pressed for his promotion to Brigadier General. Hence, the November 16, 1863 promotion to Brigadier General in the Confederate States Army made Kelly the youngest officer to attain the rank to date. Assigned a cavalry division in General Joseph Wheeler's corps, the "Boy General" was leading a September 2,

1864 raid in central Tennessee to disrupt and destroy the communications of federal forces. During an engagement near the town of Franklin, he became the prime target of a Union sharpshooter. Astride his horse, he was toppled by a bullet to his chest and was borne from the field in a blanket. The mortally wounded General was relocated to the Harrison Home where his death occurred presumably on the 4th of September, 1864. Interred on the Harrison's property, his remains were moved to his native state and re-interred in Mobile, Alabama in 1866.

William Wirt Allen Chapter #199 – Montgomery, AL

The Major General William Wirt Allen Chapter is the local chapter for the Montgomery, Alabama area. The chapter was named in honor of William Wirt Allen. He was born in Montgomery, Alabama in 1835. His father, Wade Allen went from South Carolina to Alabama in 1818 and became a planter near Montgomery. His mother was a Miss Sayre, sister of Daniel Sayre, a prominent citizen of Montgomery County. With a preparatory education in the schools of his city, young Allen entered Princeton College in New Jersey. After graduation he studied Law but with no view of practicing. He preferred the life of a planter, and in that employment he was engaged when the South's call to arms aroused her sons from the sea board to the mountains. The enthusiasm with which our people, from beardless youths to gray haired sires, responded to that call has seldom, if ever been equaled in the history of the world. Without the least hesitation young men of education and fortune marched and fought in the ranks by the side of the poor and ignorant, and were proud of the sacrifice thus made, submitting without complaint to the hardships of a soldier's life, and obeying without a tinge of shame the orders of men who at home were their companions, and, in some instances, their inferiors in social rank. Some of them, of course, were fortunate enough to be elected by their comrades to positions of command, but in large armies brought into the field, the greater part were privates from first to last. Young Allen was one of the first to respond, and had the good fortune to be elected first lieutenant of the company of which General Clanton went in as Captain. When the First Alabama cavalry was organized he was elected Major. This was some time after the company had enlisted. Many of the companies of the cavalry, at first, were not put into regiments. His commission as Major dates from March 18, 1862. Later in the same year he was promoted to Colonel of the regiment. He fought at Shiloh, and was engaged in the subsequent operations of that company. When the advance into Kentucky was made, he went as Colonel of the regiment. At the battle of Perryville he received a slight wound. At Murfreesboro he commanded a brigade and received a severe wound that disabled him for some time. On the 26th of November 1864, he was commissioned Brigadier General and took command of a brigade. Allen took command at Dalton. The regiments of the brigade consisted of the First, Third, Fourth, Ninth, Twelfth, and Fifty-First Regiments of Alabama Cavalry, Wheeler's Corps Army of Tennessee. He was in charge of this brigade through all of the arduous duties of the mounted men in the Atlanta Campaign. In August 1864, Crews Georgia Brigade was added to this command, and subsequently Anderson's Confederate Brigade. At the head of this division, under the command of Wheeler, he followed Sherman in his march through Georgia and into the Carolinas, earning by his fidelity to duty, the commission of Major-General, conferred upon him in 1865. He surrendered at Salisbury, North Carolina, May 13, 1865. Returning home, he devoted himself to agriculture. For several years, he was adjutant-general of the State. As a soldier he was cool and fearless in danger and tireless in the performance of duty. As a citizen he was cordial in manner and of ardent public spirit. In peace, as well in war, he merited and received the confidence and esteem of his people. He died in Shelfield, Alabama November 21, 1894. His wife was the sister of Colonel Charles P. Ball, of Montgomery, Alabama.

Brigadier General St. John Richardson Liddell Chapter # 271 – Bay Minette, AL

The St. John Richardson Liddell Chapter # 271 was chartered in Bay Minette, Alabama on April 8, 2002. The Chapter rapidly grew to become one of the largest in the State of Alabama. The Chapter now serves all of Baldwin County Alabama.

The Chapter sponsored the *Gulf Coast Civil War Expo* three times in Bay Minette. It has also sponsored Confederate Memorial Services, Lee Jackson Dinners and hosted the State MOSB Convention in 2003. The Chapter has procured Confederate History Proclamations each year from the City of Bay Minette and Baldwin County and recently from the Cities of Foley, Robertsdale, Spanish Fort, Gulf Shores and Summerdale It has also arranged for re-enactors to march in the Veterans Day Parades.

The Chapter also actively searches for graves of Confederate Officers and, where necessary, cleans and maintains them. The Chapter is currently ordering tombstones for those Confederate Officers in our area who need them. The major ongoing project of the Liddell Chapter is to identify, mark and care for the graves of Confederate officers and officials in our area. The Chapter has identified numerous graves of Confederate Officers and is in the process of ordering stones and Crosses of Honor for those who do not have them. While we are an organization descended from the Officers Corp of the Confederate Army, we also honor our enlisted ancestors and care for their graves along with those of their officers.

On May 11, 2012 the Chapter presented the H.L. Hunley Award to an outstanding ROTC student from Baldwin County High School. The award is an SCV award and was prepared by the Fort Blakeley Camp, SCV. This has become a yearly event and is done in the spring at the ROTC "Formal Mess". It is a rather popular medal and there were two other cadets proudly wearing theirs.

On October 6, 2012 the Liddell Chapter hosted a highly successful Bass and Crappie Tournament at Hubbards Land on Tensaw Lake. The chapter will use the proceeds to purchase and install Confederate Crosses of Hone on the graves of Baldwin County's Confederate Dead.

Brigadier General Josiah Gorgas Chapter #299 – Tuscaloosa, AL

The Gorgas Chapter is named in honor of General Josiah Gorgas, a Confederate Patriot and CSA Chief of Ordinance during the War Between the States. He served for 20 years in the Ordnance Service of the U.S. Army until he resigned in April of 1861 after which he was appointed Chief of Ordnance for the Confederate Government. After the War, he then joined the teaching staff of the University of the South in Tennessee where he became Vice-Chancellor in 1872. In 1878 he was selected as President of the University of Alabama but resigned a year later because of ill health. He died on May 15, 1883 in Tuscaloosa, AL and is buried in Tuscaloosa's Evergreen Cemetery.

The organizational meeting for the Chapter was held at 2:00 pm on Sunday, March 3, 2006 at the Dockery Museum, Tuscaloosa, Alabama. Fourteen people attended the meeting and voted to establish the chapter. The chartering ceremony for the Gorgas Chapter was held on July 18, 2006 in the Gorgas House, the former home of General Gorgas and his family which was constructed in 1829 and located on the campus of the University of Alabama. Mr. Walter Dockery was elected as Commander. Chapter Charter members are John W. Adkison, Starkey E. Armistead, James K. Barksdale, Paul W. Bryant Jr., John W. Coleman Jr., Burton K. Curry, Frank Delbridge Jr., Walter E. Dockery, James D. Dunn, Joe A. Eady, John L. Fleming, Samuel C. Gambrell, Jr., Eugene G. Gravlee, Wiley D. Hales, Hampton E. Stewart Jr., Winfield S. Hughes Jr., Hugh D. McDaniel, Richard K. McLain, Thornton L. Neathery, Daryl C. Patterson, James F. Preskitt III, Norman G. Preskitt, and Richard W. Rhone.

Those who have served as Commanders of the Chapter have been Walter Dockery, Dr. John Fleming, Dr. Richard Rhone and John Coleman. Through most of the Chapter's existence Dr. Sam Gambrell served as the Chapter's most able Adjutant.

An extremely active group the Gorgas Chapter meets monthly and has numerous projects. The Chapter held the first annual President Jefferson Davis Banquet in June 2009 and has continued to do so every year. In addition, with the Robert Rodes SCV Camp, the Chapter sponsors the annual Lee-Jackson banquet in January. Each Christmas the Chapter places wreaths on the graves of Confederate soldiers buried in various cemeteries in the area and on the large Confederate monument in Greenwood cemetery. Gorgas Chapter replaced the grave marker in Greenwood Cemetery in Tuscaloosa for Sallie Ann Swoope, a nurse for the 11th Alabama as well as restored the grave site and markers for Capt. Benjamin Eddins and his daughter in Greenwood Cemetery. Eddins was the only Confederate soldier killed in the Battle of Tuscaloosa in April, 1865. The Chapter installed a grave marker for an unknown Confederate soldier buried in the Evans cemetery at Vance as well erected a monument to the Confederate soldiers who died at Bryce Hospital in Tuscaloosa. A monument honoring Gen. Robert Rodes was placed in Evergreen Cemetery by the Chapter. In additional, Gen. Rodes' wife's grave was marked. The Chapter is a proud sponsor of the 5th Alabama Infantry Regiment Band.

The Chapter sponsored and held the dedication ceremony of a large granite monument to General Nathan B. Forrest at Gainesville, AL where he surrendered his troops in 1865. Engraved on the monument is his complete farewell address to his troops and on the reverse is a list of major donors. Approximately 150 people attended the dedication which was followed by a reenactment of the Battle of Cuba Station.

Each April at the University of Alabama John Calhoun Sanders Series, the Chapter presents the General Robert E. Lee Leadership Sabers to the Outstanding Army and Air Force Cadets at the opening of the lectures. The event is held annually to honor the University Confederate Corp of Cadets,

Over the past years, the Chapter has received the Col. Walter Hopkins Award as a distinguished Chapter, the Lt. Gen. Simon Boliver Buckner Chapter Membership Retention Award as well as the Gen. Thomas "Stonewall" Jackson Award. Individuals in the Chapter members have received the Robert E. Lee Chalice, Gold Star, Commander General's Award, Patrick Cleburne Meritorious Service Award, John Pelham Award, Henry Timrod Southern Culture Award, Charles Read Legion of Merit, Rebel Club Award and War Service Medals. Two members, Walter Dockery and Richard Rhone, have been named as Distinguished Commanders.

Florida Society

The Florida Society is still searching for documents to accurately establish the date it was started. There is no recorded history and it must be recreated as documents are found. Even our oldest members are uncertain as to the date indicating it goes back many years. The earliest documentation we have found so far is 1971.

The Society Commanders are as follows:

1984-1986	Commander	Don Wehr
1986-1988	Commander	Robert McLendon
1988-1990	Commander	Evan Price Landrum, III
1990-1992	Commander	Renaldo Hamilton
1992-1994	Commander	John Lane
1994-1996	Commander	A. Robert Kuykendall, Jr.
1996-2003	Commander	Dr. C. Fred McNary
2003-2012	Commander	James Randall Kerlin
2012- present	Commander	Raleigh Worsham

It is with deep regret that the Florida Society announces in this Anniversary Edition the passing of Past Society Commander J. Randall Kerlin. Not only had he served the Florida Society as Society Commander for nearly 10 years, he also served as Genealogist General of the Military Order of the Stars and Bars for six years.

The Florida Society has been active in numerous projects over the years. In 1975 the Society was instrumental in establishing the Museum of Southern History. Society member #683, Giles J. Patterson, Jr., provided space for the initial location and in February 1996 the museum was moved to its present location with 3500 square feet of display area. In addition to the display of historical artifacts, the museum has a 6,000 book library focused on the War Between the States era. It is one of the most complete libraries for research on individual members of the Confederate military and the battles in which they participated. The Florida Society and the local Jacksonville Chapter Capt. J. J. Dickison #29 continue to raise funds to support the museum through such events as the annual Confederate Ball held in the spring of the year.

The Florida Society together with the Museum of Southern History participates in the annual Olustee Battle reenactment by sponsoring a table displaying historical information; artifacts and information on the activities of the MOS&B. Members of the Florida Society have a prominent place in the annual parade at the start of the event.

The Florida Society has placed several plaques such as the one in the Ocala Veterans Park with its 55 foot Confederate wall. The Society has worked to catalog the location of all Confederate officers buried in the state as well as a directory of Confederate officers from Florida that are buried outside of the state. The Florida Society participated in the restoration and rededication of the grave of Major William B. Hundley, II CSA in Warrenton, GA on 24 March 2007. Major Hundley was the final commander of the 5th Georgia Infantry and prior to this the Captain of Co. D, 5th Georgia.

Many of our members are active in giving talks to various heritage groups. These are too numerous to mention but include all of Florida and from time to time we intrude on our northern (geographically only) neighbor, Georgia.

The Florida Society was the sponsor of the 2011 MOS&B Sesquicentennial Convention at Jacksonville, Florida. To the best of our knowledge, The Florida Society is the only Society to have its own seal and membership pin.

Current Florida Society Officers are:

Commander	Raleigh Worsham
Lt. Commander	Joe Clark
Adjutant	Jeffrey L. Sizemore
Chief of Staff	Ben H. Willingham
Chaplin	R. Gordon Grant
Brigade Commander	Billy Nicholson

The Florida Society has active chapters in 14 Florida communities:

Alachua	Colonel David Lang	#289
Bartow	Colonel Francis S. Bartow	#65
Daytona Beach	Captain John N. Maffitt	#252
Brevard County	Brigadier General Theodore W. Brevard	#10
Gainesville	General William Miller	#111
Jacksonville	Captain J. J. Dickison	#29

Kissimmee	Captain William J. Rogers	#212
Lake City	Captain Asa A. Stewart	#24
Miami	Captain John "Sea Ghost" Wood	#288
Ocala	Marion Dragoons	#164
Orlando	Colonel L. M. Park	#52
Sarasota-Bradenton	Major William I. Turner	#161
St. Augustine	Lt. Colonel William Baya	#140
St. Petersburg	Lt. James Duke	#145

The other chapters that were chartered in Florida are as follows: General Joseph Finegan Chapter #95 – Orlando, FL; Lt. James Monroe Dupree Chapter #146 – Brandon, FL; Lt. Nelson N. Sumner Chapter #147 – Tavares, FL; Major General James Patton Anderson Chapter #156 – Pensacola, FL; Nathan Bedford Forrest Chapter #168 – St. Augustine, FL; Capt. Richard Bradford Chapter # 215 – Madison, FL; and Captain Leslie T. Hardy Chapter #278 – Fort Lauderdale, FL.

Brigadier General Theodore W. Brevard Chapter #10 – Brevard County, FL

Theodore Washington Brevard was born 26 August 1835 as was a graduate of the USMA. He raised the Brevard Partisan Rangers in 1861 and attained the rank of Major in 1863. Brevard later became colonel in command of the 11th Florida following their victory at Olustee. With his regiment, he joined Lee's army on the eve of Cold Harbor, taking part in the famous counterattack by the newly reconstituted Florida Brigade that saved the day for the Confederate cause. He became Adjutant General to General Robert E. Lee and was captured with most of his regiment at the battle of Sayler's Creek in April 1865. He had been a general for a little more than a week. He died 20 June 1882 and is buried in the St. John's Episcopal Church Cemetery in Tallahassee, Florida. Brevard County, Florida is named in his honor.

The Brigadier General Theodore W. Brevard Chapter of the Florida Society received its Charter at Indialantic, Florida on 19 October 1989 and was assigned Chapter Number 10. The Charter Members were; Major Aubrey R. Bates, Walter E, Hall, Carl E. Smith, Charles H. Bronson and John G. Spooner. At the Chartering Ceremony Dr. Richard M. Lancaster was sworn in as a member.

The Commanders of the Chapter have been, in chronological order, John E. Spooner, James L. Patton, Carl E. Smith, Dr. Richard M. Lancaster and James E. Rowe, Jr. Commander Lancaster passed away 17 November 2005 and with him a great deal of chapter knowledge. The Chapter has nine active members and is restructuring itself currently so as to begin regular meetings and activities.

One of the Chapter's projects was expanded into the General Society's Ancestral Research Committee and we are looking forward to founding the General Society's Ancestral Research Library.

Captain Asa A. Stewart Chapter #24 – Lake City, FL

The Chapter was chartered 23 February 1988 by Commander Kenneth Havird, Lt. Commander Kurt Barvo Havird, Adjutant C. F. Johns, III, C. F. Johns, Jr. and Christopher M. Johns. It was named for Captain Asa A. Stewart who has become a legend in Florida. As a Captain, he commanded a Company in the 2nd Regiment, Brigade of Florida Foot Militia during the Florida Seminole Indian Wars from November 29, 1840 to February 28, 1841. With the outbreak of hostilities in 1861 Capt. Stewart served with the 2nd Florida Battalion Partisan Rangers. He then raised an Independent Company that was mustered in on March 4, 1863. This same company was one of eight that formed the 6th Florida Infantry Battalion on September 11, 1863. Later this battalion would become the 9th Florida Infantry and fight at Olustee on 20 February 1864. At the age of 51, Captain Stewart resigned his position on 7 June 1864 due to his health but he remained in the Florida Home Guard until the end of the war. The 9th Florida went to Virginia where they fought at Cold Harbor, Petersburg Siege, Weldon Railroad, Reams Station, Bellfield, Hatchers Run, Farmville and surrendered at Appomattox Courthouse April 9, 1865.

The Chapter was instrumental in having an historical marker and iron cross in honor of Captain Stewart dedicated at the Chambers Cemetery, Columbia County, Florida on Saturday, November 9, 2002. Currently Robert Tucker is the Commander and Adjutant. The Chapter has five active members.

Captain John J. Dickison Chapter #29 – Jacksonville, FL

Captain J. J. Dickison of Orange Lake, Florida, after whom the chapter was named, was born in Georgetown, SC and lived there through early manhood before moving to Florida. He served as a 1st Lt with the Marion Light Artillery and then as a Captain commanded Company "H", 2nd Florida Cavalry, CSA, and other additional troops which from time to time were placed under his command. He led his cavalry with such courage, tactical skill, and extraordinary success against far superior Yankee forces in Florida that his exploits read like fiction. In his own time, he became a legend throughout the State of Florida. After the war, he served as Major General of State Troops, as Adjutant General of the State of Florida and as Commander of the Florida Division of the United Confederate Veterans. He is buried in Evergreen Cemetery in Jacksonville, FL.

Through the efforts of Dean Boggs on July 13, 1971, the following male descendants of Commissioned Officers who served in the Confederate States Army petitioned the Commander-In-Chief of the Military Order of the Stars and Bars for a charter in Jacksonville, FL to be known as the Captain J. J. Dickison Chapter: Kenneth W. Ackis, Sr., Dean Boggs, Thomas Jonathan Jackson Christian, Horace Mann Emerson, Henry Hollingsworth Harris, Jr., Charles Cook Howell, Jr., John Joseph Powell, Jr., Joseph A. Livingston, Jr., James H. Mabry, Giles J. Patterson, Jr., and R. Kirven Slade. The chapter was chartered on July 26, 1971.

Besides directly supporting the activities of the Museum of Southern History, Compatriots specifically recognize the heroic contributions of their officer ancestors and Southern leadership at all levels at their Annul Dining-In that is held in the October/ November time frame. In recent years, they have provided support for the efforts to recover and preserve historical artifacts from the *USS Maple Leaf,* sunk by a Confederate Torpedo/Mine team off Mandarin Point in the St. Johns River on April 1864. The chapter co-sponsors the Annual Confederate Ball. The proceeds from this Ball help to support the Museum of Southern History.

Colonel L. M. Park Chapter #52 – Orlando, FL

Lemuel M. Park was born (Nov. 1851) in Greenville, Meriwether Co., GA and as a very young man joined the Confederate Army as a private. He was assigned to Camp Sumter in Andersonville, GA and soon found himself on the staff of the Camp Commander, Captain Wirz, as a clerk. Park was with Captain Wirz for the final year of the war. Tragically, Captain Wirz was given a quick military trial without the opportunity of defense and hung 10 November 1865, an event that caused Park to spend his life trying to vindicate the good name of Captain Wirz. Following the war, Park was active in the UCV becoming a Camp Commander and later a Regimental Commander where he was given the title of Colonel. Park wrote many articles defending Captain Wirz and Camp Sumter against the criticism that was widely circulated through the north, perhaps our first experience in having the victor write history as he wanted to see it. Many of his articles were published in the early issues of The Confederate War Journal and The Confederate Veteran. They describe life at Camp Sumter in a way not found in other publications. He died and is buried in Atlanta, GA.

The Colonel L. M. Park chapter was chartered on 17 December 1984 by Commander Donald Lee Wehr, Lt. Commander William D. Hogan, Adjutant John B. Baumgardner, III, James H. Brannon, Dr,

Charles C. Carleton, MD, Dr. Rev. Daniel C. Coleman, DD, John Crozier, Eli Madison Dews, William A. Evans, Joseph S. White, III, Gordon Albert Griggs, Joseph S. Guernsey, Daniel J. LeFevre, James Kirk Lowe, Jeffrey Kent Smith and J. Lester Williams, Jr.

Lemuel was married twice. His second wife Louise H was born Apr 1877 and they had two children, Harold H. b. 29 Jan 1897 d. 3 Oct 1975 Atlanta and Arther b. Jun 1899 and Madison b. 1902. With his first wife, he had two sons, Howard P. b. May 1879 (1920 Pres. Cotton Mill, LaGrange, Troup Co., GA) and Emery R. b. Jun 1882 and a daughter, Mary b. Jul 1884. In 1900, he was living in Rough Edge, Troup Co., GA and engaged in textile manufacturing.

Colonel Francis S. Bartow Chapter #65 – Bartow, FL

The Francis S. Bartow Chapter, Military Order of the Stars and Bars was chartered on June 17, 1985 in Bartow, Florida. The Chapter was named for the Francis S. Bartow Camp of the United Confederate Veterans which was organized on June 17, 1893 at the Polk County Court House in Bartow. The Chapter and City were both named to honor Colonel Francis S. Bartow who was born September 6, 1816 in Savannah, Georgia and who gave his life for the Confederacy in the First Battle of Manassas July 21, 1861. He was the first Confederate Brigade Commander to be killed.

One of the first projects of the Chapter was to identify Confederate Officers and enlisted soldiers buried in local cemeteries. A total of 35 officers were located in Bartow alone and were honored by publication of an Honor Roll. On January 19, 1990 the Chapter erected and rededicated a granite monument marking the site of the home of Confederate Major General Evander M. Law who resided in the city from 1893 to 1920. In addition the Chapter was instrumental in the City of Bartow's Proclamation and establishment of Major General E.M. Law Day. Confederate Memorial Day, April 26th, is annually observed by the placement of flags on the graves of confederate veterans and Confederate Monuments located in the city.

General William Miller Chapter #111 – Gainesville, FL

William Miller was born August 3, 1830 in Ithaca, NY. As a young man he relocated along with his family to Louisiana. He attended Louisiana College and served with Zachary Taylor in the Mexican War. For his service, he was given 40 acres in Florida by the U. S. Government. He studied law and engaged in a private practice in Santa Rosa Co., FL. He was active in the timber and lumber business in northwest Florida prior to the War.

Miller recruited a militia unit and became its major. He and his men eventually joined the 1st Florida Infantry where he became its first colonel in August 1862. Later that year, he fought at the Battle of Perryville, KY 8 October 1862, suffering a minor wound. During the Battle of Murfreesboro (December 31, 1862 – January 2, 1863), he was severely wounded. He returned home to Florida to recuperate for several months prior to being placed in charge of the Confederate Conscript Bureau for Alabama and Florida.

On August 2, 1864, Miller was promoted to brigadier general and asked to organize the state's reserve troops as the new commander of the Florida District. He raised and commanded the 1st Florida Reserves, a regiment recruited to help defend the state, as most of the regular Confederate troops were serving elsewhere. His most prominent action came at the Battle of Natural Bridge (Woodville, FL) 6 March 1865, where he was the tactical field commander in defeating Union forces under John Newton. His men repelled three separate Union attacks during the 12-hour battle. It was the second time Union forces were denied in their effort to capture the Florida State Capital in Tallahassee. Thus Florida became the only Confederate State east of the Mississippi to retain its State Capitol until the end of the War when General Miller and his men were finally compelled to surrender in Tallahassee, May 1865.

After the war, Miller returned to his timber business and established a farm. He eventually settled in Point Washington in Walton County, where he became the Justice of the Peace. Miller served two terms in the Florida House of Representatives and/or the State Senate. He died 8 August 8, 1909 and was initially buried in Point Washington Cemetery, but in 1922, he and his wife were exhumed and reinterred in St. Johns Cemetery in Pensacola, Florida.

The Chapter was chartered 7 May 1984 in Gainesville, FL. The first Chapter Officers and Charter Members were Commander Ernest W. "Buddy" Burch, Jr., Lt. Commander Robert G. "Bob" McLendon, Adjutant Michael D. Harden, William A. Bessent, III, Ernest W. "Trey" Burch, III, Robert G. McLendon, Sr. and John N. Reames.

The Chapter shares its functions and events with the 2nd Florida Cavalry Camp, Confederate Sons Association of Florida and the Kirby Smith Chapter 202, United Daughters of the Confederacy. Annual events include the Lee - Jackson Dinner and Confederate Memorial Day festivities. Meetings are monthly and held jointly with the 2nd Florida Cavalry Camp, CSA of Florida.

Lt. Colonel William Baya Chapter #140 – St. Augustine, FL

Lieutenant Colonel William Baya, the son of Menorcan settlers, was born in St. Augustine, Florida on 23 January 1834. He served as an Orderly Sergeant early in the war. He then served as 1st Lieutenant, Confederate Marines aboard the CSS Jeff Davis until the ship ran aground at the entrance to St. Augustine and was lost. He then organized and commanded Grayson's Artillery which was re-designated as Company D, 8th Florida Infantry Regiment where he was commissioned a Captain. This company was mustered into Confederate Service in May 1862. Promoted to Lieutenant Colonel in January 1863, he commanded the 8th Florida Infantry at the Battle of Gettysburg. They served under GEN A. P. Hill's Corps where on the third day they participated in Pickett's Charge. He was wounded twice and captured three times, the last being at Saylor's Creek, Virginia on 6 April 1865. Lieutenant Colonel Baya died on 1 July 1903 and is buried in Evergreen Cemetery, Jacksonville, Florida.

The Lieutenant Colonel William Baya Chapter 140, Military Order of the Stars and Bars # 140, was charted on 26 April 1991. Chartering ceremonies were held on 18 December 1991 at the home of its first Commander, Colonel John J. Masters, Sr., U. S. Army Retired, at 3000 Usina Road, St. Augustine, Florida. The Charter was presented by E. Price Landrum III, Commander, Florida Society, Military Order of the Stars and Bars.

Charter members were Colonel John J. Masters, Commander, and his two sons Major John J. Masters, Jr., Florida Army National Guard, Adjutant/ Treasurer and Captain Burton L. Masters U. S. Army; Kenneth Beesen, N. Putnam Calhoun, Lieutenant Commander Michael H. Charles, Captain Benjamin Hudgens, James V. Perry, Sr., John G. R. Rountree and his son Robert L. Shreve-Rountree. Four of the charter members, the three Masters and Kenneth Beeson are cousins of Lieutenant Colonel William Baya and another cousin would join later.

Commander Masters has been a committee of one in locating the graves of over 167 Confederate Soldiers and Sailors in St. Johns County and mounting 57 Veterans Administration Head Stones on graves of Confederate Soldiers in the County. As the Graves Chairman for the Florida Society, Colonel Masters has been instrumental in locating the graves of 9,820 Confederate Soldier's and Sailors buried in the state and over 4,200 Florida Soldiers who died outside the state of Florida.

The Chapter donated part of the funds for the purchase of the just published "Biographical Rosters of Florida's Confederate and Union Soldiers, 1861-1865" to be donated to the St. Augustine Genealogical Society to be put in the Main Public Library of St. Augustine.

Commander Masters has attended eight State and seven National MOSB Conventions. The Chapter co-hosted the Florida Society, Military Order of the Stars and Bars annual Convention in St. Augustine, Florida in June 1994.

The Chapters losses are mostly from deaths, namely Robert Shreve-Rountree and N. Putnam Calhoun. One member, Michael Charles transferred out but remains an associate member. The Chapter gained three members Fred Chauvin, Charles E. Stevens, Jr. and one transfer Robert Kuykendall, Jr. Commander of the Florida Society Military Order of the Stars and Bars.

At the election on 30 March 1995 Colonel Masters was reelected Commander, Major John J. Masters, Jr. was elected Adjutant/Treasurer and Fred Chauvin elected Lieutenant Commander, due to the resignation of N. Putnam Calhoun on 21 March 1995, and Charles E. Stevens, Jr. was elected Chaplain. Colonel Masters continued as Chapter Commander until the election in 2002 when Mike Pomar was elected Commander and James S. Davis was appointed Adjutant/Treasurer to replace John J. Masters Jr. Meanwhile, Commander Pomar had been elected Lieutenant Commander of the Florida Society. The Chapter was very active under Commander Pomar's leadership and even published a Chapter newsletter on 7 June 2004.

In 2006, since Commander Pomar did not call for the annual election of Chapter Officers the then Adjutant/Treasurer Talmadge S. Skinner called a special election to select Camp Officers. Elected were James S. Davis, Commander, Richard Lee, Lieutenant Commander and Talmadge S. Skinner, Adjutant/Treasurer. The Chapter continued to prosper under Commander Davis's leadership until circumstance caused Richard Lee and James S. Davis to resign from the Military Order of the Stars and Bars. The Chapter was then left leaderless and adrift. Charter Commander Colonel John J. Masters, Sr. assumed the position of Acting Commander and sent all nine members a notice of what happened and a ballot and a list of nominated members for office. The response was very encouraging. Elected were Herbert M. Greenleaf, Commander; Lt. Colonel John J. Masters, Jr. Lieutenant Commander; and Colonel John J. Masters, Sr. Adjutant/Treasurer.

The Chapter has participated in all the Sons of Confederate veterans Camp and the Ancient City Chapter, United Daughters of the Confederacy activities since its founding including Lee/Jackson/ Baya birthdays dinner in January, Confederate Memorial Day in April, cemetery ceremonies when mounting head stones throughout the year; General Loring's birth and death in December and marking the birth of General E. Kirby Smith at his home where he was born on Aviles Street in downtown St. Augustine.

In the fall of 2007 Donald Booth and Colonel Masters decorated the graves of Confederate Officers in Evergreen, Cemetery. In February 2008 Colonel Masters decorated the graves of Confederate Officers in San Lorenzo Cemetery.

The Chapter is financially sound and healthy. All dues are paid up to date to State and National. It would be well if the Chapter could be more active but, the Chapter has only nine members and four of them live out of the County and State.

Lt. James Duke Chapter #145 – St. Petersburg, FL

The chapter was chartered on 1 March 1991 by Dr. Duke N. Stern, Lawton Swan and Russell Waters. The Chapter is named in honor of 3rd Lieutenant James B. Duke who served in Capt. Edwin M. Holloway's Alabama Calvary Company. The Charter members continue to be active. The Commander since its beginning is Dr. Duke N. Stern and Lawton Swan has served as Adjutant. The Chapter meets on an irregular basis due to the geographic separation of the members but they have been active in supporting the Confederate Memorial Hall in New Orleans, the Confederate Museum in Richmond and the Order of the Southern Cross.

Major William I. Turner Chapter #161 – Sarasota-Bradenton, FL

The Chapter was named for William I. Turner, 8th Florida Infantry. The 8th Florida was at Gettysburg along with the Florida 2nd and 5th and suffered terrible losses. The 8th Florida was involved in some of the most difficult fighting as a member of the Army of Northern Virginia.

The Chapter chartered before 1980 but unfortunately no exact date is known. The Chapter has thirteen active members. The Commander has been Jack Boland since 1980 and the Adjutant has been James Hayward since 1980 as well. The Chapter has thirteen active members and meets 3 to 4 times a year.

Marion Dragoons Chapter #164 – Ocala, FL

The FLORIDA MARION DRAGOONS CAVALRY COMPANY was organized at Marianna on 14 March 1862. It mustered in there for three years or the duration of the war on 26 April 1862. Its battle flag was a 4 X 6 foot 2nd National which was made by the ladies of Citra, Florida and received much use. The Dragoons were later assigned, as Company C, of the 2nd Florida Cavalry Regiment. Its first Commander was Captain Richard L. Smith and it was part of the Department of Middle and Eastern Florida and later the District of Middle Florida, Department of South Carolina, Georgia and Florida. It saw its first combat on 7 April 1863 at St. Andrew's Bay, Florida.

The 2nd Florida Cavalry Regiment was organized with 1,190 men during the late spring of 1862. Its members were from Melton and Tallahassee, and the counties of St. John, Marion, Gadsden, and Madison. The unit was attached to the Department of South Carolina, Georgia, and Florida, and served in Florida throughout the war. It fought at Olustee, Gainesville, and Braddock's Farm, and surrendered at Tallahassee on 10 May 1865. Colonel Caraway Smith, Lieutenant Colonel Abner H. McCormick, and Major Robert Harrison were in command.

The Marion Dragoons Chapter #164 located in Ocala, Florida was chartered on 8 January 1983. The Dragoons meet on the second Tuesday evening of each month together with other Confederate heritage interest groups so as to assure a better program.

The Marion Dragoons Chapter along with the support of the Florida Society MOS&B have honored the memory of the Confederate Officer Corps in Headstone and Cemetery Dedications within Marion County and at our local Veterans Park. The Chapter has placed the MOS&B colored logo on the fifty-five foot section of the Confederate wall located on the East end of the park on street side seen by thousands every day.

The chapter flies the Confederate flags on the three Florida Confederate holidays; 19 January (Robert E. Lee's Birthday), 26 April (Confederate Memorial day) and 3 June (President Jefferson Davis' Birthday). General Lee's HQ flag is also flown on 19 June. We hold Memorial services at our Chapter meetings including the use of candlelight and remember our Confederate officers by name, rank and unit. We have participated in local parades and put on educational programs for the local schools and history groups in the area. We have supplied displays at our local library on Confederate history and in some Museums.

The Marion Dragoons Chapter #164 and the Florida Society MOS&B take great pride in support of the Florida Division Children of the Confederacy through their local Chapter (The Marion Hornets) and on the State level in the Educational Stand to preserve the History and Heritage of the Confederate Officer Corp and its Government Leaders for future generations.

Captain William J. Rogers Chapter #212 – Kissimmee, FL

The Chapter was named for William J. Rogers. From The History of Brooks County Georgia 1858-1948 (p. 112) Rogers joined Co. I, 13th Georgia Infantry in 1861. It was reorganized in May 1862 as 26th Georgia Infantry and shortly after designated as Company C. The date is not shown for his election to 2nd Lieutenant but he was promoted to 1st Lieutenant 2 February 1863 and to Captain 1 October 1863. His muster card shows he was taken as a Prisoner of War near Petersburg, VA Oct 1864.

The Capt. William J. Rogers Chapter 212 was organized March 15, 1995 in Kissimmee, Osceola County, Florida. Charter members consisted of Murray L. Rogers, Mark A. Rogers, M. Randolph Prine, John E. Carroll III, and Reidy Williams.

The chapter presently has nine active members. Current officers are: Commander Marshall L. Brewton, Jr., Lt. Commander Mark A. Rogers, and Adjutant William W. Pearce, Jr. The chapter has located the gravesites of ten Confederate officers buried in Osceola County, Florida. The chapter co-sponsors "The Battle at Narcoossee Mill" annual War Between The States reenactment which includes an Education Day for area schoolchildren. It also contributes annually to "Confederate Christmas" which consists of blind monetary donations to needy families, the families being selected by a local Church. The chapter also participates in Confederate Memorial Day services.

Captain John N. Maffitt Chapter #252 – Daytona Beach, FL

The CAPT John Maffitt Chapter was established July 1, 1991 by Charter members Commander Dr. Fred McNary, Lt. Commander Paul Steven Baltzegar, Adjutant James Yates, William G. Rose and Robert Elliott in Daytona Beach, Florida.

It was named after CAPT John Newland Maffitt, the commander of the Confederate Navy's first commerce raider, CSS Florida which in a single cruise destroyed or captured 47 U. S. merchantmen. He was born at sea on 22 February 1819 and entered the U. S. Navy as a Midshipman in February 1832. In May 1861 Lieutenant Maffitt resigned his commission and became a First Lieutenant in the Confederate States Navy. Maffitt attained the rank of Commander in the Confederate Navy and commanded the ironclad ram USS Albemarle and ended the war commanding blockade runners. After the war he became a merchant ship captain and in 1870 commanded a warship for the Cuban revolutionaries. He died in Wilmington, NC 15 May 1886.

Captain John "Sea Ghost" Wood Chapter #288 – Miami, FL

John Taylor Wood was born in Minnesota on 13 August 1830. He was the nephew of President Jefferson Davis and joined the U.S. Navy at the USNA in April 1847, graduating second in his class in 1853. He served at sea during the latter part of the Mexican War off the coast of Africa and the Mediterranean. He resigned from the U.S. Navy in April 1861.

At the outbreak of hostilities, he sold his Maryland farm and moved his family to Richmond where in October 1861 he received a commission as a First Lieutenant in the Confederate Navy. He had been training gunners for CSS Merrimack in Portsmouth, VA and was on board Merrimack for the historic battle with Monitor. He was promoted to Commander in May 1863. Simultaneously he held the rank of Colonel in the cavalry.

Having been built in England, Atlanta launched on the Thames in March 1864 and made four trips from April to July 1864 with war supplies for the South. She was purchased in Wilmington, NC for $125,000 and converted to a Confederate Cruiser (Merchant raider) and renamed CSS Tallahassee. Commander Wood was named her Captain and on 4 August 1864 began the famous breakout through the fifty ships used to blockade Wilmington and began her impressive career as a commerce raider on the east coast. Being unable to load adequate coal in Halifax, she headed toward Bermuda hoping to refuel. On board yellow fever broke out and Captain Wood decided to return to Wilmington where Tallahassee arrived on 28 August 1864 and anchored under the guns of Fort Fisher. Tallahassee's days as a raider under Wood were at an end. He was promoted to Captain in February 1865 and at the end of the war, he assisted his uncle, President Jefferson Davis, in his attempt to escape and evade capture. Wood made his way to Cuba and later to Halifax where he became a business man and died there 19 July 1904.

The Capt. John "Sea Ghost" Wood Chapter #288 of the Florida Society MOS&B was chartered on 11 May 2004 in Miami, Florida. The Charter was presented at the Annual State Convention in Palatka and was one of the last documents that Dr. Fred McNary signed before his passing.

The Chapter was chartered with five members who are still active today. The Chapter has had representatives at Confederate Memorial Day and local events involving Confederate Heritage. The Chapter has also been represented at every State convention since it was chartered.

Colonel David Lang Chapter #289 – Alachua, FL

Few have walked across the stage of history in such grand fashion as David Lang. He was the second oldest of eight children, born to Robert and Margaret Atkinson Lang in Camden County Georgia in 1838.

He was educated at the Georgia Military Institute, in Marietta, Georgia, and graduated in 1857 at the age of 19. After his graduation, he came to Florida and was elected surveyor of Suwannee Co., Florida. After Florida seceded from the Union, he enlisted as a private with the Gainesville Minuteman (more commonly known as Company H, 1st Florida infantry). He was appointed 1st Sergeant and served for one year.

In the spring of 1862, after raising a company, he was elected Captain and moved with his unit to Richmond, Virginia. Captain Lang and his men saw action in some of the heaviest fighting during the next three years. He was severely wounded in the battle of Sharpsburg, where his courage and leadership were recognized. He commanded the 8th Florida Infantry during the fighting at Fredericksburg, where he was once again wounded. He was cited for bravery and was promoted to full Colonel.

After General Perry's illness, Colonel Lang took command of the Florida Brigade at the beginning of the Pennsylvania campaign. On the third day of fighting at Gettysburg, Colonel Lang and his Florida Brigade wrote their special part of history. Along with Wilcox's brigade of Alabamians, Colonel Lang's unit was called upon to make one last push against the Yankees. Although the command to advance over the same ground that three divisions had failed to win (including General Pickett and his division) was absurd, Lang and Wilcox did advance, with misgivings. They were met with stiff resistance and ultimately had to retreat, but not before many men were killed or captured by the Union forces.

The Army of Northern Virginia never recovered from the defeat at Gettysburg, and finally, in April, 1865, Colonel David Lang and the Florida Brigade surrendered with the rest of Lee's army at Appomattox.

After the war ended, Colonel Lang married Mary Quarles Campbell, with whom he had four children. He worked as a civil engineer until his former brigade commander, the newly elected governor of Florida, E. A. Perry, appointed him Adjutant General of State Militia. He was instrumental in changing militia law when the new Florida constitution was adopted in 1885 and he started the Florida

National Guard. He stepped down as Adjutant General in 1893, but never lost his responsibility for the soldiers of Florida. He then served as the private secretary for Governors Mitchell (1893-1897) and Bloxham (1897-1901), as well as serving on the State Board of Pensions. He served as cashier of the Florida State Hospital in Chattahoochee from 1901 until his death in December 1917.

He lived a long and full life, and left a great legacy of courage, leadership and compassion for the soldiers and citizens of Florida. We are truly honored to have his name grace our chapter's name.

On 17 July 2004 then late-Commander Al Hammond Jr. had an organizational meeting of the Military Order of Stars & Bars at his home. Up for discussion was the formation of an MOS&B chapter. The name that was chosen for the chapter was the Colonel David Lang Chapter #289, as Compatriot Al Hammond, Jr. and his wife Frankie had done existence research on Colonel David Lang.

The inaugural officers for the chapter were Al Hammond Jr., Commander; Archie Matthews, 1st Lt. Commander; Arnold O'Steen, 2nd Lt. Commander and Chaplain; Wilbur O'Steen, Adjutant; and Allen O'Steen, Treasurer.

The chapter was chartered on October 7, 2004. In attendance to present the charter and install the officers were Randy Kerlin, Commander Florida Society MOS&B & MOS&B National Genealogist General; Mike Pomar, State 1st Lt. Commander; Ed Page, State Adjutant; and Eric Hague, 7th Brigade Commander. Mrs. Frankie Hammond read the history of Colonel David Lang.

It was decided that all chapter meetings would be held quarterly (January, April, July and October) on the first Thursday night of the quarter at a place to be determined.

The Chapter works closely with the John Hance O'Steen SCV Camp #770 and participates in roadside clean-ups, as well as recruitment tables at various events around North Central Florida. The Chapter is also involved in headstone dedications, living history events and cemetery clean-ups.

Georgia Society

Three Georgians were present at the organizational meeting of the then Order of Stars and Bars, August 30, 1938, at the Columbia Hall, Columbia, SC: Dr. William R. Dancy of Savannah, John Ashley Jones of Atlanta, and Judge Alexander W. Stephens of Atlanta. Dancy would be Commander of the Military Order of the Stars and Bars. Jones would be Commander-in-Chief of the Sons of Confederate Veterans.

The Georgia Society was named for Captain William A. Fuller, the Confederate hero depicted in the Disney movie, *The Great Locomotive Chase*. The Fuller Society of Georgia began as an Atlanta based chapter, organized by Clyde A. Boynton during the centennial in 1961. When the chapter split into a Society in the 1970s, Boynton would serve as the first Commander of the Society. He served into the 1980s.

In 1993, under the command of Charles Lunsford, the Georgia Society began a new program, an oratory contest, showing off the brilliance of Southern oratory. It was the Robert Toombs Oratory competition. Today, the Georgia Society holds several major events during the year that is advertised nationally. At the first of the year, the Alexander H. Stephen's Birthday Celebration is held in Crawfordville, GA. Then around the middle of the month of April, the National Confederate Memorial Day Service is held at Stone Mountain, GA. Lastly in November, the Georgia Society holds the Wirz Annual Memorial Service in Andersonville, GA.

The chapters that had been chartered in the State of Georgia as part of this Society are as follows:

Captain William A. Fuller "The General" Chapter #4	Atlanta, GA
Colonel Allen S. Cutts Chapter #45	Americus, GA
Colonel George W. Rains Chapter #50	Augusta, GA
General Alfred Holt Colquitts Chapter #70	Macon, GA
General John B. Gordon Chapter #88	Atlanta, GA
General Lafayette McLaws Chapter #97	Savannah, GA
General William T. Woffard Chapter #112	Marietta, GA
General Paul Jones Semmes Chapter #104	Columbus, GA
King Cotton Chapter #134	Thomaston, GA
Lt. General William J. Hardee Chapter #143	Jonesboro, GA
Captain Jacob Phinizy Chapter #153	Evans, GA
Robert Toombs Chapter #176	Athens, GA
The Atlanta Council Chapter #188	Atlanta, GA
General Stonewall Jackson Chapter #201	Sandy Springs, GA
Jefferson Davis Memorial Chapter #206	Irwinville, GA
Brigadier General James P. Simms Chapter #244	Conyer, GA
Lt. Colonel Robert P. Taylor Chapter #245	Newnan, GA
Colonel Emory Best Chapter #265	Cassville, GA
President Jefferson Davis Chapter #272	Gainesville, GA
Capt. William L. Walthour/Liberty Independence Troop Chapter #290	Heinsville, GA

General Alfred Holt Colquitt Chapter #70 – Macon, GA

The General Alfred Hole Colquitt Chapter was founded in 1995, and was named after Confederate Brigadier General, Congressman, U.S. Senator, and Governor of Georgia, A. H. Colquitt. The chapter projects include the donating of books on southern history each year to a library and maintaining the grave of General Colquitt at the Rosehill Cemetery.

Lt. General William J. Hardee Chapter #143 – Jonesboro, GA

The Lieutenant General William J. Hardee Chapter was founded in 1993 after the great-grandfather of charter member William Elder. The chapter projects include the donating of a Georgia State flag to the City of Lake City, GA in Clayton County; the donating of books to the library in McDonough, GA in Henry County; and holding Jefferson Davis Birthday dinners.

Robert Toombs Chapter #176 – Athens, GA

The Robert Toombs Chapter was chartered in Athens Georgia the 29th of January 1992 at a Dinner Ceremony held at Trumps. The first Commander was Toombs DuBose Lewis, Jr., Great Great Grandson of Robert Toombs. Robert N. Hale, Senior Adjutant. There was a total of 23 Charter Members. Of those eight are still active members. Several members have passed over the river to rest in the eternal life promised by our Lord and Savior Jesus Christ.

Our roster as of March 23, 2008, with three applications in progress, consisted of 16 members. For many years we met quarterly at various locations. Over the years since chartered, many members have attended the ceremony of the birth of Alexander Stephens in Crawfordville. Most chapter members are also members of the Brig. Gen. T.R.R. Cobb Camp # 97 SCV which meets monthly. As joint members of the MOS&B and SCV chapter members are involved in many projects including the marking of Confederate Graves of the 427 Veterans buried at

Oconee Hill Cemetery on Confederate Memorial Day and the Memorial Service held there on Confederate Memorial Day at the Brig. Gen. T.R.R. Cobb burial site. Over 100 officers of the Confederacy are buried in Oconee Hill Cemetery including 2 Brig. Generals and 2 Major Generals.

Illinois Society

The chapters that had been chartered in the State of Illinois as part of this Society are as follows:

Jefferson Davis Chapter # 243   Springfield, IL
Deo Vindice Chapter #270   Chicago, IL

The roots of an MOS&B presence within Illinois lie with the founding of the oldest existing Illinois SCV organization, that which became Camp Douglas 1507. Jim Barr, along with Andy Wilson, were the moving force(s) in that organizational endeavor in the mid 1980's, at which time Jim realized that there was no opportunity for the descendants of the Confederate Officer Corps to gather organizationally, as his MOS&B membership was originally begun in the Texas Society under Tulane Gordon in 1980. Some twenty years later he approached the then IL SCV Division Commander Charles Edward Briggs to request his assistance to organize an Illinois Chapter, and address the men of Illinois at a Divisional Convention.

With the unqualified support of the succeeding Illinois Division Commanders, Gale Franklyn Red and Robert F. Herr, the one Chapter, named "Deo Vindice" soon flourished to become a full Society under CDR Barr's leadership. The name was chosen as it was the least controversial of any Chapter name suggested. The remarkable growth and success of the Chapter and Society would not have been possible without three national officers, whose support was unwavering. Those were Genealogist General Rodney Patrick Williams, COS GEN Curtis Hopper, and PCG Albert Jones and Jeff Massey, all of whom had supported the infant Illinoisans as their numbers had exponentially grown. At its highest point, there were forty-six (46) members of the Illinois Society.

The originally petitioners and officers were: James F. Barr, CDR, the Very Rev. William W. Barr, MA. M Div as ADJ and the Hon. Gary L. Corlew, Esq. as Judge Advocate. Joining them to form the original Chapter 270 were Gale Franklyn Red, and Karl Federer. The Illinois Society and Deo Vindice Chapter 270 were installed on May 10th, 2003 at Springfield, Illinois by COS GEN Curtis Hopper, IN SOC CDR John Forrest, and Physician GEN Neal Pitts, MD. There were 17 members at that time. Elected at the installation for a full term were: CDR James F. Barr; Lt CDR Roger Heinrich; ADJ Charles Edward Briggs. The Society and Chapter function as one unit, with joint officers and compatible Constitutions, with grateful acknowledgement to Dr. Fred McNary of the Florida Society for his assistance with documentation.

At the Memphis Annual Meeting the Chapter presented its first report, reflecting nine members and various outreach programs for membership. At the Asheville Annual Meeting the Society and Chapter then numbered 21, and reported joint participation in several Illinois and national events. They were nationally awarded Best Newsletter and Best Scrapbook at that time, and also awarded the Distinguished Chapter Award for the Year 2003. (This was the first time a new Chapter had ever won the award, as well as the first time a chapter located in a Northern State had won this prestigious award.) At the Nashville Annual Meeting again the Distinguished Chapter Award went to Illinois, as was the Distinguished Commander Status awarded to CDR. Barr. We continue to jointly sponsor an $1000 Illinois High School Scholarship annually.

The future of the MOS&B in its entirety is dependent upon the adaptability of their leadership corps to integrate new projects and new ideas into the ever present changing role of the hereditary society within the counter culture of today's society.

Mississippi Society

The Mississippi Society holds a prayer breakfast as a means to further the cause of preserving Confederate history. These prayer breakfasts are held for such events as Confederate Memorial Day, Confederate heritage month, and Lee-Jackson birthdays. The Society has been encouraging each chapter to meet on a regular basis.

The chapters that have been chartered in the State of Mississippi as part of this Society are as follows:

Captain Ike Whitaker Chapter #28	Vicksburg, MS
Captain William H. Hardy Chapter #38	Hattiesburg, MS
Father Abram Ryan Chapter #63	Biloxi, MS
General Jacob Sharp Chapter #86	Columbus, MS
General Nathan B. Forest Chapter #100	Corinth, MS
General William Barksdale Chapter #110	Jackson, MS
President Jefferson Davis Chapter #173	Hernando, MS
William R. Mitchell Chapter #197	Holly Springs, MS
Captain Rufus K. Clayton Chapter #213	Heidelberg, MS
Brigadier General Charles Clark Chapter #253	Indianola, MS
Lt. Colonel William H. Luse Chapter #257	Yazoo City, MS
Captain James Albert Bass Chapter #275	Brookhaven, MS
Colonel Arasmus R. Burt Chapter #292	Jackson, MS

Ohio Society

The chapters that have been chartered in the State of Ohio as part of this Society are as follows:

Major General Howell Cobb Chapter #155	Middleton, OH
Major George Downs Chapter #159	Cincinnati, OH
Generals Lee and Jackson Chapter #256	Akron, OH

Tennessee Society

The Tennessee Society was first named the General John Hunt Morgan Society. Its first Society Commander was Dr. B. H. Webster of Nashville, TN who had proposed the name for the society to honor his relative who had served under General Morgan during the War Between the States.

The first meeting of this society was held on September 14, 1980 in the Senate chambers of the State Capitol. Among the items approved at this meeting was setting up society dues, society awards programs, and the appointment of a constitutional committee. The society newsletter, The Vidette, was started shortly thereafter. By the spring of 1981, a constitution had been proposed and later approved.

The chapters that have been chartered in the State of Tennessee as part of this Society are as follows:

Brigadier General A. J. Vaughan Chapter #13	Somerville, TN
Smith/Shy Chapter #14	Nashville, TN
Captain A. K. Miller Chapter #23	Lebanon, TN
General Cadmus M. Wilcox Chapter #73	Covington, TN
Shaw Battle Chapter #81	Brownsville, TN
General John Hunt Morgan Chapter #91	Nashville, TN

General Joseph B. Palmer Chapter #94	Smyrna, TN
General William B. Bates Chapter #109	Brentwood, TN
Knoxville Chapter #135	Knoxville, TN
Lt. Dabney M. Scales Chapter #141	Memphis, TN
Lt. General Nathan B. Forrest Chapter #142	Parker's Crossing, TN
Lt. Henry M. Doak CSN Chapter #144	Strawberry Plaines, TN
Major General Patrick Cleburne Chapter #158	Chattanooga, TN
Major General William D. McCain Chapter #163	Columbia, TN
Morton/Vaughn Chapter #166	Sevierville, TN
Colonel James W. Starnes Chapter #210	Tullahoma, TN
Captain Zillman Voss Chapter #223	Medon, TN
Colonel R. D. Allison Chapter #230	Smithville, TN
Brigadier General Alexander W. Campbell	Jackson, TN

Major General Patrick Cleburne Chapter #158 – Chattanooga, TN

The chapter was founded August 29, 1993 and named after Major General Patrick Cleburne. The chapter has provided leadership in the Chattanooga Confederate Cemetery renovations in the 1990s; as well as, co-hosted the SCV/MOS&B reunion in Chattanooga.

Captain Zillman Voss Chapter #223 – Medon, TN

The chapter was founded on April 15, 1995. The first and largest chapter project was the placing of a large brick marker with marble insert upon which this was for the Confederate Burial Trench at Mercer, TN. Herein lay the remains of 28 Confederate soldiers killed at a nearby crossing on the Hatchie River. We have dedicated and re-dedicated numerous graves and sites in the area also. The chapter also formed the 154th Senior Tennessee Infantry Regiment Honor Guard for services conducted by the chapter. Other memorial services have been held over the years to honor Confederate and Union soldiers that were killed in the area.

Army of Trans-Mississippi Department

At the General Convention in New Orleans in 1980, the Order amended its constitution and created Departments. At the first meeting of the Trans-Mississippi Department, Military Order of the Stars and Bars, Compatriot George Hawes Sutherlin Jr. of New Orleans, was elected Commander. At the 1984 General Convention in Biloxi, Mississippi, Compatriot Joseph A. Winkler Jr., was elected Department Commander, Commander Winkler died in 1985 and Compatriot Edward Overton Cailleteau was appointed by the Commander-in-Chief, Mark Lee (Beau) Cantrell, to fill the unexpired term. At the 1990 General Convention in Fayetteville, Arkansas, Compatriot Joseph A. Winkler III, of Lafayette, Louisiana, was elected commander of the Trans-Mississippi Department. In 1992, at Wilmington, North Carolina, Pat Hardy of St. Louis, Missouri, was elected commander. In 1994, at Mobile, Alabama, James Troy Massey of Harrison, Arkansas, Was elected commander. Officers elected in 1996 at Richmond, Virginia, were Commander Evetts Hailey Jr. of Midland, Texas and Councilman Pat Sohrwide, of Stillwater, Oklahoma. In 1998, Commander Gene Dressell of Jonesburg, Missouri was elected Commander at the General Convention in St. Louis with Pat Sohrwide as Councilman.

At the 2000 Convention in Charleston, SC, the ATM elected Curtis Hopper of Missouri as Commander. Commander Hopper would also serve as Councilman-ATM and Chief of Staff of the national MOS&B. Curtis had served as Missouri Society Commander and was a very dedicated member of the MOS&B, traveling extensively on behalf of the Order. Commander Hopper passed away September 17, 2010.

In 2002, at Memphis, TN, the ATM elected Michael McCulloch as Commander and J. David Massey as Councilman. The 2004 General Convention was in Dalton, GA, where Dale Fowlkes was elected Commander and Robert W. Crook of LA as Councilman. Commander Fowlkes had previously served as Texas Society Commander following the death of long-time MOS&B stalwart Ronald Aldis of Houston.

In 2006, the MOS&B-ATM convened in Mobile, Alabama where Robert W. Crook became Commander and Nick Warren of Colorado was Councilor. In 2008 the general convention met in Springdale, AR. The ATM elected Gary Loudermilk of Texas was elected Commander and David Whitaker of Houston as Councilman. In 2010, the MOS&B ATM elected Don Lee as Commander, and Patrick Sohrwide (Oklahoma) and Howard Jones of California as Councilmen. In 2012 at the San Antonio Convention, Gary L. Loudermilk was elected Commander, Dr. Philip Isett (Oklahoma) and David Holcombe (Louisiana) were elected as Councilmen.

The ATM has contributed the following leaders as Commander-in-Chief or Commander General over the past quarter century. Mark Lea Cantrell (OK), Edward O. Cailleteau (LA), Robert L. Hawkins (MO), Charles H. Smith (OK), Troy Massey (AR), and Jeff Massey (OK).

The Department hereby known as the Army of Trans-Mississippi is comprised of seven Societies. The active State Societies in the Army of Trans-Mississippi Department are the Arkansas Society, the California Society, the Colorado Society, the Louisiana Society, the Missouri Society, the Oklahoma Society and the Texas Society. The active chartered chapters in the Army of Trans-Mississippi that has no State Society are Captain James Iredell Waddell Chapter #259 – Anchorage, Alaska and Captain Jeff Standefer Chapter #35 – Seattle, Washington. Note that there have been several chapters chartered in the State of Arizona that are not active at this time.

General Patrick R. Cleburne, Arkansas Society

The Arkansas Society was formed on April 13, 1985, at the Arkansas Division, Sons of Confederate Veterans Convention in Harrison, Arkansas. Elected officers were Commander James Troy Massey, 1st Lieutenant Commander Bill Ferguson, and Adjutant E. Wayne Cone. The two chapters chartered into the new society were: Abner-Cone-Langston-Shaver-Wright Chapter of Harrison with fourteen members and the Wayne Van Zandt Chapter of Little Rock with nine members. At that convention, they voted to place a Military Order of the Stars and Bars plaque in the Arkansas History Commission in Little Rock to honor their Confederate officer ancestors and government officials. Also, an ongoing project was undertaken to name all known Confederate Arkansas officers and government officials in Arkansas. The next year a new chapter chartered and was named the General Dandridge McRae chapter, at Searcy, Arkansas, and formed with seven new members.

In 1993, the Arkansas Society had a name change. A vote was taken by the membership to be renamed the General Patrick R. Cleburne, Arkansas Society. Past commanders include: James Troy Massey, Jeff Massey, Sammy Joe Massey, Thomas Yoder, Samuel Alexander Massey, Jr., Bill Elmore and Jerry Lawrence. The officers for the General Patrick R. Cleburne, Arkansas Society, for 2012-2014 are Commander Gordon Hale of the Captain James Tyrie Wright Chapter No. 6 of Harrison and who resides in Berryville; 1st Lieutenant Commander Daniel James Massey of the Captain James Tyrie Wright Chapter No. 6 of Harrison who resides in Conway; 2nd Lt. Commander Steve Bailey of the Captain James Tyrie Wright Chapter No. 6 of Harrison and who resides in Bentonville; and Adjutant J. Troy Massey of the Captain James Tyrie Wright Chapter No. 6 of Harrison and resides in Harrison.

The Arkansas Society meets annually in November for their reunion. Annual projects include supporting the Confederate Cemetery at Fayetteville, where they are Life Members. Manpower and annual financial donations are given annually to the cemetery. Donations have been made to the Lee project on the Washington and Lee University campus in Lexington, Virginia. The society is a member of the Museum of the Confederacy in Richmond, Virginia. Periodically the Arkansas Society hosts a memorial service with the Indian Territory Society and societies in the Trans-Mississippi to honor General Stand Watie, at his gravesite in Oklahoma. With 2011 beginning the Sesquicentennial years of the War Between The States, the Arkansas Society has already had a print of its namesake, General Patrick R. Cleburne, etched by Past Commander Sammy Joe Massey, and approved from the Sesquicentennial Commission for sales. The funds will be used for a college scholarship for Arkansas high school seniors in Arkansas. This scholarship will be given at the Sesquicentennial banquet for General Cleburne in November 2014.

In celebration of the Sesquicentennial in Arkansas, the General Patrick R. Cleburne, Arkansas Society, MOS&B, has had the honor of sponsoring six Sesquicentennial markers at Eureka Springs, Berryville, and Green Forest in Carroll County, Arkansas. In addition, they have sponsored markers in Boone County, Arkansas at the Boone County Courthouse, Lead Hill where the 14th Arkansas Infantry Regiment was organized and at the Skirmish of Rolling Prairie. A seventh marker is in the works to be placed in 2013 at the Walker Cemetery next to the Confederate Cemetery in Fayetteville, Arkansas honoring the Walker Family. David Walker was Arkansas' Secession President and lead the state out of the Union in May 1861. Several Walker family members were enlisted in the Confederate States of America and buried in the Walker Cemetery. The site is now on the Register of Historical Places. They participated at Yellville and Clinton for their marker dedications.

The Arkansas Society is working on markers near Gravette and Richland Creek for Sesquicentennial projects. Also, they are working to name all the Killed In Action at Elkhorn Tavern and Prairie Grove.

The chapters that have been chartered in the State of Arkansas as part of this Society are as follows:

Captain James Tyrie Wright Chapter #6	Harrison, AR
Battle of Jenkins Ferry Chapter #20	Leola, AR
S. Wayne Van Zandt Chapter #178	Little Rock, AR
Lt. Silas A. Henry Chapter #231	Dardanelle, AR
General John Edward Murray Chapter #262	Pine Bluff, AR
Major General James F. Fagan Chapter #280	Jonesboro, AR

Captain James Tyrie Wright Chapter #6 – Harrison, AR

This chapter was originally named the Abner-Cone-Langston-Shaver-Wright chapter when it was formed on November 4, 1983 from Confederate officer's corps ancestors of charter members of the chapter. Abner was the ancestor of Steve Muller; Lt. Cone, an ancestor of E Wayne Cone; Langston, an ancestor of Charles and Harold Hammett; Colonel Robert G. Shaver, a great-great uncle of Ron Shaver; and Captain James Tyrie Wright, a great-great-great-grandfather of James Troy Massey, Sammy Joe Massey, Jeffery Wayne Massey, and John David Massey.

In 1994, the name was changed to the Captain James Tyrie Wright Chapter of Company C, 11th Regiment, 8th Division, Missouri State Guard. Past Commanders of this chapter are James Troy Massey, and John David Massey.

Lieutenant Silas A. Henry Chapter #231 – Dardanelle, AR

The Lt. Silas A. Henry Chapter was organized in Dardanelle, Arkansas in May of 1996. The Charter was presented by Commander General J. Troy Massey in November 1996. The original meetings of this chapter were held monthly at the Dardanelle Public Library.

California Society

California is proud to be approved as a new State Society within the Military Order of the Stars and Bars. Our application to create a Society was approved by the General Executive Council on March 30, 2008.

The idea of creating a California Society was first advanced at the 2006 National Convention in Mobile, Alabama. Former AOT Commander, John Mason, addressed the members in attendance and pointed out that California already had enough members to qualify as a Society. His remarks were well received by everyone at the convention.

On January 28, 2008, Commander Philip Law appointed Howard Jones – Commander of the General John B. Hood Chapter #89 in Los Angeles, CA to the position of Provisional California Society Commander. Commander Jones worked closely with Adjutant General Max Waldrop, Jr. to organize and create a new California State Society. On March 10, 2008, the formal application for Society status was submitted to ATM Commander Robert Crook for his approval. The application was subsequently approved by both Commander Crook and the General Executive Council.

The California Society was created by 21 members who belonged to State's only Chapter in Los Angeles. One of the first acts of the new Society was to create a second Chapter in San Francisco. This chapter was named the Captain Alonzo Ridley Chapter # 303. Our members were enthusiastic and are looking forward to a bright future.

The charter officers of the California Society are: Commander Wm. Howard Jones; Lt Commander James William Monroe; and Adjutant Gary Dewain Stephens. The charter members of the California Society are: Joseph Victor Alarid; James Nelson Bardin; Lee Edward Bishop, Jr.; Rev. Louis V. Carlson; Leslie Allen Cofer, III; Elmo Levy Draughon, Jr.; Leroy Vincent Epperson; Randall Craig Epperson, PhD; Neil Douglas Estes; Preston Leon Gilliam, Dr. Rowland Rutherford King; Charles Kenneth Maness; Roy Robert Nunn; Michael Andrew Schooling; William Elbert Steger; Manor Lawton Thorpe, PhD; Fred Henry White, IV; and John Owen White.

Colorado Society

Colorado is the most recent state to be organized as a Society. Our request for Society status was approved by the General Executive Council meeting in October 2012.

Historically, there have been two Chapters formed in Colorado. In Denver, the Captain John S. Sprigg Chapter # 263 was established in 2001, and remained active for about four years. In Colorado Springs, the Major Chatham R. Wheat Chapter #297 was established in 2005 and reached a total of eight active members by 2011. Several of the members had transferred from Chapter 263.

During 2012, Chapter #297 has been re-energized to focus on the Sesquicentennial celebrations and bring new life into Colorado activities. We currently have 16 members (8 from 2011, 5 reinstalled, 2 transfers, and one new member) plus we have two new member applications in the final preparation/ review process.

The "revived Chapter #297" members also qualified to become a full Society. At our Chapter Fall Meeting we elected the Chapter officers; then, recognized the Society Charter Members and elected the Society Officers:

CO Society Commander   David Wayne Snodgrass
CO Society Lt. Commander   John Copeland Luedecke
CO Society Adjutant   David Joseph Rodgers
CO Society Chaplain   Robert Leland Atkinson

Other Charter Members:

Stephen Dale Boyett   Oscar Jeter Mooneyham, III
Garry Wayne Brewer   Gary Eugene Parrott
James Francis Bush   William Ormsby Rutledge
William Lee Caynor, Sr.   Myron Crenshaw Smith
William Joseph Fillingim   Robert Burwell Starke
John Jackson Hedrick, IV   Thomas Adam Wellborn

Our near term activities include: Christmas Party, Lee-Jackson Dinner, Confederate Memorial Day Celebration, Jefferson Davis Dinner and educational opportunities with local middle schools. Our mission includes cooperating with other Colorado Confederate groups including: The Sons of Confederate Veterans, The United Daughters of the Confederacy, The Colorado Order of the Confederate Rose, and the Sesquicentennial Society.

Colorado had just become a "Territory" when the War Between The States began and many citizens returned to their South to defend their homes. However, some remained and formed militia groups to seize the Colorado gold which was needed by the Southern Cause. The militia groups had several successes and failures.

At least 470 graves of Confederate Veterans have been identified in the state. There were many C.S.A. veterans who came to Colorado after the war ended and then served in developing Colorado as it became a state in 1876 and through out the following decades: 2 State Governors, 1 US Senator, 1 US Congressman, 6 Colorado State senators/legislators, 10 State Judges, 12 Public Safety Officials, 39 City/County Officials, and 44 prominent Colorado business leaders. There were many Southerners who came west for a better life during the Reconstruction Era.

Our mission includes honoring our own ancestors in their home states as well as those Confederate Veterans who settled in Colorado.

Louisiana Society

The Louisiana Society, MOS&B was organized in 1979-80 by the late George Hawes Sutherlin, Jr. and Edward Overton Cailleteau. Both men are sons of Alexandria, Louisiana. In fact, when COL George Sutherlin and his wife were married, their only attendant was the lady who later was the mother of Edward Overton Cailleteau. Sutherlin, a relative of the man who owned the home in Danville, VA in which the last meeting of the Confederate Cabinet took place, had done some preliminary work toward organization earlier in 1979. Cailleteau became a member of Headquarters Camp No. 584, SCV and a member at-large of the General Society, MOS&B earlier in 1979. Sutherlin was appointed Organizing Commander of the LA Society by then Commander-in-Chief Dr. Ralph W. Widener of Dallas. Sutherlin appointed Cailleteau as Adjutant. The Society held its first meeting on June 28, 1980 at Toby's Four Corners Restaurant in Lafayette. Over dinner, those in attendance considered and adopted a Constitution which had been drafted by Adjutant Cailleteau.

When the 1980 General Convention at New Orleans amended the Constitution of the Order to create Departments, George H. Sutherlin, Jr. was elected the first Commander of the Trans-Mississippi Department and Edward O. Cailleteau became Commander of the Louisiana Society.

Those who have served as Commander are: George H. Sutherlin, Jr. of New Orleans, 1979-80 (died 1986, age 46); Edward Overton Cailleteau of Baton Rouge, 1980-83; Joseph A. Winkler, Jr. of Hammond, 1983-85 (died 1985); Bruns D'Aunoy Redmond of New Orleans, 1985-89; Joseph A. Winkler, III of Lafayette, 1989-95; Alvin Young Bethard of Lafayette, 1995-97; Miller D.M.F. Dial of Baton Rouge, 1997-99; Charles E. McMichael of Shreveport, 1999-2001; Robert Williams Crook of Baton Rouge, 2001-2003; Dr. Ernest St. Clair Easterly, III of Watson (Livingston Parish), 2003-2005; and Reinhard J. Dearing of Slidell, 2005-2007. Currently serving as Commander is Joe Thompson Walters, Jr. of Winnsboro. Those who have served as Adjutant include: Edward Overton Cailleteau, Charles Owen Johnson and Claudius Augustus Mayo.

The chapters that have been chartered in the State of Louisiana as part of this Society are as follows:

CSS Arkansas Chapter #21	Baton Rouge, LA
Governor Alexandre Mouton Chapter #120	Lafayette, LA
Major General Earl Van Dorn Chapter #154	New Orleans, LA
Lt. Issac Ryan Chapter #205	Lake Charles, LA
Col. Leon Dawson Marks -	
Major Winfrey B. Scott Chapter #214	Shreveport-Minden, LA
Brigadier General Henry Gray Chapter #218	Shreveport, LA
Isaac Harrison Texsas Cavalry Chapter #286	St. Joseph, LA

The **C.S.S. Arkansas** was an ironclad gunboat the construction of which was contracted by the Confederate Government to John T. Shirley of Memphis. As federal naval forces approached Memphis, the Arkansas was ordered up the Yazoo River to Greenwood, Mississippi for completion. No effort was made to save the Tennessee and that ship burned before it was ever launched. In Greenwood, completion of the Arkansas proceeded slowly. Secretary of the Navy Stephen Mallory placed Lt. Isaac N. Brown, CSN in command of the Arkansas with orders to complete her as soon as possible.

The Arkansas sailed for the first time on July 14, 1862. The Arkansas moved from the Yazoo into the Mississippi River and ran past the federal gunboats before Vicksburg. Facing federal naval forces of 3,000 men, 300 guns and over 50 ships, the Arkansas, with 10 guns and 200 men, succeeded in running past the federal naval force. The Arkansas arrived at the wharf in Vicksburg on the morning of July 15. The townspeople had observed the exploits of the Arkansas and the ironclad gunboat received a tumultuous welcome in Vicksburg. For several days, federal gunboats shelled the Arkansas and enjoyed only limited success. Finally, the federal fleet departed Vicksburg, Farragut returned to New Orleans and the first seige of Vicksburg was broken by the Arkansas. Lt. Isaac Brown was promoted to the rank of Commander. Repairs to the Arkansas commenced and Brown took a sick leave to go to his family in Grenada, Mississippi.

Shortly after Brown began his sick leave, Major General Earl Van Dorn sent John C. Breckinridge down to retake Baton Rouge from the Federals. Breckendridge's troops left Memphis by train on July 27, 1862 for Camp Moore, Louisiana. The federal force in Baton Rouge consisted of some 5,000 men and the ironclad gunboat Essex. In the action at Vicksburg, the Essex was hit 42 times by the Arkansas. Lt. Stevens, second in command to CDR Brown, was ordered to proceed downriver to arrive simultaneously with Breckenridge's force on August 5. Stevens refused and cited orders from CDR Brown that the Arkansas was not to be moved until Brown returned and was able to check the engines on the ship. Van Dorn caused Brown's order to be countermanded and the Arkansas set out for Baton Rouge.

On the early morning of August 5, the engines of the Arkansas stopped just north of Port Hudson. At daylight, the Arkansas was underway again and within the sound of Breckenridge's guns. Then, the starboard engine stopped. The engines were fixed by nightfall. Communications with Breckenridge were established. Breckenridge reported that he had defeated the federals on the 5th and had driven them to the river where they could be protected by the guns of the Essex. Breckenridge would renew his attack on the following morning and the Arkansas would join in. The Arkansas began moving toward Baton Rouge at 3:00 A.M. The engines failed again. At 7:00 A.M. the ship got underway again. Just as the engagement with the Essex commenced, the engines on the Arkansas failed again. Lt. Stevens ordered the crew ashore and, before he was the last to leave the ship, he ignited the explosives which blew up the Arkansas.

CDR Brown left his sickbed and came to Vicksburg by cattle car only to learn that the Arkansas had departed for Baton Rouge. Brown arrived at Baton Rouge just before the Arkansas was blown up.

The **C.S.S. Arkansas Chapter No. 21 of Baton Rouge** was organized to commemorate the feisty ironclad which, if it had been in good running order, might well have provided invaluable aid to John C. Breckinridge in the expulsion of the federal forces occupying Baton Rouge. The Charter, dated January 19, 1987, was presented at a luncheon in Baton Rouge on February 20, 1987. The Organizing Commander was Edward Overton Cailleteau. The Adjutant was Joseph A. Winkler, III.

The second Commander was Miller D.M.F. Dial who served from 1994 to 1998. At a meeting held on January 14, 1998 Dr. Ernest St. Clair Easterly, III was elected Commander and Robert Williams Crook was elected Adjutant. In 2000 William Glen Griffin was elected Commander and John A.R. Hébert was elected Adjutant. Serving as Commander since 2002 is Compatriot John A. R. Hébert of Gonzales.

In recent times, the Chapter has held luncheon meetings, once per year in the early summer. Recently, the Chapter has undertaken projects to more assertively mark, or re-mark, historical sites in Southeast Louisiana.

The **Governor Alexandre Mouton Chapter No. 120** of Lafayette applied for Charter under date of May 12, 1987. Commanders have included Joseph A. Winkler, III and Alvin Young Bethard.

The **Major General Earl Van Dorn Chapter No. 154** of New Orleans was the first MOS&B chapter in Louisiana and was chartered on January 6, 1983. Organizing Commander was David Wayne Powell. Organizing Adjutant and the only Adjutant the Chapter has ever had is Edward Overton Cailleteau. CDR Powell was succeeded by Edward Church Bush. When he became Commander of the Col. Charles Didier Dreux Camp No. 110, SCV, Bush was succeeded by the great nephew of the Chapter's namesake, Hon. Earl Van Dorn Wood. CDR Wood died in office on May 15, 1997. At a special meeting of the Chapter held at Antoine's Restaurant on October 10, 1997, Dr. Philip D. Mollère was elected to fill the unexpired term of CDR Wood as Commander of the Chapter.

The **Brigadier General Henry Gray Chapter No. 218** of Shreveport

The **Lt. Isaac Ryan Chapter No. 205** of Lake Charles was chartered in 1994. The Organizing Commander was Claudius Augustus Mayo. Compatriot G. Scott Thorn has served as Commander of the Chapter. After a period of dormancy, the Chapter has revived and the Commandancy has devolved to Compatriot Michael Dan Jones of Iowa, Louisiana, a byline reporter with the Lake Charles *American Press.*

The **Major Winfrey Bond Scott - Colonel Leon Dawson Marks Chapter No. 214** of Shreveport and Minden was organized in 1997. In 2002 the Winfrey B. Scott Chapter was renamed the Colonel Leon Dawson Marks - Major Winfrey B. Scott Chapter and the bases of the Chapter became Shreveport and Minden. Several members of the Brigadier General Henry Gray Chapter transferred to the Marks - Scott Chapter. The Commander of the Chapter is George Mark Camp.

The **Isaac Harrison's Tensas Cavalry Chapter No. 286** was organized in 2004 under the leadership of Dr. Joel E.M. Jackson of St. Joseph, Tensas Parish and Joe Thompson Walters, Jr. of Winnsboro.

Missouri Society

The Missouri Society would like to Congratulate the Men of the MOS&B, both past and present, on 75 years of fine representation of the Officer Corps and Elected Officials of the Confederate States of America. For 75 years now we have lived up to our pledges to commemorate and honor the service of the Confederate Leadership. May God bless our future endeavors as we continue to perpetuate the true history of what our Confederate Ancestors fought for, the fundamental American principles of self-determination and States Rights.

The first Chapter of the Missouri Society was formed on September 26th, 1987 in Keytesville, Missouri. That Chapter was the Brigadier General Francis M. Cockrell Chapter and is still in existence today. In a month, the Chapter had grown to sufficient numbers to be granted Society Status, and our Society Constitution was ratified at our first Society Convention on September 30th, 1988

The Society had grown to 8 chapters thru the years, with 3 Chapters eventually going defunct. Today, on January 14th, 2013 we reinstated a 6th Chapter, the Claiborne Fox Jackson Chapter 267. The Society welcomes Jackson Chapter back into the fold and we are excited to have its many valuable members on the Society team!

The Missouri Society Chapter Roster is as follows:

BG Francis Marion Cockrell 84 - Billy Ed Bowden, Commander, St. Peters, MO
MG John Sappington Marmaduke 150 - Royal Cooper, Commander, Jefferson City, MO
MG John S. Bowen 157 - Dale Wiseman Commander, St. Louis, MO
Col. Upton Hayes 235 - Charles Wood, Commander Springfield, MO
LTC John R. Boyd 236 - Kurt Holland, Commander, Independence, MO
Gov. Claiborne Fox Jackson 267- Gary Ayers, Commander, Stockton, MO

1.BG Francis Marion Cockrell 84 - Bill Bowden Commander 636-456-0009.
Now meeting in- St. Peters, MO
2. MG John Sappington Marmaduke 150 - Royal Cooper Commander 573-635-8897 - Jeff City
3. MG John S. Bowen 157 - Dale Wiseman Commander 636-281-1332 - St. Louis
4. Co. Upton Hayes 235 - Charles Wood - 417-357-8302 - Springfield
5. LTC John R. Boyd 236 - Larry Yeatman - 816-728-2291- Independence

The Missouri Society Command is as follows:
Larry Yeatman-Commander
Billy Ed Bowden-Lt. Commander
Keith Daleen-Adjutant

The Missouri Society has worked in the past to place books in Libraries and has also reprinted books about the history of the Southern Cause that were out of print. This helps to fulfill our MOS&B mission of chronicling our Confederate Officers' contributions in the history books.

Our current project the Society is working on is to buy a piece of land on a major interstate to use for a large flag pole. Good people properly displaying the Flags of the Confederacy will help to preserve our history and serve as a reminder to the public that Missouri was a former Confederate State.

Going forward, the Society needs to reach out to young men, sons, and our Grandsons to foster a sense of pride in their Confederate Heritage. This will help get them interested in joining the MOS&B and provide us with future generations of membership to carry on the legacy of the Confederacy. As an organization, we need to capitalize on the 150th Anniversary period of the war while interest is high. With many towns throughout the South holding 150th Anniversary events, this gives us many opportunities to set up recruiting and information booths.

Indian Territory (Oklahoma) Society

The Indian Territory Society had its beginning with the formation of Brigadier General Douglas H. Cooper Chapter, Oklahoma City. During a meeting at the 45th Infantry Division Museum, Oklahoma City, in March 1981, Commander Mark Lea "Beau" Cantrell advanced to Commander, Indian Territory Society. Later chapters formed in the Indian Territory Society were Major George Washington Caddo's Frontier Battalion Chapter, General Douglas H. Cooper Chapter, Roswell W. Lee Chapter, Brigadier General Eppa Hunton Chapter, Colonel William Penn Adair Chapter, Major General Patrick R. Cleburn and General Stephen D. Lee Chapters.
Indian Territory Society Commanders:

1981-82 Mark Lee "Beau" Cantrell
1983-84 Alvin Lee Baker
1985-86 Charles H. Smith*
1986-87 Richard B. Rea
1987 -88 Daniel K Almond
1988-90 Richard Almond**
1991-93 Robert E. Henson Jr.**
1995-97 K Patrick Sohrwide
1997-2001 Dr. James G. Caster
2001-2005 Dr. Philip Isett
2005-2009 David Massey
2009-Current Jeff Massey

*Resigned to become Lieutenant Commander-in-Chief, Military Order of the Stars and Bars.
**Deceased

The following members of the Indian Territory Society have served as Commanders-in- Chief, Military Order of the Stars and Bars:

1968-70 Dr. James M. Edwards
1984-86 Mark L. "Beau" Cantrell
1992-94 Charles H. Smith
2002-2004 Jeffery W. Massey

Other members of the Indian Territory Society serving on the National Military Order of the Stars and Bars Staff:

1996-1998	David Massey, Chief of Staff
1994-2012	Jeff W. Massey, Judge Advocate General, Comptroller General
1986-88	Daniel K. Almond, Chief of Staff
1992-94	Robert E. Henson, Chief Aide de Camp
1996-98	K. Patrick Sohrwide, Department Trans-Mississippi Councilman
2008-2014	Dr. Philip Isett, Archivist General

2002-2012	Dr. James G. Caster, Inspector and national literary committees
2006-2008	Col. Patrick Banks, Inspector
2010-2012	Nicholas Massey, National Boy Scout Awards member

The chapters that have been chartered in the State of Oklahoma as part of this Society are as follows:

Brigadier General Douglas H. Cooper Chapter #15	Oklahoma City, OK
Brigadier General Eppa Hunton Chapter #16	Tulsa, OK
Caddo Frontier Battalion Chapter #22	El Reno, OK
General Patrick R. Cleburne Chapter #25	Edmond, OK
Colonel Roswell W. Lee Chapter #56 & #177	Edmond, OK
Colonel William Penn Adair Chapter #200	Oklahoma City, OK

Brig. Gen. Douglas H. Cooper Chapter #15 – Oklahoma City, OK

The Brig. Gen. Douglas H. Cooper Chapter was formed in Oklahoma City on March 23, 1979. Chartering members included Charles H. Smith, Dr. C.W. Buck, Mark L. "Beau" Cantrell, Rev. Alvin Lee Baker, Donald G. Church, Richard B. Harris and Hale Bicknell, Jr. The first officers included Charles H. Smith as Commander, Adjutant Donald G. Church and Lieutenant Commander Dr. C.W. Buck.

Prominent past commanders of the D.H. Cooper Chapter include PCIC Charles H. Smith, Dr. C.W. Buck, Rev. Alvin Baker, Daniel K. Almond, Robert E. Henson, Jr., K. Patrick Sohrwide, Maj. H.B. "Barney" Larkin, Dr. Philip Isett, David Massey and Jeff Massey.

The Cooper Chapter played an important role in the formation of the other chapters in Oklahoma. The Cooper Chapter was instrumental in the eventual formation of the Indian Territory Society. The Cooper Chapter is responsible for hosting the Lee-Jackson Memorial celebration at the Confederate Hall at the Oklahoma Historical Society. This Confederate celebration is the longest running event at the historical society as of 2012.

The Cooper Chapter was selected as the Most Outstanding Chapter in the MOSB for 1995 and 1996. The chapter newsletter, "Officer's Call" was established in April 1985 and is published bi-monthly. The Chapter has been active in securing the construction of the Confederate Memorial Hall in the Oklahoma History Center. The Chapter regularly upkeeps and maintains the MOSB Archives and storing historical documents and manuscripts.

The chapter has provided numerous national officers to the Military Order of the Stars and Bars. Past Commanders-in-Chief Mark L. "Beau" Cantrell and Charles H. Smith, Judge Advocate General Jeff W. Massey, Chief of Staff David Massey and Trans-Mississippi Councilman K. Patrick Sohrwide, Past Chief of Protocol Charles Britton, Emeritus Chief of Staff Dr. James G. Caster, Dr. Philip Isett and Past Chief of Staff Robert E. Henson, Jr. have all been members of the Brig. Gen. D.H. Cooper Chapter.

General Patrick R. Cleburne Chapter #25 – Edmond, OK

The Cleburne Chapter was formed in 1998 and is composed primarily of dedicated Life Members of the MOS&B. The Chapter has been active in securing the construction of the Confederate Memorial

Hall in the Oklahoma History Center. The Chapter regularly upkeeps and maintains the MOS&B Archives and storing historical documents and manuscripts.

Charter members include David Massey, Sam Massey, Jeff Massey, Mark Atchley and Charles Atchley. Current Life Members Nicholas Massey and Matthew Massey are also members.

Colonel Roswell W. Lee Chapter #177 – Edmond, OK

The exact date of the founding of the Colonel Roswell W. Lee Chapter of the Military Order of the Stars and Bars is unknown but the adjutant has records starting in 1988. Colonel Roswell W. Lee is the namesake of the Chapter.

Charter members include Edwin L. Deason, Jamie Howard, Forest Schooling, Charles H. Smith and Roy P. Stewart.

Texas Society

Our Society is doing well. We have gained a few members, and continue with our "Recruit, Retain & Reunite" goals. We currently have 10 Active Chapters; one was reactivated in 2012 and is going strong. Our Society has 200 plus members. Some of our activities are grave marker dedications, Living History Presentations and speaking to Heritage groups. The Color Guard in our Chapters remains active. We also bring our Color Guard to UDC Chapters' special events, often in partnership with SCV. Our Texas Society also has a State Color Guard. The Texas Society and Texas Chapter #5 were hosts of the 2012 National MOS&B Convention held in San Antonio, Texas. A record number of over 160 attended. Dr. Toni Turk of the Texas Chapter #5 was elected Commander General. We had a very good year.

Texas Society Chapters MOS&B Chapters January 2013

Alvin	Isaac Avery #282
Comanche	John Loudermilk #264
Ennis	Wm. H. Parsons #273
Ft. Worth	Benjamin Morris #279
Ft, Worth	Felix H. Robertson #68
Houston	Texas #5
Midland	Haley Holt #121
Orange Benjamin	Norseworthy #276
San Antonio	Lawrence S. Ross #184
Tyler	Richard B. Hubbard #261

Texas Society Past COMMANDERS

1995-1997	John B. Meadows
1997-1999	James B. Moore
1999-2001	Walter Nass DCS
2001-2003	G. Ronald Aldis DCS (Deceased)
2003-2005	Hugh Dale Fowlkes DCS
2005-2007	Dr. Gary M. Loudermilk DCS
2007-2009	James Templin
2009-2011	Gary L. Loudermilk
2011-2013	Glenn W. Toal

The chapters that have been chartered in the State of Texas as part of this Society are as follows:

Texas Chapter #5 & #186	Houston, TX
General Felix H. Robertson Chapter #68	Fort Worth, TX
General Jerome B. Robertson Chapter #87	Hillsboro, TX
General Sul Ross Chapter #106	San Antonio, TX
General Thomas N. Wauls Texas Legion Chapter #107 & #194	Fort Worth, TX
Haley-Holt Chapter #121	Midland, TX
Jeb Stuart Chapter #124	Carthage, TX
John H. Reagan Chapter #127	Austin, TX
Lone Star Chapter #137	Dallas, TX
Lawrence Sullivan Ross Chapter #184	San Antonio, TX
Captain Ike Turner Chapter #211	Livingston, TX
Major Chatham Roberdeau Wheat Chapter #224	Plano, TX
The General Tom Green Chapter #225	Corsicana, TX
Captain Christopher Cleburne Chapter #241	Cleburne, TX
Captain David Whitfield Snodgrass Chapter #254	Fort Worth, TX
Colonel Richard Bennett Hubbard Chapter #261	Tyler, TX
Major John Loudermilk Chapter #264	Comanche, TX
Colonel W. H. Parsons Chapter #273	Ennis, TX
Colonel Benjamin H. Norsworthy Chapter #276	Orange, TX
Colonel Benjamin Morris Chapter #279	Fort Worth, TX
Colonel Isaac E. Avery Chapter #282	Alvin, TX
Major Henry Wyncoop Raguet Chapter #293	Longview, TX

Texas Chapter #5 – Houston, TX

The Texas Chapter, Military Order of the Stars & Bars, the first chapter in Texas, was chartered on June 30, 1970, in Houston, Texas. In those days MOS&B chapters affiliated with SCV Camps and the Texas Chapter affiliated with the now defunct Dick Dowling camp #1305. In the beginning thirty eight members of the MOS&B came together to form this once great chapter. A number of notable Texans were among that group including Msgr. Anton Frank of the Houston-Galveston Diocese and two future CICs of the MOS&B, Dennis W. Rainoshek and Dr. Ralph W. Widener, Jr. One of the charter members of this Chapter is our current Commander General, Dr. Toni R. Turk.

About 1999 the original Chapter ceased to exist because of attrition. The Albert Sidney Johnston Chapter #5 of Houston, Texas, on December 1st, 2009, decided to change the name of the ASJ#5 to The Texas Chapter #5 for two reasons: 1) eliminate the similar name confusion with the local SCV camp and 2) restore the great traditions of the Texas Chapter. The Texas chapter is still the largest Chapter in the MOS&B and is one of the most active with a membership of over 60 compatriots. In 2012 the Texas Chapter #5 joined hands with the Texas Society and hosted the National MOS&B Convention in San Antonio, Texas, at the famous Menger Hotel to a record crowd of over 160 people.

When the old Texas Chapter first organized the idea was conceived to present a replica of the Davis Guard Medal to any person who made a substantial contribution to preserving Southern Heritage. The Davis Guard Medal was the only medal awarded by the CSA during the War Between the States. It was given to Lt. Dick Dowling and his small group of men who defeated the Yankees as they attempted to invade Texas at Sabine Pass. The Davis Guard Medal that the old Texas Chapter presented is similar in intent to the Ron Aldis Award that was conceived after Ron's death several years ago. These two honors have been merged into one. We have a list of all the past recipients of the Davis Guard Award and it looks like a Who's Who of great Texas compatriots. Included on that list of 33 are Dr. Frank Vandiver, Ralph Green, Pete Orlebeke, Jim Vogler, several UDC presidents, and Dr. William McCain, to mention a few. Recent additions to that list are PCG Charles Smith, John Lewis Moncure, CG Dr. Toni R. Turk, David G. Whitaker, Don Edward Lee, PCG Max Waldrop Jr., and William Bryan Roehrig III.

It is the intent of the reformed Texas Chapter #5, to restore the honor and greatness of this old Chapter and the honor of the men who put the Texas Chapter in the forefront of the Military Order of the Stars & Bars.

Haley-Holt Chapter #121 – Midland, TX

This chapter was chartered October 1, 1986 in Midland, TX with fifty charter members. John L. Echols was the MOS&B Commander-in-Chief at the time of the chapter chartering. In 1990, the chapter sponsored a new award program for the benefit and support of the entire Texas Society. A bronze medallion, called the M. E. Bradford MOS&B Bronze Service Award, is to be presented to a deserving individual who by his or her endeavor with the written word is effective in the preservation of southern history and traditions. It is the intent with this award to honor those individuals who have actively defended southern culture in writing, or through other thoughtful action, have helped to accurately portray and preserve southern history for future generations. It is also appropriate for those individuals who have helped provide a forum for accurate portrayal of southern history. Dr. M. E. Bradford was the first recipient of this award.

Lawrence Sullivan Ross Chapter #184 – San Antonio, TX

The original date the Lawrence Sullivan Ross Chapter was founded is unknown, but it was reactivated May 1, 1989 under the same name. Chapter members continue to help maintain the local Confederate Cemetery. Members have also participated in the Pilgrimage to the Alamo, the King William Parade, the Leon Valley 4th of July Parade; as well as, attended the Civil War Artillery School at Fort Weesatche where they certified for safety and use of Civil War Artillery.

Major Chatham Roberdeau Wheat Chapter #224 – Plano, TX

The chapter was chartered on January 8, 1996 in Plano, TX. Major Wheat commanded the famed 1st Louisiana Special Battalion, "Louisiana Tigers". He was seriously wounded at 1st Manassas on July 21, 1861 while leading his troops, but returned to command during the Peninsular Campaign on March-July 1862. When his brigade commander, Colonel Seymour, was killed in the battle at Gaines's Mill on June 27th, Major Wheat took command and was also killed with a bullet through the brain. He is buried in Hollywood Cemetery, Richmond, VA.

The chapter participates in a variety of events such as marking graves at the Pecan Grove Cemetery in McKinney, TX, holding an ancestor dinner banquet, etc.

General Tom Green Chapter #225 – Corsicana, TX

On November 15, 1995, a chapter charter application was submitted to General Headquarters for the formation of a chapter in Corsicana, TX, to be known as the General Tom Green chapter. There were six charter members.

Col. Richard Bennett Hubbard Chapter #261 – Tyler, TX

This chapter charter meeting took place on February 6, 2001 at the Potpourri House, located in Tyler, TX. The chartering officers were Past Commander General Edward Cailleteau of New Orlean, LA and Texas Division Commander Walter Nass of Houston, TX. The charter members were Thomas S. McCall, H. Patrick Porter, John D. Haynes, Waymon Larry McClellan, Carl D. McClung, Bob G. Davidson, Hugh Dale Fowlkes, Marvin Don Majors, Leland Carter, James E. Rheudasil, Joe Parker Harris, and Andrew Wayne Jones.

Commanders

2000	Organization Commander	Bob G. Davidson
2001-2002		Dale Fowlkes
2003-2004		Larry McClellan
2005-2007		Charles Hayes
2008-2010		Dan Horton
2011-		Tom Clinkscales

Adjutants

2000-2002	Dale Fowlkes
2003-	John Haynes

The Colonel Richard Bennett Hubbard Chapter was chartered February 6, 2001, with twelve members. Dale Fowlkes and Bob G. Davidson were the driving forces behind the formation of the Chapter, with Bob acting as Founding Commander. After the chartering of the Chapter, Dale was elected as its first regular Commander, followed by Larry McClellan, Charles Hayes, Dan Horton and Dr. Tom Clinkscales. Officers for 2011-2015 are Commander Dr. Tom Clinkscales, Lt. Commander Dan Horton, Adjutant John Haynes. We currently have fourteen members.

The Hubbard Chapter acts in close concert with the Captain James P. Douglas Camp #124 of Sons of Confederate Veterans, Mollie Moore Davis Chapter #217 of United Daughters of the Confederacy and Emma Sansom Chapter #31 of the Order of Confederate Rose, also centered in Tyler. Four of the Chapter's Charter members are former Commanders of the Captain James P. Douglas SCV Camp. Members of the Hubbard Chapter help promote Southern history in numerous ways. Each year on Heritage Day at the Goodman Museum, MOSB members man tables, pass out literature about the War Between the States, and promote respect for Southern heritage. Members give programs at area schools; participate in battery reenactments; participate in marker dedications. Our Chapter sponsors a Lee-Jackson dinner each January.

Some facts give special pride: both Dale Fowlkes and Bob Davidson have been awarded Distinguished Commander Status, and both have been named Honorary Commander General. Dale Fowlkes is Past Texas Society Commander and Past ATM Commander, and has been awarded the prestigious Silver Chalice. Bob Davidson has been Texas Society Chief of Staff for twelve years, and Texas Society Editor-Publisher for ten years.

INTERNATIONAL DISPATCHES – UNITING CONFEDERATES GLOBALLY

Why the new Department?

When our Commander General Max L Waldrop, Jr took the reins of our Order in 2010, he conceived a scheme whereby we would try to liaise with other Members at Large who live or serve overseas and to establish meaningful contact with other Confederate Heritage and Military History groups.

To this end I was approached to start the movement overseas and as I live "downunder" and on the other side of the world, it seemed very apt. I am still based in Melbourne Australia and thus far I have made good contact with the local American Civil War Roundtable of Australia, The Military Historical Association of Australia and gained knowledge of an SCV Camp (for Australia and New Zealand). On the Continent I have enjoyed considerable support from Colonel Heinrich Wirz of Switzerland and Hubert Leroy of the Confederate Historical Society of Belgium. Associated with this assistance came approaches to SCV Europe Camp # 1612 and support from Commander Aachim "Archy" Bänsch.

As regards the United Kingdom, I met and have been attached to the 290 Foundation of Liverpool. 290 was the hull number of the eventual Confederate commerce raider CSS Alabama. Liverpool was virtually part of the Confederacy at times with secret agents such as James Bulloch doing their best to gain support for our new nation. This group, which I have christened the C.I.A. (Confederate Intelligence Agency), was extremely active in Liverpool and many a commerce raider was purchased in Liverpool and fitted out in a neutral port and re-named to do its duty on the high seas. I envisage that quite a number of articles will be generated by this Society.

Through International Dispatches I have also made American contacts of interest. Dr E C "Curt" Fields of Memphis, Tennessee belongs to the SCV Nathan Bedford Forrest Camp # 215, Memphis, Tennessee. Dr Fields portrays General U S Grant in various reenactments in Tennessee, and is well known for his resemblance to the Federal General. Curt has been an excellent source of photographs and information over recent times, and has introduced me to many Confederate contacts.

I have been asked to provide a contact base for various people world-wide and see the Department – International Dispatches – acting as a small de facto Confederate Embassy here in Australia. This has allowed promotion of the MOS&B to all manner of people and will hopefully draw some membership enquiries. As Headquarters has always known, we tend to look for recruitment opportunities in all activities and that is the secondary function of International Dispatches.

Why Melbourne, Australia?

Although the formation of International Dispatches could well have been established in any country other than the United States, Melbourne is of particular interest to the Confederacy primarily due to the arrival on January 25, 1865, of *CSS Shenandoah*, the Confederate commerce raider which carried the last armed forces to surrender in the WBTS.

The two main Confederate presences internationally during and immediately after the War were the Confederate Navy, and Confederate Diplomatic Services. The former were either blockade runners or commerce raiders and this fledgling Navy achieved astounding success which belied its minimal resources. It caused enormous financial and propaganda damage to the Union who angry with the help given to the Confederacy by Great Britain launched the prolonged legal battle over the accumulated damages called collectively The *Alabama Claims*. The first claim was for $2 billion plus the ceding of Canada! However the claims were eventually settled in 1872 for $15, 500,000 (and no

Canada!). This action was the prime mover behind the eventual creation of The Hague Convention and the International Court.

The visit of the *CSS Shenandoah* received an extraordinary volume of publicity for both Melbourne (Australia was then a British colony), and the Confederate Cause as public sympathy came to lie with the "rebels". The motive behind the visit has been a matter of conjecture ever since the arrival of the ship. Captain James Iredell Waddell announced that the propeller or propeller shaft had been damaged and the sympathetic authorities allowed him to place the ship up on the slips at a private dockyard in Williamstown and even today there is a plaque describing the visit at the site. However repairs were guarded from a curious public who were not allowed in the dockyard until whatever actions deemed necessary had been carried out. But then came the re-victualing and taking on of other stores, and more provocatively, some 45 stowaways (read enlistments). There were sightings of a mysterious American believed to be a Confederate Agent and it is not beyond belief that the whole affair was possibly a last ditch attempt to sour relations between the Union and Great Britain. Captain Waddell's log offers no such reasoning, but circumstantially, the hand of diplomacy or Confederate Intelligence Agency, (my "pioneer C.I.A."), can be easily imagined.

In any event after an epic voyage during which she captured 38 prize ships, the *Shenandoah* was surrendered in Liverpool, Great Britain on November 6, 1865, the last to surrender in the WBTS, some six months after Appomattox. She was the only Confederate ship to have circumnavigated the world, having sailed 58,000 miles under the Confederate Flag. Viewed from today's perspective the entire proceedings read like an orchestrated act, and because of the Colony's generally favorable reception of a Confederate vessel, Melbourne is a particularly appropriate place to launch International Dispatches. Australia generally is extremely interested in the WBTS and the studies of the War are in depth and there is much communication between there and the United States on that matter.

And so the first home of International Dispatches was established in Melbourne, Australia and has been well received to date with positive expectations for the future. We anticipate greater bonds with more and more Confederates and hope that one day we will be able to offer a home to overseas "At Large" members.

The Mystery Cannon of Churchill Island: Experts say "No" to *CSS Shenandoah.* Can you identify this Gun?

In Western Port lies the very popular tourist attraction, Phillip Island, about a 90 minute drive from Melbourne, and just off the shore on the eastern end of this island lies Churchill Island, now accessible by vehicle bridge. This little island presents a period farm from the early 1800's with a Farmers Market and all manner of rural activities.

There is an old homestead built by Samuel Amess, one-time Mayor of Melbourne and outside this restored building is a six pounder cannon fully mounted. Legend (and at times the government tourist people) has it that this unusual little gun came off *CSS Shenandoah*, which famously visited Melbourne in January 1865. Some say James Waddell gave this cannon to Samuel Amess in return for hospitality.

Local historians have taken issue with this supposition, pointing out that it was never specified as armament on the Shenandoah, that the cannon appears to be typical of European manufacturers of the approximate time, and that it is an illogical proposition too state that Amess was capable of moving the cannon in secret to its current situation.

The promoters of the story would appear to have supported the story to increase the cannon's tourist pulling power, but that leaves us with the question: "Who *did* make the cannon and how did it get there?"

A report by J R Fielding, Curator of Arms, Science Museum of Victoria, presents the following appraisal of the piece:

Location: - Churchill Island, Westernport Bay.
Type of carriage – Wood (unusual) – Platform with wheels traversing slide on top, wooden truck with no wheels.

Gun Stamped		
(To left of vent)	–	860
		38
		F RECK
Overall length of Gun	–	5 feet 9 inches
Length of barrel (Base ring to muzzle)	–	5 feet
Caliber	–	3.773 inches

Percussion Lock fitted to the right of the vent, Brass body, steel hammer fitted for lanyard cord

Solid Shot for gun	
Caliber	3.565 inches
Weight	5.978 pounds

Gun is claimed to have been given to Samuel Amess by Captain James Waddell, Commander of the CSS Shenandoah, 1865

Comments

1. I consider the stamped letters and numerals on the gun were struck at the completion of its manufacture and to have been made with the same set of punches.
   860   -   Weight of the gun in pounds
   38   -   I consider this to be the number of the piece
   F RECK -   Probably manufacturer's name, (unidentified).
2. I consider the percussion lock fitted at the right of the vent to be original equipment for firing the piece. Percussion tubes as a means of ignition were in use from the 1830's until the 1860's. This is an interesting feature on the gun as these locks were used almost exclusively for sea service.
3. The gun does not resemble any English artillery piece of which I am aware, either service or those used on merchant vessels
4. The design and light construction of the gun conforms to the artillery pieces developed n the USA during the 1830's. This together with the weight of the piece being recorded in pounds supports the theory that it was produced in that country. (NOTE: Other experts favor Europe)
5. The gun is not a service weapon and appears to have been made for use on board merchant ships. The breaching loop and the fitting of a percussion lock support this opinion.
6. The carriage may well be original to the gun. It is not a service type, but it could have been designed for use on a merchant vessel of the mid 19th century.

J R Fielding
Curator of Arms
11 June, 1982

I am indebted to Dr Henry Gordon-Clark for supplying this report.

Yet so far no American foundry has been identified. I have more diagrams of the gun should you need them, I can send them to anyone if requested, but there is enough to start a search in the above report. I am of the opinion that the tube at least was possibly made by the Finspong (now owned by the Bofors Group) Iron Works in Sweden. Their mark was an F inscribed on cannon near the trunnions. This of course does not explain how the cannon arrived on Churchill Island! While efforts have been made in USA, have we considered Northern foundries?

There is another factor which is not generally known and that is the 12 pounder cannon were the only weapons that could be safely fired by the *Shenandoah*. This came about as a result of a design fault discovered when fitting the ordnance to the ship; the other guns' recoil would have sent the cannon right across the gun deck with disastrous results.

In any event here is a puzzle which would be wonderful to solve.

International Dispatches' Sesquicentennial Celebration for 2015

Since the series of subjects discussed by International Dispatches have been heavily influenced by the visit of *CSS Shenandoah* to Melbourne in January 1865, the department has planned a suggested visit to this City and surrounding goldfield towns.

In particular, I suggest that we should travel to Ballarat, about 60 miles west of Melbourne. In that city there is a fine, restored hotel, Craig's Royal Hotel and it possesses the original ballroom where a Grand Ball was held for the officers of the *Shenandoah.* This event could be duplicated in 2015. The manager of the Hotel is enthusiastic about this idea and it would make a great re-enactment. Ballarat also offers Sovereign Hill, a reconstruction of the old gold field of about 160 years ago. There is even an authentic hotel in which people may stay. At nights, a Light Show is presented after sundown and talented people re-enact the battle of Eureka Stockade, once part of this very goldfield and the only armed insurrection ever to occur in Australia. Some 30 people were killed and the re-enactment is spectacular. The show is called rather aptly, "Blood on the Southern Cross" The rebelling miners created a banner under which to fight, a vertical blue cross on a white field with stars on the cross. Their own "Stars and the Bars", and so I feel that we will view this event with sympathy!

We could travel by bus or train or a mixture of both, a great way to see the countryside.

I recommend continuing into the "Goldfields" area of small mining towns eventually arriving in Bendigo, another extremely successful gold mining city. There are some wonderful tourist attractions and the city is a fascinating reminder of the past.

Then a quick return to Melbourne and a tour of Williamstown (where the Shenandoah was put up on slips) then if time permits a day trip to Phillip and Churchill Islands. Maybe check out that cannon, someone has to identify it soon enough.

Naturally since nothing is exactly set in braze as yet, and bearing in mid the current global financial situation, I cannot give anyone a firm estimate of the costs involved. I will discuss a package deal later in the piece with a travel consultant as the time draws closer. This part of the world is not the cheapest place in the world in which to live and some costs will shock you but with package deals the shock can be minimized. The one thing I can advise is that you would not regret taking the trip and you would never forget it either.

The time of the trip, i.e. January onward means warm to hot weather although Ballarat is capable of surprising you with chilly nights; otherwise think the Texas gulf in summer.

International Dispatches – where to now?

Firstly may I present the current team:

Commander: Commander General Max L Waldrop, Jr
Chairman; Roger P Thornton, DCS, ADC
Committee Member: Hubert Leroy
Committee Member: Colonel Heinrich Wirz, ADC
Committee Member: John Sims, ADC

To all of my compatriots above I thank you for your generous support in all areas.

We have come quite a long way, but as you know there are articles awaiting granting of copyright and permission to reprint in process at the moment. I am sure that we will obtain even more international articles.

I hope that the current members wish to continue service in this Department in the coming administration, and that we have the same goal to improve our performance continuously.

Finally we are tempted to confront the status of overseas Members and there are many ideas in the pipeline including the formation of an International Chapter which could meet by internet video, today's possibilities are endless. Maybe a Confederate Foreign Legion – who knows? March on!

"Remember the past with reverence, hold your ground in the present with tenacity, and consider the future with optimism granted by the purity of your intentions".

DEO VINDICE

Roger P Thornton, DCS
ADC International Dispatches
P O Box 796
Niddrie, Victoria 3042
AUSTRALIA

Life and Turmoil Leading Up to the War till 1865

This section is dedicated to our ancestors who lived and served during the period we know today as the "War Between the States", the "War of Northern Aggression" and the "Civil War" in which the north and the south fought for what they believed during the years from 1861 to 1865. History tells us that there was an apparent winner, but in the end all lost and paid a heavy cost as it is with any major war. Herein are some stories that will help you to relate to what our ancestors faced, the conditions they lived in, and the sacrifices that they made.

Constitution of the Confederate States of America
March 11, 1861

Preamble

We, the people of the Confederate States, each State acting in its sovereign and independent character, in order to form a permanent federal government, establish justice, insure domestic tranquility, and secure the blessings of liberty to ourselves and our posterity invoking the favor and guidance of Almighty God do ordain and establish this Constitution for the Confederate States of America.

Article I

Section 1

All legislative powers herein delegated shall be vested in a Congress of the Confederate States, which shall consist of a Senate and House of Representatives.

Section 2

(1) The House of Representatives shall be composed of members chosen every second year by the people of the several States; and the electors in each State shall be citizens of the Confederate States, and have the qualifications requisite for electors of the most numerous branch of the State Legislature; but no person of foreign birth, not a citizen of the Confederate States, shall be allowed to vote for any officer, civil or political, State or Federal.
(2) No person shall be a Representative who shall not have attained the age of twenty-five years, and be a citizen of the Confederate States, and who shall not when elected, be an inhabitant of that State in which he shall be chosen.
(3) Representatives and direct taxes shall be apportioned among the several States, which may be included within this Confederacy, according to their respective numbers, which shall be determined by adding to the whole number of free persons, including those bound to service for a term of years, and excluding Indians not taxed, three-fifths of all slaves. ,The actual enumeration shall be made within three years after the first meeting of the Congress of the Confederate States, and within every subsequent term of ten years, in such manner as they shall by law direct. The number of

Representatives shall not exceed one for every fifty thousand, but each State shall have at least one Representative; and until such enumeration shall be made, the State of South Carolina shall be entitled to choose six; the State of Georgia ten; the State of Alabama nine; the State of Florida two; the State of Mississippi seven; the State of Louisiana six; and the State of Texas six.

(4) When vacancies happen in the representation from any State the executive authority thereof shall issue writs of election to fill such vacancies.

(5) The House of Representatives shall choose their Speaker and other officers; and shall have the sole power of impeachment; except that any judicial or other Federal officer, resident and acting solely within the limits of any State, may be impeached by a vote of two-thirds of both branches of the Legislature thereof.

Section 3

(1) The Senate of the Confederate States shall be composed of two Senators from each State, chosen for six years by the Legislature thereof, at the regular session next immediately preceding the commencement of the term of service; and each Senator shall have one vote.

(2) Immediately after they shall be assembled, in consequence of the first election, they shall be divided as equally as may be into three classes. The seats of the Senators of the first class shall be vacated at the expiration of the second year; of the second class at the expiration of the fourth year; and of the third class at the expiration of the sixth year; so that one-third may be chosen every second year; and if vacancies happen by resignation, or otherwise, during the recess of the Legislature of any State, the Executive thereof may make temporary appointments until the next meeting of the Legislature, which shall then fill such vacancies.

(3) No person shall be a Senator who shall not have attained the age of thirty years, and be a citizen of the Confederate States; and who shall not, then elected, be an inhabitant of the State for which he shall be chosen.

(4) The Vice President of the Confederate States shall be president of the Senate, but shall have no vote unless they be equally divided.

(5) The Senate shall choose their other officers; and also a president pro tempore in the absence of the Vice President, or when he shall exercise the office of President of the Confederate states.

(6) The Senate shall have the sole power to try all impeachments. When sitting for that purpose, they shall be on oath or affirmation. When the President of the Confederate States is tried, the Chief Justice shall preside; and no person shall be convicted without the concurrence of two-thirds of the members present.

(7) Judgment in cases of impeachment shall not extend further than to removal from office, and disqualification to hold any office of honor, trust, or profit under the Confederate States; but the party convicted shall, nevertheless, be liable and subject to indictment, trial, judgment, and punishment according to law.

Section 4

(1) The times, places, and manner of holding elections for Senators and Representatives shall be prescribed in each State by the Legislature thereof, subject to the provisions of this Constitution; but the Congress may, at any time, by law, make or alter such regulations, except as to the times and places of choosing Senators.

(2) The Congress shall assemble at least once in every year; and such meeting shall be on the first Monday in December, unless they shall, by law, appoint a different day.

Section 5

(1) Each House shall be the judge of the elections, returns, and qualifications of its own members, and a majority of each shall constitute a quorum to do business; but a smaller number may adjourn from

day to day, and may be authorized to compel the attendance of absent members, in such manner and under such penalties as each House may provide.

(2) Each House may determine the rules of its proceedings, punish its members for disorderly behavior, and, with the concurrence of two-thirds of the whole number, expel a member.

(3) Each House shall keep a journal of its proceedings, and from time to time publish the same, excepting such parts as may in their judgment require secrecy; and the yeas and nays of the members of either House, on any question, shall, at the desire of one-fifth of those present, be entered on the journal.

(4) Neither House, during the session of Congress, shall, without the consent of the other, adjourn for more than three days, nor to any other place than that in which the two Houses shall be sitting.

Section 6

(1) The Senators and Representatives shall receive a compensation for their services, to be ascertained by law, and paid out of the Treasury of the Confederate States. They shall, in all cases, except treason, felony, and breach of the peace, be privileged from arrest during their attendance at the session of their respective Houses, and in going to and returning from the same; and for any speech or debate in either House, they shall not be questioned in any other place. Senator or Representative shall, during the time for which he was elected, be appointed to any civil office under the authority of the Confederate States, which shall have been created, or the emoluments whereof shall have been increased during such time; and no person holding any office under the Confederate States shall be a member of either House during his continuance in office. But Congress may, by law, grant to the principal officer in each of the Executive Departments a seat upon the floor of either House, with the privilege of discussing any measures appertaining to his department.

Section 7

(1) All bills for raising revenue shall originate in the House of Representatives; but the Senate may propose or concur with amendments, as on other bills.

(2) Every bill which shall have passed both Houses, shall, before it becomes a law, be presented to the President of the Confederate States; if he approve, he shall sign it; but if not, he shall return it, with his objections, to that House in which it shall have originated, who shall enter the objections at large on their journal, and proceed to reconsider it. If, after such reconsideration, two-thirds of that House shall agree to pass the bill, it shall be sent, together with the objections, to the other House, by which it shall likewise be reconsidered, and if approved by two-thirds of that House, it shall become a law. But in all such cases, the votes of both Houses shall be determined by yeas and nays, and the names of the persons voting for and against the bill shall be entered on the journal of each House respectively. If any bill shall not be returned by the President within ten days (Sundays excepted) after it shall have been presented to him, the same shall be a law, in like manner as if he had signed it, unless the Congress, by their adjournment, prevent its return; in which case it shall not be a law. The President may approve any appropriation and disapprove any other appropriation in the same bill. In such case he shall, in signing the bill, designate the appropriations disapproved; and shall return a copy of such appropriations, with his objections, to the House in which the bill shall have originated; and the same proceedings shall then be had as in case of other bills disapproved by the President.

(3) Every order, resolution, or vote, to which the concurrence of both Houses may be necessary (except on a question of adjournment) shall be presented to the President of the Confederate States; and before the same shall take effect, shall be approved by him; or, being disapproved by him, shall be re-passed by two-thirds of both Houses, according to the rules and limitations prescribed in case of a bill.

Section 8

The Congress shall have power:

(1) To lay and collect taxes, duties, imposts, and excises for revenue, necessary to pay the debts, provide for the common defense, and carry on the Government of the Confederate States; but no bounties shall be granted from the Treasury; nor shall any duties or taxes on importations from foreign nations be laid to promote or foster any branch of industry; and all duties, imposts, and excises shall be uniform throughout the Confederate States.

(2) To borrow money on the credit of the Confederate States.

(3) To regulate commerce with foreign nations, and among the several States, and with the Indian tribes; but neither this, nor any other clause contained in the Constitution, shall ever be construed to delegate the power to Congress to appropriate money for any internal improvement intended to facilitate commerce; except for the purpose of furnishing lights, beacons, and buoys, and other aids to navigation upon the coasts, and the improvement of harbors and the removing of obstructions in river navigation; in all which cases such duties shall be laid on the navigation facilitated thereby as may be necessary to pay the costs and expenses thereof.

(4) To establish uniform laws of naturalization, and uniform laws on the subject of bankruptcies, throughout the Confederate States; but no law of Congress shall discharge any debt contracted before the passage of the same.

(5) To coin money, regulate the value thereof, and of foreign coin, and fix the standard of weights and measures.

(6) To provide for the punishment of counterfeiting the securities and current coin of the Confederate States.

(7) To establish post offices and post routes; but the expenses of the Post Office Department, after the 1st day of March in the year of our Lord eighteen hundred and sixty-three, shall be paid out of its own revenues.

(8) To promote the progress of science and useful arts, by securing for limited times to authors and inventors the exclusive right to their respective writings and discoveries.

(9) To constitute tribunals inferior to the Supreme Court.

(10) To define and punish piracies and felonies committed on the high seas, and offenses against the law of nations.

(11) To declare war, grant letters of marque and reprisal, and make rules concerning captures on land and water.

(12) To raise and support armies; but no appropriation of money to that use shall be for a longer term than two years.

(13) To provide and maintain a navy.

(14) To make rules for the government and regulation of the land and naval forces.

(15) To provide for calling forth the militia to execute the laws of the Confederate States, suppress insurrections, and repel invasions.

(16) To provide for organizing, arming, and disciplining the militia, and for governing such part of them as may be employed in the service of the Confederate States; reserving to the States, respectively, the appointment of the officers, and the authority of training the militia according to the discipline prescribed by Congress.

(17) To exercise exclusive legislation, in all cases whatsoever, over such district (not exceeding ten miles square) as may, by cession of one or more States and the acceptance of Congress, become the seat of the Government of the Confederate States; and to exercise like authority over all places purchased by the consent of the Legislature of the State in which the same shall be, for the . erection of forts, magazines, arsenals, dockyards, and other needful buildings; and

(18) To make all laws which shall be necessary and proper for carrying into execution the foregoing powers, and all other powers vested by this Constitution in the Government of the Confederate States, or in any department or officer thereof.

Section 9

(1) The importation of negroes of the African race from any foreign country other than the slave holding States or Territories of the United States of America, is hereby forbidden; and Congress is required to pass such laws as shall effectually prevent the same.

(2) Congress shall also have power to prohibit the introduction of slaves from any State not a member of, or Territory not belonging to, this Confederacy.

(3) The privilege of the writ of habeas corpus shall not be suspended, unless when in cases of rebellion or invasion the public safety may require it.

(4) No bill of attainder, ex post facto law, or law denying or impairing the right of property in negro slaves shall be passed.

(5) No capitation or other direct tax shall be laid, unless in proportion to the census or enumeration hereinbefore directed to be taken.

(6) No tax or duty shall be laid on articles exported from any State, except by a vote of two-thirds of both Houses.

(7) No preference shall be given by any regulation of commerce or revenue to the ports of one State over those of another.

(8) No money shall be drawn from the Treasury, but in consequence of appropriations made by law; and a regular statement and account of the receipts and expenditures of all public money shall be published from time to time.

(9) Congress shall appropriate no money from the Treasury except by a vote of two-thirds of both Houses, taken by yeas and nays, unless it be asked and estimated for by some one of the heads of departments and submitted to Congress by the President; or for the purpose of paying its own expenses and contingencies; or for the payment of claims against the Confederate States, the justice of which shall have been judicially declared by a tribunal for the investigation of claims against the Government, which it is hereby made the duty of Congress to establish.

(10) All bills appropriating money shall specify in Federal currency the exact amount of each appropriation and the purposes for which it is made; and Congress shall grant no extra compensation to any public contractor, officer, agent, or servant, after such contract shall have been made or such service rendered.

(11) No title of nobility shall be granted by the Confederate States; and no person holding any office of profit or trust under them shall, without the consent of the Congress, accept of any present, emolument, office, or title of any kind whatever, from any king, prince, or foreign state.

(12) Congress shall make no law respecting an establishment of religion, or prohibiting the free exercise thereof; or abridging the freedom of speech, or of the press; or the right of the people peaceably to assemble and petition the Government for a redress of grievances.

(13) A well-regulated militia being necessary to the security of a free State, the right of the people to keep and bear arms shall not be infringed.

(14) No soldier shall, in time of peace, be quartered in any house without the consent of the owner; nor in time of war, but in a manner to be prescribed by law.

(15) The right of the people to be secure in their persons, houses, papers, and effects, against unreasonable searches and seizures, shall not be violated; and no warrants shall issue but upon probable cause, supported by oath or affirmation, and particularly describing the place to be searched and the persons or things to be seized.

(16) No person shall be held to answer for a capital or otherwise infamous crime, unless on a presentment or indictment of a grand jury, except in cases arising in the land or naval forces, or in the militia, when in actual service in time of war or public danger; nor shall any person be subject for the same offense to be twice put in jeopardy of life or limb; nor be compelled, in any criminal case, to be a witness against himself; nor be deprived of life, liberty, or property without due process of law; nor shall private property be taken for public use, without just compensation.

(17) In all criminal prosecutions the accused shall enjoy the right to a speedy and public trial, by an impartial jury of the State and district wherein the crime shall have been committed, which district shall have been previously ascertained by law, and to be informed of the nature and cause

of the accusation; to be confronted with the witnesses against him; to have compulsory process for obtaining witnesses in his favor; and to have the assistance of counsel for his defense.

(18) In suits at common law, where the value in controversy shall exceed twenty dollars, the right of trial by jury shall be preserved; and no fact so tried by a jury shall be otherwise reexamined in any court of the Confederacy, than according to the rules of common law.

(19) Excessive bail shall not be required, nor excessive fines imposed, nor cruel and unusual punishments inflicted.

(20) Every law, or resolution having the force of law, shall relate to but one subject, and that shall be expressed in the title.

Section 10

(1) No State shall enter into any treaty, alliance, or confederation; grant letters of marque and reprisal; coin money; make anything but gold and silver coin a tender in payment of debts; pass any bill of attainder, or ex post facto law, or law impairing the obligation of contracts; or grant any title of nobility.

(2) No State shall, without the consent of the Congress, lay any imposts or duties on imports or exports, except what may be absolutely necessary for executing its inspection laws; and the net produce of all duties and imposts, laid by any State on imports, or exports, shall be for the use of the Treasury of the Confederate States; and all such laws shall be subject to the revision and control of Congress.

(3) No State shall, without the consent of Congress, lay any duty on tonnage, except on seagoing vessels, for the improvement of its rivers and harbors navigated by the said vessels; but such duties shall not conflict with any treaties of the Confederate States with foreign nations; and any surplus revenue thus derived shall, after making such improvement, be paid into the common treasury. Nor shall any State keep troops or ships of war in time of peace, enter into any agreement or compact with another State, or with a foreign power, or engage in war, unless actually invaded, or in such imminent danger as will not admit of delay. But when any river divides or flows through two or more States they may enter into compacts with each other to improve the navigation thereof.

Article II

Section 1

(1) The executive power shall be vested in a President of the Confederate States of America. He and the Vice President shall hold their offices for the term of six years; but the President shall not be re-eligible. The President and Vice President shall be elected as follows:

(2) Each State shall appoint, in such manner as the Legislature thereof may direct, a number of electors equal to the whole number of Senators and Representatives to which the State may be entitled in the Congress; but no Senator or Representative or person holding an office of trust or profit under the Confederate States shall be appointed an elector.

(3) The electors shall meet in their respective States and vote by ballot for President and Vice President, one of whom, at least, shall not be an inhabitant of the same State with themselves; they shall name in their ballots the person voted for as President, and in distinct ballots the person voted for as Vice President, and they shall make distinct lists of all persons voted for as President, and of all persons voted for as Vice President, and of the number of votes for each, which lists they shall sign and certify, and transmit, sealed, to the seat of the Government of the Confederate States, directed to the President of the Senate; the President of the Senate shall, in the presence of the Senate and House of Representatives, open all the certificates, and the votes shall then be counted; the person having the greatest number of votes for President shall be the President, if such number be a majority of the whole number of electors appointed; and if no person have such majority, then from the persons having the highest numbers, not exceeding three, on the list of those voted for as President, the House of Representatives shall choose immediately, by ballot, the President. But in choosing the

President the votes shall be taken by States, the representation from each State having one vote; a quorum for this purpose shall consist of a member or members from two-thirds of the States, and a majority of all the States shall be necessary to a choice. And if the House of Representatives shall not choose a President, whenever the right of choice shall devolve upon them, before the 4th day of March next following, then the Vice President shall act as President, as in case of the death, or other constitutional disability of the President.

(4) The person having the greatest number of votes as Vice President shall be the Vice President, if such number be a majority of the whole number of electors appointed; and if no person have a majority, then, from the two highest numbers on the list, the Senate shall choose the Vice President; a quorum for the purpose shall consist of two-thirds of the whole number of Senators, and a majority of the whole number shall be necessary to a choice.

(5) But no person constitutionally ineligible to the office of President shall be eligible to that of Vice President of the Confederate States.

(6) The Congress may determine the time of choosing the electors, and the day on which they shall give their votes; which day shall be the same throughout the Confederate States.

(7) No person except a natural-born citizen of the Confederate; States, or a citizen thereof at the time of the adoption of this Constitution, or a citizen thereof born in the United States prior to the 20th of December, 1860, shall be eligible to the office of President; neither shall any person be eligible to that office who shall not have attained the age of thirty-five years, and been fourteen years a resident within the limits of the Confederate States, as they may exist at the time of his election.

(8) In case of the removal of the President from office, or of his death, resignation, or inability to discharge the powers and duties of said office, the same shall devolve on the Vice President; and the Congress may, by law, provide for the case of removal, death, resignation, or inability, both of the President and Vice President, declaring what officer shall then act as President; and such officer shall act accordingly until the disability be removed or a President shall be elected.

(9) The President shall, at stated times, receive for his services a compensation, which shall neither be increased nor diminished during the period for which he shall have been elected; and he shall not receive within that period any other emolument from the Confederate States, or any of them.

(10) Before he enters on the execution of his office he shall take the following oath or affirmation:

Section 2

(1) The President shall be Commander-in-Chief of the Army and Navy of the Confederate States, and of the militia of the several States, when called into the actual service of the Confederate States; he may require the opinion, in writing, of the principal officer in each of the Executive Departments, upon any subject relating to the duties of their respective offices; and he shall have power to grant reprieves and pardons for offenses against the Confederate States, except in cases of impeachment.

(2) He shall have power, by and with the advice and consent of the Senate, to make treaties; provided two-thirds of the Senators present concur; and he shall nominate, and by and with the advice and consent of the Senate shall appoint, ambassadors, other public ministers and consuls, judges of the Supreme Court, and all other officers of the Confederate States whose appointments are not herein otherwise provided for, and which shall be established by law; but the Congress may, by law, vest the appointment of such inferior officers, as they think proper, in the President alone, in the courts of law, or in the heads of departments.

(3) The principal officer in each of the Executive Departments, and all persons connected with the diplomatic service, may be removed from office at the pleasure of the President. All other civil officers of the Executive Departments may be removed at any time by the President, or other appointing power, when their services are unnecessary, or for dishonesty, incapacity, inefficiency, misconduct, or neglect of duty; and when so removed, the removal shall be reported to the Senate, together with the reasons therefore.

(4) The President shall have power to fill all vacancies that may happen during the recess of the Senate, by granting commissions which shall expire at the end of their next session; but no person rejected by the Senate shall be reappointed to the same office during their ensuing recess.

Section 3

(1) The President shall, from time to time, give to the Congress information of the state of the Confederacy, and recommend to their consideration such measures as he shall judge necessary and expedient; he may, on extraordinary occasions, convene both Houses, or either of them; and in case of disagreement between them, with respect to the time of adjournment, he may adjourn them to such time as he shall think proper; he shall receive ambassadors and other public ministers; he shall take care that the laws be faithfully executed, and shall commission all the officers of the Confederate States.

Section 4

(1) The President, Vice President, and all civil officers of the Confederate States, shall be removed from office on impeachment for and conviction of treason, bribery, or other high crimes and misdemeanors.

ARTICLE III

Section 1

(1) The judicial power of the Confederate States shall be vested in one Supreme Court, and in such inferior courts as the Congress may, from time to time, ordain and establish. The judges, both of the Supreme and inferior courts, shall hold their offices during good behavior, and shall, at stated times, receive for their services a compensation which shall not be diminished during their continuance in office.

Section 2

(1) The judicial power shall extend to all cases arising under this Constitution, the laws of the Confederate States, and treaties made, or which shall be made, under their authority; to all cases affecting ambassadors, other public ministers and consuls; to all cases of admiralty and maritime jurisdiction; to controversies to which the Confederate States shall be a party; to controversies between two or more States; between a State and citizens of another State, where the State is plaintiff; between citizens claiming lands under grants of different States; and between a State or the citizens thereof, and foreign states, citizens, or subjects; but no State shall be sued by a citizen or subject of any foreign state.
(2) In all cases affecting ambassadors, other public ministers and consuls, and those in which a State shall be a party, the Supreme Court shall have original jurisdiction. In all the other cases before mentioned, the Supreme Court shall have appellate jurisdiction both as to law and fact, with such exceptions and under such regulations as the Congress shall make.
(3) The trial of all crimes, except in cases of impeachment, shall be by jury, and such trial shall be held in the State where the said crimes shall have been committed; but when not committed within any State, the trial shall be at such place or places as the Congress may by law have directed.

Section 3

(1) Treason against the Confederate States shall consist only in levying war against them, or in adhering to their enemies, giving them aid and comfort. No person shall be convicted of treason unless on the testimony of two witnesses to the same overt act, or on confession in open court.
(2) The Congress shall have power to declare the punishment of treason; but no attainder of treason shall work corruption of blood, or forfeiture, except during the life of the person attainted.

ARTICLE IV

Section 1

(1) Full faith and credit shall be given in each State to the public acts, records, and judicial proceedings of every other State; and the Congress may, by general laws, prescribe the manner in which such acts, records, and proceedings shall be proved, and the effect thereof.

Section 2

(1) The citizens of each State shall be entitled to all the privileges and immunities of citizens in the several States; and shall have the right of transit and sojourn in any State of this Confederacy, with their slaves and other property; and the right of property in said slaves shall not be thereby impaired.
(2) A person charged in any State with treason, felony, or other crime against the laws of such State, who shall flee from justice, and be found in another State, shall, on demand of the executive authority of the State from which he fled, be delivered up, to be removed to the State having jurisdiction of the crime.
(3) No slave or other person held to service or labor in any State or Territory of the Confederate States, under the laws thereof, escaping or lawfully carried into another, shall, in consequence of any law or regulation therein, be discharged from such service or labor; but shall be delivered up on claim of the party to whom such slave belongs,. or to whom such service or labor may be due.

Section 3

(1) Other States may be admitted into this Confederacy by a vote of two-thirds of the whole House of Representatives and two-thirds of the Senate, the Senate voting by States; but no new State shall be formed or erected within the jurisdiction of any other State, nor any State be formed by the junction of two or more States, or parts of States, without the consent of the Legislatures of the States concerned, as well as of the Congress.
(2) The Congress shall have power to dispose of and make all needful rules and regulations concerning the property of the Confederate States, including the lands thereof.
(3) The Confederate States may acquire new territory; and Congress shall have power to legislate and provide governments for the inhabitants of all territory belonging to the Confederate States, lying without the limits of the several Sates; and may permit them, at such times, and in such manner as it may by law provide, to form States to be admitted into the Confederacy. In all such territory the institution of negro slavery, as it now exists in the Confederate States, shall be recognized and protected be Congress and by the Territorial government; and the inhabitants of the several Confederate States and Territories shall have the right to take to such Territory any slaves lawfully held by them in any of the States or Territories of the Confederate States.
(4) The Confederate States shall guarantee to every State that now is, or hereafter may become, a member of this Confederacy, a republican form of government; and shall protect each of them against invasion; and on application of the Legislature or of the Executive when the Legislature is not in session) against domestic violence.

ARTICLE V

Section 1
(1) Upon the demand of any three States, legally assembled in their several conventions, the Congress shall summon a convention of all the States, to take into consideration such amendments to the Constitution as the said States shall concur in suggesting at the time when the said demand is made; and should any of the proposed amendments to the Constitution be agreed on by the said convention, voting by States, and the same be ratified by the Legislatures of two- thirds of the several States, or by conventions in two-thirds thereof, as the one or the other mode of ratification may be proposed by

the general convention, they shall thenceforward form a part of this Constitution. But no State shall, without its consent, be deprived of its equal representation in the Senate.

ARTICLE VI

(1) The Government established by this Constitution is the successor of the Provisional Government of the Confederate States of America, and all the laws passed by the latter shall continue in force until the same shall be repealed or modified; and all the officers appointed by the same shall remain in office until their successors are appointed and qualified, or the offices abolished.

(2) All debts contracted and engagements entered into before the adoption of this Constitution shall be as valid against the Confederate States under this Constitution, as under the Provisional Government.

(3) This Constitution, and the laws of the Confederate States made in pursuance thereof, and all treaties made, or which shall be made, under the authority of the Confederate States, shall be the supreme law of the land; and the judges in every State shall be bound thereby, anything in the constitution or laws of any State to the contrary notwithstanding.

(4) The Senators and Representatives before mentioned, and the members of the several State Legislatures, and all executive and judicial officers, both of the Confederate States and of the several States, shall be bound by oath or affirmation to support this Constitution; but no religious test shall ever be required as a qualification to any office or public trust under the Confederate States.

(5) The enumeration, in the Constitution, of certain rights shall not be construed to deny or disparage others retained by the people of the several States.

(6) The powers not delegated to the Confederate States by the Constitution, nor prohibited by it to the States, are reserved to the States, respectively, or to the people thereof.

ARTICLE VII

(1) The ratification of the conventions of five States shall be sufficient for the establishment of this Constitution between the States so ratifying the same.

(2) When five States shall have ratified this Constitution, in the manner before specified, the Congress under the Provisional Constitution shall prescribe the time for holding the election of President and Vice President; and for the meeting of the Electoral College; and for counting the votes, and inaugurating the President. They shall, also, prescribe the time for holding the first election of members of Congress under this Constitution, and the time for assembling the same. Until the assembling of such Congress, the Congress under the Provisional Constitution shall continue to exercise the legislative powers granted them; not extending beyond the time limited by the Constitution of the Provisional Government.

Adopted unanimously by the Congress of the Confederate States of South Carolina, Georgia, Florida, Alabama, Mississippi, Louisiana, and Texas, sitting in convention at the capitol, the city of Montgomery, Ala., on the eleventh day of March, in the year eighteen hundred and Sixty-one.

HOWELL COBB, President of the Congress. South Carolina: R. Barnwell Rhett, C. G. Memminger, Wm. Porcher Miles, James Chesnut, Jr., R. W. Barnwell, William W. Boyce, Lawrence M. Keitt, T. J. Withers. Georgia: Francis S. Bartow, Martin J. Crawford, Benjamin H. Hill, Thos. R. R. Cobb. Florida: Jackson Morton, J. Patton Anderson, Jas. B. Owens. Alabama: Richard W. Walker, Robert H. Smith, Colin J. McRae, William P. Chilton, Stephen F. Hale, David P. Lewis, Tho. Fearn, Jno. Gill Shorter, J. L. M. Curry. Mississippi: Alex. M. Clayton, James T. Harrison, William S. Barry, W. S. Wilson, Walker Brooke, W. P. Harris, J. A. P. Campbell. Louisiana: Alex. de Clouet, C. M. Conrad, Duncan F. Kenner, Henry Marshall. Texas: John Hemphill, Thomas N. Waul, John H. Reagan, Williamson S. Oldham, Louis T. Wigfall, John Gregg, William Beck Ochiltree.

Florida in the War – 150 Years Ago
By Ben H. Willingham, DCS

FLORIDA ON THE EVE OF WAR

While the following chronicles the political activity and public sentiment in Florida, it is felt that this same scenario would likely have been the case in the other Southern States during the period leading up to President Lincoln's unfortunate war.

Keep in mind, when the Nation was established in 1789, the States were the creators of the Federal Government. By 1860, the Federal Government was the creator of the large majority of the States. In 1789 the Federal Government had derived all the powers delegated to it by the Constitution from the states; in 1860 a majority of the states derived all their powers and attributes as states from Congress under the Constitution. Power was the object, even back then. States were admitted to increase the power of regions and politicians. By 1860 the controlling power in the Federal Government had been transferred from the South to the industrialized North and taxation policies penalized the South to the advantage of the North.

FLORIDA ONE HUNDRED AND FIFTY YEARS AGO

1860 was a year of crisis. In the North and South, states were rapidly severing the invisible bonds which had held the Union together for seventy years. The emotion packed events of the 1850's foreshadowed the tragic years that were soon to engulf the nation. The great Whig party which had so strongly upheld the national idea disintegrated, and the Republican Party, which rose to take its place, accepted a platform which inflamed an already agitated South. The Kansas-Nebraska controversy, the Dred Scott decision, the Lincoln-Douglas debates were coals added to fires already blazing under cauldrons of suspicion and distrust. And then on October 16, 1859, John Brown, the man who many thought was a victim of mental delusions, and his followers seized the United States arsenal in Harper's Ferry. Although this plan to free the slaves was doomed from the start, the news of the Raid caused a wave of fear and revulsion to spread throughout the South. Secessionists used it to win over many conservatives who were still reluctant to support any action that might destroy the Union. Here was concrete evidence that abolitionists intended to set the slaves upon their masters and to forcibly overthrow the institution which was at the base of society. The tensions between North and South had become so great that the admirable art of compromise, which had hitherto preserved the American experiment of democratic government, was failing to function. Only disaster could result. No part of the country was isolated from the slavery and state rights controversies which were raging. The people of Florida, although they were living in the newest of the slave-holding territories, were caught up in this maelstrom and they became a part of the surging tide that carried the country into the War Between the States.

SIGNIFICANT EVENTS OF 1860

January 5, 1860 - Volunteer military companies organize in Fernandina and Tallahassee because of "the critical state of national affairs."

January 19, 1860 - The Fernandina *East Floridian* publishes article on the cost of raising and equipping a brigade for active military service.

February 16, 1860 - Enthusiasm for Stephen A. Douglas has almost completely disappeared in Florida and only the Jacksonville *Republican* still favors his nomination for president on the Democratic ticket.

April 9, 1860 - Constitutional Union Party meets in Quincy and acknowledges "the wrongs inflicted on the South" but advocates the use of "pacific, rational, and judicial methods" for righting these wrongs.

April 9, 1860 – The Democrat convention convenes in Tallahassee and appoints as delegates to the Democrat Convention to meet in Charleston: T. J. Eppes, B. F. Wardlaw, John Milton of Jackson County, Charles E. Dyke, Editor of the Tallahassee *Floridian*, James B. Owens of Marion County, and G. L. Bowne. The convention adopts a resolution condemning the Douglas slave doctrine, and declares slavery to be a necessary domestic institution. The convention insists upon the strict enforcement of the Fugitive Slave Law.

April 14, 1860 - All but 18 miles of the Florida Railroad line completed, and a crew of one hundred hands was trying to complete the job quickly. Tallahassee paper predicts that "Soon the dim and gloomy recesses of those primeval and almost impenetrable forests will re-echo the startling scream of the locomotive, and their affrighted denizens will tremble with terror as the unusual sound penetrates their hidden lairs."

April 30, 1860 - Cotton state delegations secede from the national democratic convention.

May 8, 1860 - The Pensacola and Georgia Railroad Company begins laying track for a line to run from Lake City to the Suwannee River.

May 9, 1860 - Constitutional Union Party meets in Baltimore and nominates John Bell for president and Edward Everett for vice president. Several West Florida counties are represented.

May 10, 1860 - Editor of the Fernandina *East Floridian* says that the dismemberment of the Union is only a matter of time, and that the South "is as well prepared for that grave issue now, as she will be one or ten years hence."

May 15, 1860 - A political meeting in Jacksonville declares "we are of the opinion that the rights of the citizens of Florida are no longer safe in the Union and we think she should raise the banner of secession and invite her southern sisters to join her."

May 21, 1860 - Democrats meet in Gainesville and declare "if in consequence of Northern fanaticism the irrepressible conflict must come we are prepared to meet it."

May 23, 1860 - The *U.S.S. Crusader* captures a French slaver off the coast of Cuba carrying 422 Negroes from the Congo. The vessel and its cargo will be hauled into Key West where there were already more than a thousand Negroes captured earlier in the month. "All of these," according to the editor of the Key of the Gulf," are perfectly happy and content."

May 26, 1860 - Senator Yulee says "if the modern Republicans succeed in acquiring possession of the Federal Government, it will be the duty of the Southern State to secede."

June 4, 1860 - Democratic state nominating convention at Quincy endorses the radical southern position and appoints delegates to the Richmond convention: John Milton of Jackson County is nominated for governor on the 23rd ballot. R. B. Milton of Leon County and coeditor of the Tallahassee Floridian, is nominated for Congress.

June 7, 1860 - Editor of Cedar Key *Telegraph* reports, after a recent tour of the State, "The crops are in an unusually promising state."

June 16, 1860 - Democrats hold a second convention in Baltimore and nominate Douglas and Johnson; endorse the doctrine popular sovereignty.

June 27, 1860 - Constitutional Union Party holds convention at Quincy presided over by former Governor Thomas Brown - 22 counties are represented. Edward Hopkins of Duval County nominated for governor, and B. F. Allen of Leon County, editor of Tallahassee *Sentinel,* for Congress. The Platform charges the Democrat Party with deliberately planning disunion and the state is cautioned against resorting to "extreme measures."

July 26, 1860 - State press indicates an overwhelming enthusiasm for the Democratic ticket: According to a report appearing in the Quincy *Republic,* the following are supporting the Breckingridge-Lane ticket: Pensacola *Tribune,* Marianna *Patriot, Apalachicola Times,* Quincy *Republic,* Tallahassee *Floridian,* Monticello *Family Friend,* Madison *Messenger,* Newnansville *Dispatch,* Ocala *Home Companion,* Lake City *Herald,* Jacksonville *Standard,* Cedar *Keys Telegraph,* Fernandina *East Floridian,* Tampa *Peninsular,* St. Augustine *Examiner,* and Key West *Key of the Gulf.* Supporting Bell and Everett are the Pensacola *Gazette,* Milton *Courier,* Marianna *Enterprise Sentinel,* and Lake City *Press.* The only paper which seems to be supporting Doulas and Johnson and there is considerable doubt even about this, is the Jacksonville *Mirror.*

October 1, 1860 - State election results for governor - Milton, 6,994; Hopkins, 5,248. For Congress - Hilton, 7,722; Allen, 5,172. October 5, 1860 - Governor W. H. Gist of South Carolina queries Southern governors as to their planned action if Lincoln is elected. Governor Perry of Florida says that his state would not take the lead in seceding but that Florida would follow the lead of another state.

November 7, 1860 - Florida presidential vote results: Electoral vote 3, Lincoln 0, Douglas 367, Breckenridge 8,543, Bell 5,437.

November 8, 1860 - Citizens of Waldo hold meeting and pledge themselves "to march to the assistance of the first State that may secede." They announce that they will burn Abe Lincoln in effigy tomorrow.

November 9, 1860 - Public meeting at Fernandina declares that Lincoln's election is the first step in the dissolution of the union.

November 10, 1860 - The Federal commander at Key West expresses his concern in a letter to General Winfield Scott: "I believe the temper of the South is excited- dangerous."

November 12, 1860 - Meeting at Madison Courthouse and 83 men join volunteer militia company.

November 14, 1860 - The Fernandina *East Floridian* reflects popular appeal of secession movement when it prints on its masthead the following: "The Secession of the State of Florida, The Dissolution of the Union, The Formation of a Southern Confederacy."

November 17, 1860 - St. Augustine meeting supports the calling of a Convention of Delegates "to consider the expediency of dissolving our connection with the Federal Union."

November 19, 1860 - Governor Perry formally accepts first Minute Men organization for the "defense of the State."

November 26, 1860 - People of Ocala support secession and unfurl a flag with a single blue star and the inscription "Let Us Alone." In Quincy there is a flag flying with the inscription "Secession, Florida, Sovereignty, Independence."

Legislature assembles and reads letter from Senator Yulee indicating his desire to return home "promptly and joyously" as soon as Florida secedes.

Governor Perry says in his opening message: "The crisis expected by men of observation and reflection has at last come. The only hope that the Southern states have for domestic peace or for future respect of property is dependent on . . . secession from faithless, perjured confederates.". Further delay, he said, might give rise to slave uprisings in which whites would suffer the fate of those in Santo Domingo. He further recommends that militia be revised and that $100,000 be appropriated to purchase arms.

November 28, 1860 - A bill calling for a constitutional convention to meet in Tallahassee on January 3, 1861 is introduced simultaneously in both houses. It passes unanimously. Motions to defer convention until January 17 fail in the House by a vote of 31 to 16 and in the Senate by a vote of 12 to 7. A motion in the Senate to table the bill also fails and a resolution proposing popular ratification of the convention's action is defeated by 12 to 4.

November 30, 1860 - Legislative bill signed into law by Governor Perry. He issues proclamation naming December 22 as the day for the election of delegates.

December 1, 1860 - Richard Keith Call issues a pamphlet condemning the legislature's action. He calls secession "high treason against our constitutional government."

December 12, 1860 - The Bank of St. Johns in St. Augustine suspends specie payment.

December 13, 1860 - Southern congressmen, including Hawkins of Florida, caucus and then issue a letter to their constituents declaring that all hope of relief for the South has been exhausted. Speedy secession and the formation of a southern confederacy is strongly recommended.

December 14, 1860 - Congressman Hawkins announces his refusal to serve on any congressional conciliation committee. The time for compromise, he says, has passed.

December 20, 1860 - South Carolina secedes. The Convention unanimously declares "that the Union now subsisting between South Carolina and other states under the name of The United States of America is hereby dissolved."

December 22, 1860 - Election to select delegates to secession convention held. 69 men chosen; of whom at least 25 are considered cooperationists.

Richard Call, in a letter to Tallahassee Sentinel, expresses hope that "reason may not be dethroned by passion - that no attempt will be made rashly to strike the American flag - that no attempt will be made to declare Florida a Nation alien and foreign to the American people."

U. S. Senate Committee of Thirteen meet to consider the Crittenden Compromise which would restore the Missouri Compromise line in the federal territories. It is opposed by both Republicans and Democrats.

The Florida Baptist State Convention, meeting in Monticello, adopts a resolution expressing their "cordial sympathy with, and hearty approbation of those who are determined to maintain the integrity of the Southern States, even by a disruption of all existing political ties."

December 26, 1860 - Florida hears that South Carolina Convention is considering calling a meeting of slave states at Montgomery, Alabama, to form a Southern Confederacy.

December 28, 1860 - Florida papers report that Union soldiers have left their garrison at Fort Moultrie, Charleston, South Carolina, and are occupying Fort Sumter.

December 29, 1860 - In a New Year editorial, the St. Augustine Examiner reflects on the many efforts made by the South in the past to prevent disunion and war. "Our political sky as we enter upon a new year," the editor writes, "is overcast with clouds indicating a political tempest; and along the northern horizon is written the demon declaration "IRREPRESSIBLE CONFLICT." Well, let it come and with stout hearts and armed nerves in defiance of freemen's rights, we will encounter it."

He predicts that the New Year will bring with it "the establishment of a Southern Confederacy, having resources ample to insure prosperity, strength and durability within, and to command respect without."

Texas Joins the CSA
By David G. Whitaker DCS

Texas Governor Sam Houston, the hero of the Battle of San Jacinto where he defeated the President of Mexico, General Santa Anna and got Texas free from Mexico so Texas could become the Republic of Texas, was against seceding from the Union because he felt Texas didn't have much of a dog in that fight and that the benefits of staying in the Union far outweighed the consequences. Many Texans today agree with him.

So why did the Texans want to leave the Union? First you must know the heritage of these people. They were mostly all of Scotch-Irish descent and many had close families in the eastern part of the south. Being clannish as they were they were automatically in the fight too. It gets to be very personal when blood kin are involved. By a vote of three to one Texas voted to secede in a statewide referendum. But to live in Texas at that time was neither for man nor beast that was faint of heart. Texas was a wild frontier and the men and women who lived here were able to take care of themselves, regardless of the situation whether it was Mexican bandits, Comanche Indians or Yankees, or... they didn't last long. Every day was a test of survival for these very rugged individuals and shying away from a fight was not in their makeup.

There were a number of reasons for the southern states to secede, including slavery but there was only one reason the war started. When Lincoln called for 75,000 troops to invade the south the war was on. Actually the issue to free the slaves was somewhat of an after-thought by Lincoln because the Emancipation Proclamation stated that, unless the rebellious states returned to the Union by January 1, 1863, freedom would be granted to slaves within those states. Not the northern states but only the southern states. Another thing that is rarely mentioned is that the CSA took the first step in addressing the slavery issue by forbidding the importation of slaves from any foreign country except the United States. This is in the CSA Constitution, adopted March 11, 1861. See Section 9. Texas joined the Confederacy on March 2, 1861, Texas Independence day.

In 1862, the Confederate Congress in Richmond, Virginia, passed a conscription law that ordered all males from 18 to 45 years of age to be placed in the service. All persons holding 15 slaves, or more, were exempt. Texas abolitionist north of Dallas protested this exemption and 40 of them got themselves hung. Over 75,000 Texans served in the Confederate army and Texas regiments fought in every major battle throughout the war. Some men were veterans of the Mexican-American War; a few had served in the earlier Texas Revolution and a number of them had been Texas Rangers and Indian fighters. In addition to tens of thousands of horses and mules, Texas furnished 45 regiments of cavalry, 23 regiments of infantry, 12 battalions of cavalry, four battalions of infantry, five regiments of heavy artillery and 30 batteries of light artillery for the Confederacy. Also, the state maintained, at its own expense, some additional troops that were for home defense to protect mostly those on the western frontier from Mexican bandits, and Comanche and Apache Indian raids. These included 5 regiments and 4 battalions of cavalry, and 4 regiments and one battalion of infantry. Texas actually fought three wars, first they fought the Indians, then the Yankees, and following these two wars, the

Reconstruction that lasted until 1877. Reconstruction was mostly a punitive war against the civilian population; starvation and intimidation being the Yankee's favorite weapons. Yankees got a big kick out of dropping dead animals down water wells.

Not a lot of battles were fought in Texas because of our location west of the Mississippi River and because to send infantry to Texas required fighting through Arkansas, Oklahoma, or Louisiana, not a very pleasant thing to do. However the battles that were fought had the Texans mostly winning. They fought twice in Galveston, twice at Sabine Pass and the last battle of the war at Palmetto Ranch down near Brownsville. Fortunately Sibley's New Mexico campaign is not counted as a Texas battle even though it was. General Henry Sibley (an alcoholic) started off in San Antonio with about 3400 men, marched to El Paso, then up the west side of the Rio Grande River (the New Mexico side) and fought their way to Santa Fe. The object was to eventually get the gold in California. At the Battle of Glorieta Pass, Sibley won the battle but lost his supply wagons and had to retreat back to San Antonio with little food or water, arriving back with 1800 sick and emaciated men who looked like death warmed over. The retreat was costly in that the Indians were capturing the stragglers and killing them in horrible ways while another group of Indians were out in front of the retreating troops dropping dead animals into the few available watering holes. This horror lasted for almost 600 miles. The U.S. Troops just followed the Indians letting them do their dirty work.

One of the most celebrated fighting units noted for it bravery was Terry's Texas Rangers (8th Texas Cavalry) led by Colonel Benjamin Franklin Terry. These young cowboys fought with two pistols, a carbine rifle, two sawed off shotguns and a Bowie knife. They became famous for their cavalry charge at breakneck speed getting into the enemy lines and using their shotguns first, then their pistols, then their rifles, and finally their Bowie knifes. Their horses knew what a Yankee was and knew the game plan was to kill them. They fought just as hard with their hoofs. Many Yankees ran when they heard the Rebel yell and saw the charge coming. Needless to say, the majority of these cowboys did not return to the Houston Area after the war, including Colonial Terry. It's fair to also say that many more Yankees did not return home either.

At the beginning of the war when the first companies of Texas soldiers reached Richmond, Virginia, CSA President Jefferson Davis greeted them with these words: "Texans! The troops of other states have their reputations to gain, but the sons of the defenders of the Alamo have theirs to maintain. I am assured that you will be faithful to the trust."

And they were.

Texas 1830 – 1880

Texas suffered through no less than five major wars between 1830 and 1880 and many minor wars during that same period. Texas was literally a killing field. Most people do not realize what Texas went through during those 50 years. This is a brief on each of those five wars.

1) The first and the longest war was with the **Comanche Indian tribes** that lived in the southern great plains area that included west Texas. These Indians were probably the best horsemen and the fiercest warriors on the North American continent and, like the southerners when faced with the Yankees in 1861, their attitude was, you are on our land and we will drive you off. This war started when Steven F. Austin, considered the Father of Texas, was granted permission by the Mexican government to bring in 300 families and start colonizing Texas. The Comanche took this as an invasion of their land and they started killing and capturing Anglos, making slaves of them and treating them in the most brutal and sadistic ways. Females were especially treated in horrible ways. This war lasted roughly from 1830 to 1880 when finally the Comanche warriors were mostly all killed. The statement about the Comanche being the fiercest warriors on the North American Continent is evidenced by the

Comanche's defeat of the Spaniards from Mexico, the Mexicans, the French from Louisiana, the Apaches and other Indian tribes and finally the settlers coming into Texas from the east. The Settlers, the U.S. Cavalry and the Texas Rangers were their Waterloo though. Yes, the Comanche were very fierce warriors.

2) The second significant war was the **Texas Revolution** with Mexico. The Federal Government of Mexico granted Moses Austin permission to bring colonist to Texas in 1824. Steven F. Austin, his son, took on this task after his father died. 300 families came to Texas and were given large plots of land after they pledged allegiance to Mexico and became Catholics. Eventually Mexico changed the tariff laws, was not satisfied with the immigration policies and also wanted to unite Texas with the Mexican state of Coahuila.

Texas wanted to be a state with their own government. In 1833 Steven F. Austin went to Mexico City to try and resolve some of these issues and was put in jail for two years. President Santa Anna moved toward overthrowing the Constitution of 1824 and establishing a dictatorship. He then sent troops to occupy Texas and the war was on. This eventually led to the Battle of Gonzales where 342 Texas citizen soldiers were massacred. Many other smaller skirmishes occurred and finally the Battle of the Alamo where 189 men were killed. After this battle Santa Anna moved troops east to fight General Sam Houston. He found them at San Jacinto and it took 18 minutes for the Texas Army to win independence from Mexico and become the Republic of Texas in 1836.

3) The third war was the **Mexican - American War.** This was an armed conflict between the United States of America and Mexico from 1846 to 1848 in the wake of the December 29, 1845, U.S. annexation of Texas, which Mexico considered part of its territory despite the 1836 Texas Revolution. Old Santa Anna is still in the picture but so were the Texas Rangers who fought along side the U.S. troops.

Combat operations lasted a year and a half, from spring 1846 to fall 1847. American forces quickly occupied New Mexico and California, then invaded parts of Northeastern Mexico and Northwest Mexico; meanwhile, the Pacific Squadron conducted a blockade, and took control of several garrisons on the Pacific coast further south in Baja California. After Mexico would still not agree to the cession of its northern territories, another American army led by General Winfield Scott captured Mexico City, and the war ended in a victory for the U.S. Many West Point Officers that fought together in this war would fight against each other during the South's quest for independence that started in 1861.

The Treaty of Guadalupe Hidalgo was the major result of the war: the territories of California, Arizona, and portions of Utah, Nevada, Colorado plus all of New Mexico would be ceded to the U.S. in exchange for $18 million. In addition, the United States forgave debt owed by the Mexican government to U.S. citizens. Mexico accepted the Rio Grande as its national border, and the loss of Texas.

4) War number four was the **War Between the States.** Texas Governor Sam Houston, the hero of the Battle of San Jacinto where he defeated the President of Mexico, General Santa Anna and freed Texas from Mexico, was against seceding from the Union because he felt Texas didn't have much of a dog in that fight and that the benefits of staying in the Union far outweighed the consequences. However, by a vote of three to one Texas voted to secede in a statewide referendum. Over 85,000 Texans served in the Confederate army and Texas regiments fought in every major battle throughout the war. Some men were veterans of the Mexican-American War; a few had served in the earlier Texas Revolution and a number of them had been Texas Rangers and Indian fighters. In addition to tens of thousands of horses and mules, Texas furnished 45 regiments of cavalry, 23 regiments of infantry, 12 battalions of cavalry, four battalions of infantry, five regiments of heavy artillery and 30 batteries of light artillery for the Confederacy. Also, the state maintained, at its own expense, some additional troops that were for home defense to protect mostly those on the western frontier from Mexican bandits, and

Comanche and Apache Indian raids. The South lost the war in April of 1865 and the fifth war started. It was called Reconstruction.

5) **Reconstruction** was mostly a punitive war against the civilian population; starvation and intimidation being the Yankee's favorite weapons. Yankees got a big kick out of dropping dead animals down water wells. This war lasted until about 1877 but the effects of the "War Between The States" lasted many years after 1877. At the end of the Civil War, in which Southerners had fought valiantly against the brutal invasion forces of the North in an effort to protect local institutions and states rights, the South lay broken and destitute. Rather than trying to reunite the country as peacefully and quickly as possible, the victorious North set out on a deliberate policy of rape, pillage, plunder, and vindictive punishment.

Texas and the South was invaded and controlled during Reconstruction by vengeful Union soldiers, opportunistic carpetbaggers, and treasonous scalawags. The Yankee carpetbaggers were opportunists who came to the South to get rich in the aftermath of conquest through theft of money, land, property, etc. Their allies were the treasonous scalawags - Southerners who had always favored the Union, had opposed secession, and in some cases had even taken up arms against their countrymen during the Civil War. These traitors were now placed by military force into political power in the South.

These forces - the Union army of occupation, the carpetbaggers, the scalawags, and the ex-slaves they easily manipulated - subjected Southerners to unethical, unprincipled, and inhumane punishment during Reconstruction. Representative Southern leaders were displaced by African-American politicians and Yankee Republicans. They stood the South on its head - ruining the economy, raising taxes, and using military force to savagely perpetuate their control. The effects were to last for decades, making the South a subjugated colony of the North - no longer the equal it had been before. But Southern people are tough. We got over it.

The Georgia Home Guard and the Battle of Griswoldville
By Ben H. Willingham, DCS

The Confederate Home Guard, in theory at least, was an organized militia serving under the direction and authority of the Confederate States of America, tasked with the defense of the home front. Their function varied with the needs of the area and home state. Although many states did not initially organize a Home Guard, by 1863 all eleven Confederate states had a Home Guard in place. As this article will focus on the Battle of Griswoldville, we will concentrate on the Georgia Home Guard.

In the early stages of the War Between the States, companies and regiments were formed all over Georgia and after very limited training, sent out of the state. Initially, it was thought the war would be of short duration and men were recruited for a period of one year. This practice of one year enlistments lasted only until April 1862 when the Confederate Congress passed a conscription law automatically extending army enlistments to three years. The majority of the early Georgia troops were sent to the Army of Northern Virginia and the remaining to the Army of Tennessee. At the end of their one year obligation, soldiers had the opportunity to leave and return home while others elected to remain for the duration. Later as the war progressed and more men were required these veteran soldiers would join other units and be sent as replacements or formed into companies that would augment existing regiments. Responsibilities changed with other departments being formed so it becomes difficult to generalize. Units were sent to the Department of South Carolina, Georgia and Florida but again most of these men were sent out of the State of Georgia to meet demands elsewhere.

In early 1864 Governor Joe Brown had 25,000 men ostensibly exempt from the 17-50 age group in the "Militia Proper." Since their service was restricted to the State of Georgia and they could not be sent elsewhere, they were unfairly called, "Joe Brown's Pets." The third Conscription Act of

February 1864 had taken most of these men from Brown while giving boys of 17-18 and men 45-50 to General Howell Cobb to organize Confederate defenses for Georgia. This left Governor Brown with the "Militia Reserve" consisting of boys 16-17 and men 50-60 and numbering about 16,000 for local protection. These units were very loosely organized and their members were all volunteers who were enlisted for six month terms and received no salary for their service. These Home Guard units were thought to be the last defense against an invading Federal army so it fell upon the boys and older men to defend the homeland. In Georgia these units served throughout the state. Although there were units of Cavalry, Artillery and Infantry, they were all poorly equipped and trained. As an effort to arm the home front, pikes were issued in lieu of guns which had become almost impossible to find. These too became known as "Joe Brown's Pikes." These medieval defenses were fine as long as all was quiet. There was little activity in the state away from the coast so the Home Guard spent its time trying to capture deserters from units serving elsewhere as they would be paid a bounty for each deserter they caught and turned over to the Confederate forces.

Two great armies were locked in a struggle for Chattanooga, TN as its loss would open Georgia to invasion. Georgia Governor Joe Brown called for more Home Guard troops to be sent to the central and northwest areas of the state. The Home Guard stationed along the Chattanooga-Atlanta axis was not placed in immediate danger. All of this changed in May of 1864 when Federal Major General William T. Sherman and his army invaded the state from the vicinity of Chattanooga in its march on Atlanta. The initial defense was conducted by the Army of Tennessee under General Joseph Eggleston Johnston. After Johnston withdrew from northwest Georgia to the surrounding areas of Atlanta, he was relieved by President Jefferson Davis and replaced by Lieutenant General John Bell Hood who had earlier been severely wounded in Virginia. It was thought Hood would be more aggressive and indeed Hood challenged the Federal force in a series of damaging frontal assaults. Hood's army was finally besieged in Atlanta and the city fell on 2 September. At this point, Hood and the Army of Tennessee withdrew with approximately 30,000 men moving north on a circuitous route toward Tennessee. They headed first to north Georgia in an attempt to cut off Sherman's supplies and then west toward Gadsden, AL to avoid having to cross the Cumberland Mountains that lay between north Georgia and central Tennessee.

Although Sherman was victorious in his Atlanta campaign, he was criticized for not having destroyed the Army of Tennessee with his far greater force of 81,000. The capture of Atlanta became a great boost to Northern morale and surely was an important factor in Lincoln's reelection in 1864.

Since Confederates under Hood were threatening Sherman's supply line from Chattanooga, he detached about 20,000 men under the command of Major General George H. Thomas to deal with Hood in what would later become the Franklin-Nashville Campaign. With the remaining 62,000 men (55,000 infantry, 5,000 cavalry and 2,000 artillerymen manning 64 guns) Sherman started his Savannah Campaign which became known as the "March to the Sea." Defending against Sherman was Lieutenant General William J. Hardee's Department of South Carolina, Georgia and Florida with the 13,000 men remaining at Lovejoy's Station south of Atlanta and Major General Gustavus W. Smith's Georgia Militia consisting of 3,050 soldiers, most of whom were boys and older men. The Confederate Cavalry Corps under Major General Joseph Wheeler reinforced by a brigade under Brigadier General William H. Jackson had about 10,000 troupers. During this campaign the Confederate War Department brought in men from Florida and the Carolinas but they were never able to increase the effective force beyond 13,000.

The Georgia Home Guard was to remain outside of the actual area of fighting and attempt to restrict the damage to property in the path of Sherman's march. To more easily follow this, I will use the example of my great grandfather 1st Lieutenant William A. Shields who was 35 at the time hostilities broke out but wanting to participate, he joined the Georgia Home Guards in 1862. The Guards were obligated to serve only six months but Shields continued to renew his commitment after brief visits home after each enlistment term to check on his family and property. Thus he served during the duration of the war. Records indicate his unit was stationed in Decatur, GA from early 1863 until at least August of 1864. Thus we know Shields was in the Atlanta area during the battle before being ordered to Macon to slow the advance of Sherman.

The Confederates were uncertain as to the actual destination of Sherman's advance. After Atlanta was Sherman going toward Macon, Augusta or Savannah? All of these avenues had to be protected and thus Confederate Major General William J. Hardee had ordered the local Militia in Macon to reinforce Augusta.

At the time of Sherman's march through Georgia, Griswoldville had been the home of the Confederate Pistol factory. The plant had been converted in 1862 from the production of cotton gin machinery to producing revolvers of the Colt pattern and during the course of the war had produced a total of about 3,500. On 21 November 1864 Federal Brigadier General Judson Kilpatrick's Cavalry, operating on the Federal right flank during the "March to the Sea" destroyed this beautiful town with wide streets and lovely homes and factory areas burning down everything.

On 22 November 1864, the Home Guard troops made up of 4,350 inexperienced boys and men with artillery under the command of Brigadier General Pleasant J. Philips, marched eastwards on the Georgia Central Railroad toward Augusta. Just past the smoldering ruins of Griswoldville they ran into detachments of the Federal Army. Thinking these were an isolated and unsupported brigade and contrary to direct orders from superiors, Phillips formed his lines for battle and attacked across an open field, trying to cross a swampy creek and charge up a hill. His men made seven assaults, coming within 50 yards of the Yankees before being repulsed by blistering fire. Federal Colonel Charles Wills later wrote of the battle, "Old gray haired men and weakly looking men and little boys, not over 15 years old, lay dead or writhing in pain." The old men and boys attacked with great courage and vigor, but failed to change any part of Sherman's plan in the only pitched battle on the "March to the Sea." Some call this battle the "Gettysburg of Georgia" referring to Pickets Charge where troops ran into a terrific fire and fearful execution as they moved forward.

Philips' commander, Major General Gustavus Woodson Smith, had ordered the militia not to engage the advancing Federal army but Philips seeing his chance chose to disobey his clear orders.

It was into this horrible one sided battle that Shields and the men of Co. B, 8th Georgia Infantry (State Guards) entered that fateful day of 22 November 1864. In the report following the battle, it was written that Shields was "pierced in the right breast and expired instantly." Little is known about what occurred after the battle and it is assumed that Shields was interred in one of the mass graves without any marker to identify his location.

Little is said about the service and sacrifice of the men in the Georgia State Guards but they served the cause in home defense. While there was no holding back Sherman's massive force, the Home Guard tried to contain the Federals who would burn anything they could not haul away. The Home Guard did manage to keep the looting Federals from straying from the main force thus saving a number of towns and many homes on the periphery of Sherman's march. This action, no doubt, reduced the damage caused by Sherman's tragic tramping through Georgia.

Griswoldville may have been the only full-fledged battle on the "March to the Sea" but there were a number of major skirmishes between units of Sherman's army and the Confederate cavalry, many of them being significant Confederate victories. Never the less, Sherman with such a large army under his command was not to be deterred in his devastating drive to destroy the very heart of Georgia. It would take many years to rebuild the senseless damage done by the Federal army in its desire to punish the women and children of the Southland.

Life in the Confederate Navy
By Ben H. Willingham, DCS

Too little is known or written about the efforts of the confederate Navy during the war. The Navy was established by the Confederate Congress on 21 February 1861 and President Jefferson Davis appointed the 49 year old lawyer, Stephen Russell Mallory of Pensacola, Florida to become the Secretary of Navy, a post that he held throughout the war. President Davis knew Mallory in the U.S. Senate from 1851 to 1861. During that period, Mallory served as Chairman of the Naval Affairs Committee. In that capacity, Mallory kept abreast of Naval Improvements around the world. When Florida seceded, Mallory came home to Pensacola and was there when word came of his appointment.

The responsibilities were the protection of the Southern harbors and coastlines, making the sea lanes of commerce difficult for the United States by attacking merchant vessels world-wide and breaking the Federal Blockade by forcing U.S. Navy ships to withdraw from blockade duty to pursue the Confederate raiders. In 1861, the Confederate Navy was non-existent with the exception of the almost destroyed and abandoned U.S. Navy's installations at Norfolk, VA and at Pensacola, FL; the Charleston Navy Base was taken over by South Carolina troops intact before hostilities actually began. The South was without naval facilities and the future Navy consisted of thirty ships of which only fourteen were seaworthy. Before the war ended the Navy reached 101 ships but this was not sufficient or fast enough to overcome the massive Federal fleet. The Confederacy had no port equipment. Not a single marine engine was being manufactured in the South, but Secretary Mallory immediately started to rectify that situation.

There were 16 captains, 34 commanders, 76 lieutenants, and 111 midshipmen present for duty. In every United States ship, without exception, these officers returned their U.S. Naval ships to their home ports before resigning their commissions to serve the South. Around these officers and men from nearly every Confederate State (Florida's share was almost 2,000 men) Secretary Mallory built the Confederate Navy. The demand for more officers was solved by the establishment of the Confederate Naval Academy on board the CSS Patrick Henry anchored in the James River of Virginia.

As early as May 10, 1861, Secretary Mallory urged the construction of an iron-clad Confederate Navy to off-set the superiority of the Federal Navy. He stated: "that the Confederate Navy must have quality, strength, & invulnerability."

Under Secretary Mallory's leadership, his staff including Captain James D. Bullock and Lieutenant James H. North negotiated in England for the purchase of 3 sail and steam cruisers. They were the *CSS Florida* commanded by Captain James Newland Maffitt, who despite of neutrality problems with British and Spanish authorities and a bout with yellow fever sailed his ship to Mobile to complete its outfitting as a ship of war. On the night of 15 January 1863, the *CSS Florida* finally broke out onto the high seas to become a terror to Federal merchant vessels. After 7 months of raiding, Maffitt put his ship into dock at Brest, France where he asked to be relieved. The *CSS Florida* had captured 55 prizes and had sunk many other ships carrying goods for the Federal Army. Maffitt was succeeded by Cdr. Joseph N. Barney and a few weeks later by Lieutenant Charles M. Morris. On 4 October 1863, the ship put into Bahia, Brazil and anchored near the *USS Waschusett,* assuming safety under the rules of international warfare. The Southern crew of officers and men went ashore. The United States committed an act of international outrage against the neutral nation of Brazil and seized the *CSS Florida* in the harbor; she was lost after a collision in Chesapeake Bay. Brazil received only an apology.

The second sail and steam cruiser delivered to the Confederacy by British sympathizers was the *CSS Alabama* commanded by Captain Raphael Semmes who took command of his ship in the Azores. During the next 22 months (from August 1862 to June 1864) the *CSS Alabama* captured and sank more enemy ships (a total of 92) than any other Confederate raider. The *CSS Alabama* even sank the *USS Hatteras* in a 13 minute battle off of Galveston, TX. In June 1862, he brought the *CSS Alabama* into Cherbourg, France for repairs. Shortly after his arrival, the *USS Kearsarge* appeared off Cherbourg and after being challenged by Captain Semmes gave battle outside of the port; after a little over an hour of battle, the *CSS Alabama* was sunk and Semmes was taken away to England by a private yacht.

The third sail and steam cruiser delivered to the Confederacy was the *CSS Shenandoah* commanded by Captain James Iredell Waddell that joined the Confederate Navy on 19 October 1864. On a cruise to Australia, the *CSS Shenandoah* captured 36 prizes. After repairs in Melbourne in January and February 1865, Waddell sailed the Pacific, sinking and rounding up more prizes and moved on into the Bering Sea and the Arctic Ocean where the *CSS Shenandoah* virtually destroyed the whaling fleet; scoring the last victories on 28 June 1865 against 11 Yankee Whalers. In August 1865, he learned from a British vessel that the war was over, and sailed to Liverpool where the *CSS Shenandoah* lowered her flag for the last time – the last Confederate Combat unit to do so on 6 November 1865.

Collectively, these three Confederate cruisers sank, burned, or captured almost 200 Federal ships forcing the Federal Navy to assign some of its ships from the Blockade of Southern ports to protect their merchant marine. The loss of Federal shipping forced Marine Insurance Underwriters and ship owners to bring pressure on the Lincoln government for an end of the war.

Iron-clad rams were under construction for the Confederate Navy by the Lairds of Birkenhead and in other British shipyards. Pressure from the Lincoln government eventually forced Lord Russell to support their neutral status seized these rams turned them over to the British Navy.

Secretary Mallory encouraged the development of the Torpedo or Marine Mine. It was a magazine of powder equipped with a detonator. The Confederate Navy used anchored torpedoes to mine harbors at New Orleans and at Mobile; as well as, in other harbors along the entire coastlines. More than 30 Federal ships were sunk by Confederate torpedoes during the war.

It was through Secretary Mallory's efforts that private marine engineers built and launched 4 successful submarines from 1862 to 1864. Of these the CSS Pioneer was built by McClintock and Watson in New Orleans only to be scuttled in April 1862 in Lake Pontchartrain to prevent her from falling into enemy hands when New Orleans was taken over by Federal Forces. A sister ship was built in Mobile and lost at sea before being commissioned in bad weather. The *CSS H. L. Hunley* was also built in Mobile and shipped to Charleston by rail car to expedite the defenses of that city. She sank twice, drowning her crew of five each time; raised once more, she crashed her torpedo against the hull of the Federal steam sloop of war the *USS Housatonic* in Charleston Harbor on the night of 17 February 1864. She sank near her target, carrying her crew with her. Now hear this, the *CSS Hunley* was the last American Submarine to sink an enemy warship until World War II!

Secretary Mallory also experimented perfected the *CSS David*. This was a 50 ft long, cigar shaped steamer, an iron torpedo boat that was built in Charleston in 1863. Operated by a crew of 4, it was capable of a maximum speed of 7 knots. The CSS David was armed with a torpedo carrying 100 pounds of explosives connected to a 10 foot spar at the bow. There were several other torpedo boats built and operated in and around the port of Charleston. They damaged Federal ships, but failed to sink a single ship.

After the Confederate occupation of the all but destroyed and abandoned Norfolk Navy Yard, the scuttled *USS Merrimac* renamed the *CSS Virginia* was brought into service. The *CSS Virginia* was originally a wooden frigate that was burned at the water's edge and sunk by the Federals. She was raised and rebuilt inside; strengthened in every way and armored with such iron as could be obtained. A slanting deck house was constructed, and an iron bow or beak was added for ramming purposes.

To the able Confederate Naval ship designers: Chief Engineer William P. Williamson, Lieutenant John L. Porter (Chief Naval Constructor), and to Lieutenant John M. Brooke (the inventor of the Brooke rifled gun) goes the credit for assisting Secretary Mallory to introduce the iron-clad battle ship into Naval Warfare history. Brooke placed the guns on the *CSS Virginia*. One 7" pivotal Brooke rifle at each end and 8 guns, 4 to the side, and 6 of these 8 were 9" Dahlgren plus 2 more 32 pound rifles.

The USS Monitor was commissioned one day ahead of the *CSS Virginia* on 25 February 1862. Flag officer, Captain Franklin Buchanan, CSN was assigned to the *CSS Virginia*. Her speed was about 5 knots; she required 22 feet of water under her keel to clear the bottom.

The *CSS Virginia* carried a crew of 325 officers and men. She had never been given a complete trial run on the day of her initial baptism of fire. Even her gun crews were fresh from the Confederate Army Artillery units. They did not know their officers & had never fired a gun together and she was hard to steer.

The Confederate flotilla that moved towards Hampton Roads from the Norfolk Navy base consisted of the *CSS Virginia,* the *CSS Patrick Henry,* the *CSS Jamestown,* the *CSS Teaser,* the *CSS Raleigh* and the *CSS Beaufort.* Midshipman Mallory, the son of the Secretary, was to see action for the first time on the *CSS Beaufort.*

On the morning of 9 March 1862, the *USS Monitor* and the *CSS Virginia* fought for four hours mercilessly, but ineffectively. Early in the afternoon the *CSS Virginia* turned towards Norfolk leaving the USS Monitor in possession of the roads. Earlier in the day the *CSS Virginia* had attacked the *USS Cumberland* and sank her by ramming; in fact when she reversed engines, she left most of the iron ram wedged into the *USS Cumberland;* next she attacked the *USS Congress* and ran her aground. Next came the battle with the *USS Monitor.*

When the Federals re-occupied Norfolk Navy Yard, the *CSS Virginia* was scuttled on 11 May 1862 to prevent capture.

When the war ended, Stephen Russell Mallory left Richmond with President Davis and the other cabinet members. He was taken prisoner at LaGrange, GA en route to Pensacola on 20 May 1865 and taken to Fort Lafayette, New York until March 1866 when he was released. He returned to Pensacola where he practiced law until he died on 9 November 1873.

The entire world and especially the naval forces thereof, owe to Secretary Stephen Russell Mallory their gratitude for his efforts in bringing naval warfare to a more perfect state than ever before. At the end of the war, the Confederate Navy consisted of 315 ships of which 104 were gunboats. While the Confederate Blockade Runners consisted of 101 ships and cruisers such as the *CSS Shenandoah* numbered 22 ships. There were 9 torpedo boats plus 25 iron-clad rams – all this in four years. Oh yes, after the *CSS Hunley,* the Confederate Navy ended the war with 3 submarines.

Section

4

Honor the Remaining Real Sons

Eulogy to the Confederate Soldier
By Lt. General Jubal Anderson Early, CSA

I believe that the world never produced a body of men superior in courage, patriotism, and endurance to the private soldiers of the Confederate armies. I have repeatedly seen these soldiers submit with cheerfulness to privations and hardships which would appear to be almost incredible; and the wild cheers of our brave men when their lines sent back opposing hosts of Federal troops, staggering, reeling, and flying, have often trilled every fiber of my heart. I have seen with my own eyes ragged, barefooted and hungry Confederate soldiers perform deed which if performed in days of yore by mailed warriors in glittering armor, would have inspired the harp of the minstrel and the pen of the poet.

All Living Real Sons

As with each year, it comes to mind that we are getting older with each passing day. The sons listed herein most likely reminded their fathers of the hope of the future that would be most different from the hardship and tough times that they faced before and after the War Between the States. Some of these individuals may have learned about these experiences that helped them forge for a better future. We all have much to learn from the past. We must decide whether to learn from it or ignore it. Let us remember these men and learn from them so that we can share their knowledge and the knowledge of other American veterans. Today's generation and those generations ahead are dependent on us to record the historical facts.

Per the records that the Military Order of the Stars and Bars has on hand, a listing of all known living real sons of Confederate Veterans are:

H. V. Booth	Elberton, GA
Thomas Newton Bruce	Knoxville, TN
Albert Lee Comer	Lavale, MD
Calvin Crane	Roanoke, VA
Tyus K. Denney	Tarrant, AL
Henry O. Gober	Millbrook, AL
Clifford Blair Hamm	Gastonia, NC
Thomas Keith	Franklin, KY
Luther Otto Lucas	Caledonia, MO
Bufford Sims	Marianna, FL
Francis H. Vittetow	Winter Park, FL
Mike Y. Yancey	Cardova, TN

Member Ancestor Listing & Biographies

Over the past couple years; the Military Order of the Stars and Bars has requested that members of the Order consider writing a short article about their ancestor. The biographies that appear in this Anniversary Book are the ones received and have been included for your reference.

Ancestor: 2nd Lt. David L. Brannan, Co. C. 37th MS. Infantry
(Great Grandfather of Glenn Wayne Toal)

David Brannan was born in about 1827, in Greene County, Mississippi. His parents were Henry and Unity Brannan. Henry was a Methodist minister and a farmer.

David married Louisa Kelley in 1847 and they lived in Clarke County, Mississippi. David was also a farmer. They had a large family. (David's son Francis Marion, born in 1854, was my maternal grandfather.)

On December 1, 1861 he enlisted in the Confederate Army in **Capt. Patton's "Army of 10,000 Volunteers"**, Co. A, as a Corporal. (He is listed as having his double barrel shotgun to carry with him.) David's enlistment card states he travelled 220 miles to "place of rendevous", which was Corinth, Ms. This unit was soon disbanded due to an extreme outbreak of the measles.

Determined to serve the Confederacy, on March 13, 1862, David joined **Co. C, 37th Mississippi Regiment** as a 2nd Lieutenant. He was later offered a promotion in rank, but declining health made it impossible for him to accept.

David and some of his family came to Hill County, Texas in the 1880's. The exact date of his death is not known. He has a Confederate stone in Bell Springs Cemetery in Bynum, Texas; but sadly, as with many of these stones, there are no dates listed. The application for his Confederate stone was made in September of 1941; his date of death is listed as 1914.

Ancestor: Major B. F. Brown, Regimental Surgeon, 2nd S. C. Rifles (Volunteers)
(Submitted by Dan Brown)

Benjamin Franklin Brown was born February 4, 1833, "first male child" in Anderson, S. C. and was graduated from the Medical College of the State of S.C. in Charleston in 1854. B. F. Brown enlisted as a private in Company L, S. C. Rifles (Volunteers) on March 17, 1862 at Anderson, receiving a $50 signing bonus of April 7th and 25 cents per day thereafter. On May 12th he was commissioned Captain and Assistant Surgeon. His military occupation was "Physician Detailed" and his pay rose to $110 a month. He was promoted to Surgeon with the rank of Major on February 7, 1863 and assigned to staff, 2nd Regiment, S. C. Rifles.

The 2nd Regiment was part of Jenkins' Brigade, Longstreet's Corps, Lee's Army of Northern Virginia. From the Field and Staff Muster Roles, and receipts for feed obtained for his horse (12lbs a day of corn and 14lbs a day of oats, hay or fodder, as available) his duties took him to Winchester, VA, in 1862, and to Chester, Franklin Depot and Richmond, VA and Morristown, TN, in 1863. He was "absent, sick" once in 1863. He was also "absent, on approved 60 day furlough" in 1863 to represent his wife in his mother-in-law's probate proceedings regarding the disposition of their slaves. In 1864 he was at Bull's Gap, TN and Cobhams, Petersburg and near Richmond, VA. His last Muster was also near Richmond in February 1865.

His name appears in a list of prisoners of war surrendered at Appomattox Court House on April 9, 1865. His signature appears on a list of parolees at Appomattox that same day. B. F. Brown died in Williamstown, S. C. on May 23, 1919. On his headstone, besides his name and dates, it says simply "Served in the War between the States as Regimental Surgeon with rank of Major in Jenkins' Brigade, Longstreet's Corps, Lee's Army, and surrendered with his command at Appomattox."

His military records were photocopied in 1987 from microfilm obtained from the National Archives and Records Service and from the S. C. Department of Archives and Records.

Ancestor: Col. William Reuben Butler, CSA
(Submitted by Judge Edward F. Butler, Sr.)

William Reuben Butler was born 22 Sep 1834 in Rutherford Co., TN. He and Isadora Smith were married 1 Nov 1859 in Rutherford Co., TN. He died on 15 Nov 1883 in Rutherford Co., TN

He served as Postmaster under president Pearce. His term began in 1854. President Buchanan reappointed him, and he served throughout Buchanan's administration.

At age 28, he served as Field and Staff Captain in Company C of the Tennessee 18th Infantry Regiment, which was organized at Camp Trousedale, Sumner County on 11 Jun 1861. He was elected Company Commander on 7 Aug 1861. at Fort Donelson, the regiment surrendered on 16 Feb 1862.

After four days of pitched battle, he was among the 1104 officers and men taken prisoner at the surrender of Fort Donelson on 6 Feb 1862. He was received at Camp Chase on 1 Mar 1862. He was imprisoned at Johnson Island, Sandusky, OH on 10 Apr 1862, and was among the prisoners transferred to Vicksburg, MS on 1 Sep 1862 on the riverboat Steamer John H. Bone, which arrived near Vicksburg on 20 Sep 1862. After being held prisoners for just over seven months, the entire unit was paroled at Vicksburg, MS on 26 Sep 1862. He was elected Lt. Colonel on 10 Oct 1862.

The unit was reorganized. They fought at Murfresboro, Tullahoma, and at Chickamauga. While engaged in the Chattanooga Siege, they were consolidated with the 26th Infantry Regiment. They fought in the Rocky Face Ridge battle, Resaca, New Hope Church; and the Atlanta Campaign including fights at Powder Springs Road, Kennesaw Mountain, and Chattahoochee River. Their last hurrah was during the Carolinas Campaign from Feb to April 1865, during which time they were again consolidated with 17 other units and designated as the 4th Infantry Regiment Consolidated.

He was wounded in action in Jul 1864 and sent to hospital in Griffin, GA. In 1870 he was elected as a member of the seven men Board of Aldermen of Murfresboro, TN, and served as treasurer. He was a Master Mason and served as Grand Commander of Grand Commandery of Tennessee. He is buried in the Old Butler Graveyard in Rutherford Co., TN.

Ancestor: Lt. Henry Stuart "Hall" Crockett
(Submitted by George Crockett)

Henry Stuart "Hal" Crockett was a CSA Lieutenant who was born September 22nd, 1846, in Wythe County, Virginia, to John Stuart and Margaret (Taylor) Crockett on a large cattle farm. Of six children, Hal and two sisters survived childhood.

James Ewell Brown married first, Hal's aunt, second, JEB Stuart's aunt.

Hal enrolled in Virginia Military Institute, September 1863. During late summer and fall, VMI cadets were called upon to hunt deserters and to block the advance of Republican army raiders, encountering no raiders. Hal was a Cadet Private, Company D, VMI Cadet Battalion in the Battle of New Market. Cadet Charles Gay Crockett, killed in that battle, was Hal's first-cousin.

Hal campaigned with the VMI Cadet Battalion through January 1865, including brief periods in the Richmond defenses but no combat.

On January 29th, 1865, Hal resigned from VMI, in Richmond, to join the Confederate Army. In April, he joined a cavalry company forming in Logan County, Va., to join the command of Col. V.A. Witcher. Probably, this company was being raised by Hal's first-cousin, Charles Fulton, also a New Market cadet. My aunt told me that my great-grandfather was an army recruiter in the Holston River Valley before joining the army. Maybe that was during February and March, 1865. When the company heard of Lee's surrender, it disbanded without surrendering.

Hal's father died in 1864, possibly heavily invested in the war effort; at any rate, there was no farm for Hal to return to. To earn money for medical school at Washington College, Baltimore, Md., he worked in a cousin's general store in Mississippi, studying medical books by night.

Dr. Crockett married Minnesota Howe, May 28th, 1873. They had six sons and one daughter, and lived some years in Rural Retreat, Wythe Co., Va., then in Wilmore, Ky., where Mrs. Crockett died in May 1907. Dr. Crockett remarried and moved to Americus, Ga., where he and two sons owned a pharmacy. Dying September 8th, 1908, he is buried in Americus's Oak Grove cemetery.

Ancestor: Dr. John Emory Douthit, MD
(Submitted by Robert D. Brazier)

Dr. J. E. Douthit was born in 1836 in North Carolina. He served in the 21st NC Infantry as an Assistant Surgeon. He was a physician before the war, during and after the war was over.

When the war ended, he traveled to Mexico, then to Missouri where he married Medora Crenshaw. They later came to Rockdale, Texas; where he practiced medicine and also operated a drug store for many years.

As reported in the Dallas Morning News, The Necrology of Physicians in Texas – 1885, "Dr. J. E. Douthit died suddenly from heart disease on February 1, 1885. He served as surgeon in the Confederate Army."

He is buried beside his wife, in the Old City Cemetery in Rockdale, Texas.

Ancestor: Captain William Patton Fortune
(Submitted by great-grandson David Wayne Snodgrass)

William Patton Fortune (1833-1901) and his brother Benjamin Fletcher Fortune (1838-1915) were 2 of 10 siblings living and farming at Black Mountain near Asheville , NC when the War Between the States began. Both of these brothers enlisted as Privates with the "Rough and Ready Guard". Company F of the 14th Infantry Division North Carolina in May 1861. William P. Fortune was promoted to Division Quartermaster Sergeant in June of 1861. The NC 14th Infantry Division served in Lee's Army of Northern Virginia from the Peninsula Campaign all the way through the end at Appomattox. The Fortune brothers transferred in 1863 to a newly formed 14th NC Battalion (only three companies) where William P. Fortune was Captain of the Third Company and his brother Benjamin was a Second Lieutenant. The 14th Battalion was responsible for protecting western North

Carolina from invasion by opposing raids of the Union Army stationed in eastern Tennessee. This required guerilla type of warfare, picketing roads, fighting bushwhackers, conducting raids into east Tennessee, and significant brushes with the enemy, but no pitched battles. These three companies were soon joined by three additional companies making a full Battalion. The service was a peculiar service and a particularly hard one in 1864 and 1865 amidst the hardships of mountain campaigns where no assurances of safety and rather independent companies confronted opponents with no accurate intelligence of opponents capabilities. Many men were killed and wounded and in April 1864 the battalion reported 221 present out of a total of 510. Early in 1865 the 14th Battalion was joined with four additional companies which created the 79th NC Regiment (also referred to as the NC Eighth Cavalry). The regiment's last service was around Asheville repelling raids by Union forces. On being made certain of Lee's and Johnston's surrender, the 79th Regiment quietly dissolved and the men went home without being paroled.

Ancestor: Major William Britton Hundley, II CSA
(Submitted by Great grandson Ben H. Willingham, DCS)

William Hundley was born in 1827 and educated at the University of Georgia; he married Mary Elizabeth Jones the daughter of the first medical doctor in Georgia to have actually received an education at a medical university. Together they began a very successful business of importing dresses and fine apparel for the wealthy ladies of the Anti Bellum South. By 1860, they had accumulated a comfortable estate and Hundley had been elected a Superior Court Judge. All of this was not enough to keep Hundley at home when his country called.

On 5 May 1861, the Confederate Congress formally declares a state of War exists with the United States. The patriots of Warren County, Georgia raise their first company of soldiers and only five days after War has officially been declared, these soldiers who were initially known as the McDuffie Rifles, are incorporated into the 5th Georgia Infantry Regiment in Macon, GA under the command of Colonel John King Jackson (promoted to Brigadier General 14 January 1862) and mustered into Confederate service. The 5th Regiment was composed of ten companies of volunteer infantry raised in the counties around Augusta.

In the election of company officers, Judge William Hundley was elected a 2nd Lieutenant. After being mustered into service, the 5th Georgia entrained at Macon for Pensacola, FL. The trip to Pensacola was long and complicated needing to travel on four different train lines. In garrison at Pensacola they would received their basic training. General Braxton Bragg would often come from his headquarters eight miles away to watch them drill. The ten companies were all from cities or towns, and nicely uniformed, though each in a different style. After the 5th Georgia had been in Pensacola a while their uniforms led General Bragg to name them the "Pound Cake Regiment." After a bit of hard campaigning in the West, hardly two men in the 5th Georgia were dressed alike.

On 9 October 1861 the 5th Georgia receives its baptism under fire at the Battle of Santa Rosa (Fort Pickens) outside of Pensacola, FL. That day, the 5th Georgia had its first casualties when four men, one of them the brother in law of Lieutenant Hundley, are killed in action. Others are wounded including Lieutenant Hundley. The 5th Georgia would remain in Florida for the balance of 1861. After a period of recovery and garrison in Pensacola, the 5th Georgia is sent to Grand Junction, TN. There they are assigned to guard Cumberland Gap and to organize brigades on their way to Corinth, MS. Now under the command of Brigadier General John King Jackson (Jackson's Brigade is composed of: 2nd Battalion, 1st Georgia, 5th Georgia, 2nd Battalion of Sharpshooters, 5th Mississippi, 8th Mississippi), in April, the 5th Georgia participates in the Battle of Shiloh and was one of the last Confederate regiments in contact at the end of the day. Out of ammunition, the 5th Georgia along with the other regiments of Jackson's Brigade had run into heavy fire. With bayonets only, the 5th Georgia ascended the last ridge nearly to the crest, but without support, the exhausted men could go no further.

Following this engagement the initial enlistment of the 5th Georgia terminated and the original captain resigned to resume his law practice and Hundley, who chose to remain, was elected captain. Later in the war the commander of the 5th Georgia, Colonel Charles P. Daniel, will be wounded and Hundley will assume command of the 5th Georgia. Following Shiloh the 5th Georgia was involved in the Kentucky Campaign of 1862, General Jackson and his Brigade were ordered from Knoxville to Bridgeport, AL where they were to guard Confederate communications along the railways and railroad bridges between Murfreesboro and Chattanooga. With Confederate Major General Braxton Bragg starting Kentucky Campaign, the 5th Georgia starts a history making forced march from Chattanooga to Bardstown, KY and then to the eastern part of Kentucky and down through Cumberland Gap, 800 miles in two months July and August. General Bragg withdraws through Cumberland Gap putting the 5th Georgia back in Tennessee just in time to see action in the Stones River Campaign of late 1862 where during the Battle of Murfreesboro (31 December 1862 – 02 January 1863). Hundley was again wounded, this time in the shoulder but he was able to continue on with the regiment.

After the Battle of Murfreesboro Jackson's Brigade was sent back to Bridgeport, AL to defend communications from Atlanta, GA to Tullahoma, TN. This led to the Battle of Chickamauga on 19-20 September 1863 where the 5th Georgia lost sixty-one per cent of her effective force in a single battle. Hundley was again wounded. Following Chickamauga the 5th Georgia participated in the Chattanooga Campaign in October and November and most notably the Battle of Missionary Ridge where Jackson's Brigade and that of Brigadier General John C. Moore greatly slowed the Federal breakthrough on 25 November 1863. General Jackson's Brigade was involved in the Atlanta Campaign with the Army of Tennessee until 2 July 1864 when Jackson and two of his regiments, the 5th and 47th Georgia were detached and ordered to Charleston to report to Major General Samuel Jones. There Jones gave Jackson orders to proceed to Lake City, FL where Jackson along with the two Georgia regiments relieved Brigadier General James P. Anderson taking charge of the Department of Florida. During Sherman's March to the Sea in late 1864, Jackson and his command were sent to Savannah, GA and participated in the siege of Savannah where they were given the responsibility for the center line of the Confederate defenses. When the city of Savannah was abandoned in December 1864 the remains of Jackson's Brigade was sent to Branchville, SC where they were to establish military depots as the quartermaster of the Army of Tennessee. As the end was nearing, the remnants of the Army of Tennessee, including Jackson's Brigade moved on to North Carolina for the Battle of Bentonville on 19-21 March 1865. Colonel Charles P. Daniels became wounded causing Major Hundley to assume command of the 5th Georgia Infantry Regiment. Although the Confederates acquitted themselves well in battle, the war was over and Major Hundley was forced to surrender the men of the 5th Georgia with General Joseph E. Johnston at Bennett Place near Durham Station, NC.

After the war, Hundley returned to his family in Warren County, GA. Having been wounded three times and under the restrictions of Federal occupation and reconstruction, he was unable to return to his earlier occupation nor was he allowed to serve again as a judge. He is listed in the 1870 census as without occupation and living in his father-in-law's home. Shortly after the census was taken, he died at the age of 42.

This is the story of one Confederate officer but surely this story was repeated many times throughout the South. Hundley believed in the cause and was willing to fight for his principles, even if it cost him his life.

Ancestor: Captain James Jackson

Capt. James Jackson was born on the 4th day of September 1832 and joined the Confederate Army on the 1st day of March 1862 as Capt. of Company E, 45th Alabama, went first to Mississippi, was there at the battle of Shiloh; then to Kentucky and was in all the battles in Tennessee and Georgia; was wounded at Mufreesboro and Atlanta; wounded again at Franklin Tennessee, the day General Cleburne was, killed in which Division he was. At that time he was acting Major of the Regiment. He had his sword hilt shot off and the ball went through the fleshy part of his thumb and shot out some of the bones in his wrist. He was promoted to Lieutenant Colonel before the war closed. He died in Montgomery, Alabama, April 5th, 1895.

Ancestor: Daniel Malone
(Submitted by Francis J. Sypher, Jr.)

Daniel Malone, Justice of the County Court of Dinwiddie Co., Va., was born in 1801/1802 and died April 11, 1868 in his 67th year, that is, aged 66 (gravestone at Malone cem., Rte #667, Dinwiddie Co.; census records suggest birth circa 1805). He was the son of William Malone (ca. 1771– ca. 1850) whose will, dated 1849, naming his children, was probated in 1851 (Dinwiddie Co. Will Book 4, pp. 567–568). Daniel Malone appears on Dinwiddie Co. census returns of 1830, 1840, 1850, and 1860. His farm was near Stony Creek and the Rowanty River. He married Wilmuth Ann Pace; children were: Lucinda Malone (b. ca. 1830), William J. Malone (b. ca. 1833), John D. Malone (b. ca. 1836), Robert G. Malone (b. ca. 1844), and Ella V. Malone (b. 1850). Daniel Malone—known as "Major Malone," apparently from antebellum militia service—was elected to four-year terms as county justice in 1852, 1856, and 1860; in 1858 he served on a committee for a new courthouse building. See *Dinwiddie County: "The Countrey of the Apamatica"* (Federal Works Agency, 1942), pp. 118, 229, 244. In 1863 Major Malone provided the Confederates with timber for gun carriages (letter, J. R. Anderson & Co. to C. O. Sanford, Jan. 6, 1863, in Tredegar Records, Lib. of Va.). In the summer of 1864, Major Malone's farm was the camp ground for the 9th Virginia Cavalry, which then saw action at the railroad line to Petersburg, including a skirmish at Malone's Crossing and a battle at Reams's Station. See William Campbell, "Autobiographical Sketch," *William and Mary Quarterly,* 2nd series, vol. 9, no. 2 (April 1929), p. 105; Marshall A. Moncure, in *Richmond Dispatch,* March 15, 1896, p. 6 ("Our Confederate Column"); Louis N. Boudrye, *Historic Records of the Fifth New York Cavalry* (Albany, N.Y., 1865), pp. 154–155. May 1868 administration proceedings on Daniel Malone's estate list a full inventory, including a piano (Will Book 8, pp. 302–306).

Ancestor: General Samuel McGowan

Story about William Matthew's great-grandfather taken from Confederate Military History, edited by Gen. Clement A. Evans, Atlanta, Confederate Publishing Co., 1899, Volume V, page 412:

Brig. Gen. Samuel McGowan was born of Scotch-Irish parentage near Cross Hill in Laurens County on Oct. 9, 1819. He graduated from South Carolina College in 1841, studied law with T. C. Perrin in 1842, was admitted to the Bar in the fall of 1842 and embarked upon the practice of law at Abbeville.

He answered the call of his country in 1846 and started for the Mexican War as a private in the Palmetto Regiment. He was soon appointed to the General Quartermaster's Staff with the rank of captain, serving during the war first on the staff of General Quitman and afterward with Generals Worth and Twiggs. As volunteer aide to General Quitman at the storming of Chapultepec and the capture of Garita de Belem, he was distinguished for gallantry.

After his return to South Carolina in 1848 he continued with much success the practice of his profession, and sat twelve years in the lower house of the State Legislature; but also retained his connection with military matters, becoming Major General in the State Militia. Upon the secession of South Carolina he was commissioned Brigadier General in the State army and assigned to command of one of the four brigades first formed and in that capacity assisted General Beauregard during the reduction of Fort Sumter. Upon the transfer of the troops to the Confederate service he joined General Bonham in Virginia and served as a volunteer aide at the battles of Blackburn Ford and First Manassas.

Then, returning to South Carolina, he was elected lieutenant colonel of the Fourteenth Regiment and in the spring of 1862 while in service on the coast, was promoted to colonel. Soon afterward, with Gregg's Brigade, he began a distinguished career in the Army of Northern Virginia. He was wounded at Cold Harbor where he led his regiment in several daring charges, retrieved the ground lost by another brigade at Frayser's Farm, and continued on duty in spite of his injury until after Malvern Hill. For his gallantry in these battles he was recommended by General Gregg for promotion.

After fighting at Cedar Run he was wounded at Second Manassas, and for some time disabled, but he rejoined his regiment after the battle of Sharpsburg and commanded it at Fredericksburg. There General Gregg was killed, and in January 1863, Colonel McGowan was promoted Brigadier General and became Gregg's successor in command of the gallant brigade. In this capacity he served until the end of the war, receiving several wounds, the most severe of which befell him at Chancellorsville and during the fight at bloody angle at Spotsylvania Courthouse.

After the surrender at Appomattox he returned to his home and resumed the "profession from which he had twice been diverted by war." He was elected to Congress in 1865, but was not permitted to take his seat, made a thorough canvass of the State as an elector at- large on the Democratic Presidential ticket in 1876; in 1878 he was elected to the Legislature, and in 1879 he was elected associate justice of the Supreme Court. In the latter office he won lasting honor and distinction as he had upon the field of battle. His death occurred Aug. 9, 1897.

Ancestor: Colonel John Thomas Mercer, 21st Georgia State Infantry

(Submitted by Dr. Donald Watson)

John Thomas Mercer was born February 7, 1830 in Taliaferro County, Georgia to Dr. Leonidas Bennington Mercer and Lovicia Janes Mercer. John received an appointment to West Point in 1850, and graduated in 1854. Upon graduation, he was commissioned a Lieutenant in the United States Army in the First Dragoons, and was sent out to the American West.

First Lieutenant Mercer served honorably in the U. S. Army in California until his home state of Georgia seceded from the Union. Lt. Mercer resigned his commission and reported to Montgomery, Alabama to tender his services to the Confederate Army. He was subsequently given command of the 21st Georgia State Infantry with the rank of Colonel. Colonel Mercer led his men in battles at Winchester, Virginia, Cross Keys, Malvern Hill, and was mentioned for gallantry at the Battle of Chancellorsville and Gettysburg.

In early 1864, the 21st Georgia, led by Colonel Mercer was assigned to Dole's Brigade, was sent to New Bern, then on to Plymouth, North Carolina in April of 1864, to engage the enemy, and take back control of the town on the Roanoke River, from Union forces who captured Plymouth in 1862. On April 18, 1864, Colonel Mercer led an assault on Fort Sanderson, near Welch's Creek Swamp, and received a fatal gunshot wound in the head. Moments later, Fort Sanderson was taken by the Confederates, and Plymouth was once again, under the control of the Confederate Army. Colonel Mercer was the highest ranking officer killed in the Battle of Plymouth.

All of Colonel Mercer's family lived in Georgia, except for a distant cousin, and West Point classmate, General William Dorsey Pender, who was wounded at Gettysburg, and died days later from his wound. Colonel Mercer was taken to Goldsboro, then on to Tarboro, North Carolina, and laid to rest next to General Pender at Calvary Episcopal Church.

As a descendant of Colonel Mercer, and member of the MOS&B, I visit his grave each year as I travel to Plymouth to participate in the Plymouth Living History Weekend, held on the anniversary of the battle.

Ancestor: Robert A. B. Munson
(Submitted by Michael Bates)

Robert A.B. Munson numbers among those relatively few Confederate officers of Northern heritage. Born in 1839 in Elizabeth, NJ, Munson moved to Winchester, VA in the 1850s, probably to live with a maternal relative who had settled there in 1826. He received his medical training in Frederick County, and on 18 Apr 1861, enrolled for active service in VA 2nd Infantry, Co. F, Stonewall Brigade. On 5 Feb 1862 he was promoted to Assistant Surgeon in the Medical Department and served honorably in that capacity until the end of the war. In 1871 he married Mary Buckmaster, a native of Winchester. Robert and Mary had three children. By 1875 he had moved his family to New Jersey where he spent the rest of his life. Munson died in Millington, NJ on 1 Feb 1904 and is buried alongside his wife at the cemetery adjacent Millington Baptist Church.

Ancestor: Major Josiah P. Parrott
(Submitted by Gary E. Parrott)

Josiah Rhoton Parrott served the Confederate States of America as a military officer and a government official. He was commissioned as a major in Brigadier General William T. Wofford's Brigade (of Major General Lafayette McLaw's Division in Lieutenant General James Longstreet's Corps, the 1st Corps - Army of Northern Virginia-CSA) on February 16, 1863.

Major Parrott served as a brigade quartermaster until January 26, 1864, when he resigned his commission to accept a government position (Solicitor General of the Cherokee Judicial District, Bartow County, Georgia) and served in that capacity until the end of the War.

Josiah R. Parrott was born in February 1826 in Cocke County, Tennessee. He was one of six children of Jacob and Amelia (Swaggerty) Parrott. He was educated at Emory and Henry College, one of the oldest and prestigious colleges in southwest Virginia.

After graduating from college, Josiah moved to Georgia with one of his brothers (Charles Parrott). Soon, thereafter, he married Mary M. Trammell, the daughter of Jehu and Elizabeth (Fain) Trammell. Over the years they would have seven children.

By 1850 Josiah was a teacher in Gordon County, Georgia, however his ultimate goal was to become a lawyer. So, when he was not teaching, he spent his time studying law. In 1851 he was admitted to the Georgia State Bar.

Josiah became a successful lawyer and very active in the local community. He was a delegate to the 1856 and 1860 Georgia State Presidential Conventions. And, after the War, he was a member of the Georgia State Constitutional Convention in 1865.

In 1868 Josiah Parrott was appointed Judge of the Cherokee Circuit Court in Georgia and served in that capacity until his death. He passed away on June 10, 1872, the result of a chronic illness he had contracted during the War. His final resting place is at the Oak Hill Cemetery in Cartersville, Bartow County, Georgia.

Note: Josiah's father (Jacob Parrott) was the younger brother of John Parrott (the great-great-great grandfather of MOS&B - Colorado Society charter member Gary E. Parrott).

Ancestor: Brigadier Peter Burwell Starke
(Composed by Robert Burwell Starke, Jr., Great grandson)

Peter Burwell Starke was born about 1815 in Brunswick County, Virginia. He and his brother, William Edwin Starke (Brigadier General, CSA, killed at Sharpsburg in 1862), ran a stage line in their youth. About 1835, he removed to Columbus, MS, obtaining U.S. Government mail contracts in Alabama, Mississippi and Arkansas.
An ardent supporter of Henry Clay, he rose to prominence as a Whig in 1840. In 1846, he was requested and authorized to raise a regiment of dragoons in Mississippi for the Mexican War. The war ended before the regiment was organized.

In December 1846, he lost as the Whig candidate to fill the Congressional seat of Jefferson Davis, who had resigned to fight in the Mexican War. About this same time, he was wounded, refusing to shoot, in a duel with Thomas G. Blewett in Alabama. By 1849, he had removed to Bolivar County, Mississippi, establishing at large plantation.

From 1850 to 1854, Starke served in the Mississippi State Legislature; and from 1856 to 1862 in the State Senate. In February, 1860 Starke was appointed by Governor Pettus as Commissioner from Mississippi to the Virginia Convention considering actions with other slave holding States.

In 1862, Colonel Starke raised and organized the 28th Mississippi Cavalry Regiment. They participated in the Vicksburg Campaign until Vicksburg's surrender. In early 1863, Starke participated with Van Dorn's Cavalry campaign in Middle Tennessee. Starke was in charge of the investigation into the assassination of Van Dorn.
Under General W. H. Jackson's Division, Starke fought Sherman across Mississippi during Sherman's Meridian campaign. He was with Brigadier General Frank C. Armstrong as his brigade moved into Alabama and Georgia in the spring of 1864. Promoted to Brigadier General in November, 1864, and now a part of Forrest's command, Starke participated in the march into Tennessee, including the Battle of Franklin. Starke remained under Forrest's command until Forrest's surrender in May, 1865.

His wife and five children having died by 1865, he returned to Brunswick County, Virginia. There he participated in the Virginia legislature, married, had one son and died there in 1888.

Ancestor: Captain Joel Gilmore Wood

Joel Gilmore Wood enlisted in Craighead County, Arkansas on March 11, 1862. His company completed its organization in March 1862 and Joel Wood was elected Captain. The Company was assigned to Lieutenant-Colonel Batt L. Jones' 8th Arkansas Infantry Battalion as Company F (Wood's Rifles) on April 9. As a result of the battalion's reorganization a month later, Wood's Rifles was re-designated as Company E on May 10, 1862 with Joel remaining as captain of the company. In October, 1862, the battalion was assigned to Cabell's Brigade, Price's Corps, and covered the Confederate withdrawal from the battle of Corinth. The battalion suffered significant losses in this rear-guard action of October 5, 1862. The battalion was then transferred to the brigade of Brigadier-General William Nelson Rector Beall in the Department of Mississippi and East Louisiana, and formed part of the garrison of Port Hudson, Louisiana. They endured the siege of that place from May to July, 1863, only surrendering when the fall of Vicksburg rendered the defense of Port Hudson irrelevant. The garrison capitulated on July 9, 1863. This company did not rejoin the battalion after the surrender at Port Hudson.

Captain Wood returned to northeast Arkansas and organized Company A, Davies' 7th Arkansas Cavalry Battalion, in Craighead and Greene counties, and several members of his former company enlisted. It was organized with 5 companies (at least). The battalion was surrendered by Jeff Thompson on May 11, 1865. It's only assignments were: Northern Sub-District of Arkansas, District of Arkansas, Trans-Miss (Apr 1865) Northern Sub-District of Arkansas, District of Arkansas and West Louisiana, Trans-Miss (Apr-May 1865). Joel Gilmore Wood received his official parole on May 25, 1865 at Wittsburg, Arkansas.

Following The War of Northern Aggression, Joel served with credit one term as sheriff of Craighead County, Arkansas. Besides the operation of the family farm, Joel owned and operated a grocery store/ general store in Jonesboro. Ten (10) children were born to Joel and his wife Maria (Evans). He died from an accident November 16, 1882.

Ancestor: WHR Workman of Camden, SC: 2nd Lt, Co D, 15th SC Infantry

THE CAPTURE OF THE 19 YANKEES - Hand written account, attributed to daughter Bettie Coats Workman.

I remember in 1876 when there were in [the Law Offices of Kershaw and Workman] six or more Confederate generals: Hampton, Butler, James Connor, Anderson, Kershaw, Chesnut, and J. D. Kennedy. When my father stayed so long, my mother sent me to tell him dinner was waiting. On the way back, my father remarked on what wonderful exploits and experiences they related. My brother said, "Father, why didn't you tell what you did?" He replied, "Who, me? Speak before those great generals?" Then I said, "Papa, what did you do?" "Well, nothing much. Just marched nineteen men to headquarters, General Kershaw's tent." Then I began begging him to tell how he did it.

After the battle [Chancellorsville?] he went out to get away from everything, but everywhere he went the sight of human bodies lay mangled and torn to pieces. He said, "I was so overcome with sorrow and distress that I kept wandering, and soon I realized that I was lost as to what direction the camp was. I kept going and to my surprise and great fear I came upon a group of twenty Yankee soldiers, resting in a quiet and secluded spot. I know I had to do something right away so I said 'Surrender!' To my relief they surrendered without protest. Then they said, 'What about our guns?' I said, 'Each one take his gun and do as I command. One man broke away. One said, 'Why are we prisoners of one man?' I called, 'One single shot and the whole regiment of Confederates will be upon you and shoot everyone of you.' I was scared I tell you for I didn't know but that I might be marching them to their own lines. As we marched to the crest of the next hill, to my great relief, there was General Kershaw who saw me. Throwing up his hands, he cried, 'Hurrah for Workman!'

I was so proud of my father. I never forgot his telling us this in such a humble way - always saying, 'I was not brave, just scared to death.'

The rest of this anniversary book lists all of our member's ancestors who served as Confederate Officers and Government Officials during the War Between the States. We herein list these ancestors as a tribute to them for their bravery during the War Between the States.

Listing of Member's Ancestors

Name	Rank	Unit
ABBITT, GEORGE W.	CAPT	VA 46TH INF, CO B
ABBOTT, ELI	CAPT	MS CAV (CHICKASAW COUNTY)
ABELL, CHARLES ALEXANDER	2LT	SC 1ST CAV, CO H
ABERNATHY, ALFRED HARRIS	COL	TN 53RD INF, F&S, CO C
ABERNATHY, BUCKNER	CAPT	AR 12TH INF, CO G
ABERNETHY, JOHN WESLEY	2LT	TX 1ST PARTISAN RANGERS, CO L
ABNEY, JESSE MERCIER	1LT	MS CLAYTON'S CO (JASPER DEFENDERS)
ABNEY, JOSEPH	LT COL	SC 27TH INF, F&S
ACKER, ELIHU H.	2LT	SC INF (HAMPTON'S LEGION), CO D
ACKERSON, THOMAS J.	1LT	TN 11TH INF, CO E,A
ACREE, JAMES G., MD.	SURG/1LT	TN 50TH INF, CO D
ACTON, RUFUS MCCRAFT	2LT	AL 30TH INF, CO K
ADAIR, EPHRIAM MARTIN	CAPT	OK 2ND CHEROKEE MTD RIFLES, CO D, K
ADAM, HORTON B.	CAPT	GA 1ST INF, CO D
ADAMS, J. M.	2LT	VA 34TH BN CAV (WITCHER'S NIGH HAWKS), CO A
ADAMS, JAMES THEOPHILUS	LT COL	NC 26TH INF, CO D
ADAMS, JAMES WYATT	CAPT	AR 25TH INF, CO B
ADAMS, JAMES	2LT	VA 34TH BN CAV (WITCHER'S NIGHTHAWKS), CO E
ADAMS, JOHN Q. JR	CAPT	NC 39TH MILITIA (WAKE COUNTY)
ADAMS, JOHN W.	1LT	GA 44TH INF, CO A
ADAMS, NON QUINCY	2LT	MS 27TH INF, CO A
ADAMS, THOMAS JEFFERSON	CAPT	MS JEFF DAVIS LEGION CAV, CO A
ADAMS, WILLIAM CARROLL	CAPT	MO 3RD INF, CO G
ADAMS, WILLIAM TOWNSEND	2LT	SC HARTS BTRY (HAMPTON'S LEGION)
ADDISON, ARMISTEAD LEWIS	CAPT	CSA - AQM
ADDISON, CHARLES B., MD.	ASST SURG	SC 2ND ARTY, CO D
ADDISON, JOEL JACKSON	SHERIFF	FL MANATEE COUNTY
ADERHOLD, JACOB WILSON	LT COL	CSA 1ST INF, CO A
ADKERSON, JOHN H.	1LT	TN 45TH INF, CO I
ADKINS, STANLEY A.	2LT	VA 34TH BN CAV (WITCHER'S NIGHTHAWKS), CO A
ADKINS, WILSON	2LT	NC 29TH INF, CO G
ADKISON, JOHN E.	CAPT	AL 4TH RESERVES, CO I
AGENT, GEORGE WASHINGTON	1LT	MS 1ST INF, CO C
AGNEW, ANDREW J.	1LT	TX 28TH CAV, CO F
AGURS, JOHN L.	1LT	SC 6TH INF, AFS - AQM
AIKEN, D. WYATT	COL	SC 7TH INF, F&S
AIKEN, HUGH KERR	COL	SC 6TH CAV, F&S
AIREY, JOHN DORSEY, MD.	ASST SURG	AL 20TH INF
AKERS, AMOS	2LT	VA 54TH INF, CO F
ALBERT, HENRY ST GEORGE	COL	VA 146TH INF, 7TH BDE MILITIA, F&G
ALBRIGHT, HENRY CLAY	CAPT	NC 26TH INF, CO G
ALBRIGHT, JOSEPH HENRY LUMPKIN	2LT	CSA 1ST INF
ALCORN, JAMES LUSK	BRIG GEN	MS STATE MILITIA
ALDIS, HORACE	2LT	TX 13TH INF, CO C
ALDREDGE, JOEL H.	2LT	TX 17TH CAV, CO I
ALEXANDER, CLAUDIUS SIMONTON	CAPT	NC 4TH INF, CO C
ALEXANDER, EDWARD PORTER	BRIG GEN	CSA, LONGSTREET'S CORPS - CHIEF OF ARTY
ALEXANDER, ISAAC WESTLEY	BVT 2LT	GA 11TH CAV, CO A
ALEXANDER, JOHN CAIN	1LT	TN 35TH INF, CO E

ALEXANDER, MILTON ELBERT	CAPT	TN 53RD INF, CO K
ALEXANDER, THOMAS R.	1LT	VA 40TH INF, CO C
ALFORD, BRITTAIN WASHINGTON	JR 2LT	GA 27TH INF BN (NON-CONSCRIPTS), CO E
ALFORD, PIERCE LAFAYETTE	1LT	AL 47TH INF, CO C
ALLEN, AUSTIN	2LT	LA 3RD CAV, CO K
ALLEN, CORNELIUS TACITUS	CAPT	VA LUNENBURG REBEL ARTY & VA 20TH INF, CO B
ALLEN, EDWIN	CAPT	TN 26TH INF, CO C
ALLEN, GEORGE WASHINGTON	ENSIGN	AL 14TH INF (JACKSON'S AVENGERS), CO A
ALLEN, HENRY WATKINS	GOV	LA GOVERNOR 1864-1865
ALLEN, JOHN BRYAN	1LT	AL 29TH INF, CO I
ALLEN, JOHN M.	1LT	KY 13TH CAV, CO F
ALLEN, JOHN PRICE	CAPT	GA 55TH INF, CO H
ALLEN, LARKIN J.	CAPT	NC 38TH MILITIA (WAKE COUNTY)
ALLEN, LEWIS CLAYTON	CAPT	GA 65TH INF, CO B
ALLEN, RUFUS F.	1LT	NC 38TH INF, CO C
ALLEN, SAMUEL WARNER	1LT	TX 2ND INF, CO B
ALLEN, WILLIAM CARNEY	CAPT	TN 50TH INF, CO A
ALLEN, WILLIAM WIRT	BRIG GEN	AOT WHEELER'S CAV CORPS
ALLEY, SAMUEL JAMES	BVT 2LT	TN 11TH INF, CO F
ALLISON, JOHN	2LT	GA 39TH INF, CO D
ALLISON, ROBERT TURNER	DELEGATE	SC SIGNER SECESSION ORDINANCE, DELEGATE YORK COUNTY
ALLISON, WILLIAM BARRY	LT COL	SC 18TH INF, CO H
ALLISON, WILLIAM M.	LT COL	NC 78TH MILITIA (IREDELL COUNTY)
ALLRED, CHARLES	1LT	TN 25TH INF, CO H
ALLTOP, LEWIS	1LT	VA 19TH CAV, CO K
ALLUISI, JULIAN	1LT	VA 2ND STATE RESERVES, CO K
ALMAND, GRAVES BENNETT	CAPT	GA 35TH INF, CO B
ALMAND, JOHN	2LT	GA 42ND INF, CO E
ALSTON, MICAJAH THOMAS JOSEPH	CAPT	LA RESERVE CORPS, CO K
ALSTON, PHILIP S.	MAJ	MS 4TH CAV MILITIA
ALSTON, ROBERT WILLIAMS	MAJ	NC 12TH INF, CO K
ALSUP, JOSEPH F.	MD	ASST SURG/CAPT TN 18TH INF, CO I
ALTIZER, JOHN	2LT	VA 34TH BN CAV (WITCHER'S NIGHTHAWKS), CO E
ANCRUM, JOHN L., MD	ASST SURG	CSA PACS
ANDERSON, ALEXANDER C.	CAPT	SC 1ST MTD MILITIA
ANDERSON, ALFRED	1LT	VA 38TH INF, CO C (PITTSYLVANIA)
ANDERSON, ANDREW BROADDUS	1LT	VA 53RD INF, CO F
ANDERSON, BENJAMIN	CAPT	AL 38TH INF, CO D
ANDERSON, JAMES PATTON	MAJ GEN	AOT BDE CMDR
ANDERSON, JOHN C.	1LT	SC 13TH INF, F&S
ANDERSON, JOSEPH REID	BRIG GEN	ANV
ANDERSON, P. E.	1LT	AR MTD VOLS, BAKER'S CO
ANDERSON, PETER	2LT	TX 2ND INF (WAUL'S LEGION), CO E
ANDERSON, PIERCE BUTLER	CAPT	VA L ARTY, HARDWICKE'S CO
ANDERSON, RICHARD HERON	LT GEN	ANV IST & IV CORPS
ANDERSON, THOMAS MELVILLE	2LT	FL 2ND INF, CO L
ANDERSON, WILLIAM M.	1LT	TN 28TH CAV, CO A
ANDERSON, WILLIAM THOMAS	1LT	NC 39TH INF, CO B
ANDERSON, WILLIAM W., MD	SURG/MAJ	CSA - MEDICAL INSPECTOR OF HOSPITALS
ANDREWS, ALEXANDER BOYD	CAPT	NC 1ST CAV, CO B, E
ANDREWS, DAVID C.	2LT	GA 55TH INF, CO G

ANDREWS, GEORGE W.	CAPT	NC 50TH INF, CO G
ANDREWS, ROBERT N.	1LT	VA 42ND INF, CO D
ANDREWS, WINSTON	2LT	AL 39TH INF, CO C
ANGELO, FRANCIS MARION	LT	VA MOSBY'S CAV, CO C
ANTHONY, DANIEL	1LT	SC 5TH INF, CO I
ANTHONY, JOHN THOMAS	2LT	AL 26TH INF, CO H
ANTHONY, WHITMEL HILL II	CAPT	NC 1ST CAV, CO B
APPLEWHITE, JOHN	1LT	MS 38TH CAV, CO I
APPLING, SAMUEL BURWELL	1LT	AL 8TH CAV (HATCH'S), CO A
ARBUCKLE, JOHN DAVIS	2LT	VA 14TH CAV, CO K
ARCHER, FLETCHER H.	LT COL	VA 3RD BN RESERVES, F&S
ARCHER, FRANCIS M.	1LT	AL MORELAND'S CAV, CO I
ARCHER, JAMES J.	BRIG GEN	CSA - ANV, 3RD CORPS, HETH'S DIV, 3RD BDE
ARCHER, JOSEPH	1LT	AL 41ST INF, CO C
ARLEDGE, CLEMENT	CAPT	TN 1ST INF, CO F
ARMESY, THOMAS G.	MAJ	VA 17TH CAV, CO B
ARMISTEAD, LEWIS ADDISON	BRIG GEN	ANV GEN PICKETT'S DIV
ARMISTEAD, THOMAS S.	1LT	FL 8TH INF, CO E
ARMSTRONG, ANDREW JACKSON	1LT	AL 46TH INF, CO I
ARMSTRONG, KAIDES A.	1LT	MS 10TH CAV,CO C
ARMSTRONG, RICHARD FIELDER	1LT	CSN
ARMSTRONG, ROBERT A J	1LT	AL 28TH INF, CO K
ARNOLD, AMERICA JOHN	CAPT	TN 44TH INF, CO F
ARNOLD, ARTHUR J.	1LT	VA 5TH INF, CO J
ARNOLD, GEORGE W.	CAPT	AL 50TH INF, CO D
ARNOLD, HENRY S.	1LT	MS 16TH INF, CO B
ARNOLD, JOHN A.	2LT	TN 8TH CAV, CO D
ARNOLD, JOHN FREDRICK	MAJ	CSA QM
ARNOLD, JOHN Q.	CAPT	TN 29TH INF, CO F
ARRINGTON, GEORGE WASHINGTON	2LT	GA 16TH INF, CO K
ARRINGTON, GEORGE WASHINGTON	2LT	NC 32ND INF, CO H
ARRINGTON, JOHN DOUGLAS	2LT	NC 32ND INF, CO H
ARRINGTON, NICHOLAS WILLIAMS	LT COL	NC 32ND MILITIA (NASH COUNTY), F&S
ARTHURS, CALVIN WINKFIELD	2LT	NC 79TH INF (IREDELL COUNTY), CO I
ASBURY, RUFUS REID	CAPT	GA 52ND INF, CO C
ASBURY, WILLIAM B.	CAPT	VA 34TH BN CAV (WITCHER'S NIGHTHAWKS), CO E
ASH, JOHN H.	SR 2LT	GA 5TH CAV, CO A
ASHBY, EDWARD L.	2LT	TX 10TH INF, CO H
ASHBY, HENRY MARSHALL	COL	TN 2ND CAV, CO D
ASHBY, TURNER	BRIG GEN	VA 7TH CAV
ASHCRAFT, JOHN BENJAMIN	LT COL	NC 37TH INF, CO D
ASHCRAFT, WILLIAM LEROY	JR 2LT	AR 26TH INF, CO D
ASHE, SAMUEL A'COURT	CAPT	CSA - AAG
ASHLEY, GEORGE	LT	AR 2ND MTD RIFLES, CO F
ASHLEY, GEORGE	2LT	TN 44TH CONSOLIDATED INF, CO D
ASHMORE, WILLIAM W.	CAPT	AR GUNTER'S BN CAV, CO D
ATHEY, WILLIAM W.	1LT	VA 17TH INF, CO C
ATKINSON, ALEXANDER SMITH	CAPT	GA 26TH INF, CO B
ATKINSON, ANDREW A.	LT	MO POINDEXTER'S CAV, CO A
ATKINSON, WILLIAM HARRISON	3LT	MS 1ST INF, CO E
ATWOOD, JOSEPH HARVEY	JP	AL JEFFERSON COUNTY
AULT, JOSEPH N.	2LT	MS 16TH, CO I

AUSTIN, GALITEN	1LT	VA 8TH CAV, CO D
AUSTIN, ELIJAH COLEMAN	2LT	NC 28TH INF, CO C
AUSTIN, ELIJAH	3LT	AR SPAVINE'S RIFLES (MILITIA)
AUSTIN, JOHN JAMES T	1LT	TN 22ND CAV, CO F
AUSTIN, JOSIAH	1LT	NC 4TH SENIOR RESERVES, CO I
AUSTIN, MILTON STANHOPE	CAPT	NC 52ND INF, CO E
AUSTIN, NATHANIEL III	2LT	SC 14TH INF, CO E
AUSTIN, RICHMOND PEARSON	CAPT	MS 8TH INF (PICKNEY GUARDS), CO B,I
AUSTIN, SAMUEL HUNTER, MD	ASST SURG/1LT	VA 22ND INF, CO B
AUSTIN, WILLIAM COLLINS	BVT 2LT	VA 18TH INF, CO E
AUSTIN, WILLIAM M.	2LT	NC 58TH INF, CO C
AUTREY, JAMES LINDSAY	CAPT	NC 25TH MILITIA (SAMPSON COUNTY)
AUTREY, THOMAS ANDREW	2LT	GA 22ND INF
AVEGNO, JEAN BERNARD	CAPT	LA 13TH INF, CO D
AVERY, ISAAC ERWIN	COL	NC 6TH INF, CO E
AWALT, WILLIAM J.	CAPT	TN 1ST INF (TURNEY'S), CO D
AYCOCK, RICHARD JACKSON	1LT	AL 19TH INF, CO F
AYER, LEWIS MALONE JR.	REPRESENTATIVE	SC REPRESENTATIVE TO CONFEDERATE CONGRESS
AYLETT, WILLIAM ROANE	COL	VA 53RD INF, CO D
AYMETT, HANCE HAMILTON	MAJ	TN 53RD INF, CO C
AYRES, ELI JAMES	2LT	MS 30TH INF, CO D (DIXIE HERONS)
AYRES, GEORGE WASHINGTON	CAPT	AL 20TH INF, CO C
BACHMAN, JONATHAN WAVERLY	CAPT	TN 60TH INF, CO G
BADHAM, WILLIAM JR.	CAPT	NC 3RD ARTY, CO B
BAGBY, ARTHUR PENDLETON	COL	CSA PACS
BAGBY, JOHN ROBERT	MAJ	VA 34TH INF, CO K
BAGBY, JOHN WARD	CAPT	MO 3RD INF, CO H
BAGLEY, ALVIN	1LT	NC 66TH INF, CO K
BAHNSON, CHARLES FREDERICK	AQM	NC 2ND INF, CO G
BAILES, WILLIAM HENRY	1LT	AL 4TH CAV (RUSSELL'S), CO C
BAILEY, ABIJAH P.	CAPT	LA 18TH INF, CO F
BAILEY, ANGUS WALLACE, MD	SURG	SC 1ST PALMETTO SHARPSHOOTERS, F&S
BAILEY, AUGUSTUS F.	1LT	GA 9TH BN INF, CO D
BAILEY, GADI S.	1LT	SC 3RD STATE TROOPS, CO C
BAILEY, GRIFFIN	2LT	GA 16TH INF (COBB'S LEGION), CO C
BAILEY, ISAAC H.	CAPT	NC 58TH INF, CO B
BAILEY, JAMES JACKSON	CAPT	AL 16TH INF, F&S
BAILEY, JOSEPH M.	1LT	AR 16TH INF, CO D
BAILEY, ROBERT AUGUSTUS	MAJ	VA 22ND INF, CO K
BAILEY, WILSON	1LT	NC 47TH INF, CO A
BAIRD, DAVID FRANKLIN	2LT	NC 58TH INF, CO D
BAKER, ALPHEUS ESTES	1LT	AL 4TH INF (CONEUCH GUARDS), CO K
BAKER, DICKSON LELAND	1LT	GA 24TH INF, CO B
BAKER, ELI A.	1LT	AL 47TH INF, CO B
BAKER, HENRY HYER	CAPT	FL 1ST INF, CO E
BAKER, JANADIUS H.	CAPT	NC 24TH INF, CO K (POPLAR SPRING GRAYS)
BAKER, JOSEPH T.	BVT 2LT	TX 19TH INF, CO E
BAKER, LAURENCE SIMMONS	BRIG GEN	NC COMMISSARY GENERAL
BAKER, THOMAS HUDSON	2LT	GA 18TH INF, CO K
BALCH, ROBERT M.	MAJ	TN 3RD CAV (FORREST'S), CO C
BALDRIDGE, WILLIAM THOMAS	2LT	TN 31ST INF, CO A
BALDWIN, BENJAMIN J., REV	CHAPLAIN/CAPT	GA 31ST INF, F&S

BALDWIN, CYRUS BRISCOE	1LT	MS 31ST INF, CO C
BALDWIN, JACOB	CAPT	VA 34TH BN CAV (WITCHER'S NIGHTHAWKS), CO A
BALDWIN, MARION AUGUSTUS	ATTY GEN	AL 1847-1865
BALDWIN, THOMAS ROPER	1LT	NC 52ND INF, CO E
BALDWIN, WILLIAM GASTON	CAPT	NC 20TH INF, CO K
BALL, DABNEY	CHAPLAIN	VA 5TH CAV, F&S
BALL, MOTTROM DULANEY	LT COL	VA 11TH CAV, CO I
BALLARD, FRANCIS MARION	2LT	TX BORDER'S CAV (ANDERSON'S), CO I
BALLARD, JOHN CAMPBELL	CAPT	VA 166TH MILITIA
BANE, JOHN P.	COL	TX 4TH INF , CO D
BANKHEAD, ARCHER CHRISTIAN	CAPT	MO 2ND INF, CO B
BANKHEAD, JOHN HOLLIS	1LT	AL 16TH INF, CO K
BANKS C. B.	CAPT	MS 39TH INF, CO F
BANKS, GEORGE T.	1LT	MS 9TH CAV, CO K
BANKSTON, THOMAS JEFFERSON	1LT	MS 16TH INF, CO F
BARBEE, JAMES GASTON, MD	ASST SURG	TX FRONTIER CAV REGT (McCORD'S), F&S
BARBEE, JAMES MONROE SR	2LT	VA 4TH CAV, CO A
BARBEE, WILLIAM A.	1LT	NC 6TH SENIOR RESERVES, CO E
BARBER, GREENSBY W.	1LT	GA 9TH INF, CO H
BARBER, WILLIAM MORGAN	COL	NC 37TH INF, CO F
BARBIN, LUDGER	2LT	LA 8TH CAV, CO B
BARBOUR, THOMAS M.	MAJ	AL 43RD INF, CO D
BARDWELL, EZEKIEL	1LT	MS 8TH CAV, CO I
BAREFOOT, THOMAS DUNCAN	CAPT	MS 2ND CAV, CO E
BARKER, JAMES HAMILTON	1LT	SC 1ST INF, CO C
BARKER, THOMAS MERIWHETHER	1LT	KY 1ST CAV, CO H
BARKLEY, WILLIAM ANDREW	2LT	MS 7TH CAV, CO F
BARKSDALE, COLLYAR DOUGLAS	CAPT	SC 1ST INF, CO L
BARKSDALE, HENRY P.	1LT	TN 9TH INF, CO E
BARKSDALE, WILLIAM	BRIG GEN	MS 13TH INF
BARNARD, PATTON ABNER	1LT	AL 48TH INF, CO D
BARNER, GEORGE WASHINGTON	2LT	MS 1ST INF, CO C
BARNES, FRANK P.	2LT	TX WALLER'S CAV, CO B
BARNES, HENRY M.	CAPT	NC 10TH BN H ARTY, CO B
BARNES, NATHAN B.	CAPT	MS STUBBS BN CAV, CO C
BARNETT, JOEL	1LT	LA 3RD CAV (WINGFIELD'S), CO F
BARNETT, JOHN HENRY	2LT	MS 40TH INF, CO B
BARNETT, JOHN	1LT	KY 4TH MTD INF, CO F
BARNETT, WILLIAM HUMPHREY	2LT	AL 6TH CAV, CO H, F
BARR, JAMES JR.	COL	MS 10TH INF, CO A
BARRETT, ANDREW J.	1LT	VA 22ND INF, CO I
BARRETT, BENJAMIN FRANKLIN	1LT	TN 18TH INF, CO D
BARRETT, JAMES HURT	2LT	VA 37TH INF, CO I
BARRETT, ROBERT LEIGHTON, MD	ASST SURG	CSA VA MANASSAS HOSPITAL
BARRETT, THOMAS G.	1LT	GA 5TH INF, CO C
BARRETT, THOMAS G.	2LT	VA 34TH BN CAV (WITCHER'S NIGHTHAWKS), CO I
BARRINGER, RUFUS CLAY	BRIG GEN	NC 1ST CAV
BARRON, HARRISON CABINESS	1LT	GA 45TH INF, CO F
BARRON, SAMUEL III	FLAG OFFICER	CONFEDERATE STATES NAVAL FORCES IN EUROPE
BARROW, BENJAMIN LEWIS	1LT	VA 20TH INF, CO I
BARROWS, DAVID NYE	DEPUTY TREASURER	CSA
BARTLETT, FRANK A.	MAJ	LA MILITIA - CRESCENT BLUES (BEAUREGARD'S)

BARTON, J H. M.	1LT	GA 7TH INF, CO B
BARTON, JAMES MADISON	LT COL	TX 10TH CAV, F&S
BARTON, ROBERT T.	ASST SUPT	CSA - NITRE & MINING BUREAU, WAR DEPT
BASHAM, OLIVER	LT COL	AR 7TH INF, F&S
BASINGER, WILLIAM STARR	MAJ	GA 18TH INF, CO A
BASS, JAMES ALBERT	CAPT	MS 38TH CAV, CO E
BASS, JAMES EDWIN	CAPT	SC 8TH INF, CO F
BASS, JAMES ORIN	CAPT	TN 7TH INF, CO I
BASYE, NATHAN JOHN	2LT	VA 7TH CAV, CO K
BATE, WILLIAM BRIMAGE	COL	TN 2ND INF (ROBINSON'S)
BATEMAN, GEORGE WASHINGTON	2LT	NC 32ND INF, CO A
BATEMAN, MANNAH WHEATON	MAJ	LA 26TH INF, CO B
BATES, ALEXANDER RALEIGH	2LT	GA 12TH CAV (WRIGHT'S), CO C
BATES, GEORGE WASHINGTON	1LT	MO 4TH INF, CO K
BATES, JEFFERSON	2LT	AR 4TH INF, CO C
BATES, JOSEPH	COL	TX 13TH VOLS, F&S
BATES, MABRY NATHANIEL	JR 2LT	LA 28TH REG, CO A
BATES, MARTIN VAN BUREN	1LT	VA FRENCH'S BN INF
BATES, ROBERT	CAPT	MS 2ND INF, CO E
BATTLE, FRED	1LT	TN 9TH INF, CO E
BATTLE, JOEL ALLEN, SR.	COL	TN 20TH INF, F&S
BATTS, WILLIAM WOODARD ESQ	COL	NC 33RD MILITIA (WILSON COUNTY)
BAUGH, WILLIAM FIELDING	1LT	VA 61ST INF, CO G
BAXTER, OSCAR FITZ-ALAN, JR, MD	ASST SURG/MAJ	VA 5TH CAV, F&S
BAXTER, PETER ZIMMERMAN	CAPT	NC 49TH INF, CO K
BAXTER, STEPHEN H., JR	2LT	GA 16TH MILITIA DIST (EMAUEL COUNTY)
BAXTER, WILLIAM B.	CAPT	TN 41ST INF, CO K
BAYA, WILLIAM	LT COL	FL 8TH INF, CO D
BAYLOR, WARNER LEWIS, MD	SURG	VA 32ND INF, F&S
BAYNE, THOMAS LEVINGSTON	MAJ	CSA - CHIEF OF BUREAU OF FOREIGN SUPPLIES
BAYS, GEORGE W.	2LT	VA 34TH BN CAV (WITCHER'S NIGHTHAWKS), CO H
BEALE, NOBLE NEWMAN	1LT	GA 2ND STATE TROOPS
BEALL, JAMES J.	CAPT	GA 19TH INF, CO C
BEALL, JOHN YATES	ACTING MASTER	CSN PRIVATEER
BEALL, THADDEUS SOLEN	MAJ	CSA - 8TH CAV (WADE'S)
BEALL, WILLIAM NELSON RECTOR	BRIG GEN	ATM - MG EARL VAN DORN
BEALL, WILLIAM ORLANDO	CAPT	GA 3RD INF, CO F
BEALS, JOSEPH A.	CAPT	GA 22ND H ARTY, CO C
BEAM, GEORGE WASHINGTON	2LT	NC 49TH INF, CO K
BEAM, OLIVER PERRY	2LT	NC 38TH INF, CO I
BEAN, WILLIAM BENNETT	1LT	MD 2ND BALTIMORE L ARTY
BEARD, DANIEL M.	1LT	AR 4TH INF, CO I
BEARD, JOHN	CAPT	NC 57TH INF, CO C
BEARD, WILLIAM KELLY	LT COL	FL 1ST INF, F&S
BEARD, WILLIAM WILEY	CAPT	LA 17TH INF, CO G
BEARDEN, MARCUS JOSEPH	CAPT	NC 58TH INF, F&S - QM
BEARDEN, NAPOLEAN MONROE	CAPT	TN 8TH INF, CO E
BEASLEY, ABRAHAM JR.	ENSIGN	GA 12TH CAV
BEASLEY, ISAIAH	1LT	GA 7TH CAV, CO H
BEASLEY, JAMES HENRY	2LT	TN 51ST INF, CO B
BEASLEY, JOSEPH T.	2LT	MS 6TH INF, CO F
BEASLEY, WILLIAM R.	2LT	NC 44TH INF, CO A

BEATON, GEORGE E.	CAPT	VA 41ST INF, CO H
BEATTIE, FOUNTAIN	1LT	VA 43RD CAV (MOSBY'S RAIDERS), CO E
BEATTY, THOMAS SHOOK	CAPT	TN 19TH CAV (BIFFLE'S), CO H
BEATY, JOHN PEEL	CAPT	GA 46TH INF, CO F
BEATY, WILLIAM ALEXANDER	2LT	AL 48TH INF, CO K
BEAUREGARD, PIERRE GUSTAFE TOUTANT	GEN	DEPT OF THE WEST
BEAVERS, JOHN W.	2LT	VA 34TH BN CAV (WITCHER'S NIGHTHAWKS), CO C
BEAZLEY W. HERBERT	CAPT	TX MORGAN'S CAV, CO K
BECK, SAMUEL M.	CAPT	GA 52ND INF, CO F
BECKHAM, JAMES MINOR	2LT	CSA 1ST ENGINEERS, CO D
BECKHAM, ROBERT FRANKLIN	COL	CSA AOT ARTY
BECKHAM, WILLIAM M.	1LT	SC 24TH INF, CO G
BEDENBAUGH, JACOB HAZELIUS	2LT	GA 7TH INF, CO A
BEDINGER, HENRY CLAY, JR.	1LT	MO 10TH CAV, CO E
BEESON, WILLIAM BAKER	CAPT	AL 49TH INF, CO G
BEGGS, CHARLES	CAPT	FL 11TH INF, CO E
BELCHER, EDWARD LITTLETON	AQM	TN 4TH INF, CO A
BELIN, JACOB HARRELL	2LT	SC 10TH INF, CO F
BELL, AUGUSTUS J.	1LT	GA 31ST INF (CROWDERS), CO F
BELL, DEMOSTHENES	CAPT	NC 4TH CAV, CO G
BELL, ERASMUS LEE	LT	VA 10TH INF, CO K
BELL, FRANCIS (FRANK) TETRALAFAYETTE	2LT	TX 8TH CAV, CO L
BELL, HOLLAND MIDDLETON	CAPT	AL 41ST INF, CO H
BELL, JAMES EDWARD	LT	AL 41ST INF, CO H
BELL, JAMES EWELL	2LT	VA 6TH INF, CO B
BELL, JAMES MADISON	LT COL	CSA 2ND CHEROKEE MTD VOLS, CO F&S
BELL, JOHN HENRY	1LT	AR HARDY'S INF, CO I
BELL, JOHN T.	CAPT	AL 14TH INF (JACKSON'S AVENGERS), CO I
BELL THOMAS R.	2LT	GA 39TH MIL DISTRICT, CHEROKEE COUNTY, 10TH CO
BELL, TYREE HARRIS	BRIG GEN	TN CAV, BELL'S BDE - (FORREST'S)
BELSCHES, BENJAMIN W.	MAJ	VA 13TH CAV, F&S
BELVIN, JAMES PETER	CAPT	GA 11TH INF (WALTON'S), CO K
BENAVIDES, SANTOS	COL	TX BENAVIDES' CAV
BENHAM, JOHN	1LT	MO CLARDY'S BN CAV, CO B
BENJAMIN, JUDAH PHILIP	SECRETARY	CSA - WAR & STATE
BENNETT, ALVA THURMAN	CAPT	GA 34TH INF, CO E
BENNETT, DEWITT CLINTON	1LT	TN 23RD INF, CO C
BENNETT, JOSHUA S.	2LT	MS 35TH INF, CO G
BENNETT, RICHARD	CAPT	GA 54TH INF, CO K
BENTLEY, ANDREW J.	1LT	GA 35TH INF, CO A
BENTLEY, DAVID E.	2LT	AL 16TH INF, CO I
BENTLEY, THOMAS JEFFERSON	SR 2LT	AR 12TH INF, CO K
BENTLEY, WILLIAM W.	MAJ	VA 24TH INF, CO E
BENTON, PETER GOODWIN	1LT	MO 11TH INF, CO C
BERKELEY, F. CARTER	1LT	VA McCLANAHAN'S CO HORSE ARTY
BERRIER, WILLIAM A.	1LT	NC 65TH MILITIA (DAVIDSON COUNTY)
BERRY, ANDREW JACKSON	1LT	TX MORGAN'S CAV, CO A
BERRY, JAMES MADISON	CAPT	VA 25TH INF, CO G
BERRYHILL, WILLIAM H.	1LT	MS 43RD INF, CO D
BERRYMAN, NEWTON MONROE	2LT	TX 1ST INF, CO I
BERRYMAN, RICHARD C.	MAJ	MO 12TH INF, F&S
BESHOAR, MICHAEL, MD	SURG/MAJ	AR 7TH INF, F&S

BETHUNE, WILLIAM CALVIN	LT COL	AL 57TH INF, CO D
BEVILL, JAMES THOMPSON	CAPT	GA 50TH INF, CO D
BICKERSTAFF, WILLIAM JEFFERSON	CAPT	AL 34TH INF, CO I
BICKLEY, E. L.	2LT	VA 34TH BN CAV (WITCHER'S NIGHTHAWKS), CO H
BICKLEY, JOHN H.	CAPT	VA 34TH BN CAV (WITCHER'S NIGHTHAWKS), CO H
BILBREY, JOSIAH S H	CAPT	TN 25TH INF, CO B
BILLINGTON, JAMES M.	CAPT	TN 24TH INF, CO G
BILLS, JOHN DANIEL	2LT	MS 32ND INF, CO B
BILLS, ROBERT D.	SR 2LT	TX 19TH CAV, CO I (BURFORD'S)
BILLUPS, HENRY CARLTON	CAPT	GA 3RD INF, CO K
BILLUPS, JOHN EDEN	2LT	CSN
BIRD, PICKENS BUTLER	MAJ	FL 9TH INF
BISHOP, CARTER R.	CADET	VMI
BISHOP, JOHN A.	1LT	VA 59TH INF, CO H
BISHOP, JOHN EDWARD	2LT	TX 7TH CAV, CO I
BISHOP, WILLIAM PRESTON	CAPT	SC HOLCOMBE'S LEGION INF, CO I
BISSELL, JOHN BENNETT	2LT	SC 17TH MILITIA INF (PALMETTO GUARDS), BUIST'S CO
BIVENS, JAMES MONROE	MAJ	GA 19TH INF BN (STATE GUARDS, CO C
BIVINGS, CLEVELAND	1LT	SC JUNIOR RESERVES, SPARTANBURG RANGERS CAV CO
BIZZELL, WOOTEN	LT	NC 27TH INF, CO C
BLACK, DUNCAN A.	2LT	NC 38TH INF, CO K
BLACK, EPHRAIM	CAPT	NC 87TH MILITIA, CO 11 (GASTON COUNTY)
BLACK, JOHN LOGAN	COL	SC 1ST CAV, F&S
BLACK, JOHN,	JR 2LT	AR 34TH INF, CO F
BLACK, WILLIAM MARTIN	CAPT	NC 49TH INF, CO D
BLACKBURN, AMBROSE	1LT	AR GORDON'S CAV, CO F
BLACKBURN, ANDREW JACKSON	2LT	TX MTD EXEMPTS CO (WASHINGTON COUNTY)
BLACKERBY, JAMES BOYD	LT	AR 2ND BN CAV (BARNETT'S), CO B
BLACKMAN, SIR WILLIAM	2LT	NC 117TH MILITIA (JOHNSTON COUNTY)
BLACKSTOCK, JAMES ERWIN	2LT	GA 56TH INF, CO E
BLACKSTONE, ARGILE	1LT	GA INF (RICHMOND FACTORY GUARDS), BARNEY'S CO
BLACKWELDER, MOSES	2LT	FL 1ST CAV, CO D
BLACKWELL, THOMAS GEORGE	1LT	GA 32ND INF, CO A
BLACKWOOD, WILLIAM ROBERT	1LT	VA 45TH INF, CO F
BLAINE, THOMAS A.	1LT	MO 1ST CAV, CO D
BLAIR, COLUMBUS	BVT 2LT	GA INF, ALEXANDER'S CO
BLAIR, GEORGE WASHINGTON	2LT	MS 35TH INF, CO I
BLAIR, JAMES DESS	LT COL	LA 2ND CAV, CO B
BLAIR, JAMES O.	2LT	GA 41ST INF, CO G
BLAIR, LOVICK WILLIAM ROCHELLE	MAJ	SC 7TH INF, CO A
BLAKENEY, JAMES MADISON	1LT	AR 47TH CAV, CO K
BLAKEY, DAVID T.	COL	AL 1ST CAV, F&S
BLALOCK, ALFRED	1LT	NC 7TH SENIOR RESERVES
BLALOCK, JAMES MARION	CAPT	GA 1ST CAV, CO E
BLALOCK, JAMES SEWELL	2LT	FL 10TH INF, CO B
BLALOCK, WILLIAM A.	1LT	NC 50TH INF, CO A
BLANCHARD, ALBERT GALLATIN	BRIG GEN	LA 1ST INF
BLANCHARD, JEREMIAH	1LT	GA 10TH INF, CO F
BLAND, JOSEPH J.	1LT	NC 44TH INF, CO I
BLANKENSHIP, THOMAS C.	1LT	VA 34TH BN CAV (WITCHER'S NIGHTHAWKS), CO C
BLANTON, JASPER N.	CAPT	TN 17TH INF, CO A
BLEDSOE, FRANCIS MARION	CAPT	GA 11TH INF (WALTON'S), CO I

BLEVINS, HARRISON	1LT	AR 46TH CAV, CO B
BLEVINS, HAYWOOD	1LT	VA 45TH INF, CO C
BLEVINS, POINDEXTER	CAPT	NC 58TH INF, CO F
BLICK, WILLIAM ALEXANDER	2LT	VA 56TH INF, CO E
BLOUNT, JOHN THOMA, JR	2LT	GA 4TH INF, CO A
BLOUNT, NATHAN SNOW	MAJ	FL 7TH INF, CO E
BLOW, WILLIAM J. MD	SURG	NC 27TH INF
BOARD, FRANCIS H.	COL	VA 58TH INF, CO I
BOARD, GEORGE FRANK	1LT	VA 2ND RESERVES BN, CO F
BOATWRIGHT, BENJAMIN SESSION	2LT	GA 12TH L ARTY BN, CO E
BOATWRIGHT, JAMES	CAPT	SC 14TH INF, CO B
BOAZ, WILLIAM RUTHERFORD	1LT	KY 12TH CAV, CO C
BOGAN, GEORGE WASHINGTON	CAPT	GA 6TH CAV, CO C
BOGGS, AARON	1LT	SC 10TH CAV BN, CO B
BOGGS, JAMES M.	1LT	VA 9TH INF BN (HANSBROUGH'S), CO C
BOGGS, THOMAS HAMILTON	LT COL	SC 2ND RIFLES, F&S
BOGGS, WILLIAM R.	BRIG GEN	ATM, GEN. E KIRBY SMITH COS
BOHLMAN, WILLIAM F.	CAPT	VA 22ND, CO K
BOISSEAU, ROBERT H.	CAPT	VA 5TH BN INF (ARCHER'S), CO E
BOLAND, JAMES F.	2LT	GA 27TH INF, CO F
BOLES, JAMES D.	2LT	AL MEAD'S CAV, CO B
BOLT, THOMAS D.	CAPT	VA 45TH INF, CO I
BOLT, WILLIAM H C	CAPT	VA 45TH INF, CO I
BOLTON, JOHN, MD	ASST SURG	TN 9TH INF
BOND, CHARLES WRIGHT	CAPT	GA CAV (STATE GUARDS), BOND'S CO
BOND, JAMES	BVT 2LT	TN 7TH CAV (DUCKWORTH'S), CO D
BOND, JOSEPH BRYAN	2LT	CSA - ENGINEERS
BOND, LEWIS	CAPT	CSA, ORD OFFICER OF GEN WM H JACKSON
BONDURANT, ALBERT	CAPT	LA 3RD CAV (HARRISON'S), F&S
BONHAM, BETHEL JARRELL	CAPT	AL 2ND CAV, CO F
BONHAM, MILLEDGE LUKE	GOV	SC GOVERNOR 1862-1864
BONVILLAIN, ERNEST LEANDRE	1LT	LA 26TH INF, CO K
BOON, JOSEPH MARION	2LT	GA 1ST CAV, CO E & F
BOONE, JERRY B F	MAJ	CSA
BOONE, NATHAN	1LT	TN CAV JACKSON'S CO
BOONE, SQUIRE	COL	AR 15TH INF (NORTHWEST), F&S
BOONE, WILLIAM R.	2LT	TN 17TH INF, CO B
BOOTH, DAVID WINFIELD, MD	SURG	MS 21ST INF, F&S
BOOTH, DEWITT CLINTON	CAPT	VA 58TH INF, CO D
BOOTH, JOHN FLETCHER	CAPT	MS 2ND INF, CO E
BOOTH, THOMAS JEFFERSON	CAPT	MS 15TH INF, CO B
BOOTON, JOHN KAYLOR	CAPT	VA LIGHT ARTY, CHAPMAN'S CO (DIXIE ARTY)
BOOZER, HENRY SHEPPARD	CAPT	SC HOLCOMBE LEGION INF, CO H
BORDEN, JAMES COLE	CAPT	NC 1ST CAV, CO H
BORDEN, THOMAS JAMES	MAJ	MS 6TH INF, F&S
BORN, WILLIAM J.	SR 1LT	GA 9TH BN L ARTY, CO D
BOST, JACKSON LAFAYETTE	MAJ	NC 37TH INF, CO D
BOSTICK, THOMAS JAMES LANIER	2LT	NC 43RD INF, CO A
BOSWELL, JAMES K.	CAPT	CSA - ENGINEERS
BOSWELL, JOHN C.	1LT	GA 23RD INF, CO C
BOTTOMS, RILEY S.	2LT	AL 5TH CAV, CO K
BOUDINOT, ELIAS CORNELIUS	MAJ	CSA CHEROKEE 1ST MTD RIFLES, F&S

BOUDINOT, WILLIAM PENN	CAPT	CSA CHEROKEE 1ST MTD RIFLES, CO E
BOULDIN, HAMMOND	2LT	TX 8TH CAV (TERRY'S RANGERS), CO K
BOUNDS, JOSEPH A.	2LT	MS 19TH INF, CO F
BOURLAND, ROBERT H.	1LT	MS 24TH INF, CO F
BOURQUINE, THOMAS ELKINS	1LT	GA 47TH INF, CO I
BOUSHALL, JOSEPH DOZIER	1LT	NC 33RD INF, CO E
BOVENDER, JOHN V B	CAPT	NC 75TH MILITIA (YADKIN COUNTY)
BOWDEN, BENJAMIN C	2LT	NC 1ST BN H ARTY, CO B
BOWDEN, CONSTANTINE SEBASTIAN	2LT	TN 54TH INF, CO E
BOWDEN, DOCTOR JEFFERSON	1LT	TN 5TH INF, CO H
BOWDOIN, JOHN THOMAS	LT COL	GA 5TH INF MILITIA
BOWEN, CHARLES	CAPT	AR 23RD CAV, CO A
BOWEN, CHARLES	CAPT	AR 9TH INF, CO I
BOWEN, JOHN HALLUM, JR.	CAPT	SC HAMPTON LEGION INF, CO K
BOWEN, WALTER	CAPT	VA 7TH CAV, CO E
BOWEN, WILLIAM DRURY	1LT	AL 16TH INF, CO H
BOWEN, WILLIAM J.	CAPT	SC 6TH RESERVES, CO G
BOWERS, MICHAEL E.	1LT	VA 25TH INF, CO K
BOWLES, PETER TINSLEY	JR 2LT	VA 15TH INF, CO C
BOWLES, ROBERT LETCHER	2LT	KY 9TH INF, CO C
BOWLEY, CHARLES Y.	1LT	MS 3RD CAV, CO E
BOWLING, HENRY A.	CAPT	ANV - BG JOHN R CHAMBLISS - ADC
BOWLING, ROBERT LERAY	CAPT	AL 32ND INF, CO A
BOWMAN, ANDREW JACKSON	2LT	VA 29TH INF, CO D
BOWMAN, BENJAMIN LEE	CAPT	MO LIGHT ARTY (PARSON'S CO)
BOWMAN, HENRY FARRAR	CAPT	TN 5TH INF CO G
BOWMAN, JOHN A.	CAPT	MO 1ST INF, CO C
BOWMAN, JOHN PARKER	MAJ	MO 6TH INF, F&S
BOYCE, GEORGE	1LT	TN 19TH INF, CO E
BOYCE, KER	AQM	GA 12TH BN L ARTY, F&S
BOYD, CHARLES WESLEY	CAPT	SC 15TH INF, CO F
BOYD, ROBERT C.	CAPT	VA 34TH BN CAV (WITCHER'S NIGHTHAWKS), CO H
BOYD, SAMUEL	2LT	AR 45TH INF, CO C
BOYD, THEODORE BELLE	CAPT	CSA - ACS
BOYD, THOMAS JEFFERSON	1LT	VA 4TH INF, CO C
BOYD, WARREN	1LT	SC 2ND RIFLES, CO K
BOYD, WILLIAM JAMES	2LT	VA 1ST LIGHT ARTY BN, CO C
BOYETTE, LARRY B.	2LT	NC 2ND INF, CO B
BOYKIN, ALEXANDER HAMILTON	CAPT	SC 2ND CAV (BOYKIN'S RANGERS), CO A
BOYLAN, GEORGE WASHINGTON	1LT	LA 13TH INF, CO BDI
BOYLE, FRANCIS A.	ADJ	NC 32ND INF, CO AFG
BOYLSTON, S. CORDEN	ADJ	SC 1ST ARTY, BFD
BOYNTON, JAMES STODDARD	MAJ	GA 30TH INF, CO A
BOYNTON, WILLIAM W.	2LT	GA 2ND INF, CO K
BRABHAM, JOHN M.	CAPT	SC 2ND STATE TROOPS, CO E
BRACEY, THOMAS WRIGHT	1LT	SC 1ST INF, CO N
BRACKENRIDGE, JAMES MADISON	CAPT	TX 33RD CAV, CO K
BRADEN, WILLIAM WARREN	1LT	TN 11TH CAV, CO C
BRADFIELD, WILLIAM	AQM	TX 7TH INF
BRADFORD, JAMES WATT	1LT	AR 15TH INF (JOSEY'S), CO B
BRADFORD, NATHANIEL GUY	CAPT	NC 26TH INF, CO I
BRADHAM, DANIEL JUDSON	2LT	SC 23RD INF, CO I

BRADLEY, BENJAMIN F.	MAJ	KY 1ST MTD RIFLES BN
BRADLEY, LUCIUS DE YAMPERT	CAPT	TX WAUL'S LEGION, CO B
BRADSHAW, JOHN W.	2LT	MS 12TH CAV, CO K
BRAGG, BRAXTON T.	GEN	AOT AND COUNCIL TO PRESIDENT DAVIS
BRAGG, JUNIUS NEWPORT, MD	ASST SURG	AR 33RD INF, F&S
BRANCH, JOHN	1LT	FL 1ST INF RESERVES, CO E
BRANCH, LAWRENCE O'BRYAN	BRIG GEN	ANV - BRANCH'S BDE, HILL'S LIGHT DIV
BRANCH, MICHAEL	2LT	GA 54TH INF, CO B
BRAND, JAMES WALKER	2LT	VA 4TH INF, CO A
BRANDON, NATHAN	LT COL	TN 14TH INF
BRANDON, WILLIAM L.	BRIG GEN	MS 21ST INF (HURRICANE RIFLES)
BRANHAM, ISHAM HARRIS	CAPT	GA 57TH INF, CO E
BRANHAM J. W.	1LT	CSA CONFEDERATE TROOPS
BRANNAN, DAVID L.	2LT	MS 37TH INF, CO C
BRANNEN, WILLIAM ALEXANDER	CAPT	GA 12TH CAV (WRIGHT'S)
BRANSCOME, FRANKLIN	2LT	VA 54TH INF, CO G
BRANSON, THOMAS ALLEN	CAPT	NC 46TH INF, CO F
BRASHEARS, SAMUEL RAY	CAPT	KY 13TH CAV, CO H (BRASHEARS)
BRASINGTON, GEORGE CAUTHEN	2LT	SC 2ND INF (PALMETTO SHARPSHOOTERS), CO H
BRASWELL, ASA GORDON	BVT 2LT	GA 28TH INF, CO A
BRASWELL, ROBERT JOSEPH	1LT	VA H ARTY, CAPT COLEMAN'S CO
BRAUGHN, GEORGE HORACE	CAPT	LA CRESCENT INF, CO F
BREATHED, JAMES	MAJ	VA HORSE ARTY, SHANK'S CO
BREAZEALE, STEPHEN A.	2LT	SC 2ND RIFLES, CO L
BRECKENRIDGE, JAMES	CAPT	VA 2ND CAV, CO C
BRECKINRIDGE, CARY	LT COL	VA 2ND CAV, CO CFS
BRECKINRIDGE, JOHN CABELL	MAJ GEN	CSA - SECRETARY OF WAR
BRECKINRIDGE, PEACHY GILMER	MAJ	VA 28TH INF, CO K
BRELAND, OLIVER FRANKLIN	1LT	MS 5TH INF, CO E
BREVARD, THEODORE WASHINGTON, JR	COL	FL 11TH INF, F&S
BREWER, CHARLES, MD	SURG	CSA - TREATED GEN STUART AT HIS DEATH
BREWER, LEROY	2LT	AL 1ST MOBILE VOLS, CO A
BREWER, STEPHEN WILEY	CAPT	NC 26TH INF, CO E
BREWER, WILLIAM	2LT	NC 15TH INF, CO G
BREWTON, BENJAMIN	DELEGATE	GA SIGNER SECESSION ORDINANCE, DELEGATE TATTNALL COUNTY
BREWTON, MARTIN B.	2LT	GA 61ST INF, CO H
BRIAN, JAMES P.	2LT	KY 3RD MTD INF, CO A
BRICE, JAMES MICHAEL	2LT	SC 6TH INF, CO D, G
BRICE, ROBERT WADE	2LT	SC 6TH INF, CO H
BRICE, THOMAS WILLIAM	2LT	SC 6TH INF, CO D
BRIDEWELL, CHARLES AUGUSTINE	CAPT	AR 7TH INF, F&S AQM
BRIDGES, GOODRUM LUCAS	1LT	TN 32ND INF, CO F
BRIDGES, JAMES SIDNEY	CAPT	NC 89TH MILITIA, CO O (CATAWBA COUNTY)
BRIDGEWATER, JOHN CHAMBERS	MAJ	TN 35TH INF
BRIGHT, GEORGE W.	CAPT	TN 31ST INF, CO H
BRIGHT, ROBERT A.	CAPT	VA 53RD INF, CO B
BRIGHT, WILLIS OLLINS	CAPT	TN 8TH INF, CO E
BRINKLEY, ROBERT BEVERLY	CAPT	VA 41ST INF, CO I
BRISTOL, LAMBERT AUGUSTUS	CAPT	NC 3RD JUNIOR RESERVES, CO G
BRISTOL, ROBERT ALEXANDER	2LT	NC 39TH INF, CO E
BRITTON, DANIEL	1LT	TN 61ST MTD INF, CO A

BRITTON, EDWARD WHARTON MD.	SURG	TX 3RD INF (LUCKETT), F&S
BROADHURST, DAVID JON	CAPT	NC 20TH INF, CO E, K
BROADNAX, EDWARD TRAVIS	1LT	NC 5TH CAV, CO D
BROCK, JOHN P.	CAPT	VA 10TH CAV, CO H
BROCK, NOAH MONROE	2LT	VA 10TH CAV, CO B
BROCKMAN, HENRY	CAPT	MO 10TH INF, CO K
BROGDON, NOAH RICHARD	2LT	GA 42ND INF
BROOKE, JOHN MERCER	CMDR	CSN, CHIEF ORDNANCE & HYDROGRAPHY
BROOKS, ALBERT GREEN	2LT	GA 49TH INF, CO F
BROOKS, JAMES	1LT	TN 30TH INF, CO G
BROOKS, JOHN R.	2LT	VA 56TH INF, CO A (MECKLENBURG GUARDS)
BROOKS, LEWIS P.	1LT	GA 7TH INF, CO B
BROOKS, SAMUEL W.	1LT	VA 22ND CAV, CO H
BROOKS, WILLIAM PARAM	CHIEF ENGR	CSN CSS STONEWALL
BROWDER, EDWARD CABELL	CAPT	TX 18TH CAV (DARNELL'S REG), CO C
BROWN, ALEXANDER H.	COL	SC 1ST MILITIA (RESERVES)
BROWN, BENJAMIN FRANKLIN, MD.	SURG/MAJ	SC 2ND INF, CO L
BROWN, EPAMINONDAS	2LT	FL 2ND INF BN, CO C
BROWN, GEORGE BARTLETT	CAPT	TX 6TH CAV, CO C
BROWN, HAMILTON ALLEN	LT COL	NC 1ST INF, CO B
BROWN, HARRY W., MD	SURG	CSA
BROWN, JACKSON VAN BUREN	BVT 2LT	TN, 16TH INF, CO H
BROWN, JAMES MOREAU	COL	CSA - PURCHASING AGENT IN MEXICO
BROWN, JAMES T.	CAPT	CSA - AAG
BROWN, JAMES WILSON	CAPT	KY 8TH MTD INF, CO B
BROWN, JOHN JONES	CAPT	SC PALMETTO SHARPSHOOTERS, CO H
BROWN, JOSEPH E.	GOV	GA GOVERNOR 1861-1865
BROWN, NATHANIEL LANE	1LT	NC 47TH INF, CO C
BROWN, R. C.	CAPT	VA 34TH BN CAV (WITCHER'S NIGHTHAWKS), CO F
BROWN, RIDGELY	LT COL	MD 1ST CAV
BROWN, THOMAS BENJAMIN	CAPT	TN 26TH INF, CO I
BROWN, W. B.	2LT	MS 41ST INF, CO C
BROWN, WILLIAM ALEXANDER	1LT	MO 15TH CAV, CO L
BROWN, WILLIAM GAINER	2LT	GA 59TH INF, CO D
BROWN, WILLIAM H.	CAPT	GA 2ND SHARPSHOOTERS, CO B
BROWN, WILLIAM HENDERSON	2LT	TN 3RD CAV (FORREST'S), CO H
BROWN, WILLIAM	CAPT	GA 18TH INF, CO K
BROWNING, GEORGE W.	1LT	AR 8TH INF, CO H
BROWNLEE, JOHN M.	2LT	MS 35TH INF, CO K
BROWNLOW, WILLIAM W J	MAJ	TN 32ND INF, CO H
BROYLES, CHARLES EDWARD	MAJ	GA 36TH INF, F&S
BRUCE, ELI METCALFE	REPRESENTATIVE	KY CONFEDERATE CONGRESS
BRUCE, FREDERICK H.	2LT	VA 49TH INF, CO K
BRUCE, SAMUEL JOHNSON	CAPT	AL 49TH INF, CO C
BRUMFIELD, HENRY SIMMS	CAPT	MS 38TH INF, CO K
BRUMMETT, JOHN	2LT	KY 4TH KY MTD INF, CO B
BRUX, JAMES AUGUSTUS	JR 1LT	SC MANIGAULT'S ARTY BN, CO A
BRUYN, DEWITT	CAPT	GA 47TH INF, CO E
BRYAN, DANIEL O.	1LT	NC 2ND CAV, CO I
BRYAN, GUY MORRISON, SR	MAJ	ATM CAV; JUDGE MILITARY COURT; CONFIDENTIAL ADJ GEN
BRYAN, JOSEPH DAKOTA	2LT	GA 49TH INF, CO B

BRYAN, ROBINSON CRUSOE	CAPT	CSA
BRYANT, ALFRED BROWN	CAPT	SC INF HOLCOMBE LEGION, CO B
BRYANT, ELIJAH L.	1LT	GA 4TH RESERVES, CO B
BRYANT, JOHN ELBERT	2LT	GA 4TH MILITIA DIST, 1ST CO
BRYANT, JOHN W.	CAPT	NC 47TH INF, CO A
BRYANT, WILLIAM JACKSON	1LT	MS 21ST INF (HURRICANE RIFLES), CO F&S
BRYARS, RED BERRY	REPRESENTATIVE	AL STATE REPRESENTATIVE - BALDWIN COUNTY
BRYNE, DAVID CRAWFORD	2LT	AL 23RD INF, CO I
BRYSON, ANDREW WILBUR	CAPT	NC 39TH INF, CO K
BRYSON, WALTER M.	CAPT	NC 35TH INF, CO G
BUCHANAN, JOHN B.	CAPT	NC 18TH INF, CO F
BUCHANAN, P. C., JR	CAPT	VA 50TH INF, CO L
BUCK, HENRY L.	CAPT	SC 26TH INF, CO A
BUCKHOLTS, CHARLES B.	CAPT	TX 4TH CAV, CO E
BUCKNER, SIMON BOLIVAR	LT GEN	ATM GEN E KIRBY SMITH COS
BUDD, ABRAHAM VANWYCK, MD.	ASST SURG	NC 32ND INF, CO I
BUELL, JAMES	CAPT	AL 1ST CAV, CO B
BUFFKIN, JAMES THOMAS	2LT	SC 26TH INF, CO K
BUFORD, ABRAHAM II	BRIG GEN	AL 2ND DIV, FORREST'S CAV
BUIE, JAMES DUNCAN	ACTING CAPT	NC 2ND BN LOCAL DEFENSE TROOPS, CO G
BULL, WILLIAM IZARD, SR.	COL	CSA GEN BEAUREGARD'S - ADC
BULLITT, THOMAS WALKER	1LT	KY 2ND CAV (DUKE'S), CO C
BULLOCK, CHARLES WILLIAM	CAPT	TX 24TH CAV, CO G
BUNCH, JEREMIAH JACKSON	CAPT	SC CAV (HAMPTON'S LEGION), CO A
BUNTING, JAMES VINSON	1LT	NC 66TH INF, CO B
BURBRIDGE, JOHN Q.	COL	MO 4TH CAV, F&S
BURCHETT, ELISHA CLARK	CAPT	VA 50TH INF, CO B
BURCHFIELD, ANDREW JACKSON	CAPT	AL 26TH INF, CO G
BURFORD, ELISHA SPRUILLE	MAJ	CSA - AG DEPT
BURGESS, ELIAS M.	1LT	AL 13TH INF, CO K
BURGESS, JOSEPH C.	LT	SC 21ST INF, CO C
BURGWYN, HARRY K. JOHN	COL	TX STATE ADJ GEN
BURKETT, ELI V.	2LT	GA 32ND INF, CO I
BURKS, JESSE SPINNER	COL	VA 42ND INF
BURKS, ROBERT F.	2LT	MS 17TH INF, CO A
BURNAM, JAMES HINES	CAPT	KY CAV (BUCKNER GUARDS)
BURNAM, JOHN	TREASURER	CSA
BURNETT, JOHN ADAM	1LT	VA 51ST INF, CO D
BURNETT, JOHN H.	COL	TX 13TH CAV, CO B
BURNITT, EDWIN	JR 2LT	MS 20TH INF, CO B
BURNS, BENJAMIN F.	3LT	LA 16TH INF, CO D
BURNS, ROBERT	CAPT	TX 5TH INF, CO A
BURRIS, SOLOMON	2LT	NC 83RD MILITIA (STANLEY COUNTY)
BURROUGHS, EDGAR	MAJ	VA 15TH CAV, CO I
BURROUGHS, RICHARD BERRIEN, MD.	ASST SURG/CAPT	GA 63RD INF, F&S
BURROW, REUBEN JR.	LT COL	TN 12TH CAV, CO E
BURT, ERASMUS R.	COL	MS 18TH INF, CO K
BURT, SAMUEL HARDY, SR.	CAPT	VA 13TH CAV, CO K
BURTON, ANDREW J.	2LT	GA 55TH INF, CO D
BURTON, ELIJAH MARQUESSE	1LT	AL PRISON GUARDS, CAPT FREEMAN'S CO
BURTON, JAMES HENRY	COL	CSA ARMORIES SUPERINTENDENT
BURTON, JAMES MONROE	2LT	NC 24TH INF, CO A

BURTON, JOHN WINSTON	CAPT	AL 6TH INF, CO E
BURTON, MAY MEDLEY	CAPT	MO PERKINS' INF BN, F&S - AQM
BURTON, ROBERT M.	CAPT	TN 52ND INF, CO F
BURWELL, JOHN BOTT	CAPT	NC 53RD INF, F&S
BURWELL, ROBERT TURNBULL	2LT	NC 43RD INF, CO B
BUSBEE, WILLIAM REESE	CAPT	GA 10TH INF (FAYETTE RIFLE GRAYS), CO D
BUSBY, NATHANIEL	1LT	TN 18TH CAV (NEWSON'S), CO H
BUSH, GRIFFIN, JR	3LT	VA 58TH INF, CO D
BUSH, JACOB A.	2LT	NC 26TH INF, CO I
BUSH, STEPHEN, COLUMBUS LINCOLN	1LT	SC 2ND ARTY, CO G
BUSH, THOMAS	CAPT	AL 5TH INF, CO B
BUSH, W. G.	COM AGENT	CSA - COMMISSARY OF SUBSISTENCE
BUSH, WILLIAM MARTIN	LT COL	TX 34TH CAV, CO G
BUSHONG, ISAAC A.	2LT	VA 52ND INF, CO H
BUSHONG, JOHN M.	CAPT	VA 8TH BN RESERVES, CO D
BUSICK, ANDREW J.	1LT	NC 22ND INF, CO E
BUSKERK, JAMES V	2LT	VA 34TH BN CAV (WITCHER'S NIGHTHAWKS), CO A
BUSSELL, JOHN	2LT	TN MILLER'S CO, LOCAL DEFENSE TROOPS
BUSSEY, CHARLES EARLE	CAPT	AL 38TH INF, CO I
BUSSEY, JOHN BURGAMY	CAPT	TX 20TH CAV, CO A
BUSWELL, GEORGE DANIEL	2LT	VA 33RD INF, CO H
BUTCHER, WILLIAM F.	1LT	VA SWANN'S CAV BN, CARPENTER'S CO
BUTLER, JOSIAH BLACKMAN	1LT	GA 621ST MILITIA DIST (DECATUR COUNTY)
BUTLER, THOMAS HARVEY	CAPT	TN 25TH INF - CS
BUTLER, WILLIAM REUBEN	LT COL	TN 18TH INF, CO C
BUTT, EDGAR M.	COL	GA 2ND INF, F&S
BUTT, THOMAS JEFFERSON	CAPT	GA 6TH CAV, CO F
BUTT, WILLIAM GORDON LESTER	CAPT	GA 23RD INF, CO K
BUZBEE, JEREMIAH	2LT	AL 2ND CAV, CO G
BYERLY, DANIEL CORT	2LT	LA 30TH INF, CO C
BYLER, JOHN R.	2LT	AR 27TH INF, CO C
BYNUM, WILLIAM P.	COL	NC 2ND INF
BYRD, JOHN THOMAS	1LT	VA 18TH CAV, CO G
BYRD, THOMAS OWEN	AQM	MS 4TH INF, F&S
CABANISS, HARVEY DEKALB	AQM	NC 15TH INF, CO D
CABELL, WILLIAM LEWIS	BRIG GEN	ATM - CAV CMDR
CADENHEAD, JAMES MARTIN	1LT	MS 40TH INF, CO F
CAIN, ISAAC J.	2LT	NC 2ND ARTY, CO I
CAIN, JAMES FREDERICK	1LT	NC 3RD ARTY, CO G
CAIN, LORENZO DOW	1LT	NC 30TH INF, CO C
CAIN, WILLIAM ANDERSON	CAPT	GA 10TH CAV (STATE GUARDS), CO H
CALDWELL, J. F J	2LT	SC 1ST INF (MCCREARY'S), CO B
CALDWELL, JOHN HENRY	JR 2LT	LA 31ST INF, CO C
CALDWELL, JOHN	2LT	NC 33RD INF, CO E
CALDWELL, THOMAS J., MD	ASST SURG	MS 26TH INF F&S
CALDWELL, THOMAS J.	MAJ	LA 8TH CAV F&S
CALHOUN, JOHN ALEXANDER	LT	SC 23RD INF, CO G
CALHOUN, JOHN C.	1LT	VA 62ND MTD INF, CO I
CALLAHAN, WILLIAM, REV.	CHAPLAIN	GA 53RD INF
CALLAWAY, JOHN SANDERS	CAPT	GA 15TH INF, CO A
CALLAWAY, JONATHAN WILSON	1LT	AR 2ND MTD RIFLES, CO E

CALLEN, HUGH JACKSON	2LT	AL 44TH INF, CO H
CAMFIELD, CALEB HALSTEAD	MAJ	GA 29TH CAV BN
CAMP, DAVID A.	CAPT	GA 13TH CAV, CO D
CAMP, DAVID COLLIN	JR 2LT	NC 3RD CAV, CO G
CAMP, JOHN LAFAYETTE	COL	TX 14TH CAV, F&S
CAMP, RALEIGH SPINKS	MAJ	GA 40TH INF, F&S
CAMPBELL, A. G.	CAPT	AL 40TH INF, CO G
CAMPBELL, ANDREW JACKSON	MAJ	TN 48TH INF (VOORHEES'), CO F
CAMPBELL, GEORGE BARMER	1LT	TX 28TH CAV, CO G
CAMPBELL, GEORGE WASHINGTON	2LT	SC 22ND INF, CO K
CAMPBELL, JASPER J.	1LT	SC 19TH INF, CO G
CAMPBELL, THOMAS JEFFERSON, JR.	MAJ	TN 5TH CAV BN (McCLELLAN'S)
CAMPBELL, WILLIAM PEYTON	MAJ	AR 1ST MTD RIFLES, CO D
CANDLER, CHARLES NEWTON	CAPT	NC 64TH INF, CO C
CANDLER, JOHN HENRY	CAPT	VA 48TH INF, CO K
CANNADY, ISAAC G., MD	ASST SURG	NC 55TH INF, F&S
CANTEY, EDWARD BREVARD	CAPT	SC 6TH INF, CO C
CANTRELL, ABRAHAM PATTERSON	2LT	TN 23 INF, CO C
CANTRELL, ISAAC	2LT	TN 35TH INF, CO I
CANTRELL, JOHN MARSHALL	2LT	TN 22ND CAV, CO D
CANTRELL, ROBERT	LT COL	TN 23RD INF, CO C
CAPEHART, WILLIAM RHODES, MD.	SURG	CSA - POAGUES ARTY BN
CAPERS, ELLISON	BRIG GEN	SC 24TH INF
CAPPS, SPENCER W.	2LT	AL 1ST BN HILLIARD'S LEGION, CO B
CARAKER, JACOB M.	CAPT	GA 4TH INF, CO H
CARAWAY, NATHANAEL JACKSON	MAJ	TX 11TH INF, FFS
CAREY, GEORGE WILLIAM	CAPT	GA 4TH INF, CO F
CARLETON, MONTGOMERY	CAPT	MS 5TH INF, CO A
CARLISLE, JOHN MILLARD, REV.	CHAPLAIN/CAPT	SC 7TH INF, F&S
CARMACK, THOMAS K.	CAPT	TX MARTIN'S CAV (5TH PARTISAN RANGERS), CO G
CARNEY, JOHN L.	CAPT	TN 10TH/11TH CONSOLIDATED CAV, CO D
CAROTHERS, SAMUEL M.	1LT	TN 42ND INF, CO B
CARPENTER, FREDERICK HAMBRIGHT, MD	SURG	MS ASHCRAFTS INF
CARPENTER, JOHN N.	LT COL	AL 2ND CAV, CO C
CARPENTER, WYLIE	1LT	AL 30TH INF, CO B
CARR, GEORGE WILSON	COL	VA 57TH INF, F&S
CARR, JOHN F.	CAPT	AR 9TH INF, CO K
CARR, OVED WILLIAM	CAPT	NC 46TH INF, CO G
CARR, SAMUEL FREDERICH	2LT	MS 7TH BN INF, CO E
CARROLL, EDWIN BENAJAH	CAPT	GA 29TH INF, CO G
CARSON, JOHN	1LT	NC 6TH INF, CO D
CARSWELL, JAMES ALEXANDER	2LT	GA 1ST INF, CO H
CARSWELL, REUBEN WALKER	BRIG GEN	GA 1ST MILITIA BDE
CARSWELL, WILLIAM EDWARD, II	CAPT	GA 3RD INF, CO I
CARTER, BARNETT	CAPT	VA 34TH BN CAV (WITCHER'S NIGHTHAWKS), CO D
CARTER, BERNARD HILL, JR.	2LT	VA 3RD CAV, CO C
CARTER, FRED	CAPT	VA 46TH INF (WISE LEGION), CO A
CARTER, HALEY MCCALISTER	1LT	LA 4TH INF, CO F
CARTER, HENRY CLAY	1LT	VA 1ST ARTY, CO D (RICHMOND HOWITZERS)
CARTER, JAMES	REPRESENTATIVE	GA STATE REPRESENTATIVE - LOWNDES COUNTY
CARTER, JESSE M.	CAPT	GA 4TH INF, CO I
CARTER, JOHN C.	COL	AL 24TH INF

CARTER, JOHN CALVIN	MAJ	TX 2ND BN CAV, RAGSDALE CO (RED RIVER DRAGOONS)
CARTER, JOHN WILLIAM	MAJ	VA 2ND INF BN (LOCAL DEFENSE), F&S
CARTER, MILTON LADD	CAPT	VA 7TH CAV, CO I
CARTER, ROBERT J.	1LT	LA 18TH BN CAV, CO B
CARTER, SIDNEY	2LT	SC 14TH INF, CO A
CARTER, THOMAS	2LT	TN 25TH INF, CO G
CARTER, WILLIAM INGRAM	MAJ	SC 14TH INF, CO A
CARTER, WILLIAM PAGE	CAPT	VA L ARTY, CARTER'S CO
CARTER, WILLIAM R.	LT COL	VA 3RD CAV, F&S
CARTWRIGHT, NORVAL DOUGLAS	2LT	TX 4TH CAV, CO A
CARUTHERS, SAMUEL	CAPT	TX 30TH CAV, CO E
CARY, NATHANIEL ROBERT	MAJ	VA 39TH INF, F&S
CASEY, CHRISTOPHER COLUMBUS	CAPT	AR 10TH MILITIA, CO I
CASH, HIRAM RUSSELL	LT	GA 5TH INF, CO B
CASKEY, JAMES DIXON	CAPT	SC 17TH INF, CO I
CASNER, MARTIN	CAPT	TX 31ST BDE STATE TROOPS (BLANCO COUNTY), CAV CO
CASON, CALEB McKNIGHT	LT COL	TN 31ST INF, CO C
CASON, JOHN PEACOCK	1LT	GA 26TH INF, CO K
CASSADA, JOHN J.	2LT	VA 38TH INF, CO C
CASSELL, J. T.	MAJ	KY 2ND CAV (DUKE'S), CO A
CASTLEBERRY, JAMES VINYARD	JUDGE	GA CHATTAHOOCHEE ORDINARY
CAUBLE, HENRY ALEXANDER	CAPT	CSA COMMISSARY OF SUBSISTENCE
CAUDILL, ABNER, JR.	2LT	KY 13TH CAV, CO E
CAUDILL, BENJAMIN EVERAGE	COL	KY 13TH CAV, F&S
CAUDILL, HENRY R S	2LT	KY 13TH CAV, CO H
CAUTHORN, ANDREW B.	2LT	VA 26TH INF, CO C
CAVANAUGH, PATRICK HENRY	1LT	LA 1ST INF, CO B
CAWTHON, STEPHEN ASHLEY	CAPT	FL 6TH INF, CO H
CAYNOR, JOHN L.	CAPT	VA 60TH INF, CO F
CENTER, GEORGE FRANCIS	CAPT	FL 2ND CAV
CHADBOURNE, ALFRED HENRY	1LT	AL 10TH INF, CO C
CHADWICK, WILLIAM DAVIDSON	LT COL	AL 5TH INF, F&S
CHAFFIN, GEORGE MALLORY	1LT	GA 27TH INF, CO H
CHAFFIN, WILLIAM JOSEPH, SR.	1LT	TX STATE TROOPS, 11TH BDE, ELKHART CAV, PRIDGEN'S CO
CHALKER, SAMUEL COTTON	1LT	AL 33RD INF, CO I
CHALMERS, JAMES RONALD	BRIG GEN	MS 9TH INF
CHAMBERS, JAMES W.	CAPT	TN 39TH MTD INF, CO A
CHAMBLISS, JOHN ALEXANDER, REV	CHAPLAIN/CAPT	TN HASKELL'S ARTY BTRY
CHAMBLISS, JOHN RANDOLPH	BRIG GEN	VA 13TH CAV
CHANDLER, JOSEPH NEWTON	LT COL	GA 24TH INF, CO A
CHANEY, CHARLES	LT	MS 39TH INF, CO D
CHAPLIN, SAXBY	1LT	SC 3RD CAV, CO B
CHAPMAN, GEORGE J.	2LT	TN 1ST H ART'Y (JACKSON'S), 2ND CO D
CHAPMAN, JOHN L.	CAPT	VA 34TH BN CAV (WITCHER'S NIGHTHAWKS), CO B
CHAPMAN, JOHN RUSSELL	LT	VA 36TH INF, CO C
CHAPMAN, REUBEN, JR.	CAPT	AL 11TH INF, CO H
CHAPMAN, ROBERT DUNCAN	CAPT	GA 55TH INF, CO E
CHAPMAN, STEPHEN PUGH	1LT	AL 24TH INF, CO E
CHAPMAN, WILLIAM HENRY	LT COL	VA MOSBY'S CAV, CO C
CHAPPELL, HENRY H.	2LT	SC 12TH INF, CO F
CHAPPELL, JAMES O.	CAPT	VA 53D INF, CO F
CHARBONNET, LOUIS ADOLPH	COL	LA CONTINENTAL MILITIA, F&S

CHARLES, REUBEN H.	1LT	FL 1ST CAV, CO A
CHARLTON, RICHARD	LT COL	MS 3RD INF BN, CO K
CHASTAIN, RENE LAFAYETTE	1LT	GA 11TH CAV, CO C
CHATHAM, ALEXANDER	2LT	NC 21ST INF, CO H
CHAZAL, JOHN PHILIP, MD	SURG	CSA SC
CHEARS, BENJAMIN F.	ASST SURG	NC 48TH INF, F&S
CHEARS, VACHEL T.	1LT	NC 37TH INF, CO D
CHEATHAM, BENJAMIN FRANKLIN	MAJ GEN	AOT
CHEATHAM, THOMAS J M	2LT	VA 44TH INF, CO A
CHENAULT, HARVEY	1LT	TN 2ND INF (ROBINSON'S), CO K
CHENAULT, JOHN MURPHY	CAPT	KY 11TH CAV, CO B
CHENEY, ISAAC NEWTON, MD	ASST SURG	CSA
CHERRY, ELIJAH H.	CAPT	SC 17TH INF, CO E
CHERRY, WILLIAM P.	CAPT	TN 44TH INF, CO A
CHESNUT, CHARLES GLADNEY	CAPT	GA 53RD INF, CO B
CHESNUT, JAMES. JR.	BRIG GEN	JEFFERSON DAVIS - ADC/CMDR SC RESERVES
CHESNUTT, JOHN CHRIS	2LT	AR 1ST INF, CO I
CHESNUTT, WILLIAM HENRY	POSTMASTER	AL FERNVALE, TUSCALOOSA COUNTY
CHILDRESS, DAVID M.	2LT	MS 34TH INF, CO I
CHILTON, GEORGE W.	MAJ	TX 3RD CAV, F&S
CHILTON, ROBERT HALL	BRIG GEN	ANV - COS
CHINNIS, SAMUEL ROBERT	1LT	NC 51ST INF, CO G
CHOATE, WILLIAM THOMAS	CAPT	NC 61ST INF, CO I
CHRISMAN, GEORGE	MAJ	VA 3RD INF BN RESERVES, CO A
CHRISTIAN, ADDISON	2LT	VA 34TH BN CAV (WITCHER'S NIGHTHAWKS), CO B
CHRISTIAN, HIRAM	1LT	VA 34TH BN CAV (WITCHER'S NIGHTHAWKS), CO E
CHRISTIAN, PATTERSON	BVT 2LT	VA 129TH MILITIA, AVIS' CO
CHURCH, CALEB, I	CAPT	TX 31ST CAV, CO C
CHURCH, CHARLES W.	2LT	NC 71ST MILITIA (FORSYTH COUNTY)
CHURCH, JOSHUA PINCKNEY	CAPT	TN 48TH INF, CO K
CHURCHILL, THOMAS JAMES	MAJ GEN	AR 1ST MTD RIFLES
CLAIBORNE, JOHN HERBERT, MD	SURG	VA 12TH INF, F&S
CLAIBORNE, JOHN HERBERT, MD	SURG	VA 12TH INF, F&S
CLAIBORNE, THOMAS	COL	CSA - 1ST CAV F&S
CLANCY, MICHAEL ADAM	2LT	AL 60TH INF, CO H
CLARDY, THOMAS FLEMING, MD	SURG	KY 7TH INF, F&S
CLARK, CHARLES	GOV	MS GOVERNOR 1863-1865
CLARK, DAVID CARNEL	CAPT	NC 24TH INF, CO D
CLARK, DAVID	BRIG GEN	NC 9TH BDE MILITIA (HALIFAX COUNTY)
CLARK, EDWARD	GOV	TX GOVERNOR 1861
CLARK, FREDERICK JAMES	CAPT	FL 2ND CAV, CO K
CLARK, FUGATE MD	ASST SURG	VA 34TH BN CAV (WITCHER'S NIGHTHAWKS), F&S
CLARK, FURNEY	2LT	AL 54TH INF, CO A
CLARK, HENRY TOOLE	GOV	NC GOVERNOR 1861-1862
CLARK, JOHN MOORMAN, JR.	COL	TN 46TH INF
CLARK, JOHN POMEROY	1LT	NC 5TH INF, CO G
CLARK, JONOTHAN O.	1LT	MS 2ND CAV, CO G
CLARK, JOSEPH B.	2LT	AR 23RD INF, CO I
CLARK, THOMAS GOODE	CAPT	MS 42ND INF, CO F
CLARK, WILLIAM E.	CAPT	SC 7TH INF, CO G
CLARK, WILLIAM HENRY	LT COL	MS 46TH INF, CO D
CLARK, WILLIAM MARTIN	CAPT	TN 20TH INF, CO C

CLARKE, CHARLES HAMMETT	MAJ	VA 15TH INF, F&S
CLAY, MATHEW BOLLING	1LT	VA 9TH INF, CO C
CLAY, MATTHEW	ACS	MS 6TH CAV
CLAY, SAM	3LT	TX INF RESERVE, CO 6
CLAYTON, GEORGE MARCELLUS	SR 2LT	GA 50TH INF, CO I
CLAYTON, HENRY DELAMAR	MAJ GEN	AOT - GEN A P STEWART'S DIV
CLAYTON, JAMES H.	AQM	TN 23RD INF, F&S
CLAYTON, RICHARD ERSKINE	CAPT	MS 2ND INF, CO A
CLAYTON, RUFUS KING	CAPT	MS 40TH INF, CO A
CLAYTON, SOLOMON SMITH	CAPT	AL 9TH CAV (MALONE'S), CO H
CLEERE, GEORGE DEWITT	LT	AL 4TH CAV
CLEGG, MONTVAVILLE DAVID	1LT	NC 48TH INF, CO D
CLEGG, WILLIAM O.	CAPT	GA 14TH INF, CO F
CLENDENON, B. P.	3LT	VA 34TH BN CAV (WITCHER'S NIGHTHAWKS), CO B
CLENDINEN, JAMES AUGUSTUS	1LT	AL 6TH INF, CO B
CLIFT, JAMES WARREN	CAPT	TN 36TH INF, CO H
CLIFT, MOSES H.	CAPT	TN 36TH INF, ACS
CLIFTON, WILLIAM E.	LT	TN 14TH, CO K
CLINE, ANDREW JACKSON	1LT	AL 32ND INF, CO I
CLINGMAN, THOMAS LANIER	BRIG GEN	NC 25TH INF
CLINKSCALES, J. FLEETWOOD	3LT	SC 20TH INF, CO E
CLONINGER, WILEY MCWRISTON	1LT	NC 28TH INF, CO B
CLOUD, JOHN F.,	JR 2LT	AR 11TH/17TH CONSOLIDATED INF, CO A,B
CLOWNEY, ROBERT CHEYNE	1LT	SC 6TH INF, CO H
CLYBURN, THOMAS FRANKLIN	LT COL	SC 12TH INF, F&S
COATS, W. W., JR	2LT	AL 8TH CAV (HATCH'S), CO C
COBB, BENJAMIN F., MD	SURG	CSA
COBB, HOWELL	MAJ GEN	GA 16TH INF (COBB'S LEGION)
COBB, LEMUEL	CAPT	AL 47TH INF, CO E
COBB, SETH WALLACE	1LT	VA 18TH BN H ARTY, CO A
COBB, THOMAS READE ROOTES	BRIG GEN	GA COBB'S LEGION
COBBS, JAMES V.	JR 2LT	VA 34TH INF, CO G
COCKE, PHILIP ST GEORGE	BRIG GEN	VA STATE TROOPS
COCKERHAM, DAVID S.	CAPT	NC 54TH INF, CO H
COCKERHAM, HENRY E.	CAPT	LA 16TH INF, CO I
COCKRELL, FRANCIS MARION	BRIG GEN	MO COCKRELL'S BDE
CODY, ANDREW JACKSON	CAPT	NC 39TH INF, CO F
CODY, BARNETT HARDEMEN	2LT	AL 15TH INF, CO G
COE, JAMES ALEXANDER	2LT	AL 6TH CAV, CO E
COFER, GEORGE N.	2LT	VA 22ND INF, CO D
COFFEE, ALEXANDER DONELSON	CAPT	AL 16TH INF, CO C
COFFEE, ANDREW JACKSON	1LT	FL 11TH INF, CO E
COFFEY, CHESLEY SHELTON	CAPT	MS 19TH INF, CO D
COFFEY, THOMAS JEFFERSON	2LT	NC 58TH INF, CO E
COFFMAN, ISAAC G.	MAJ	VA 10TH INF, CO B
COFIELD, GEORGE	ENSIGN	SC HOLCOMBE LEGION CAV BN, CO A
COGBILL, WILLIAM W T	CAPT	VA 14TH INF, CO D
COGGIN, JEREMIAH	2LT	NC 23RD INF, CO C
COGHILL, JAMES LINDSAY	LT	VA 50TH INF, CO F
COHEN, ABRAHAM DAVID	CHAPLAIN	NC 46TH INF
COINER, CYRUS BENTON	CAPT	VA 52ND INF, CO G
COKER, JOSEPH WILBUR	CAPT	NC 32ND INF, CO C

COLE, ALEXANDER TROY	CAPT	NC 23RD INF, CO D (PEE DEE GUARDS)
COLE, CHRISTOPHER COLUMBUS	LT COL	NC 22ND INF, CO E
COLE, JAMES L.	AQM	VA 37TH INF, CO F
COLE, LORENZO D.	1LT	VA 6TH RESERVES, CO E
COLE, WILLIAM FERGUSON	2LT	MS 5TH CAV, CO F
COLEMAN, BENJAMIN F.	CAPT	TN 42ND INF, CO F
COLEMAN, HENRY CLAY	2LT	VA 13TH INF, CO A
COLEMAN, JOHN CLARK	CAPT	VA 20TH INF, CO H
COLEMAN, JOHN SCOTT, MD	SURG	VA 3RD CAV
COLEMAN, LEVI P.	CAPT	NC 43RD INF, CO G
COLEMAN, THOMAS WILKES	CAPT	AL 40TH INF, CO F
COLEY, ANDREW JACKSON	BVT 2LT	AL STATE RESERVES, YOUNG'S CO
COLEY, GABRIAL REDDING	CAPT	GA 19TH BN CAV, CO C
COLHOUN, NATHANIEL DICK	2LT	LA 2ND CAV, CO C
COLLIER, J. D.	CAPT	SC IST INF, CO D
COLLIER, JOHN	1LT	GA 4TH CAV, CO E
COLLIER, WILLIAM JASPER	CAPT	VA 64TH MTD INF, CO I
COLLINS, JESSE	3LT	FL 4TH INF, CO K
COLLINS, LEVI	CAPT	VA 34TH BN CAV (WITCHER'S NIGHTHAWKS), CO D
COLLINS, ROBERT ALLEN	CAPT	MS 31ST INF, CO F
COLLINS, THOMAS	1LT	MO 5TH CAV, CO H
COLLY, JOHN G.	2LT	MS 3RD INF (LIVE OAK RIFLES), CO F
COLQUITT, ALFRED HOLT	BRIG GEN	ANV
COLQUITT, JOHN ROBERT	CAPT	AL 34TH INF, CO E
COLVIN, ALLEN RILEY	CAPT	KY 10TH CAV (DIAMOND'S), CO B
COLVIN, CHARLES HENRY	COL	AL 6TH CAV, F&S
COLVIN, JOHN PETRIE	1LT	LA 28TH INF, CO I
COLVIN, PRESTON L.	1LT	GA 15TH INF, CO G
COMBS, HENDERSON M.	CAPT	KY 13TH CAV, CO G
COMBS, JAMES	2LT	FL 1ST RESERVES INF, CO G
COMMANDER, JOSEPH, JR, MD	SURG	NC 7TH INF, CO L
COMPTON, WILLIAM POOLE	CAPT	SC 13TH INF, CO F
CONE, JAMES BARNARD	LT	FL 2ND INF, CO K
CONE, JOSEPH S.	LT COL	GA 47TH INF, CO K
CONE, PETER	MAJ GEN	PRESIDENT PRO TEMPORE GA SENATE
CONE, SIMON PETER	2LT	FL 2ND CAV, CO K
CONE, WILLIAM B.	2LT	AR 19TH INF, CO E
CONNALLY, DRURY M.	3LT	TX MORGAN'S CAV, CO E
CONNALLY, JOHN CORNELIUS	2LT	CSA - 1ST INF, CO C,D
CONNER, JOHN LEWIS	1LT	MS 35TH INF, CO D
CONNER, WILLIAM P.	CAPT	KY 5TH MTD INF, CO D
CONNERLY, JAMES ZACHARIAH SIMPSON	2LT	AL 7TH CAV, CO C
COOK, HENRY BARNES	1LT	SC 8TH INF, CO I
COOK, HENRY HOWELLL	2LT	TN 44TH CONSOLIDATED INF, CO I
COOK, JAMES J.	CAPT	GA 44TH INF, CO H
COOK, JAMES M.	1LT	TN 32ND INF, CO B
COOK, JAMES PHILIP, MD	ASST SURG	AL 47TH INF, F&S
COOK, JOSEPH J.	CAPT	NC 75TH MILITIA (YADKIN COUNTY)
COOK, SAMUEL CALVIN	BVT 2LT	AL 3RD CAV, CO D
COOK, WILLIAM E.	JR 2LT	LA 8TH INF, CO A
COOKE, JAMES BURCH	COL	TN 59TH MTD INF, CO A
COOLEY, HIRMAN C., MD	SURG/CAPT	SC 4TH INF, F&S

COOMBES, ZACHARIAH ELLIS	CAPT	TX 31ST CAV, CO G
COOPER, CLARK COLUMBUS	2LT	SC 11TH RESERVES, CO E
COOPER, DUNCAN BROWN	LT COL	TN COOPER'S CAV
COOPER, JAMES GRIFFIN	1LT	GA 35TH INF, CO B
COOPER, JOHN DANIEL	2LT	MS 7TH INF, CO G
COOPER, JOHN RANDOLF	CAPT	GA 25TH INF, CO K
COOPER, JOSEPH	1LT	VA 8TH INF, CO G
COOPER, NATHANIEL A.	2LT	LA 2ND CAV, CO I
COOPER, SAMUEL	GEN	VA RICHMOND - ADJ & IG
COOPER, SYLVESTER C.	MAJ	TN 46TH INF, CO D
COOPER, THOMAS LACKINGTON	LT COL	GA 8TH INF, CO F
COPELAND, JOHN D.	1LT	SC 13TH INF, CO A
COPELAND, WILLIAM BLUFORD, III	LT	GA 2ND INF, CO E
COPPEDGE, CHARLES CLARK	1LT	TX 19TH INF, CO F
CORBETT, GEORGE W.	1LT	NC 18TH INF, CO E
CORBETT, HENRY DICKSON	1LT	SC 11TH INF, CO B
CORDING, JEROME BONAPARTE	LT COL	TN 49TH INF, CO D
CORNETT, HARDY	2LT	GA 20TH INF, CO B
CORNETT, WILLIAM E.	1LT	KY 13TH CAV, CO B
CORNWELL, BENJAMIN S.	2LT	TN 24TH INF, CO H
CORTNER, WILLIAM MATTHEW	2LT	TN CAV JACKSON'S CO
COSBY, GEORGE BLAKE	BRIG GEN	KY - COSBY'S CAV BDE
COTTLE, SOLOMON MILLS	JR 2LT	GA 17TH INF (MUSCOGEE VOL), CO B
COTTON, THOMAS SAMUEL	CAPT	MS 7TH INF, CO A
COTTON, W. F.	CAPT	TX 9TH CAV, CO F
COUCH, DAVID TERRY	2LT	GA PHILLIPS' LEGION, CO A,G
COUCH, ROBERT WAITE	2LT	TN 9TH BN CAV (GANTT'S), CO F
COULTER, FRANCIS MARION	2LT	GA 1ST CAV, CO G
COUNTS, EZEKIEL K.	CAPT	VA 21ST CAV, CO E
COURTNEY, GEORGE JACKSON	2LT	TN 61ST MTD INF, CO C
COURTNEY, JORDAN BROOKS	CAPT	SC 19TH INF, CO K
COUSINS, JEPTHA GREEN	2LT	AL 53RD CAV, CO A
COVINGTON, WILLIAM R.	2LT	NC 38TH INF, CO E
COWAN, JAMES JONES	CAPT	MS 1ST L ARTY, CO G
COWAN, ROBERT H.	COL	NC 18TH INF, F&S
COWAN, WILLIAM WADE	1LT	TN 17TH INF, CO K
COWAN, JAMES BENJAMIN, MD	ASST SURG	CSA
COWAND, DAVID GEORGE	COL	NC 32ND INF
COWARD, WILLIAM SHADRACK	2LT	AR 7TH INF, CO F
COWARDIN, JOHN LEWIS	1LT	VA 19TH H ARTY, F&S - ADJ
COWHERD, COLBY C., MD	ASST SURG	VA 13TH INF, F&S
COX, ARAS BISHOP	CHAPLAIN	NC 12TH INF, F&S
COX, CARWILE	2LT	SC HOLCOMBE'S LEGION BN CAV, CO E
COX, GEORGE WILLIAM	CAPT	SC 1ST INF (ORR'S RIFLES), CO K
COX, JAMES RILEY	2LT	VA 45TH INF, CO E
COX, JOHN HENRY	1LT	VA 21ST INF (VALLEY OF CHAMPIONS), CO I
COX, JOHN MILTON	1LT	SC 2ND RIFLES, CO G
COX, MELVILLE BEVERIDGE	CAPT	VA 4TH INF, CO C
COX, MOSES EDWARD	CAPT	MO 8TH CAV, CO D, K
COX, WILLIAM DRISCOL	3LT	TN 59TH MTD INF, CO H
COX, WILLIAM REYNOLDS	1LT	VA 64TH MTD INF, CO A
COX, AUGUSTUS A.	JR 2LT	VA 26TH INF, CO E

COZART, WILLIAM WILEY	2LT	NC 43RD MILITIA (GRANVILLE COUNTY)
CRABB, JOHN C.	CAPT	GA 1ST CAV, CO A
CRABTREE, SAMUEL M.	CAPT	TN 27TH INF, CO H
CRAFT, JOHN HENDERSON	1LT	KY 13TH INF, CO C
CRAFT, WILLIAM J.	SR LT	TX 11TH INF, CO K
CRAFTON, JOSEPH DAVID	1LT	SC CAV (HAMPTON'S LEGION), CO A
CRAIG, WILLIAM WHITE	CAPT	MO 8TH CAV, CO F
CRAIN, EPHRAIM JESSE	1LT	LA 15TH INF, CO C
CRALE, SAMUEL SPELMAN	CAPT	VA 40TH INF, CO D
CRAVENS, LAMAR MIRABEAU	CAPT	MS 1ST CAV, CO F
CRAWFORD, ANDREW BENJAMIN	CAPT	VA 23RD INF, CO K
CRAWFORD, JOHN HAMMER	COL	TN 60TH MTD INF
CRAWFORD, JOHN MOORE	1LT	NC 62ND INF, CO B,E
CRAWFORD, JOHN	CAPT	TN 26TH INF, CO E
CRAWFORD, WILLIAM C.	2LT	MS 17TH INF, CO G
CRAWLEY, WILLIAM J.	COL	SC INF (HOLCOMBE'S LEGION), CO D
CREECH, IRA	CAPT	VA 29TH BN, CO A
CREEL, PRESTON H.	JR 2LT	AL 29TH INF, CO K
CRESAP, NELSON ADAIR	2LT	TN 47TH INF, CO F
CREWS, THOMAS BISSELL	1LT	SC 1ST CAV, CO A
CRICHTON, CHARLES GILBERT	1LT	VA 21ST INF, CO G
CRICHTON, HUGH RANDOLPH	2LT	NC 47TH INF, CO F
CRIGLER, JOHN LEWIS	CAPT	MS 14TH INF, CO G
CRISLER, NELSON WEAVER	MAJ	VA 7TH INF - QM
CRISP, CHARLES FREDERICK	2LT	VA 10TH INF, CO K
CROCKER, SHERWOOD GREEN	1LT	TN 16TH INF, CO B
CROCKETT, EDWARD R.	CAPT	TN 30TH INF, CO A
CROCKETT, WILLIAM RILEY	1LT	TX 24TH CAV. CO D
CROFT, EDWARD	CAPT	GA FLYING ARTY, CROFT'S BATTERY
CROFT, RANDELL	CAPT	SC 16TH INF, CO C
CROOK, BENJAMIN FRANKLIN	2LT	MS 8TH INF, CO C
CROOK, JEREMIAH STELL	1LT	TX 9TH MTD INF, CO A
CROOK, WILLIAM JERE	MAJ	TN 13TH INF, CO I
CROOM, CHARLES SHEPPARD	2LT	NC 61ST INF, CO E
CROOM, HARDY CHURCH	2LT	FL 5TH CAV, CO C
CROOM, STEPHENS	MAJ	CSA MG FORNEY, F&S -AAG
CROOM, WILLIAM HENRY	CAPT	FL 2ND INF, CO L
CROPP, JAMES THOMAS, MD	SURG	VA 51ST INF, F&S
CROSBY, JOSIAH FRAZIER	CAPT	CSA GENERAL STAFF OF EDMUND KIRBY SMITH - AG
CROSS, GEORGE WARREN, MD	SURG	CSA
CROSS, GEORGE WARREN	2LT	NC 20TH INF, CO K
CROSS, JAMES ROBERT	CAPT	AL 46TH INF, CO B
CROSS, WILLIAM M.	1LT	MO 15TH CAV, CO B
CROSSLAND, EDWARD	COL	KY 7TH MTD INF, F&S
CROUCH, LEVIN MCDANIEL	3LT	SC 19TH INF, CO D
CROUCH, R. C.	1LT	VA 34TH BN CAV (WITCHER'S NIGHTHAWKS), CO F
CROWDER, JAMES W.	1LT	NC 23RD INF, CO A
CROWDER, MARTIN SIMS	1LT	CSA - 1ST CHOCTAW MTD RIFLES, CO E
CROWE, CHRISTIAN C.	2LT	TN 59TH MTD INF, CO C
CRUMLEY, RIAL FLEMING	1LT	TN 61ST MTD INF (PITT'S), CO K
CRUMP, GEORGE J.	JR 2LT	AR 16TH INF, CO E
CRUMPLER, THOMAS NEWTON	MAJ	NC 1ST CAV, CO A

CRUSH, JAMES E.	2LT	VA WADE'S LOCAL DEFENSE, CO A
CULBREATH, HENRY CHAPPELL	CAPT	SC 2ND ARTY, CO K
CULLOM, JAMES JOSEPH	CAPT	TN 8TH INF, CO F
CULLOM, JEREMIAH WALKER, REV	CHAPLAIN	TN 24TH INF
CULLUM, WILLIAM	ACS	AR 31ST INF, CO D
CULP, JONATHAN RIPLEY	LT COL	SC 17TH INF, CO A
CULVER, JOHN LATIMER	CAPT	GA 15TH INF, CO K
CUMMINGS, ARTHUR CAMPBELL	COL	VA 33RD INF
CUMMINGS, WILLIAM BURRELL	CAPT	TN 35TH INF, CO C
CUNNINGHAM, GEORGE A.	2LT	GA 31ST INF (CROWDERS), CO G
CUNNINGHAM, JOHN, JR.	1LT	TN 32ND INF, CO D
CUNNINGHAM, JOHN	CAPT	GA 1ST RESERVES (SYMONS), CO B
CUNNINGHAM, JOHN	1LT	KY 4TH MTD INF, CO G
CUNNINGHAM, JOSEPH L.	CAPT	AL 19TH INF, CO H
CUNNINGHAM, SOLOMON	CAPT	NC 25TH INF, CO H
CURLEE, THOMAS GOWAN	CAPT	TN 18TH INF, CO H
CURLEE, WILLIAM PEYTON	LT COL	MS HAM'S CAV, F&S
CURRENCE, MILTON HAMILTON	CAPT	SC 3RD BN RESERVES, CO C
CURREY, JOHN HENRY, MD	ASST SURG	CSA
CURRIE, ARCHIBALD A.	CAPT	MS 13TH INF, CO F
CURRIE, DANIEL WORTH	1LT	CSA - ENGINEERS
CURRIE, NICHOLAS DAVID	2LT	SC 25TH INF, CO D
CURRY, DAVID PHILLIPS	CAPT	VA 25TH INF, CO H
CURRY, WILLIAM ELLIS	CAPT	KY 8TH CAV
CURTIS, LARKIN JUNIUS	1LT	NC 1ST INF, CO B
CURTIS, THOMAS A.	CAPT	VA ARTY (FREDERICKSBURG ARTY), CURTIS' CO
CUSHMAN, BASIC CROW	ADJ	LA 30TH INF, CO E
CYPERT, JOHN WILLIAM	CAPT	MO COFFEE'S CAV, CO C
DABNEY, JOHN C.	2LT	GA 30TH INF, CO B
DABNEY, R. S.	CAPT	TX 3RD CAV, CO D
DABNEY, VIRGINIUS M.	1LT	VA 21ST INF, CO H
DAILEY, JEREMIAH	CAPT	AL 4TH CAV (RODDY'S), CO E
DALE, ANDREW C.	CAPT	TN 8TH CAV, CO F; AQM
D'ALVIGNY, PETER PAUL N, MD	SURG	GA 9TH BN ARTY, F&S
DAME, GEORGE W.	CHAPLAIN/2LT	LA 31ST INF, CO D
DAMERON, JESSE ROBERT	CAPT	TN 19TH CAV, CO D
DAMERON, WILLIAM HALL	MAJ	CSA MS - CHIEF COMMISSARY
DAMRON, MILTON WESLEY	CAPT	TX 18TH CAV, CO D
DANCE, WILLIS JEFFERSON	MAJ	VA 1ST L ARTY
DANCY, FRANCIS LITTLEBURY	CAPT	CSA - AQM
DANIEL, DAVID CHISOLM	CAPT	AL 55TH INF, CO B
DANIEL, JAMES S.	2LT	VA 21ST INF, CO A
DANIEL, JOSEPH A.	CAPT	AR 15TH INF (JOHNSON'S), CO B
DANIEL, JUNIUS	BRIG GEN	NC 45TH INF
DANIEL, REUBIN P.	JR 2LT	GA 23RD INF, CO K
DANIEL, THEODORE FLOYD	2LT	GA COBBS LEGION, CO F
DANIEL, WALTER HENRY	CAPT	AL 2ND CAV, CO I
DANIEL, WILLIAM A.	LT COL	GA 46TH INF, CO I
DANNELLY, FRANCIS, OLIN, MD	SURG	CSA SC COLUMBIA CAMP OF INSTRUCTION
DANNELLY, HARDY, EMANUEL	2LT	AL 6TH CAV, CO A
DANNER, ALBERT CAREY	CAPT	CSA - AQM
DANTZLER, DAVID HEBER	2LT	SC 14TH BN CAV, CO B

DANTZLER, OLIN MILLER	COL	SC 22ND INF, F&S
DARBY, AMES WILLIAM	CAPT	AL 4TH INF (CONEUCH GUARDS), CO E
DARDEN, JAMES MONROE L.	2LT	AL 41ST INF, CO A
DARK, JOSEPH NEAL	MAJ	TX 25TH CAV, BFS
DARK, LEROY JAMES LAWRENCE	2LT	GA 26TH BN INF, CO C
DARLEY, JAMES ADDISON	1LT	TX 5TH CAV, CO I
DARLING, THOMAS JACKSON	JR 2LT	GA 24TH BN CAV, CO A
DARST, JAMES HENRY	MAJ	VA 158TH MILITIA
DASPIT, HENRY CLAIBORNE	2LT	LA 26TH INF, CO H
DAUGHERTY, JARKIAH	CAPT	MO COL E. T. WINGOS INF BDE
DAVENPORT, HUGH MCCALL	MAJ	GA 1ST INF, F&S (OLMSTEAD'S) - QM
DAVENPORT, ROBERT RODOLPHUS	CAPT	AL 9TH CAV (MALONE'S), CO F
DAVES, EATON P.	1LT	MS MCLELLAND'S CO (NOXUBEE HOME GUARDS)
DAVES, GRAHAM	MAJ	CSA - PACS
DAVID, ALPHONSE	1LT	LA 3RD MILITIA, 2ND BDE, 1ST DIV, CO K - ACTING ADJ
DAVIDSON, GREENVILLE ROBERT	2LT	KY 10TH CAV (DIAMOND'S), CO A
DAVIDSON, HUGH HARVEY	LT COL	NC 39TH INF, F&S
DAVIDSON, JOHN MITCHELL	1LT	NC 39TH INF, CO C
DAVIDSON, NEAL	ADJ	LA 1ST BN CAV F&S
DAVIDSON, RUBEN S.	1LT	SC 5TH STATE TROOPS, CO C
DAVIDSON, WILLIAM	JR 2LT	AL 8TH CAV (HATCH'S), CO F
DAVIS, ALFRED WADE	LT	SC 21ST INF, CO E
DAVIS, BENJAMIN F.	CAPT	SC 10TH INF, CO F
DAVIS, CALEB	CAPT	AR 15TH INF (NORTHWEST), CO E
DAVIS, CHAMPION THOMAS NEAL	COL	NC 16TH INF, F&S
DAVIS, CHARLES FRANKLIN	2LT	MS 1ST INF, CO G
DAVIS, DAVID WARD	CAPT	CSA - 5TH INF - CS
DAVIS, ELIJAH PALMER	JR 2LT	TX 29TH CAV, CO G
DAVIS, EUGENE	CAPT	VA 2ND CAV, CO K
DAVIS, GEORGE	ATTY GEN	CSA CABINET - ATTY GENERAL
DAVIS, J. P.	1LT	MS CAV (STONEWALL RANGERS), CAPT KNOX'S CO
DAVIS, J. S E	CAPT	AL 14TH INF, CO E
DAVIS, J. T.	CAPT	AL 12TH INF, CO D
DAVIS, JAMES MERETT	2LT	NC 56TH INF, CO G
DAVIS, JEFFERSON FINIS	PRESIDENT	CSA
DAVIS, JOHN BOYDON	LT	MO WOODS CAV, CO H
DAVIS, JONATHAN J.	1LT	MS 4TH INF, CO K
DAVIS, JOSEPH L.	2LT	KY 1ST CAV, CO E
DAVIS, JOSEPH ROBERT	BRIG GEN	MS & LA BDE, HETH'S
DAVIS, MICAJAH C.	CAPT	NC 34TH INF, CO E
DAVIS, R. H.	1LT	VA 34TH BN CAV (WITCHER'S NIGHTHAWKS), CO B
DAVIS, REUBEN	MAJ GEN	CSA
DAVIS, RICHARD M.	LT COL	AR 47TH CAV, F&S
DAVIS, ROBERT JAMES	1LT	TN 24TH INF, CO F
DAVIS, ROBERT THOMAS	1LT	AL 38TH INF, CO B
DAVIS, ROBERT	OPERATIVE	AL PUBLIC WORKS OPERATIVE AT SELMA
DAVIS, THOMAS DIXON	2LT	CSA - DRILLMASTER
DAVIS, WELDON E.	CAPT	NC 30TH INF, CO B
DAVIS, WILLIAM FORSYTHE	CAPT	GA 51ST INF, CO H
DAVIS, WILLIAM JAMES	CAPT	VA 55TH INF, CO A
DAVIS, WILLIAM THOMAS	2LT	AL 11TH INF, CO I
DAWKINS, AARON G.	1LT	61ST MILITIA (RICHMOND COUNTY)

DAWSON, GEORGE W.	CAPT	MO 1ST INF, CO I
DAWSON, HALINGER B.	2LT	GA 17TH INF, CO I
DAWSON, JONATHAN SMITH	COL	TN 46TH INF, F&S
DAY, ROBERT J.	2LT	NC 1ST INF, CO K
DAY, WILLIAM C.	AQM	MS 7TH BN INF, CO D
DE BLANC, ALPHONSE	1LT	LA 10TH BN INF, CO H
DE BORDENAVE, CHEVALIER FULGENCE	MAJ	LA C S ZOUAVE BN, F&S
DE JARNETTE, DANIEL COLEMAN	REPRESENTATIVE	VA 1ST & 2ND CONFEDERATE CONGRESSES
DE JARNETTE, ELLIOTT HAWSE	CAPT	VA 30TH INF, CO I
DE LOACH, JOHN	CAPT	AL 36TH INF, CO F
DE POLIGNAC, CAMILE ARMAND JULES MARIE	MAJ GEN	ATM - "PRINCE POLECAT"
DE VAUGHN, JAMES ELIJAH	1LT	GA 2ND CAV, CO F
DEADERICK, A. S.	2LT	VA 34TH BN CAV (WITCHER'S NIGHTHAWKS), CO F
DEADERICK, DAVID FRANK	2LT	VA 34TH BN CAV (WITCHER'S NIGHTHAWKS), CO F
DEADWYLER, HENRY ROBINSON	CAPT	GA 38TH INF, CO H
DEAL, ALONZO	CAPT	NC 38TH INF, CO F
DEAN, AUGUSTUS AARON	2LT	SC 2ND INF, CO G
DEAN, SAMUEL JOHN	1LT	GA 47TH INF, CO H
DEAN, THOMAS PINCKNEY	1LT	GA 2ND CAV, CO I
DEANS, JOHN EDWARD	CAPT	VA 3RD INF, CO H
DEARAGON, RAMON T., MD	SURG	TX 9TH INF, F&S
DEARING, JAMES C.	BRIG GEN	NC DEARING'S BDE
DEATHERAGE, JAMES A.	1LT	NC 73RD MILITIA (SURRY COUNTY)
DEAVENPORT, THOMAS H.	CHAPLAIN	TN 4TH/5TH CONSOLIDATED INF
DEBERRY, WILLIAM L., MD	SURG/MAJ	AR 2ND MTD RIFLES, CO B
DECELL, THOMAS G.	1LT	MS 36TH INF, CO A
DEDGE, JOSEPH GORE	CAPT	GA 47TH INF, CO F
DEDMAN, ROBERT H.	CAPT	AR 3RD CAV, CO A
DEHART, JOHN HARVEY, JR	1LT	NC 7TH BN CAV, CO C
DEKLE, WILLIAM GRISSOM, JR	JR 2LT	GA 50TH INF, CO F
DELAMAR, WILLIAM W.	CAPT	GA 27TH INF, CO H
DELAWDER, SAMUEL	2LT	VA 18TH CAV, CO B
DELAY, GEORGE A.	2LT	GA 16TH INF, CO B
DELAY, RUSSELL VAN	2LT	GA 43RD INF, CO H
DELLENEY, JOHN W.	1LT	SC 12TH INF, CO C
DELOACH, JOHN B.	CAPT	AL 6TH INF, CO I
DELOACH, JOHN CALVIN, SR	CAPT	GA 5TH INF, CO G
DELOACH, ZACHARIAH	2LT	FL 2ND INF, CO I
DELOATCH, JOSEPH DANIEL	1LT	GA 61ST INF, CO H
DEMENT, WILLIAM FENDLEY	CAPT	MD 1ST ARTY BTRY
DEMONBREUN, JOHN R.	1LT	TN 30TH INF, CO H
DENBY, CHARLES L.	1LT	VA 5TH CAV, CO B
DENHAM, ANDREW, JR	LT	CSA - ORDINANCE OFFICER
DENHAM, JOSEPH W.	CAPT	MS 7TH INF, CO F
DENNIS, SUMERAL JR.	2LT	AL 6TH CAV, CO C
DENNY, DAVID	CAPT	SC 7TH INF, CO E
DENSMORE, WILLIAM HOXIE	ASST PROVOST MARSHALL	MS VICKSBURG
DENSON, CALLEY ADRIAN, MD	ASST SURG	CSA
DENTON, ELISHA H.	2LT	GA 24TH INF, CO D
DERRICK, FREDERICK W., JR	1LT	SC 15TH INF
DERRICK JOSEPH	2LT	TX EVAN'S BN RESERVES CORPS, CO C
DeSHA, BENJAMIN	MAJ	KY 9TH MTD INF, F&S

DESHAZO, JOHN MARION	CAPT	AL 30TH INF, CO K
DESHAZO, RUFUS MONROE	1LT	AL 20TH INF, CO G
DESPORTES, RICHARD S.	2LT	SC 3RD INF, CO G
DEUPREE, THOMAS WILLIAM	1LT	GA FLOYD LEGION, CO H
DEVANE, BENJAMIN MITCHELL	2LT	GA 50TH INF, CO I
DEVAUGHAN, SAMUEL H.	CAPT	VA 17TH INF, CO E
DEVEREUX, JOHN HENRY	CAPT	CSA - ACS
DEWS, SAMUEL S.	CAPT	VA 60TH INF, CO C
DEWS, WILLIAM WASHINGTON	1LT	GA 25TH INF, CO C
DEYERLE, ANDREW JACKSON	CAPT	VA 42ND INF, CO E
DIAL, WILLIAM H.	CAPT	FL 4TH INF, CO C
DIAMOND, GEORGE R.	LT COL	KY 10TH CAV, CO D
DIBRELL, GEORGE GIBBS	BRIG GEN	TN CAV BDE - GEN FORREST
DICK, JOHN STEWART	1LT	NC 21ST INF, CO M
DICK, ROBERT THORNTON	1LT	VA 9TH INF, CO E
DICKERSON, ANDREW	CAPT	VA 54TH INF, CO A
DICKERSON, BURDINE	CAPT	VA 54TH INF, CO A
DICKERSON, CALVIN	JR 2LT	NC 26TH INF, CO B
DICKERSON, EARLY	2LT	VA 54TH INF, CO A
DICKERSON, RICHARD GHOLSON	CAPT	SC 21ST INF, CO G
DICKERT, D. AUGUSTUS	CAPT	SC 3RD INF, CO H
DICKINSON, JAMES SHELTON	REPRESENTATIVE	CONFEDERATE 2ND CONGRESS
DICKSON, DAVID CATCHINGS, MD	CAPT	TX 17TH MILITIA BDE
DICKSON, JOHN Q.	2LT	VA 34TH BN CAV (WITCHER'S NIGHTHAWKS), CO A
DICKSON, THOMAS JEFFERSON	2LT	GA 43RD INF, CO B
DIGGS, ALBERT F.	2LT	VA ARMISTEAD'S L ARTY, CO A
DIGGS, BENJAMIN M.	2LT	TN 7TH CAV (DUCKWORTH'S), CO G
DILBURN, SAMUEL G.	2LT	AL 24TH BN CAV, CO L,B
DILLARD, BENJAMIN FRANKLIN, MD	SURG	LA MILITIA (UNION PARISH)
DILLARD, HARVEY H.	CAPT	TN 16TH INF, CO K
DILLARD, THOMAS J.	JR 2LT	TX 28TH CAV (RANDAL'S), CO E
DILLON, GEORGE WASHINGTON	2LT	TN 18TH INF, CO I
DISHMAN, A. T.	1LT	VA 9TH CAV, CO I
DISMUKES, BENJAMIN JACKSON	2LT	MS 1ST CAV, CO H
DISMUKES, WILLIAM HENRY	LT COL	AR 19TH INF, CO C
DIXON, JOHN ABERNATHY	MAJ	LA 12TH INF (JACKSON'S SHARPSHOOTERS), CO C
DIXON, JOHN DAVID	2LT	NC 15TH MILITIA (CRAVEN COUNTY)
DOAK, WILLIAM R.	MAJ	TN 2ND INF (ROBISON'S)
DOBBINS, ARCHIBALD S.	COL	AR 1ST CAV (DOBBINS')
DOBBS, LODOWICK ADAMS	1LT	AL 7TH/9TH CAV, CO H
DOBBS, SILAS MERCER	3LT	MS 31ST INF, CO E
DOBBS, SILAS PARKS	CAPT	AL 9TH CAV (MALONE'S), CO M
DOBYNS, THOMAS J.	CAPT	MO STATE GUARD
DOCKERY, JAMES MARION	1LT	TN L ARTY (MAURY ARTY), SPARKMAN'S CO
DODDS, JAMES CROOK	2LT	TN 21ST CAV (WILSON'S), CO D
DODGEN, ELI WASHINGTON	2LT	AR 33RD INF, CO I
DODSON, THOMAS S.	CAPT	TX MILITIA, CO F (CAMP SHILOH, HOUSTON COUNTY, TX)
DODSON, WILLIAM ESAMUEL	CAPT	AL 33RD INF, CO C
DODSON, WILLIAM V.	2LT	VA 5TH CAV, CO G
DOGGETT, ARISTIDES	CAPT	FL 3RD INF, CO A
DOLLINS, MILTON S	1LT	TN 8TH INF, CO D
DONALD, GEORGE L.	MAJ	MS 13TH INF, CO G

DONELSON, DANIEL SMITH	MAJ GEN	TN MILITIA
DOOLEY, MARTIN PEMBERTON	2LT	TN 48TH INF, CO E
DOOLEY, MCKINNEY	CAPT	TN 54TH INF
DORMAN, JAMES FLETCHER	2LT	AL 34TH INF, CO F
DORMAN, JOHN BLANTON	2LT	TX 28TH CAV, CO A
DOROUGH, THOMAS TRAVIS	COL	GA 34TH INF, CO H
DORSET, JOHN S.	2LT	VA 20TH INF, CO D
DORSEY, CALEB	COL	MO STATE GUARD
DORTCH, JOHN BAKER, II	CAPT	KY 7TH/8TH CAV, CO G
DOSS, REDDERICK PARKER	AQM	MS 9TH INF, CO K
DOSS, SEABORN PEYTON	1LT	GA 18TH INF, CO B
DOSS, WILLIAM W.	2LT	AL 41ST INF, CO C
DOTSON, JOHN WESLEY	1LT	TN 12TH CAV, CO G
DOUGHTY, LLEWELLYN G.	CAPT	GA 48TH INF, CO C
DOUGLAS, HENRY KYD	CAPT	VA 2ND INF, CO B
DOUGLASS, ISAAC C.	1LT	TX 17TH INF, CO A
DOUGLASS, JONES TARPLEY	CAPT	GA 8TH INF (STATE GUARDS), CO E
DOUTHIT, JOHN E., MD	ASST SURG	NC 21ST INF
DOWLING, AARON	2LT	GA 50TH INF, CO A
DOWLING, JOHN WESLEY	1LT	AL 7TH INF, CO F
DOWLING, RICHARD W.	1LT	TX 1ST H ARTY, CO F
DOWNS, GEORGE	MAJ	VA 19TH CAV, F&S
DOWNS, SHELLY PAYNE, JR, MD	POSTMASTER	GA NEWTON COUNTY - OAK HILL
DRAKE, JOHN ADAMS	CAPT	NC 12TH INF, CO H
DRAKE, JOHN JOSEPH	CAPT	NC 32ND INF, CO H
DRANE, JAMES WILLIAM	LT COL	MS 31ST INF, CO I
DRANE, JAMES	PRESIDENT PRO TEM	MS SENATE
DRAUGHON, THOMAS J.	CAPT	GA 13TH MILITIA, MACON COUNTY BN, 2ND CO
DRAWDY, PETER W.	BVT 2LT	SC 24TH INF, CO E
DRAYTON, THOMAS FENWICK	BRIG GEN	SC 15TH CMDG
DREBING, CHARLES L.	1LT	VA 2ND INF, CO D
DRENNEN, CHARLES	1LT	AL 28TH INF, CO F
DREW, WILLIAM W.	1LT	NC 2ND ARTY, CO K
DREWRY, SAMUEL DAVIES, MD	ASST SURG	CSN
DRISKELL, JOSEPH BETT	CAPT	MS 2ND BN CAV RESERVES, CO E
DROMEL, THEODORE MELCHIOR	CAPT	LA EUROPEAN BDE
DRUM, HOSEA H.	CAPT	NC 94TH MILITIA (ALEXANDER COUNTY), CO A
DRUM, THOMAS F.	2LT	NC 89TH MILITIA, CO K (CATAWBA COUNTY)
DU BOSE, WILDS SCOTT	CAPT	NC 2ND INF, CO E (ANTHONY'S GRAYS)
DUBARD, JOHN THOMAS	1LT	MS 3RD CAV, CO K
DUBOSE, DUDLEY MCIVOR	BRIG GEN	GA 15TH INF
DUCK, R. A W	1LT	AL 34TH INF, CO G
DUCKWORTH, MOSES A.	2LT	AR 9TH INF, CO K
DUCKWORTH, WILLIAM LAFAYETTE	COL	TN 7TH CAV, CO D
DUCOTE, HYPOLITE	SR 2LT	LA DUBECQ'S CAV
DUDLEY, RANSOM	2LT	VA 58TH INF, CO E
DUFF, GEORGE WASHINGTON	1LT	TX 35TH INF, CO A
DUFF, WILLIAM POWELL	CAPT	VA 50TH INF, CO G
DUFFEY, GEORGE	CAPT	CSA - ORDNANCE
DUGGAN, WILLIAM JACKSON	LT	LA 17TH INF, CO B
DUKE, ALEXANDER HAMILTON	2LT	GA 56TH INF, CO H
DUKE, BASIL WILSON	BRIG GEN	KY MORGANS CAV

DUKE, JAMES	CAPT	LA 31ST INF, CO B
DUKE, RICHARD THOMAS WALKER	COL	VA 46TH INF, F&S
DULA, THOMAS J.	LT COL	NC 58TH INF, CO H
DUNBAR, ROBERT J.	CAPT	SC HOLCOMBE LEGION INF, CO D
DUNCAN, BURWELL ALEXANDER, MD	SURG	CSA
DUNCAN, JOHN HAMILTON LEWIS	CAPT	TN 16TH INF, CO B
DUNCAN, JOSEPH WHITFIELD	LT COL	MO 2ND DIV, JAG
DUNCAN, MARSHALL	1LT	MS 7TH CAV, CO C
DUNKLEY, CHARLES LEE, MD	ASST SURG	CSA
DUNLAP, HENRY OVERTON	MAJ	NC 50TH MILITIA, F&S (CHATHAM COUNTY)
DUNLAP, THOMAS JEFFERSON	1LT	AL 4TH CAV (RODDY'S), CO D
DUNN, BALLARD P.	2LT	VA 34TH BN CAV (WITCHER'S NIGHTHAWKS), CO K
DUNN, JONATHAN BEVERLEY	1LT	LA 3RD CAV, CO D
DUNN, RUFUS FREEMAN	CAPT	TX 3RD CAV, CO F
DUNNAHOO, THOMAS JORDAN	2LT	GA COBB'S LEGION CAV BN, CO H
DUNNAVANT, JAMES WALDO	1LT	MS 2ND PARTISAN RANGERS, CO K
DUNSON, WALKER HARRISON	3LT	TN 50TH INF, CO C
DUPREE, THOMAS , JULES	CAPT	CSA LA ZOUAVE BN, CO F
DUPUY, JULES	CAPT	CSA LA ZOUAVE BN, CO F
DURHAM, BENJAMIN FRANKLIN	1LT	TX 3RD CAV, CO B
DURHAM, LINDSEY, JR	2LT	GA 3RD INF, CO L
DURHAM, PLATO	CAPT	NC 12TH INF, CO E
DURRANCE, JOHN RUFUS	1LT	FL MTD INF DETACHMENT - FT MEADE, FL 1861
DUVAL, JOHN R.	CAPT	MS 23RD INF, CO I
DUVAL, WILLIAM C., MD	SURG	CSA - MEDICAL DIRECTOR
DUVALL, FERDINAND	CAPT	MD 2ND BN, CO C
DWINELL, MELVIN	1LT	GA 8TH INF, CO A
DYAL, ELIJAH	1LT	GA 20TH INF, CO H
DYCHES, WILLIAM HARRISON	CAPT	SC 11TH INF, CO B
DYER, CHARLES SAMUEL	2LT	TX 14TH BDE MILITIA, CANEY CREEK MTD INF
DYER, SPILLSBY	2LT	TN 37TH INF, CO H
DYESS, JOHN JOSHUA	JR 2LT	MS 36TH INF, CO C
DYSART, JOHNSTON	2LT	TX 6TH CAV, CO D
EAGAN, HENRY J.	CAPT	LA 15TH INF, CO B
EAGLES, LORENZO DOW	2LT	NC 30TH INF, CO F
EALUM, SOLOMON	TAX COLLECTOR	AL CALHOUN COUNTY
EANES, POPE DRYDEN	CAPT	VA 57TH INF, CO I
EARLY, JUBAL ANDERSON	LT GEN	CSA - ANV 2ND CORPS
EARLY, SAMUEL HENRY	1LT	CSA - GEN JUBAL A EARLY - ADC
EASLEY, THOMAS STEWART	CAPT	TN 10TH CAV, CO G
EAST, THOMAS LANGSTON	1LT	LA 27TH INF, CO A
EASTERLING, NELSON A.	1LT	SC 21ST INF, CO F
EASTERLING, WILLIAM K.	LT COL	MS 46TH INF, CO D
EASTERLING, WILLIAM KENNON	CAPT	MS 3RD CAV, CO A
EASTMAN, JOSEPH K P	1LT	LA 25TH INF, CO I
EATON, JAMES WILLIAM	1LT	TN SHAW'S BN CAV, O P HAMILTON'S CO
EAVES, JESSE M.	CAPT	GA 14TH INF, CO K
EBERHARDT, JACOB BETSY	CAPT	GA 37TH INF, CO E
ECHOLS, JAMES WALTER	LT COL	AL 34TH CAV, F&S
ECHOLS, SAMUEL B., JR	CAPT	AL 19TH INF, CO K
EDENFIELD, EPHRAIM H.	1LT	GA 48TH INF, CO H
EDMONDSON, JAMES HOWARD	COL	TN 11TH INF, F&S

EDMONDSON, JAMES MINOR	BVT 2LT	TN 11TH CAV (HOLMAN'S), CO E
EDMONDSON, JOHN	CAPT	GA 30TH INF, CO H
EDMONDSON, THOMAS JEFFERSON	2LT	GA 44TH INF, CO G
EDMONDSON, THOMAS POLK	CAPT	CSA 3RD CAV (HOWARD'S), CO F
EDRINGTON, HENRY C.	CAPT	LA 4TH CAV, CO I
EDWARDS, CHARLES	ADJ	VA 34TH BN CAV (WITCHER'S NIGHTHAWKS), F&S
EDWARDS, DAVID W.	SR 1LT	SC MANIGAULT'S BN ARTY, CO C
EDWARDS, GEORGE COLUMBUS	2LT	MS 35TH INF, CO D
EDWARDS, MARION COLUMBUS	CAPT	GA 3RD CAV (CRAWFORD'S), CO E
EDWARDS, NICHOLAS STONE	CAPT	LA 16TH INF, CO B
EDWARDS, WILLIAM HENRY	CAPT	SC 17TH INF, CO A
EELLS, JOHN	MAJ	VA 5TH CAV, CO F
EGGER, JAMES L,	1LT	MS 24TH INF, CO D
EGGERS, JOHIEL SMITH	1LT	NC 37TH INF, CO E
EICHELBERGER, CHARLES FREDERICK	CAPT	VA 31ST INF, CO C
EIDSON, JOHN WESLEY	LT	SC 7TH INF, CO G
ELAM, THOMAS ANDERSON	1LT	MS 4TH INF, CO H
ELDRIDGE, ERWIN JAMES, MD	SURG	GA 16TH INF, F&S
ELKINS, CHRISTIAN CHRISTOPHER	CAPT	AR 14TH INF, CO D
ELKINS, LENDER L.	CAPT	GA 54TH INF, CO I
ELLER, CALVIN	CAPT	NC 58TH INF, CO L
ELLERBEE, JOHN CRAWFORD	1LT	MS 37TH INF, CO I
ELLERBEE, WILLIAM GREEN	CAPT	LA 16TH INF, CO K
ELLIOTT, BAILOR SAMPLES	1LT	GA 19TH INF, CO G
ELLIOTT, GEORGE H.	JR 2LT	SC 25TH INF, CO G
ELLIOTT, GILBERT	ADJ	NC 17TH INF, F&S
ELLIOTT, JOHN FELIX	1LT	SC 6TH INF, CO F,I
ELLIOTT, SAMUEL H.	1LT	NC 49TH INF, CO F
ELLIOTT, WILLIAM H.	1LT	CSA DRILLMASTER
ELLIOTT, WILLIAM RICHARD	CAPT	TX 29TH CAV, CO I
ELLIS, CHARLES JAMES	1LT	TN 30TH INF, CO D
ELLIS, EZEKIEL JOHN	CAPT	LA 16TH INF, CO H
ELLIS, JOHN THOMAS	LT COL	VA 19TH INF, CO H
ELLIS, JOHN WILLIS	GOV	NC GOVERNOR 1861
ELLIS, LLOYD	CAPT	VA 45TH BN INF, CO E
ELLIS, THOMAS JEFFERSON	2LT	AL 62ND INF, CO I
ELLIS, THOMAS JEFFERSON	2LT	TX 8TH INF (HOBBY'S), CO K
ELLIS, WILLIAM J.	DELEGATE	SC SIGNER SECESSION ORDINANCE, DELEGATE HORRY COUNTY
ELLIS, WILLIAM T.	CAPT	NC 24TH INF, CO B
ELLISON, JAMES HENRY	CAPT	AL 15TH INF, CO C
ELLISON, JOSEPH MATHEW	1LT	AL 15TH INF, CO C
ELLISON, WILLIAM F.	2LT	TN 32ND INF, CO C
ELLISON, WILLIAM L.	2LT	GA 30TH INF, CO G
ELMORE, THOMAS J.	CAPT	MS 4TH INF, CO G
ELMORE, WILLIAM F.	CAPT	VA 59TH INF, CO B
ELMS, CHARLES HAYWOOD	CAPT	CSA NC POST COMMISSARY CHARLOTTE - CS
EMANUEL, HILLIARD MARION	1LT	GA 17TH INF (MUSCOGEE VOL), CO D
EMBREY, JUDSON JACKSON	1LT	VA 11TH INF, CO I
EMBREY, RICHARD C.	2LT	VA 47TH INF, CO I
EMERSON, JOSEPH M.	CAPT	KY 3RD INF, CO E
ENGLAND, ENOS C.	CAPT	AL 8TH CAV (HATCH'S), CO E

ENGLAND, MATHEW M.	CAPT	AL 11TH INF, CO K
ENGLAND, WILLIAM GAYLE	CAPT	AL 41ST INF, CO E
ENGLAND, WILLIAM JASPER	1LT	GA 52ND INF, CO E
ENGLE, JACOB H.	2LT	VA 7TH CAV (ASHBY'S), GLENN'S CO
ENOCHS, JAMES BASIL	CAPT	MS 6TH INF, CO A
EOFF, JOHN JACKSON	1LT	AR HARRELL'S BN CAV, CO D
EPPS, WILLIAM JAMES	CAPT	VA 2ND STATE RESERVES, CO B
EPTING, JACOB	MAJ	SC 39TH MILITIA
ERWIN, ANDREW EUGENE	COL	MO 6TH INF, F&S
ERWIN, EPHRAIM A.	1LT	SC 1ST INF, CO A
ERWIN, JAMES ANDREW	1LT	LA 3RD CAV, CO K
ERWIN, JESSE B.	1LT	NC 64TH INF, CO K
ESTES, JOHN WINCE	LT COL	TN 52ND INF, CO H
ESTES, JOSEPH PUETT	2LT	NC 95TH MILITIA, CO C (CALDWELL COUNTY)
ESTES, WILLIAM NEWTON	LT COL	CSA 3RD CAV (HOWARD'S), F&S
ETHERIDGE, ROBERT	2LT	GA 55TH INF, CO B
ETHERIDGE, WILLIAM H.	MAJ	VA 41ST INF, F&S
ETTER, W. G.	CAPT	TN 16TH INF, CO H
EUBANK, ELIAS NEWMAN	CAPT	TX 2ND INF, CO C
EUBANKS, JAMES THOMAS	2LT	TN 16TH CAV, CO F
EVANS, CLAIBORNE E.	MAJ	AL 37TH INF, CO G
EVANS, CLEMENT A.	BRIG GEN	ANV LAWTON GORDON EVANS BDE
EVANS, DANIEL JAMES	1LT	VA 20TH BN H ARTY BN, CO A
EVANS, HIRAM MARTIN	1LT	AL 22ND INF, CO E
EVANS, JOHN W.	COL	GA 64TH INF
EVANS, JONATHAN B.	MAJ	NC 24TH INF, CO F
EVANS, ROBERT C.	1LT	GA 27TH INF, CO H
EVANS, ROBERT L.	CAPT	TN 53RD INF, CO I
EVANS, THOMAS JEFFERSON	1LT	AL 1ST BN ARTY, CO F,D
EVANS, THOMAS JEFFERSON	1LT	GA 5TH CAV, CO E
EVANS, WILLIAM D.	2LT	FL 1ST INF, CO D
EVE, MACPEHERSON BERRIEN	MAJ	CSA
EWELL, RICHARD STODDERT	LT GEN	CSA - 4TH CORPS ANV
EZELL, CULLEN R.	CAPT	GA 4TH INF RESERVES, CO G
EZELL, FRANCIS MARION	1LT	TN 9TH CAV (WARD'S), CO I
EZZELL, MASON	BVT 2LT	TN 51ST INF, COK
FAGAN, JAMES FLEMING	MAJ GEN	AR CAV DIV - ATM
FAIN, JAMES MCKINNEY	2LT	LA 11TH INF BN, CO G
FAIN, JOHN SIMPSON	COL	GA 65TH INF, F&S
FAIN, THOMAS MADISON	1LT	AL 4TH INF (CONEUCH GUARDS), CO K
FAIN, WILLIAM ISAAC	1LT	AL 51ST PARTISAN RANGERS, CO. A
FAIRFAX, JOHN WALTER	LT COL	CSA AAG
FAKES, GIDEON BRANSFORD, MD	ASST SURG	AR 1ST MTD RIFLES, CO D
FALCONER, THOMAS STERLING	2LT	MS 46TH INF, CO A
FALLIGANT, CHAMPION GUSTAVUS	1LT	GA 48TH INF, CO H
FALLIGANT, PHILIP RAIFORD	JR 2LT	GA 54TH INF, CO F
FALLIGANT, ROBERT SHICK	2LT	GA L ARTY, MILLEDGE'S BTRY
FANNIN, PETER M.	1LT	KY 5TH MTD INF, CO B
FANNING, JAMES HENRY	1LT	SC 1ST INF, CO K
FANT, ALBERT E.	COL	MS 5TH INF, CO H
FARGASON, LEONARD MASON	CAPT	TX 19TH INF, CO G
FARINHOLT, BENJAMIN LYONS	2LT	VA 53RD INF, CO E

FARLEY, FRANCIS MARION	CAPT	FL 8TH INF, CO E
FARLEY, WILLIAMS DOWN	CAPT	CSA - SCOUT FOR GEN STUART, ADC
FARMER, ABNER TAYLOR	2LT	VA 14TH INF, CO G
FARMER, LEVIN WILLIAM	CAPT	GA 38TH INF, CO G
FARMER, SYLVESTER J., MD	SURG	GA 15TH INF, CO D
FARRAR, ABSALOM WASHINGTON	CAPT	GA 53RD INF, CO F
FARRAR, DANIEL SMITH	CAPT	MS CAV, JEFF DAVID LEGION - AQM
FARRAR, HENRY HARRIS	3LT	MS 13TH INF, CO C
FARRAR, SIMON BOWDEN	CAPT	TX 4TH CAV, CO H
FARRIS, OLVIER BUCKLEY	MAJ	TN 22ND CAV, CO K
FARROW, WILLIAM T., REV	CHAPLAIN	SC 1ST INF (BUTLER'S)
FARROW, WILSON TILMAN	1LT	NC 33RD INF, CO H
FAULK, WILLIAM JASPER	2LT	AL 36TH INF, CO F
FAUST, HENRY M., MD	ASST SURG	SC 5TH CAV, F&S
FAUVER, JOHN ALEXANDER	1LT	VA 52ND INF, CO F
FEAGIN, ISAAC BALL	LT COL	AL 15TH INF, CO F
FEARS, AUGUSTUS B.	CHAPLAIN	CSA
FEATHERSTON, CHARLES HENRY	CAPT	TX 11TH CAV, CO H
FELTON, THADIUS W.	CAPT	AL 35TH INF, CO B
FENDLEY, JOSEPH H.	2LT	AL 38TH INF, CO B
FEREBEE, DENNIS DOZIER	COL	NC 4TH INF, F&S
FERGUSON, CHAMP	CAPT	CSA - AQM
FERGUSON, JAMES EDWARD	2LT	MS 14TH INF, CO H
FERGUSON, JOSEPH MARTIN	CAPT	VA 8TH CAV, CO G
FERGUSON, MILTON J.	COL	VA 16TH CAV
FERGUSON, RICHARD	LT	VA 18TH INF - ADJ
FERGUSON, SAMUEL J.	2LT	VA 8TH CAV, CO K
FERGUSON, THOMAS CURTIS	CAPT	AL 44TH INF, CO E
FERGUSON, THOMAS JOSIAH	1LT	NC THOMAS LEGION INF, CO E
FERRELL, GEORGE ARCHER	1LT	AL LT ARTY
FERRELL, T. R.	2LT	VA 34TH BN CAV (WITCHER'S NIGHTHAWKS), CO D
FERRELL, WILLIAM BOLIVAR	CAPT	MS 37TH INF, CO K
FERRELL, WILLIAM C.	2LT	NC 4TH CAV, CO H
FIELD, CHARLES W.	MAJ GEN	ANV - HOOD'S DIV
FINDLAY, WILLIAM SPILLER, MD	ASST SURG	TN 43RD INF, F&S
FINGER, M. W.	1LT	GA 4TH CAV
FINGER, SIDNEY MICHAEL	MAJ	CSA - QM
FINKS, ALEXANDER NEWTON	CAPT	VA 10TH INF, CO L
FINLEY, G. W.	2LT	TN 8TH INF, CO D
FINLEY, JESSEE JOHNSON	BRIG GEN	FL BDE
FISHBURNE, ROBERT, JR	CAPT	SC 2ND INF, CO I
FISHER, W. F.	2LT	TN 24TH INF, CO C
FITCH, WILLIAM WALKER	1LT	NC 47TH MILITIA (CASWELL COUNTY)
FITZENREITER, CHARLES F.	2LT	LA 22ND MILITIA
FITZGERALD, PATRICK HENRY	2LT	VA 3RD CAV, CO E
FITZHUGH, LAFAYETTE HENRY	CAPT	KY 1ST INF, CO H
FITZPATRICK, BENJAMIN FRANKLIN	CAPT	MS 31ST INF, CO C
FLANAGIN, HARRIS	GOV	AR GOVERNOR 1862-1864
FLANDERS, ALEXANDER CHESTNUT	CAPT	GA 48TH INF, CO H
FLANDERS, CHARLES EDGAR	2LT	GA 26TH INF, CO A
FLANERY, ELKANAH	3LT	VA 64TH MTD INF, CO G
FLEENOR, WESLEY JAYNE	3LT	VA 64TH MTD INF, CO A

FLEMING, CHARLES EDWIN, MD	SURG	SC 22ND INF, F&S
FLEMING, WILLIAM AUGUSTUS	1LT	GA 5TH CAV, CO G
FLEMING, WILLIAM BASKERVILEE	2LT	NC 12TH INF, CO C
FLEMING, WILLIAM CARPENTER	CAPT	TN 33RD INF, CO A
FLEMING, WILLIAM HORD	CAPT	TX 34TH CAV, CO K
FLETCHER, DAVID RILEY	1LT	AL 55TH INF, CO G
FLETCHER, JAMES BENJAMIN	CAPT	AL 49TH INF, CO D
FLETCHER, JAMES DYKES	1LT	VA 64TH MTD INF, CO D
FLETCHER, JOHN GOULD	CAPT	AR 6TH INF, CO A
FLETCHER, LARKIN	2LT	VA 37TH INF, CO I
FLEWELLEN, JAMES PERSONS	MAJ	CSA
FLEWELLYN, EDWARD A MD	SURG	GA 5TH INF, F&S
FLOOD, EDWARD JR	1LT	LA 6TH IRISH INF, CO K
FLOOD, JOEL WALKER	CAPT	VA 2ND CAV, CO H
FLOURNOY, EDMUND H	CAPT	VA 6TH INF, CO K
FLOURNOY, THOMAS S	COL	VA 6TH CAV, CO G
FLOWERS, ABNER	LT	AL 39TH INF, CO D
FLOWERS, JAMES	2LT	MS 5TH CAV, CO C
FLOYD, FRANCIS FULTON	2LT	NC 51ST INF, CO E
FLOYD, JOHN BUCHANAN	CAPT	AL 9TH CAV (MALONE'S)
FLOYD, JOHN COLBERT	1LT	GA COBB'S LEGION, CO A
FLOYD, JOHN JULIUS	COL	GA 10TH CAV, CO K (STATE GUARDS)
FLOYD, JOUSHA C	2LT	SC 26TH INF, CO H
FLOYD, WILLIAM JASON	CAPT	MS 18TH CAV, CO H
FLY, GEORGE WASHINGTON LAFAYETTE	MAJ	TX 2ND INF, F&S
FOARD, JOHN	2LT	NC 35TH INF, CO F
FOARD, NOAH PARTEE	CAPT	NC 1ST CAV, CO F
FOLEY, WILLIAM D	1LT	LA 1ST SPECIAL BN INF (WHEAT'S), CO D
FOLGER, ROMOLUS S	1LT	NC 28TH INF - ADJ
FOLLIN, ARTHUR W	2LT	VA 8TH INF, CO H
FOLSOM, SAMPSON	COL	CSA - 1ST CHOCTAW MTD RIFLES
FOLTS, ALEXANDER	2LT	TX 13TH VOLS, CO C
FOOTE, HENRY STUART	REPRESENTATIVE	TN REPRESENTATIVE TO CONFEDERATE CONGRESS
FORBES, JOHN C	CAPT	VA 42ND INF, CO G
FORBES, JOSEPH HARRIS	CAPT	CSA - BRAXTON'S BN ARTY - AQM
FORBIS, JOHN W	CAPT	NC 68TH MILITIA (GUILFORD COUNTY)
FORCUM, JOHN BURGESS JR	CAPT	NC 4TH INF, CO H
FORD, ABRAHAM	CAPT	TN 25TH INF, CO K
FORD, JAMES C MD	ASST SURG	CSA
FORD, JAMES C	1LT	MO 11TH INF, CO D
FORD, JOHN S	COL	TX 2ND CAV, F&S
FORD, N B	2LT	GA 22ND INF, CO G
FORD, ROBERT GRAHAM	CAPT	GA 10TH MILITIA (WORTH COUNTY)
FORE, JOHN FRANKLIN	1LT	AL 23RD INF, CO D,E
FORMAN, SAMUEL TEBBS	1LT	KY 4TH INF, CO I
FORREST, AARON H JR	CAPT	MS 6TH BN CAV
FORREST, CHARLES MATLOCK	CAPT	TN 35TH INF, CO B
FORREST, JERRY E	COL	TN 13TH CAV (GORE'S)
FORREST, JESSE ANDERSON	LT COL	TN 21ST CAV
FORREST, NATHAN BEDFORD	LT GEN	AOT CMDR
FORRESTER, JOHN E	2LT	SC 16TH INF (BUTLER'S), CO I
FORSEE, TILFORD MONROE	1LT	TN 24TH BN SHARPSHOOTERS, CO A

FORTNER, JAMES ASHLEY	2LT	GA 10TH INF, CO H
FORTUNE, WILLIAM PATTON	CAPT	NC 79TH INF, CO C
FOSTER, BENJAMIN C	2LT	AL 5TH INF, CO I
FOSTER, JAMES LACHLISON	2ND ASST ENGR	CSN
FOSTER, KINCHEN BAXTER	2LT	AR 10TH INF, CO D
FOSTER, THOMAS JOEL	CAPT	GA 40TH INF, CO G
FOSTER, ZACKARIAH N	1LT	MS 21ST INF, CO K
FOURNET, VALSIN ANTOINE	LT COL	LA 10TH INF (YELLOW JACKETS)
FOUST, ELIJAH	CAPT	TN 5TH INF, CO F
FOUTCH, MARTIN B	CAPT	TN 11TH BN CAV (GORDON'S), CO F
FOWLE, WILLIAM HOMMES JR	CAPT	VA 17TH INF, CO H
FOWLER, ALVIN	CAPT	KY 10TH CAV, CO C
FOWLER, AUGUSTUS SHERRARD MD	SURG	GA 39TH INF, F&S
FOWLER, EDWARD W	2LT	NC 18TH INF, CO C
FOWLER, HENRY BARKSDALE	2LT	NC 13TH INF, CO A (YANCEYVILLE GRAYS)
FOWLER, JOHN HENRY	2LT	NC 52ND INF, CO D
FOWLER, JOHN WESLEY	BVT 2LT	MS 27TH INF, CO A
FOWLER, JOSIAH CRUDUP MD	ASST SURG	NC 47TH INF
FOWLER, MOSES T	CAPT	SC 1ST INF, CO G
FOWLER, WILLIAM H	CAPT	AL PHELAN'S CO LIGHT ARTILLERY
FOWLER, WILLIAM HARRISON	CAPT	SC 3RD INF (JAMES'), CO E
FOWLER, ZEPHANIAL A	CAPT	GA 6TH INF, CO E
FOWLKES, EUSEBIUS	CAPT	VA 11TH INF (PRESTON GUARDS), CO F
FOWLKES, WILLIAM T	2LT	VA 18TH INF, CO C
FOX, THOMAS JEFFERSON	2LT	MS 9TH INF, CO F
FOY, CHRISTOPHER DUDLEY	CAPT	NC 67TH INF, CO H
FOY, FRANKLIN	2LT	NC 8TH BN CAV, CO A (PARTISAN RANGERS)
FRANK, B M	2LT	TX 1ST INF, CO A
FRANKLIN, JOHN A	2LT	TX 29TH CAV, CO F
FRANKLIN, LUCIUS C	1LT	MS 11TH INF, CO D
FRAZER, JOHN LELAND	2LT	GA 61ST INF, CO G
FRAZIER, CHARLES W	CAPT	CSA - AAG
FRAZIER, JOHN H	JR 2LT	MO 10TH CAV, CO B
FREEMAN, BASIL MANLY	ENSIGN	TN 38TH INF, CO G
FREEMAN, DANDRIDGE CLAIRBOURNE JR	LT COL	CSA GEN JOHN PEGRAM ADC
FREEMAN, JEREMIAH S	CAPT	GA 2ND CAV, CO A
FREEMAN, THOMAS HARVEY	1LT	TN 45TH INF, CO F
FREEMAN, THOMAS JONES SR	COL	TN 22ND INF, CO G
FREEMAN, WESLEY NEWELL	CAPT	NC 25TH INF, CO C
FRENCH, JAMES HENRY	CAPT	CSA TX GEN BEE'S STAFF, FT BROWN, BROWNS-VILLE - ACS
FRENCH, SAMUEL BASSETT	COL	CSA - GEN T. J. "STONEWALL" JACKSON - ADC
FRENCH, THOMAS BARTON	1LT	VA COOPER'S CO L ARTY
FRIEND, JOHN WESLEY	LT	CSA THIRD CORPS, F&S
FRISTOE, ROBERT HARRISON	CAPT	KY 8TH CAV, CO C
FRITTS, CLAIBORNE S	1LT	AR 17TH INF (GRIFFITHS), CO G
FRIZZELL, JOHN	CAPT	CSA AQ
FRIZZELL, WILLIAM H	1LT	MS 12TH INF, CO I
FRY, A S	1LT	VA 34TH BN CAV (WITCHER'S NIGHTHAWKS), CO D
FRY, BIRKETT DAVENPORT	BRIG GEN	AL 13TH INF
FRY, GEORGE THOMPSON	CAPT	TN 37TH INF, CO C H
FRY, JOSEPH	CAPT	CSN MOBILE SQUADRON

Name	Rank	Unit
FRY, NEILL A	3LT	NC 49TH INF, CO D
FULGHAM, JAMES MONROE	CAPT	MS 36TH INF, CO K
FULGHUM, GERRY	1LT	NC 2ND INF, CO B
FULKERSON, ABRAM	MAJ	TN 19TH INF, CO K
FULKERSON, SAMUEL VANCE	COL	VA 37TH INF
FULKERSON, WILLIAM H	LT COL	TN 63RD INF, CO A
FULLER, JAMES RICHARD	1LT	LA 12TH INF, CO E
FULLER, THOMAS CHARLES	REPRESENTATIVE	NC 2ND CONFEDERATE CONGRESS (1864-1865)
FULLER, WILLIAM A	CAPT	GA INF, FULLER'S CO (INDEPENDENT RAILROAD GUARD TROOPS)
FUNCHES, GEORGE J D	CAPT	MS 16TH INF, CO B
FUNDERBURK, GEORGE WASHINGTON	1LT	SC 22ND INF, CO E
FUNKHOUSER, MONROE P	CAPT	CSA - AQM
FUNSTUN, DAVID	COL	VA 11TH INF, F&S
FUQUA, JOSEPH WATKINS	1LT	LA CAV, COLE'S CO
FURMAN, CHARLES MANNING	CAPT	SC 16TH INF (GREENVILLE'S), CO H
FURMAN, SCRIMZEOUR CORNWALL	MAJ	LA 2ND CAV, CO E
FURR, CICERO HOLT	CAPT	GA 43RD INF (HALL LIGHT GUARDS), CO F
FURR, SOLOMON	1LT	NC 7TH INF, CO B
GAAR, BENJAMIN FRANKLIN	1LT	VA 7TH INF, CO K
GABARD, RICHMOND MURPHY	1LT	NC 75TH MILITIA (YADKIN COUNTY)
GADDES, ROBERT	2LT	AL 8TH INF, CO C
GAFFORD, ANDREW J	2LT	TX 32ND CAV, CO D
GAINES, WILLIAM F	CAPT	MS 22ND INF, GAINES' CO
GAITHER, BEALE	COL	AR 27TH INF, CO D
GALLASPY, GARLAND MILLER BURLEY	CAPT	MS 36TH INF, CO C
GALLOP, HIRAM CLYDE	CAPT	NC 1ST MILITIA (CURRITUCK COUNTY)
GALLOWAY, HENRY C	2LT	AR McGEHEE'S CAV, CO C
GALLOWAY, JAMES EARL	1LT	NC 62ND INF, CO K
GAMBLE, JOHN FRANK	1LT	NC 14TH INF, CO D
GAMBRELL, JAMES BRUTON	JR 2LT	MS 2ND INF, CO I
GAMMILL, GEORGE WASHINGTON	2LT	AL 47TH INF, CO K
GANDEE, WILLIAM ALEXANDER	LT	VA 19TH CAV, CO C
GANN, FRANCIS FRANKLIN	2LT	GA 1ST INF, CO E
GANTT, HENRY	LT COL	VA 19TH INF, F&S
GANTT, HIRAM	CAPT	AL 4TH INF (CONEUCH GUARDS), CO I
GARDINER, ALGERNON COLGATE	CAPT	TN 9TH INF, CO G
GARDINER, JOHN R	CAPT	AL 49TH INF, CO K
GARDINER, WILLIAM F	1LT	AL 49TH INF, CO A
GARDNER, JAMES M	CAPT	NC 27TH INF, CO K
GARLAND, NELSON HENRY	2LT	VA 23RD INF, CO I
GARLAND, SAMUEL JR	BRIG GEN	VA 11TH INF
GARLINGTON, BENJAMIN CONWAY	LT COL	SC 3RD INF, CO A
GARMON, JOHN H	2LT	MS 1ST INF, CO I
GARNETT, MUSCOE RUSSELL HUNTER	REPRESENTATIVE	VA CONFEDERATE REPRESENTATIVE 1862-64
GARNETT, THOMAS STUART	LT COL	VA 48TH INF
GAROUTEE, WILLIAM BABINGTON	JR 2LT	MO 3RD BN CAV, CO E
GARRETT, GEORGE WASHINGTON BROOKS	MAJ	MS 23RD INF, CO C
GARRETT, ISAAC	ENROLLING OFFICER	GA 1165TH MILITIA DIST
GARRETT, RICHARD M	2LT	VA 1ST ARTY (JAMES CITY ARTY), CO B
GARRETT, WILLIAM E	1LT	TX 1ST CAV (STATE TROOPS), CO E
GARRETT, WILLIAM J	MAJ	GA COMMISSARY DEPT, AUGUSTUS

GARRETT, WILLIAM N	LT COL	NC 64TH INF, F&S
GARRIS, JOSEPH T	JR 2LT	NC 12TH BN CAV, CO C
GARRISON, FLEMING H	MAJ	TX 14TH CAV, CFS
GARRISON, JAMES HENRY	CAPT	TX 14TH CAV, CO C
GARRISON, WILLIAM G	2LT	AR 27TH INF, CO F
GARRONTTE, WILLIAM BABINGTON	JR LT	MO 3RD CAV BN, CO E
GARTRELL, LUCIUS JEREMIAH	COL	GA 7TH INF, F&S
GARY, MARTIN WITHERSPOON	BRIG GEN	SC HAMPTON LEGION CAV
GASKINS, DANIEL	2LT	GA 50TH INF, CO I
GASQUE, HENRY A	1LT	SC 21ST INF, CO I
GASTON, JAMES MCFADDEN MD	SURG/CAPT	SC 6TH INF
GASTON, JOHN BROWN MD	SURG/CAPT	AL 14TH INF (JACKSON'S AVENGERS)
GASTON, JOSEPH LUCIUS	CAPT	SC 6TH INF, CO F
GASTON, JOSIAH PERRY	1LT	NC 64TH INF, CO I - ADJ
GASTON, WILLIAM H	CAPT	TX 1ST INF, CO H
GATES, ELIJAH P	COL	MO 1ST CAV, F&S
GATES, MICHAEL	2LT	MO 3RD CAV, CO H
GATES, SETH H	CAPT	GA 59TH INF, CO K
GATLIN, THOMAS HALL BENTON	CAPT	NC 33RD INF, CO B
GATLING, JOHN T	2LT	NC 52ND INF, CO C
GAUSE, WILLIAM R	COL	MO 3RD INF, CO B
GAVIN, GEORGE W	2LT	MS 40TH INF, CO A
GAY, HIRAM	1LT	GA 50TH INF, CO H
GAY, LITTLETON ALLEN	1LT	VA 3RD INF, CO D
GAYDEN, WILLIAM ALEXANDER	1LT	MS 6TH BN CAV
GEARHEART, ADAM	1LT	KY 13TH CAV, CO F
GEFFCKIN, ELDRED	JR 2LT	GA 63RD INF, CO B, F
GEOGHEGAN, AMBROSE DENTON	1LT	MS 19TH INF, CO D
GEORGE, JAMES Z	COL	MS 5TH CAV
GEORGE, NATHAN BASS	BVT 2LT	MO 12TH CAV, CO C
GETZEN, THOMAS W	CAPT	SC 19TH INF, CO B
GHENT, HENRY CLAY MD	SURG	VA 15TH INF
GHOLSON, SAMUEL JAMESON	BRIG GEN	MS STATE TROOPS
GHORMLEY, DEWITT CLINTON	CAPT	TN 5TH CAV, CO K
GIBBON, ROBERT MD	SURG	NC 28TH INF, F&S
GIBBONEY, ROBERT E	COMMISSIONER	CSA PRICES COMMISSION
GIBBONS, SIMEON BUFORD	COL	VA 10TH INF
GIBBS, HARMON B	2LT	AR 12TH INF, CO E
GIBBS, JULIUS GAUGE	CAPT	MS 30TH INF, CO I
GIBBS, THOMAS	REPRESENTATIVE	GA STATE REPRESENTATIVE
GIBSON, CHURCHILL CLAYTON	1LT	TX 17TH CAV, CO F
GIBSON, GEORGE B	CAPT	AR 34TH INF, CO B
GIBSON, NELSON M	2LT	SC 23RD INF, CO A
GIBSON, SAMUEL BENIAH	1LT	VA 21ST INF, CO E
GIBSON, THOMAS SHELBY	CAPT	VA 25TH CAV, CO G
GIBSON, WILLIAM RENFRO	1LT	TN 1ST CAV, CO L
GILBERT, GIDEON SHOCKLEY	CAPT	GA DOUROUGH'S CAV BATTN
GILBREATH, MONTGOMERY	LT COL	AL 31ST INF (HALES), CO E
GILES, JOHN I	1LT	GA 49TH INF, CO C
GILL, HARDY C	2LT	LA 1ST INF (NELLIGAN'S), CO B
GILL, WILLLIAM HENRY HARRISON	1LT	SC 6TH INF, CO F
GILLASPIE, CHARLES FOX REV	CHAPLAIN	MS 8TH INF, F&S

GILLESPIE, JAMES HARRISON	1LT	VA 23RD INF, CO D
GILLHAM, BENJAMIN F	2LT	GA 8TH INF, CO K
GILLHAM, ISAAC A	2LT	TN 48TH INF (VOORHIES), CO C
GILLIAM, GEORGE	CAPT	NC 52ND INF, CO C
GILLIAM, HENRY RUTLEDGE	CAPT	TX 13TH INF, CO H
GILLIAM, JAMES S	LT COL	VA 9TH INF, F&S
GILLIAM, JAMES	1LT	NC 7TH SENIORS RESERVES, BRADSHAWS CO
GILLIS, JOHN	2LT	MS 7TH INF, CO B
GILMER, JERRY FRANCIS	MAJ GEN	CSA CHIEF OF THE ENGINEER BUREAU
GILSON, WILLIAM CAMPBELL MD	SURG	MS 35 INF, F&S
GIRARDEAU, JOHN LAFAYETTE REV	CHAPLAIN	SC 23RD INF, F&S
GIRARDEAU, WILLIAM OGLETHORPE	CAPT	FL 3RD INF, CO H
GISH, GEORGE McHENRY	CAPT	VA 28TH INF, CO I
GIST, JOSEPH FINCHER	COL	SC 15TH INF, F&S
GIST, STATES RIGHTS	BRIG GEN	SC MILITIA (GIST'S BDE)
GIVEN, THEODORE	1LT	VA 17TH CAV, CO I
GIVENS, THOMAS WILKES	2LT	FL 8TH VOLS, CO K
GLASS, P T	MAJ	CSA - CS
GLASS, WILLIAM WOOD	LT COL	VA 51ST MILITIA, F&S
GLENN, JOHN EDWARD	COL	AR 36TH INF, F&S
GLOSTER, ARTHUR WILLIS	CAPT	CSA (TN) 3RD ENGR, CO C
GLOVER, JOHN THOMAS	LT	GA 6TH INF, CO I - ACTING ADJ
GLOVER, SAMUEL H	CAPT	TN 8TH CAV, CO H
GLOWER, WILLIAM THORNTON	1LT	GA 53RD INF, CO C
GOAD, AARON FLOYD	2LT	VA 54TH INF, CO G
GODWIN, AARON STRAIT	LT COL	TN 48TH INF, CO K
GODWIN, JOHN DILL	CAPT	GA 28TH SIEGE ARTY BN, CO G
GOETTEE, FRANCIS MARION	2LT	GA 26TH INF, CO E
GOFF, FELIX WALKER	1LT	MS 4TH CAV, CO F
GOGGANS, DANIEL PICKENS	CAPT	SC 1ST INF, CO B
GOLDSMITH, WASHINGTON LAFAYETTE	LT COL	GA 14TH INF, CO K
GOLDWIRE, JOHN WILLIAM KING	BVT 2LT	GA 12TH INF, CO I
GONZALES, ALFREDO JOSE	COL	CSA - GEN T G BEAUREGARD'S ARTY
GONZALES, JOSEPH MICHAEL	CAPT	LA 14TH CAV (OGDEN'S), CO D
GONZALEZ, MARTIN	2LT	TX 33RD CAV, CO H
GOODBEE, DAVID	2LT	LA MILES' LEGION, CO E
GOODE, FRANCIS MARION	CAPT	AL 44TH INF, CO H
GOODE, JOHN THOMAS	COL	VA 34TH INF, F&S
GOODGAME, JAMES ALLEN	CAPT	TX 15TH INF, CO F
GOODIN, J S	2LT	MO 1ST STATE GUARD CAV, CO D
GOODING, RICHARD McDUFFIE	CAPT	SC 11TH INF, CO D
GOODLETT, WILLIAM H	CAPT	SC 3RD INF, CO F
GOODLOE, ALBERT THEODORE	1LT	AL 35TH INF, CO D
GOODMAN, JAMES JORDON	1LT	NC 37TH INF, CO A
GOODMAN, SAMUEL H	1LT	TX MADISON'S CAV, CO G
GOODNER, JOHN FITE	COL	TN 7TH INF, F&S
GOODSON, JAMES	CAPT	TX STATE TROOPS, 17TH BDE, MONTGOMERY COUNTY, BEAT #3
GOODSON, JOAB	CAPT	AL 44TH INF, CO B
GOODWIN, EBENEZER WESCOT	DELEGATE	SC SIGNER SECESSION ORDINANCE, DELEGATE MARLBORO COUNTY
GOODWIN, EDWIN G	LT COL	AL 35TH INF

GOODWIN, ISHAM	2LT	SC 2ND STATE TROOPS, CO H
GOODWYN, ARTHUR MCCLURE	BVT 2LT	VA 9TH INF, 2ND CO H
GOODWYN, ARTHUR MONROE	CAPT	VA 12TH INF, CO I
GOODWYN, PETERS WHITTEN	CAPT	SC 6TH CAV, CO C
GOOGER, MARCUS DE LAFAYETTE	2LT	GA 49TH INF, CO D
GOOLSBY, WILLIAM J	JR 2LT	TX 2ND BN CAV (STATE TROOPS), CO A
GOOLSBY, WILLIAM J	1LT	VA 28TH INF, CO D
GORDON, ANDREW R	CAPT	TN 11TH CAV, CO E
GORDON, FRANCIS M	1LT	KY 2ND CAV (DUKE'S), CO C
GORDON, GEORGE AUGUSTUS	CAPT	GA 1ST INF (GORDON COUNTY)
GORDON, GEORGE WASHINGTON	BRIG GEN	VAUGHN'S BDE, CHEATHAM'S CORPS
GORDON, GREENBERRY G MD	SURG	GA 9TH INF, F&S
GORDON, JAMES BYRON	BRIG GEN	CSA ANV CAV
GORDON, JOHN BROWN	MAJ GEN	ANV - II CORPS
GORE, FLOYD SHANNON	2LT	VA 22ND INF (KANAWA RIFLES), CO G
GOREE, THOMAS JEWETT	1LT	CSA - GEN JAMES LONGSTREET ADC
GOULD, HORATIO NELSON	JR 2LT	AL MOBILE CITY TROOP
GOULD, WILLIAM BOND	CAPT	AR 4TH INF, CO G
GOURRIER, THOMAS G	CAPT	LA 3RD INF, CO A
GOVAN, DANIEL CHEVILETTE	BRIG GEN	AR INF
GRACE, CHRISTOPHER C	2LT	GA 12TH INF, CO I
GRACEY, EMORY AUGUSTUS	2LT	TX 1ST CAV (YAGER'S), CO H
GRACY, FRANK PATTEN	1LT	KY COBBS L ARTY
GRAHAM, ADAM	CAPT	GA 12TH INF, CO I
GRAHAM, JOHN BETHUNE	CAPT	NC 51ST MILITIA (MOORE COUNTY)
GRAHAM, ROBERT F	COL	SC 21ST INF, F&S
GRAHAM, ROBERT VIRGIL JR	COL	SC 21ST INF, F&S
GRAHAM, SAMUEL LIVINGSTON	CAPT	VA 6TH BN RESERVES (TAZEWELL COUNTY), CO B
GRAHAM, WILLIAM ALEXANDER JR	CAPT	NC 2ND CAV, CO K
GRAHAM, WILLIAM LEANDER	LT COL	VA 16TH CAV, F&S
GRANBURY, HIRAM BRINSON	BRIG GEN	TX BDE
GRANDY, CALEB L	2LT	NC 56TH INF, CO A
GRANGER, JOHN W	1LT	AL 37TH INF, CO E
GRANT, WILLIAM WATSON	CAPT	GA 65TH INF, CO K
GRAVES, CHARLES IVERSON	1LT	CSN CSS VIRGINIA II
GRAVES, EDWARD B	2LT	TN 3RD CAV (FORREST'S), CO G
GRAVES, JOHN BARRINGER	2LT	TN 43RD INF, CO I
GRAVES, WILLIAM F	MAJ	VA 2ND CAV, F&S
GRAVES, WILLIAM GRIFFIN	CAPT	NC 56TH INF, CO H
GRAVES, WILLIAM	CAPT	AL CAV, GRAVES' CO
GRAVLEE, JESSE LAFAYETTE	JR 2LT	AL 28TH INF, CO I
GRAY, DANIEL LEVI	2LT	GA 61ST INF, CO K
GRAY, HENRY VINCENT MD	SURG	CSA HUGER'S BN CAV, F&S
GRAY, OLIVER CROSBY	CAPT	AR 3RD CAV, CO A
GRAY, ROBERT H	LT COL	NC 22ND INF, CO L
GRAYDON, JOHN CLINTON	1LT	AL 6TH CAV, CO B
GREEN, ALEXANDER PORTER	1LT	GA 10TH CAV, CO D
GREEN, DANIEL SMITH MD	SURG	CSN RICHMOND STATION
GREEN, HENRY E	CAPT	AR 15TH INF, CO D
GREEN, HENRY HAINES	1LT	AL 28TH INF, CO C
GREEN, HENRY HARDIN	2LT	GA 42ND INF, CO G
GREEN, JOHN	CAPT	AL 9TH CAV (MALONE'S), CO L

GREEN, JOSEPH	CAPT	NC 30TH INF, CO C
GREEN, LEANDER PALEMICUS	1LT	TX 9TH CAV, CO K
GREEN, THOMAS	BVT 2LT	MS 1ST CAV (WIRT ADAMS'), CO M
GREEN, WILLIAM MARTIN	1LT	TN 44TH INF (CONSOLIDATED), CO A
GREEN, WILLIAM NATHANIEL	CAPT	AL 44TH INF, CO F
GREENE, ISRAEL C	MAJ	CSA - QM
GREENE, PETER ALEXANDER	1LT	GA 31ST INF (CROWDERS), CO G
GREENE, WILLIAM MACKEY	MAJ	TN 11TH, CO C
GREENHOW, ROSE O'NEAL	AGENT	CONFEDERATE AGENT
GREENWAY, GILBERT C	1LT	VA 51ST INF, F&S - ADJ
GREENWOOD, BEVERLY CARTER #2	CAPT	TX GOLIAD COUNTY HOME GUARD, CHARCO PCT
GREENWOOD, DEWITT CLINTON	1LT	MS 11 CAV, CO A
GREER, GREEN BERRY	1LT	TN 55TH INF (BROWN'S), CO A
GREER, JAMES LAFAYETTE	2LT	GA 4TH INF, CO D
GREER, SAMUEL W	CAPT	MO FRISTOE'S CAV, CO L
GREER, THOMAS JEFFERSON	1LT	SC 18TH INF, CO B
GREGG, JACOB FRANKLIN	1LT	MO 12TH CAV, CO B
GREGG, JOHN	BRIG GEN	CSA CMDR HOOD'S TX BDE
GREGG, MAXCY	BRIG GEN	CSA
GREGG, WILLIAM HENRY	CAPT	MO 1ST INF, CO M
GREGORY, J L	1LT	LA RESERVE CORPS, CO B
GREGORY, JOSEPH L REV	CHAPLAIN	KY 8TH INF
GRESHAM, JAMES FILES	CAPT	MS 26TH INF, CO H
GRICE, JOHN A	CAPT	GA 56TH INF, CO C
GRIDER, JESSE S	LT COL	AR McGEHEE'S CAV
GRIFFIN, BENJAMIN	CAPT	TX 27TH CAV, CO F
GRIFFIN, FELIX THOMAS	1LT	GA 11TH BN ARTY (SUMTER ARTY), CO C,E
GRIFFIN, HARVEY D	1LT	NC 47TH INF, CO B
GRIFFIN, J B	LT COL	GA 3RD REG RESERVES, F&S
GRIFFIN, LENN MITCHELL	2LT	GA 1ST INF (RAMSEY'S), CO G
GRIFFIN, THOMAS MASTERSON	CAPT	MS 3RD CAV, F&S - AQM
GRIFFIS, JOHN CHAPPEL	MAJ	GA 18TH INF, ADJ
GRIFFITH, JOHN SUMMERFIELD	LT COL	TX 6TH CAV, BFS
GRIGGS, GEORGE KING	COL	VA 38TH INF, CO K
GRIGGS, ROBERT DEBEL B	2LT	AL 14TH INF (JACKSON'S AVENGERS), CO A
GRIGSBY, ANDREW JACKSON	COL	VA 27TH INF, F&S
GRIGSBY, GEORGE WASHINGTON	CAPT	VA 25TH MILITIA, CO C
GRIMES, BRYAN	MAJ GEN	ANV RODES OLD DIV, 2ND CORPS
GRIMES, CAREY FRANKLIN	CAPT	VA L ARTY (PORTSMOUTH L ARTY), THOMPSON'S CO
GRIMES, GEORGE MARTIN	MAJ	SC 1ST INF (HAGOOD'S)
GRIMES, HENRY JACKSON	CAPT	VA 10TH CAV, CO B
GRIMSLEY, WILLIAM C	MAJ	MO 4TH INF, F&S
GRIMSLEY, WILLIAM D	2D ASST ENGR	CSN CSS FLORIDA
GRINER, NATHANIEL G H	2LT	FL 9TH INF, CO K
GRINNAN, GEORGE ARCHIBALD	1LT	VA 13TH INF, CO B
GRISSETT, EDWARD W	1LT	NC 8TH SENIOR RESERVES
GRISSOM, ALEXANDER	2LT	TN 35TH INF, CO C
GRISWOLD, BENJAMIN JAMES	2LT	NC 27TH MILITIA (WAYNE COUNTY)
GRIZZARD, JAMES MONROE MD	SURG/CAPT	NC 35TH MILITIA (HALIFAX COUNTY)
GRIZZARD, WALTER BOGGAN	CAPT	TN GREER'S PARTISAN RANGERS - AQM
GROVES, JOHN FERGUS	MAJ	GA 1ST INF, F&S

GRUBB, RICHARD B	CAPT	VA 35TH BN CAV, CO C
GRUBBS, WILLIAM LANCASTER	1LT	SC 2ND INF, CO D
GRUBBS, WORTHY JORDAN	1LT	MS JEFF DAVIS LEGION CAV, CO I
GUDGER, JAMES M	CAPT	NC 14TH INF, CO F
GUILFORD, JOHN C	2LT	GA 51ST INF, CO G
GUINN, JAMES MILES KILLIAN	CAPT	AL 13TH INF, CO K
GUINN, JAMES SAMUEL	1LT	KY 13TH CAV, CO I
GUINN, THOMAS D	2LT	GA 3RD BN SHARPSHOOTERS, CO A
GUNN, LUNDY REID	3LT	MS 17TH INF, CO A
GUNN, WILLIAM THOMAS	CAPT	TX 29TH CAV (DeMORSE'S), CO C
GURR, THOMAS JEFFERSON	1LT	GA 51ST INF, CO B
GUTTERY, ANDREW J	CAPT	AL 56TH PARTISAN RANGERS, CO L
GUY, L M	1LT	MS 32ND INF, CO B
GUY, WILLIAM SCOTT	LT COL	NC 13TH INF, F&S
GWIN, JESSE VANDIVER	1LT	SC 14TH INF, CO E
GWINN, ROBERT BRUCE	CAPT	VA HOUNSHELL'S CAV BN, GWINN'S CO
GWYNN, ANDREW JACKSON	CAPT	MD 2ND INF, CO F
HADDOCK, ZACHARIAH T	2LT	FL 1ST RESERVES, CO A
HADEN, ANSEL M HENRY	2LT	VA 60TH INF, CO K
HADEN, JAMES HAMBLETON	CAPT	MO CLARK'S INF - AAG
HADEN, JOEL WATKINS	1LT	CSA 7TH CAV - ADJ
HAGER, PHILIP	2LT	VA 34TH BN CAV (WITCHER'S NIGHTHAWKS), CO D
HAGLER, D S	CAPT	TX 14TH CAV, CO F
HAGLER, DAVID SMITH	CAPT	TX 14TH CAV, CO F
HAGOOD, JOHNSON	BRIG GEN	SC 27TH (HAGOOD'S BDE)
HAGUE, JAMES ABNER	3LT	NC 26TH INF, CO C
HAHR, FRANZ JOSEPH	MAJ	NC 19TH INF (BETHEL'S)
HAIGHT, THOMAS R	2LT	MS 12TH INF, CO H
HAILE, COLUMBUS CURETON	CAPT	SC 2ND INF, CO G
HAIRE, JOHN M	2LT	MS 31ST INF, CO D
HALBERT, JAMES M	CAPT	AL 41ST INF, CO K
HALE, HARRISON	1LT	MS 1ST INF, CO D
HALE, JAMES WILSON	JR 2LT	TX 22ND CAV, CO B
HALE, JOHN C	BVT 2LT	TN 18TH INF, CO E
HALEY, J M	AQM	AR 8TH INF, F&S
HALEY, JAMES H MD	SURG	MS 1ST L ARTY, CO D
HALL, ALFRED S	1LT	GA 27TH INF, CO I
HALL, BENJAMIN FRANKLIN MD	SURG	CSA
HALL, EDWARD DUDLEY	COL	NC 46TH INF, F&S
HALL, GEORGE ALEXANDER	LT COL	GA 28TH INF
HALL, HENRY GIRARD	LT COL	TX 28TH CAV, F&S
HALL, HUGH CROCKETT	1LT	MO SEARCY'S BN SHARPSHOOTERS, CO E
HALL, JAMES CHAMBERS	1LT	GA 38TH INF, CO H
HALL, JOHN M	COL	AL 5TH INF, CO I
HALL, LEMUEL HARRISON MD	SURG	MS 1ST INF, CO D
HALL, WILLIAM J	CAPT	KY 13TH CAV, CO E
HALL, WILLIAM MARLBOROUGH	CAPT	MS 6TH INF, CO C
HALLFORD, BRADLEY	1LT	GA 16TH BN CAV (STATE GUARDS), CO G
HALLFORD, JASON WILLIAM	1LT	AL 33RD INF, CO J
HALLIBURTON, JOHN WESLEY	1LT	AR 7TH CAV (HILL'S)
HALLIBURTON, UTE SHERRILL	2LT	TN 20TH INF, CO C
HALSEY, DON PETERS	CAPT	CSA - AAG

HALSEY, EDWIN LINDSLEY	CAPT	SC HART'S HORSE ARTY CO
HALSEY, JOSEPH JACKSON	COMMISSARY	VA 6TH CAV, F&S
HALSEY, STEPHEN PETERS	MAJ	VA 21ST CAV, F&S
HAM, HILLORY H	CAPT	LA 19TH INF, CO E
HAM, JOHN HARVEY	CAPT	AL 47TH INF, CO A
HAMBRICK, JOHN TURNER	MAJ	NC 13TH INF, CO D
HAMBY, JOHN HAMPTON	CAPT	KY 10TH CAV, CO K
HAMER, ALFRED WALLACE MD	ASST SURG	CSA VA RICHMOND HOSPITAL
HAMILTON, J P	2LT	LA 17TH INF, CO H
HAMILTON, JOHN LEO MD	ASST SURG	CSA - LTG ROBERT TAYLOR'S
HAMILTON, OLIVER PERRY	LT COL	TN SHAW'S CAV BN
HAMILTON, ROBERT L	2LT	NC 7TH BN CAV, CO E
HAMILTON, WILLIAM DYSON	CAPT	GA 25TH INF, CO F
HAMILTON, WILLIAM POTTER	CAPT	CSN 2ND REGT SEMME'S NAVAL BRIGADE, CO K
HAMLIN, THOMAS VI	2LT	SC 23RD INF, CO B
HAMMETT, HENRY PINCKNEY	QM	SC 1ST STATE TROOPS, F&S - REGIMENTAL QM
HAMMOND, ANDREW J	MAJ	SC 24TH INF, F&S
HAMMOND, D S	1LT	TN 32ND INF, CO F
HAMMOND, NATHANIEL I	2LT	AR 8TH INF, CO F
HAMNER, HENLEY WINGFIELD JOHN	2LT	AL 38TH INF, CO E
HAMPTON, EPHRAIM	2LT	VA 63RD INF, CO G
HAMPTON, JOSEPH TYSON	1LT	VA 8TH CAV, CO C
HAMPTON, LITRILLE HICKERSON	CAPT	VA 63RD INF, CO G
HAMPTON, THOMAS BISON	CAPT	VA 63RD INF, CO G
HAMPTON, WADE N	2LT	CSA 1ST CHOCTAW & CHICKASAW MTD RIFLES, CO G,K
HAMPTON, WADE III	LT GEN	ANV CAV CMDR
HANAHAN, JOSEPH SEABROOK	CAPT	SC 25TH INF, CO A
HANCOCK, ABRAM BOOTH	MAJ	VA 195TH MILITIA
HANCOCK, JOHN BENJAMIN	SR 2LT	TX 12TH CAV, CO D
HANE, WILLIAM CLARENCE	1LT	SC 19TH CAV BN, CO B
HANEY, JOHN G	CAPT	AL 50TH INF, CO H
HANKINS, E L	MAJ	MS 3RD CAV, CO F
HANKINS, JONATHAN	CAPT	VA 16TH CAV, CO C
HANKLA, JOHN F	1LT	TX COTTON'S CO INF (SABINE VOLUNTEERS)
HANLEITER, CORNELIUS REDDING	CAPT	GA 38TH INF, CO F
HANNA, WOODFORD ROBERT	CAPT	AL 10TH INF, CO H
HANNAH, JOHN FRUIT	CAPT	TN 3RD MTD INF (LILLARD'S), CO D
HANSON, GUSTAVE ADOLPH	CAPT	FORREST'S STAFF
HANSON, JOHN F JR	ADJ	GA 53RD INF, F&S
HARALSON, HUGH ANDERSON	CAPT	CSA - AQM
HARBIN, SAMUEL	CAPT	GA 11TH BN INF (STATE GUARDS), CO C
HARBISON, MATHEW MALCOLM	2LT	TN 48TH INF, CO G
HARD, JOHN STEWART	MAJ	SC 7TH INF, CO F
HARDEE, PARROT M	1LT	NC 10TH BN H ARTY, CO B
HARDEE, WILLIAM JOSEPH	LT GEN	AOT - HARDEE'S CORP
HARDEMAN, ISAAC	LT COL	GA 12TH INF, CO B
HARDEMAN, PETER	COL	TX HARDEMAN'S CAV
HARDEN, JAMES ABEL	ADJ	VA 23RD BN INF, F&S
HARDEN, WILLIAM PRESTON SR	SURG	CSA CMDR EMPIRE STATE HOSPITAL TRAIN - BATTLE OF ATLANTA
HARDER, WILLIAM H	CAPT	TN 23RD INF, CO G
HARDIN, WILLIAM K	2LT	NC 15TH INF, CO C

HARDING, CYRUS W JR	MAJ	VA 5TH CAV, F&S
HARDING, FREDERICK	CAPT	NC 3RD CAV, CO K
HARDING, HENRY	MAJ	NC 61ST INF, F&S
HARDISON, WILLIAM JONAHAN	1LT	NC 17TH INF, CO E
HARDWICK, ALONZO CECIL	CAPT	VA 4TH INF, CO E
HARDWICK, JOHN C	BVT 2LT	AL 46TH INF, CO F
HARDY, ELIJAH PEDIGO	1LT	GA 52ND INF, CO A
HARDY, JOHN CHRISTOPHER	2LT	AR 20TH INF, CO H
HARDY, JOHN McKIM	CAPT	VA INF RESERVES (COL KENTON HARPER'S), CO A
HARDY, WILLIAM BELL	1LT	TN 12TH BN CAV, CO E
HARGAN, JAMES N	2LT	KY 6TH MTD INF, CO H
HARGROVE, CHARLES S	POSTMASTER	GA OGLETHORPE COUNTY - CRAWFORD - 10/1862
HARLAN, JOSEPH GIST	CAPT	SC 5TH CAV (FERGUSON'S), CO K
HARLEY, JAMES PRESTON	1LT	SC 2ND ARTY, CO H
HARLLEE, ANDREW TURPIN	CAPT	SC 8TH INF, CO I
HARLOW, JOHN A	CAPT	GA 48TH INF, CO D
HARMAN, DANIEL H	CAPT	VA 34TH BN CAV (WITCHER'S NIGHTHAWKS), CO C
HARMAN, EDWIN HOUSTON	LT COL	VA 45TH INF, F&S
HARMAN, ELIAS VANCE	CAPT	VA 34TH BN CAV (WITCHER'S NIGHTHAWKS), CO C
HARMAN, FRANKLIN J	BVT 2LT	SC 20TH INF, CO K
HARMAN, JAMES	3LT	VA 25TH CAV, CO D
HARMAN, LEWIS GIVENS	CAPT	TX 11TH CAV, CO D
HARMAN, THEODORE S	1LT	SC 20TH INF, CO K
HARMAN, WILLIAM B	1LT	VA 34TH BN CAV (WITCHER'S NIGHTHAWKS), CO C
HARNED, FRANKLIN	1LT	KY 6TH INF, CO H
HARNESS, GEORGE S	2LT	VA 62ND MTD INF, CO B
HARPER, ELLIS	CAPT	TN HARPERS SCOUTS
HARPER, FRANK M	LT	NC CLARK'S SPECIAL BN, CO A
HARPER, WILLIAM PAYNOT	CAPT	LA 7TH INF, CO H
HARR, CHARLES LEONARD	2LT	TX 7TH INF, CO C
HARRELL, HAYWOOD WILLIAM	1LT	FL 6TH INF, CO E
HARRELL, J A	1LT	TX WAUL'S LEGION, CO B
HARRELL, JAMES C	2LT	MS 2ND PARTISAN RANGERS, CO C
HARRELL, JOHN A	CAPT	GA 31ST INF, CO F
HARRELL, WILLIAM BERNARD MD	ASST SURG	VA DUBLIN CAMP ON INSTRUCTION
HARRELL, WRIGHT W	CAPT	GA MILITIA, 364TH DIST, 36TH INF, 5TH CO
HARRILL, LAWSON	CAPT	NC 56TH INF, CO I
HARRILL, WILLIAM HENRY	1LT	NC 34TH INF, CO B
HARRIS, BENJAMIN TARPLEY	CAPT	AR 13TH INF, CO C
HARRIS, EMSLEY LEE	2LT	NC 42ND INF, CO I
HARRIS, HAYWOOD W	CAPT	NC 35TH INF, CO E
HARRIS, HENRY HILL	CAPT	AR 8TH INF, CO G
HARRIS, ISHAM GREENE	GOV	TN GOVERNOR 1861-1862
HARRIS, JOHN R	2LT	GA 26TH INF, CO K
HARRIS, JOHN WYATT JR	LT COL	AL 16TH INF, CO H
HARRIS, JOSEPH WEST	CAPT	AL 20TH INF, CO G
HARRIS, NATHANIEL HARRISON	BRIG GEN	MS 19TH INF, CO C
HARRIS, ROBERT BEVERLY	2LT	AL 13TH INF, CO E
HARRIS, ROBERT GILES	1LT	TN 19TH CAV, CO G
HARRIS, SEABORN D	1LT	FL 4TH INF, CO I
HARRIS, THOMAS MARCUS	CAPT	GA 49TH INF, F&S - AQ
HARRIS, THOMAS WEST	CAPT	NC 5TH CAV, CO E

HARRIS, WILLIAM H MD	ASST SURG	GA 30TH INF, F&S
HARRIS, WILLIAM P	CAPT	VA 48TH INF, CO E
HARRISON, CARTER HENRY	MAJ	VA 11TH INF, F&S
HARRISON, FRANCIS EUGENE	COL	SC 1ST RIFLES (ORR'S), CO D
HARRISON, GEORGE PAUL JR	COL	GA 32ND INF
HARRISON, ISHAM JR	COL	MS 6TH CAV, F&S
HARRISON, JAMES EDWARD	BRIG GEN	TX 1ST BDE
HARRISON, JOHN C	CAPT	VA 34TH BN CAV (WITCHER'S NIGHTHAWKS), CO E
HARRISON, JOHN REEVES	CAPT	SC 7TH BN INF, CO B
HARRISON, JOHN	2LT	TN 22ND BN INF, CO A
HARRISON, JOSEPH H	CAPT	VA 45TH INF, CO A
HARRISON, JOSEPH	1LT	VA 34TH BN CAV (WITCHER'S NIGHTHAWKS), CO E
HARRISON, MATHIAS H	2LT	VA 34TH BN CAV (WITCHER'S NIGHTHAWKS), CO E
HARRISON, RANDOLPH	LT COL	VA 34TH INF, F&S
HARRISON, WILLIAM FLEMING	CAPT	VA 23RD INF, CO F
HARSH, GEORGE	CAPT	TN 1ST INF, CO E
HART, BENJAMIN THOMAS	1LT	NC 15TH INF, CO I
HART, JOSEPH C JR	CAPT	TX 9TH CAV, CO E
HART, ROBERT DANIEL	MAJ	AL 43RD INF, CO B
HARTGRAVES, BRICE GARNER	CAPT	TX 10TH INF, CO H
HARTSFIELD, AUGUSTUS MILLEDGE	2LT	GA 4TH BN SHARPSHOOTERS, CO B,C
HARTSFIELD, WILEY F	LT COL	GA 53RD INF, CO H
HARTWICK, ALONZO CECIL	CAPT	VA 4TH INF, CO E
HARVEY, ALEXANDER T	1LT	MS 13TH, CO K
HARVEY, DANIEL W	CAPT	VA 21ST CAV, CO A
HARVEY, JAMES GLOVER JR	1LT	VA 18TH INF, CO H
HARVEY, MICHAEL WILLIAMSON	2LT	VA 23RD BN INF, CO B
HARVIE, EDWIN JAMES	COL	CSA - AIG
HARVIE, JOHN BLAIR	MAJ	CSA ENGINEERS QM
HARVIE, WILLIAM OLD	MAJ	CSA COMMISSARY OF SUBSISTENCE
HARWELL, JAMES S	2LT	TN 23RD INF, CO A
HARWELL, JOHN	2LT	NC 89TH MILITIA, CO O (CATAWBA COUNTY)
HARWOOD, JOSEPH CHRISTIAN	CAPT	VA 53RD INF, CO K
HASKINS, AARON WHARTON	LT	TN 51ST INF, CO E
HASKINS, CHRISTOPHER C	1LT	VA 3RD L ARTY (LOCAL DEFENSE), CO B
HASKINS, DAVID CALVIN	LT COL	TN 3RD MTD INF (LILLARD'S), CO D
HASSELL, GEORGE WASHINGTON	CAPT	AL 3RD INF, CO G
HASSELL, MAYNARD ALEXANDER	1LT	AL STATE ARTY, CO A
HASTINGS, JOSEPH H	2LT	TN 17TH INF, CO A
HATCH, BENJAMIN N	LT	MS PIKE'S CO
HATCHER, ELDRIDGE	2LT	GA 28TH INF, CO H
HATCHER, JOHN	1LT	FL 10TH INF, CO B
HATCHER, ROBERT S	2LT	LA 19TH INF, CO H
HATCHER, THOMAS CHARLES	2LT	VA 14TH INF, CO D
HATCHER, WILLIAM HENRY	2LT	VA 42ND INF, CO C
HATCHER, WILLIAM R	2LT	TN 28TH INF, CO C
HATFIELD, WILLIAM ANDERSON	1LT	VA 45TH BN INF, CO B "LOGAN WILDCATS"
HATHAWAY, GEORGE WASHINGTON	LT	NC 2ND CAV, CO E
HATHAWAY, JOSEPH FRANKLIN	MAJ	AR 36TH INF, F&S
HATTAN, MARK II	CAPT	VA 58TH INF, CO G
HATTEN, WILLIAM W	2LT	MS 7TH BN INF, CO G,C
HAWES, SAMUEL HORACE	2LT	VA 1ST ARTY, CO K

HAWES, THOMAS D	CAPT	GA 15TH INF, CO G
HAWKINS, PINK	LT COL	CSA 2ND CREEK MTD VOL
HAWKINS, SAMUEL	CAPT	GA 6TH CAV, CO G
HAWKS, WELLS JOSEPH	MAJ	CSA COMMISSARY OF SUBSISTENCE
HAWPE, TRESVANT CALHOUN	COL	TX 31ST CAV (HAWPE'S), F&S
HAWTHORN, ALEXANDER TRAVIS	BRIG GEN	AR 6TH INF
HAWTHORNE, E P MD	ASST SURG	TN 28TH INF
HAYES, ALLEN T	2LT	SC 26TH INF, CO C
HAYES, THOMAS H	MAJ	KY 6TH MTD INF
HAYES, THOMAS JR	3LT	TN 12TH BN CAV (DAY'S), CO C
HAYHURST, JOSEPH	CAPT	VA 20TH CAV, CO H
HAYLEY, F M	BVT 2LT	AR 25TH INF, CO C
HAYMAKER, ISAAC W	2LT	VA 4TH INF, CO B
HAYMAN, SIMON REEDER	CAPT	TN 1ST H ARTY, CO B
HAYMOND, ALPHEUS F	MAJ	CSA
HAYNES, ALEXANDER	LT COL	VA 29TH INF
HAYNES, ASA J	3LT	GA 4TH RESERVES, CO E
HAYNES, LANDON CARTER	SENATOR	TN - 1ST & 2ND CONFEDERATE CONGRESSES
HAYNES, PERIL COLUMBUS	LT COL	TN 4TH CAV (McLEMORE'S), F&S
HAYNES, WILLIAM DECATUR	CAPT	VA 16TH CAV, F&S - AQM
HAYTH, EDWARD P	2LT	VA 2ND CAV, CO C
HAYWOOD, EDMUND BURKE MD	SURG	CSA NC PETTIGREW MIL HOSP, RALEIGH - OIC
HAYWOOD, EDWARD GRAHAM	COL	NC 7TH INF, F&S
HEAD, BEDFORD JACKSON MD	ASST SURG	GA 11TH ARTY BN (SUMTER ARTY), CO A
HEAD, COTESWORTH P	2LT	AR 1ST MTD RIFLES, CO K
HEAD, JOHN W	1LT	KY 10TH CAV (MORGAN'S PARTISAN RANGERS), CO C
HEAD, THOMAS E	1LT	AL 2ND BN HILLARD'S LEGION, CO A
HEAD, WILLIAM JEFFERSON	CAPT	GA 35TH INF, CO A
HEADLEY, FRANCIS M	CAPT	KY 8TH INF, CO E
HEALY, SAMUEL LUNSFORD STRAUGHN	1LT	VA 15TH CAV, CO A
HEARD, JESSE WOODSON	2LT	TN SHAW'S BN CAV, CO F
HEARNE, ISHAM GILLIAM	CAPT	TN 27TH INF, CO G
HEATH, HOMER VIRGIL	2LT	GA 48TH INF, CO D
HEATH, JESSE HARTWELL	CAPT	VA 4TH CAV, F&S - ACTING QM
HEATH, RICHARD ALEXANDER	1LT	GA 3RD INF, CO A
HEBERT, LOUIS	BRIG GEN	LA CHIEF ENGINEER
HEDRICK, CYRUS A JR	1LT	LA 3RD INF, CO H
HEDRICK, JOHN JACKSON	COL	NC 3RD ARTY, F&S
HEFLIN, WILLIAM DAVID	CAPT	MS 2ND PARTISAN RANGERS, F&S - AQM
HEISKELL, CARRICK WHIT	COL	TN 19TH INF, F&S
HELLER, JOEL B	CAPT	SC HOLCOMBE'S LEGION, CO G
HELM, BENJAMIN HARDIN	BRIG GEN	KY 1ST BDE, BRECKINRIDGE DIV
HELMS, ALBERT LEANDER	2LT	NC 15TH INF, CO B
HEMPERLEY, ANDREW SIMPSON	1LT	AR 20TH INF, CO K
HENDERSON, ANDREW R	CAPT	NC 87TH MILITIA, CO 9 (GASTON COUNTY)
HENDERSON, ANDREW ROBINSON	CAPT	NC 88TH INF MILITIA (LINCOLN COUNTY)
HENDERSON, CHARLES HARDING	2LT	VA 58TH INF, CO F
HENDERSON, CHRISTOPHER RANKIN	1LT	MS 18TH INF, CO F
HENDERSON, DANIEL JR	CAPT	GA 10TH INF BN (WORTH REBELS), CO B
HENDERSON, JEREMIAH AUGUSTUS	DELEGATE	AL SIGNER SECESSION ORDINANCE, DELEGATE PIKE COUNTY
HENDERSON, RICHARD HENRY	1LT	CSA MARINE CORPS

HENDERSON, WILLIAM	2LT	TN 1ST CAV, F&S
HENDRIX, F M	2LT	SC 13TH INF, CO K
HENDRY, CHARLES WESLEY	1LT	FL 4TH INF, CO K
HENDRY, ENOCH DANIEL	CAPT	GA CAV, HENDRY'S CO (ATLANTIC AND GULF GUARDS)
HENDRY, FRANCIS ASBURY	CAPT	FL 1ST SPECIAL CAV BN, CO A
HENLEY, JOHN L	CAPT	MS HENLEY'S CO (HENLEY'S INVINCIBLES)
HENLEY, JOHN PETER	LT COL	TN 28TH CAV
HENLEY, PETER BRANCH	1LT	VA 23RD INF, CO B
HENLEY, THOMAS	1LT	TN 26TH INF, CO F
HENRY, JOHN F	MAJ	TN 4TH INF (NEELY), F&S
HENRY, JUSTUS REYNOLDS	1LT	MS 35TH INF, CO K
HENRY, PHILIP GEORGE	CAPT	AR 9TH INF, CO C
HENRY, THOMAS JEFFERSON	CAPT	KY 5TH INF, CO C
HENRY, WILLIAM R	1LT	GA 38TH INF, CO K
HENSON, BRYAN SAMUEL	2LT	TN 16TH CAV
HENSON, THOMAS G	CAPT	NC 62ND INF, CO K
HEREFORD, LEWIS STIRLING	1LT	LA 4TH INF, CO F
HERMAN, ADOLPHUS HENRY	2LT	NC 89TH MILITIA, CO P (CATAWBA COUNTY)
HERNDON, JOHN A	CAPT	VA 38TH INF, CO D
HERNDON, RALPH CLEMENT	CAPT	VA 38TH INF, CO D
HERREN, WADE A	CAPT	CSA - ACS
HERRING, ISAIAH	2LT	NC 46TH INF, CO I
HESS, JOSEPH T	CAPT	VA 11TH CAV, CO E
HEWITT, GOLDSMITH W	CAPT	AL 28TH INF, CO G
HEYS, SAMUEL LEACH	SR 2LT	GA 11TH BN ARTY (SUMTER ARTY), CO A
HICKMAN, DAVID PAINTER	MAJ	VA 57TH INF, CO C
HICKMAN, THOMAS	2LT	NC 2ND ARTY, CO K
HICKMAN, WILLIAM ALBERT	1LT	SC 11TH INF, CO K
HICKS, ISAAC C	2LT	AR 2ND MTD RIFLES, CO C
HICKS, JOHN S	2LT	VA 44TH INF, CO B
HICKS, RICHARD EWELL RANDOLPH	1LT	AL 40TH INF, CO H
HICKS, WILLIAM	CAPT	AR 10TH CAV, CO L
HIGGINBOTHAM, JOHN CARLTON	COL	VA 25TH INF, F&S
HIGGINS, EDWARD B	BRIG GEN	LA 21ST INF
HIGGS, JOHN WILEY ROLAND	CAPT	TN 7TH CAV (DUCKWORTH'S), CO H
HIGH, SAMUEL M	1LT	AR 50TH INF MILITIA, CO G
HIGHFILL, HEZEKIAH	SR 2LT	MO 8TH INF, CO A
HIGHTOWER, RALEIGH II	CAPT	GA 30TH INF, CO B
HIGHTOWER, RICHARD HOUSE	2LT	GA 10TH CAV (STATE GUARDS), CO F
HILBURN, FRANCIS MARION	1LT	AR 2ND MTD RIFLES, CO D
HILL, AMBROSE POWELL	LT GEN	ANV - 3RD CORPS
HILL, BENJAMIN JEFFERSON	BRIG GEN	TN CAV BDE, FORREST'S CMND AOT
HILL, CHARLES	MAJ	CSA MAGRUDER'S F&S, CHIEF OF ARTY & ORDNANCE
HILL, DANIEL HARVEY	MAJ GEN	NC 1ST INF
HILL, EDWARD SANDERS	1LT	GA 36TH INF (BROYLES'), CO C
HILL, GIBSON FLOURNAY JR	2LT	AL 37TH INF, CO B
HILL, HARVEY H	1LT	TN 48TH INF (VOORHEES'), CO A
HILL, JACOB I	CAPT	VA 31ST INF, F&S AQM
HILL, JAMES HAMILTON MD	ASST SURG	FL 3RD INF
HILL, JAMES LUDSON	SR 2LT	VA WRIGHT'S CO L ARTY (HALIFAX ARTY)
HILL, JOHN MIDDLETON	CAPT	GA 2ND CAV (STATE GUARDS), CO C

HILL, JOHN	CAPT	TN 12TH INF, CO D
HILL, JOSEPH LAFAYETTE GREENE	1LT	GA 1ST INF, F&S - ADJ
HILL, JUNIUS LEROY	LT COL	NC 7TH INF, F&S
HILL, LAURISTON H	SURG	NC 53RD INF, F&S
HILL, THOMPSON W	1LT	MS 11TH INF, CO H
HILL, WILLIAM H	1LT	MS 11TH CONSOLIDATED CAV, CO A
HILL, WYATT TUCKER	2LT	VA 3RD RESERVES, CO A
HILLHOUSE, SAMUEL WILSON	2LT	GA 28TH INF, CO D
HILLSMAN, JAMES MOSES	CAPT	VA 44TH INF, CO H
HILTON, JAMES MONROE	1LT	AR 4TH INF, CO H
HILTON, JOSEPH	CAPT	GA 26TH INF, CO B
HINDMAN, THOMAS CARMICHAEL	MAJ GEN	MS TRANS DIST
HINES, ALFRED ALEXANDER	1LT	NC 38TH INF, CO G (ROCKY FACE RANGERS)
HINES, JAMES S	MAJ	NC 1ST INF, CO C
HINSON, ALFRED F	2LT	AR 8TH INF, CO I
HINSON, JOSEPH LAWLEY	1LT	AL 6TH INF, CO M
HINSON, LEVISE	2LT	GA 13TH CAV, CO F
HINSON, ORRIN C	CAPT	SC 22ND INF, CO E
HISE, JAMES MADISON	2LT	TN 34TH INF, CO A
HITCH, ROBERT MARCUS	CAPT	GA 30TH INF, CO B
HITE, ROBERT M	BVT 2LT	VA 3RD CAV, CO A
HOBBS, JAMES ANDREW	1LT	TN 7TH INF, CO G
HOBBS, RICHARD	CAPT	GA 51ST INF, CO K
HOBBS , JOSHUA EWING	CAPT	VA 64TH MTD INF, CO A
HOBSON, WILLIAM L	BVT 2LT	AL 20TH INF, CO H
HOCKADAY, WILLOUGHBY L	1LT	NC 10TH BN H ARTY, CO B
HODGES, CHARLES W	1LT	MD 2ND BN INF, CO C
HODGES, ELI W	2LT	GA 5TH CAV, CO E
HODGES, VINCENT A	2LT	GA 26TH INF, CO K
HODGES, WESLEY CLARKE	COL	GA 17TH INF (MUSCOGEE VOL), F&S
HODGES, WILLIAM	1LT	GA 6TH INF, CO H
HODO, DYER C	CAPT	AL 19TH INF, CO A
HOFFER, HENRY NAPOLEON	2LT	TX 19TH CAV (BURFORD'S), CO K
HOFFMAN, LABAN MILES	2LT	NC 2ND JR RESERVES, CO C
HOGAN, ALEXANDER	2LT	TN 7TH INF, CO E
HOGAN, GRIFFIN	2LT	AR 45TH CAV, CO A
HOGAN, JEREMIAH	2LT	LA 6TH INF, CO B
HOGARTH, JAMES L	COMMISSIONER	FL CLAY COUNTY
HOGG, GEORGE	CAPT	KY 13TH CAV, CO B
HOGG, JOSEPH LEWIS	BRIG GEN	CSA - ATM
HOGG, ROBERT THOMAS	CAPT	VA 115TH MILITIA, CO B
HOGUE, EZEKIEL REV	CHAPLAIN	AR 11TH INF (POE'S BN)
HOGUE, JAMES SANSOM	CAPT	CSA - CS
HOKE, PHILO PETER	1LT	NC 12TH INF, CO E
HOKE, ROBERT FREDERICK	MAJ GEN	CSA
HOLBROOK, LARKIN	1LT	KY 2ND BN MTD INF, CO D
HOLBROOK, WILLIAM ALEXANDER	1LT	NC 39TH INF, CO B
HOLCOMB, THOMAS	COL	NC 78TH MILITIA (IREDELL COUNTY), F&S
HOLDER, BENJAMIN LUTHER	1LT	SC 1ST CAV, CO K
HOLDER, WILLIAM DUNBAR	COL	MS 17TH INF, CO C
HOLLAND, THOMAS CHARLES	1LT	VA 28TH INF, CO G
HOLLAND, TILLMAN HORNE	LT	AL 9TH INF, CO F

HOLLAND, WILLIAM WILSON	1LT	CSA - BG BLANCHARD'S STAFF
HOLLEY, ALBERT LAFAYETTE	LT	SC 19TH INF, CO K
HOLLEY, JAMES H	1LT	VA 34TH BN CAV (WITCHER'S NIGHTHAWKS), CO A
HOLLEY, MARTIN T	1LT	SC 14TH INF, CO H
HOLLIMAN, JAMES FLETCHER	1LT	AL 58TH INF, CO B
HOLLINGSWORTH, LEWIS HENRY	CAPT	MS 40TH INF, CO K
HOLLINGSWORTH, WILLIAM PERRY	MAJ	CSA COMMISSARY OF SUBSISTENCE
HOLLIS, EDWARD G	2LT	VA L ARTY, CAPT EILETT'S CO (CRENSHAW BTRY)
HOLLIS, WILLIAM B	JR 2LT	TX 6TH BN CAV (GOULD'S), CO E,B
HOLLOWAY, ROBERT G MD	ASST SURG	GA 38TH INF
HOLMAN, JOHN THOMPSON	CAPT	CSA AQM
HOLMAN, WILLIAM HENRY	CAPT	SC 4TH RESERVES BN, CO A
HOLMES, JOHN	1LT	MS 16TH INF, CO E
HOLMES, NOAH DORTCH	CAPT	AR 3RD CAV, CO A
HOLMES, THOMAS F	MAJ	MS 35TH INF, CO D
HOLMSLEY, JAMES MONROE	CAPT	TX 1ST CAV, CO G
HOLSTEIN, HIRAM L	2LT	SC 19TH INF, CO F
HOLT, BOLLING HALL	COL	GA 35TH INF, F&S
HOLT, JAMES HENRY	CHAPLAIN	NC FAYETTEVILLE MILITARY ACADEMY - AQM
HOLT, JOHN R	2LT	KY 1ST CAV, CO D
HOLT, JOHN OSCAR	1LT	TX 12TH INF, CO F
HOLT, RICHARD S	CAPT	AR 14TH INF, CO C
HONEA, ALBERT	1LT	GA 28TH INF, CO D
HONEYCUTT, WAIGHTELL T	2LT	NC 29TH INF, CO G
HONNOLL, JAMES WISEMAN	JR 2LT	MS HAM'S CAV, CO C
HOOBERRY, JOHN W	2LT	TN 44TH CONSOLIDATED INF, CO I
HOOD, JOHN BELL	LT GEN	AOT CMDR
HOOD, JOSEPH NATHANIEL	CAPT	AL 47TH INF, CO E
HOOD, WILLIAM HENRY	LT COL	VA HOOD'S BN RESERVES
HOOKS, WILLIAM W	2LT	GA 8TH CAV, CO I
HOOPER, THOMAS W	COL	GA 21ST INF, F&S
HOPE, SAMUEL EDWARD	CAPT	FL 9TH INF, CO C
HOPKINS, JAMES	LT	SC 9TH INF, CO B
HOPKINS, LEWIS G	1LT	NC 24TH INF, CO A
HOPSON, JAMES H	1LT	AR 1ST CAV (MONROE'S), CO D
HORN, G F	3LT	AL 30TH INF, CO G
HORNE, SIMEON	1LT	AR 21ST INF, CO G
HORNER, JAMES H	CAPT	NC 23RD INF, CO E (PEE DEE GUARDS)
HORTON, JAMES W	2LT	NC 15TH INF, CO D
HOSKINS, JAMES D	2LT	VA 20TH INF, CO E
HOSKINS, WILLIAM MD	SURG	VA 59TH INF, F&S
HOSMER, SILAS MONROE	CAPT	AL 26TH INF, CO G
HOTCHKISS, JEDEDIAH GRAPHICAL ENGR	MAJ	CSA GEN JACKSON, EARLY, & EWELL, CHIEF TOPO-
HOTTEL, JAMES MORGAN	1LT	VA 33RD INF, CO C
HOUGH, ALHANAN GIBBS	1LT	MS L ARTY, TURNER'S CO
HOUGH, MINOR J	CAPT	SC 6TH INF, CO K
HOUSE, JAMES W J	1LT	NC 30TH INF, CO F
HOUSE, WILLIAM LEWIS	2LT	GA 178TH MILITIA; GA 180TH MILITIA; GA 181ST MILITIA
HOUSTON, SAMUEL JR	LT	CSA DRILLMASTER
HOUSTON, WILLIAM JAMES	CAPT	NC 1ST CAV, CO I
HOVIS, LAWSON BERRY	LT COL	MS 7TH CAV, CO B

HOWARD, BENJAMIN DYER	1LT	NC 55TH INF, CO K
HOWARD, LARKIN	1LT	KY 5TH INF, CO K
HOWARD, WILEY C	1LT	GA COBB'S LEGION CAV, CO C
HOWARD, WILLIS III	1LT	GA 12TH CAV
HOWE, JOHN THOMAS	1LT	VA 4TH INF, CO E
HOWELL, EVAN PARK	CAPT	GA L ARTY, HOWELL'S CO
HOWELL, GEORGE W	CAPT	NC 25TH INF, CO I
HOWELL, HAMILTON S	2LT	LA 25TH INF, CO A
HOWELL, HENRY P	CAPT	VA 9TH INF, CO E
HOWELL, JOSEPH ANDERSON	AQM	TN 26TH INF, F&S
HOWELL, LAZARUS PURIFOY	2LT	GA 4TH INF, CO K
HOWELL, SYVLANUS	CAPT	TX L ARTY 11TH FIELD BTRY, HOWELL'S CO
HOWELL, WILSON PARK	CAPT	AL 25TH INF, CO I
HOWLE, THOMAS E	CAPT	SC 8TH INF, CO F, M
HOWSE, WILLIAM HENRY	1LT	MS 8TH INF, CO E
HOWZE, JAMES ALEXANDER	2LT	AL 32ND INF, CO D
HOYLE, DAVID R	CAPT	NC 34TH INF, CO F
HOYLE, JOSEPH JOEL	1LT	NC 55TH INF, CO F
HOYT, JOHN KEAIS	CAPT	AL 3RD INF, CO K
HUBBARD, DAVID	COMMISSIONER	CSA INDIAN AFFAIRS
HUBBARD, JAMES WALTER	CAPT	TN 9TH INF, CO B
HUBBARD, RICHARD B	COL	TX 22ND INF (HUBBARDS), F&S
HUBBERT, REUBEN JASPER	1LT	MS 38TH CAV, CO G
HUBERT, GEORGE ROBERT WALLACE	2LT	GA 5TH INF (MCDUFFIE RIFLES), CO D
HUBERT, ROBERT W	CAPT	TX 5TH INF, CO K
HUCK, HENRY JOSEPH	QM	TX - ATM CHIEF QM
HUDDLESTON, JOHN B	CAPT	MS 34TH INF, CO G
HUDDLESTON, STOKELY H	COL	TN 48TH MILITIA
HUDGENS, JAMES	1LT	SC 4TH INF (McGOWAN'S BDE), CO D
HUDGINS, BENJAMIN F	CAPT	VA 32ND INF (HAMPTON GREY'S), CO E
HUDGINS, FRANKLIN FINCHER	2LT	AL 41ST INF, CO D
HUDGINS, JAMES MADISON	CAPT	CSA ANV STAFF - ACS
HUDNALL, EZEKIEL T	1LT	MS 7TH INF, CO F
HUDSON, ISAAC	2LT	VA 45TH INF, CO K
HUDSON, JAMES WILSON	ASST SURG	SC 4TH INF, F&S
HUDSON, NOAH LAFAYETTE	2LT	GA COBB'S LEGION, CO E
HUEY, JAMES M	CAPT	TX 14TH BDE, CO FOR BEAT # 8 (HUNT COUNTY)
HUFF, WARREN R D	2LT	AL 22ND INF, CO D
HUFFMAN, JOSEPH NAPOLEON	CAPT	VA HOUNSHELL'S BN CAV (PARTISAN RANGERS)
HUFFMAN, MADISON L	3LT	VA 46TH INF
HUFFMAN, WILLIAM C P	2LT	GA 2ND SHARPSHOOTERS BN, CO D
HUFFMASTER, JOSEPH	CAPT	TN 43RD INF, CO E
HUFSTEDLER, ELI	LT COL	AR 25TH INF, CO A
HUGHES, IVY S	CAPT	AR 13TH INF, CO I
HUGHES, JAMES M	CAPT	VA 44TH INF (FLUVANNA GUARDS), CO K
HUGHES, JOHN H	1LT	NC 31ST INF, CO E
HUGHES, LARKIN	1LT	SC 2ND RIFLES, CO H
HUGHES, R B	1LT	TN 20TH INF, CO H
HUGHES, WILLIAM RILEY	2LT	AL 41ST INF, CO A
HUGHS, JOHN THOMAS	CAPT	GA 49TH INF, CO A
HUGUENIN, THOMAS A	MAJ	SC 1ST INF (BUTLER'S), CO A
HUIE, JOSEPH HAMILTON	CAPT	GA 30TH INF, CO E

HUIET, GEORGE DAVID	CAPT	SC 2ND STATE TROOPS, CO B
HULLIHEN, WALTER QUARRIER	CAPT	CSA LOMAX'S BRIGADE, STUART'S DIV - AAIG
HUMBLE, THOMAS C	MAJ	LA 31ST INF
HUME, THOMAS REV	CHAPLAIN	VA 3RD INF, F&S
HUMPHREYS, BENJAMIN GRUBB	BRIG GEN	MS 21ST INF (HURRICANE RIFLES)
HUMPHREYS, FREDERICK CLINTON	MAJ	GA EXECUTIVE OFFICER COLUMBUS ARSENAL
HUMPHREYS, GEORGE WASHINGTON	CAPT	TX 24TH CAV, CO K
HUMPHREYS, J H	CAPT	TN 3RD BN INF (MEMPHIS LOCAL DEFENSE), CO B
HUMPHRIES, JOHN ROBERT POWELL	1LT	VA 55TH INF, CO M
HUMPHRIES, WILLIAM MONROE	2LT	AL 19TH INF, CO G
HUNDLEY, GEORGE KAUFMAN	1LT	VA 2ND RESERVES BN, CO C
HUNDLEY, OSCAR DUNREATH	JR 2LT	MS POWER'S CAV, CO A
HUNDLEY, THOMAS SHIVERS	CAPT	GA 22ND INF, CO H
HUNDLEY, WILLIAM BRITTON II	MAJ	GA 5TH INF, CO F&S
HUNKAPILLER, JOHN C	1LT	AL 19TH INF, CO B
HUNLEY, HORACE LAWSON	CHIEF ENGR	CSN
HUNNICUTT, THOMAS HARRISON	BVT 2LT	NC 25TH INF, CO G
HUNNICUTT, WILLIAM McEWEN	1LT	GA 587TH MILITIA DIST BN (RABUN COUNTY)
HUNT, BENJAMIN FRANKLIN	MAJ	GA 8TH INF, F&S
HUNT, SIMEON	CAPT	VA 37TH INF, CO I
HUNT, WILLIAM PICKNEY	1LT	SC 2ND CAV, CO F
HUNT, ZIMRI	CAPT	TX 16TH INF, CO F
HUNTER, CLINTON H	LT	AL 2ND CAV, CO I
HUNTER, FOUNTAIN WINSTON	COL	AL 2ND CAV
HUNTER, JAMES HOWARD	1LT	NC 15TH MILITIA (CRAVEN COUNTY)
HUNTER, JOHN HENRY	CAPT	AR 26TH INF, CO C - ACS
HUNTER, JOHN THOMAS	1LT	AL 37TH INF, CO I
HUNTER, THOMAS T SR	COMMANDER	CSN CSS RALEIGH, CSS GAINES, CSS CHICORA
HUNTER, WILLIAM MILES C	3LT	FL 5TH INF, CO F
HUNTON, EPPA	BRIG GEN	VA 8TH INF
HURLEY, ELIAS	2LT	NC 28TH INF, CO E
HURLEY, WILLIAM CARROLL	CAPT	TX 37TH CAV, CO D
HURT, JAMES MANN	CAPT	TX 1ST BN SHARPSHOOTERS, CO D
HURT, WAYLES	JR 2LT	VA 3RD BN RESERVES (ARCHER'S), CO E
HURTT, DANIEL WASHINGTON	MAJ	NC 2ND INF, CO I
HUSTON, GEORGE	LT COL	VA 33RD INF, CO I
HUTCHINSON, JOHN	2LT	LA 3RD CAV (WINGFIELD'S), CO F
HUTCHISON, MARTIN VAN BUREN	1LT	VA 28TH INF (CRAIG MOUNTAIN BOYS), CO C
HUTCHISSON, JAMES HENRY	CAPT	AL 2ND BN LIGHT ARTY, CO E
HUTSON, THOMAS WOODWARD JR, MD	SURG/MAJ	SC 3RD CAV, F&S - CHIEF SURGEON
HUTTER, JAMES RISQUE	MAJ	VA 11TH INF, CO H
HYDE, TASWELLL V	CAPT	TN 21ST INF
HYDRICK, ANDREW J	CAPT	SC 2ND CAV, CO D
HYLTON, GEORGE WADE	2LT	VA 58TH INF, CO H
HYMAN, JOSEPH HENRY	COL	NC 13TH INF, F&S
IHRIE, ROSS RUFUS	LT COL	NC 15TH INF, CO I
IKARD, ELIJAH HARRISON	CAPT	TN 32ND INF, CO K
INABINET, J T	BVT 2LT	SC 20TH INF, CO D
INABNET, HENRY	CAPT	AR 20TH INF, CO C
INMAN, AARON ALLEN	3LT	NC 18TH INF, CO D
INSALL, HENRY	2LT	TX 13TH INF, CO F
INZER, JOHN WASHINGTON	LT COL	AL 58TH INF, F&S

INZER, WILLIAM MARION	CAPT	AL 58TH INF, CO D
IRBY, EDWARD	CAPT	TN 21ST INF, CO A
IRBY, RICHARD	CAPT	VA 18TH INF, CO G
IRELAND, THOMAS CHILTON	2LT	KY 8TH CAV, CO C
IRION, WILLIAM MCKINNEY	CAPT	MS 32ND INF, CO G
IRONMONGER, FRANCIS McCREADY	CAPT	VA 16TH INF, F&S - AQM
IRVIN, SAMUEL D	CAPT	GA 18TH INF, CO D
IRVINE, JAMES BENNINGTON	CAPT	AL 4TH CAV, F&S
IRVING, FRANCIS DEANE	CAPT	VA 21ST INF, CO D
IRWIN, JOHN DEWEESE	1LT	NC 20TH INF, CO A
ISAACSON, HENRY M	CAPT	LA 1ST ARTY BN (WASHINGTON)
ISRAEL, MONTRAVILLE M	CAPT	AL 19TH INF, CO E
ISRAEL, PLEASANT J	1LT	NC 60TH INF, CO A
IVES, WALTER C	2LT	VA 62ND INF, CO E
IVEY, WILLIAM H	2LT	NC 2ND CAV, CO H
IZLAR, JAMES FERDINAND	CAPT	SC 25TH INF, CO G
JACKMAN, SIDNEY DRAKE	COL	MO 7TH INF
JACKSON, ARCHIBALD A	2LT	NC 30TH INF, CO H
JACKSON, BENJAMIN FRANKLIN	LT	TX 21ST CAV, CO D
JACKSON, CLAIBORNE FOX	BRIG GEN	MO GOVERNOR
JACKSON, CRAWFORD MOTLEY	1LT	GA 2ND BN SHARPSHOOTERS, CO D
JACKSON, D C	CAPT	TN 12TH BN CAV, CO D
JACKSON, GEORGE A JR	CAPT	GA 25TH INF, CO K
JACKSON, HENRY ROOTES	BRIG GEN	GA 1ST INF
JACKSON, ISAAC M	1LT	TN 6TH INF, CO G
JACKSON, JAMES	CAPT	AL 45TH INF, CO E
JACKSON, JAMES JONATHAN	CAPT	NC 15TH INF, CO G
JACKSON, JOHN DAVIES	SURG	TN 44TH CONSOLIDATED INF, F&S
JACKSON, JOHN KING	BRIG GEN	AOT
JACKSON, MAXIMILLAN FRANK	1LT	SC 26TH INF, CO B
JACKSON, ROBERT DANDRIDGE MD	ASST SURG	CSA
JACKSON, THOMAS JONATHAN	LT GEN	ANV - II CORPS
JACKSON, WILLIAM HICKS	BRIG GEN	TN CAV - GEN FORREST
JACKSON, WILLIAM LOWTHER	BRIG GEN	ANV - LOMAX'S DIV "MUDWALL"
JACKSON, WILLIAM M	2LT	TN 49TH INF, CO H
JACO, JEREMIAH	1LT	TN 35TH INF, CO A
JACOB, EMILE	1LT	LA 18TH INF, CO A
JACOBS, JOHN TYLER	CAPT	MO THOMPSON'S COMMAND
JAMES, ASA	MAJ	MO 3RD CAV (STATE GUARDS)
JAMES, THOMAS A	CAPT	GA 62ND CAV, CO H
JAMES, WILLIAM HARRIS	2LT	MS 23RD INF, CO L
JAMES, WILLIAM N	CAPT	TN 44TH CONSOLIDATED INF, CO C
JAMISON, DAVID FLAVEL	COL	SC 16TH INF
JAMISON, HENRY J	CAPT	MS 4TH INF, CO K
JANNEY, ELI H II	MAJ	CSA ANV GEN ROBERT E LEE - QM
JARBOE, JOSEPH THOMAS REV	CHAPLAIN	TN 2ND INF
JARED, JOHN	2LT	TN 84TH INF, CO G
JARRELL, WILLIAM HAMILTON	JR 1LT	GA L ARTY (ECHOLS), TILLER'S CO
JARRETT, JAMES M	COL	NC 109TH INF, F&S
JARRETT, JAMES MONTEVAL	1LT	NC 15TH INF, CO C
JARROTT, J ALSTON	2LT	SC 21ST INF, CO I
JAYNE, WILLIAM MCAFEE	QM	MS 22ND INF, F&S

JEFFCOAT, NEEDAM PRICE	2LT	SC 20TH INF, CO D
JEFFERIES, JOHN RANDOLPH	CAPT	SC 15TH INF, CO F
JEFFORDS, ROBERT JOSIAH	LT COL	SC 5TH CAV (FERGUSON'S), F&S
JEFFORDS, THEODORE A	ADJ	SC 5TH CAV, F&S
JEFFRIES, WILLIAM H	CAPT	GA 51ST INF, CO K
JENKINS, MICAH	BRIG GEN	SC PALMETTO SHARPSHOOTERS
JENKINS, NEWTON HILL	CAPT	SC 2ND INF, CO C
JENKINS, NEWTON MADISON	1LT	TN 44TH INF, CO I
JENKINS, THOMAS F	MAJ	AL 53RD PARTISAN RANGERS, F&S
JENKINS, WILSON THOMAS	CAPT	NC 14TH INF, CO A
JENKS, JOHN	JR 1LT	AL 2ND BN L ARTY, CO A
JENNINGS, HENRY EDMUND	CAPT	VA 3RD L ARTY (LOCAL DEFENSE), CO G
JENNINGS, HENRY S JR	2LT	GA TROUP ARTY, CARLTON'S CO
JENNINGS, NEWBORN A	1LT	TN 7TH INF, CO G
JENNINGS, WILLIAM	2LT	TN 35TH INF, CO B
JERKINS, REASON WILSON	2LT	FL 7TH INF, CO I
JERNIGIN, JAMES H	2LT	TX MARTIN'S CAV (5TH PARTISAN RANGERS), CO H
JEROME, ROBERT P	MAJ	NC 15TH INF, CO B
JERVEY, HENRY MD	ASST SURG	CSA
JESSUP, SAMUEL M	1LT	NC 21ST INF, CO F
JETER, BERRY ARGIVIS	CAPT	SC MACBETH L ARTY, JETER'S CO
JETER, GILLIAM HOBSON	1LT	SC 7TH CAV, CO C
JETER, WILLIAM RYLAND	CAPT	VA 13TH CAV, CO B
JOFFRION, ELOI	CAPT	LA AVOYELLES MILITIA
JOFFRION, JOSEPH CELESTIN	1LT	LA 1ST CAV, CO G
JOHNSON, ABRAHAM MALONE	LT COL	AL 1ST CAV, F&S
JOHNSON, ADAM RANKIN	BRIG GEN	KY 10TH CAV (MORGAN'S PARTISAN RANGERS)
JOHNSON, ALFRED H	1LT	TN 1ST INF, CO C
JOHNSON, BARNETT DEVLIN	CAPT	GA 4TH INF RESERVES, CO E
JOHNSON, BENJAMIN JENKINS	LT COL	SC INF (HAMPTON'S LEGION), F&S
JOHNSON, BENJAMIN SAMUEL	CAPT	MO 3RD CAV, CO A, H
JOHNSON, CHARLES SANDERS	CAPT	TN 20TH INF, CO B
JOHNSON, HERSCHEL VESPASIAN	SENATOR	GA - 2ND CONFEDERATE CONGRESS
JOHNSON, ISAAC VASHTAW	1LT	VA 31ST INF, CO H
JOHNSON, J WESLEY	2LT	SC 22ND INF, CO I
JOHNSON, JACOB H	1LT	TN 11TH INF, CO H
JOHNSON, JEPTHA C	LT COL	AR 37TH INF (BELL'S), CO B
JOHNSON, JOHN A	CAPT	GA 28TH INF, CO H
JOHNSON, JOHN THOMAS	JR 1LT	VA 13TH BN L ARTY, CO C
JOHNSON, JOHN W	CAPT	GA 11TH INF, CO F
JOHNSON, JOHN	2LT	AR 1ST MTD RIFLES, CO F
JOHNSON, JOSEPH ALEXANDER	LT COL	MS 2ND STATE CAV, CO F
JOHNSON, JOSEPH BRYAN	CAPT	LA CONSOLIDATED CRESCENT INF, CO K
JOHNSON, JOSEPH BURTON	BRIG GEN	TX 19TH BDE MILITIA
JOHNSON, JOSEPH E	CAPT	LA 3RD INF, CO I
JOHNSON, LOUIS ASBURY	CAPT	NC 4TH CAV, CO A
JOHNSON, MARTIN VANBUREN	2LT	GA 20TH INF, CO F
JOHNSON, ROBERT	CAPT	SC 24TH INF, CO B
JOHNSON, ROWAN B	CAPT	GA 11TH CAV (STATE GUARDS)
JOHNSON, SAMUEL BENJAMIN	2LT	VA 21ST INF, CO C
JOHNSON, SEYMOUR A	2LT	VA 23RD INF, CO D
JOHNSON, THOMAS LANCASTER	1LT	AL 3RD INF, CO D

JOHNSON, WALDO PORTER	LT COL	MO 4TH INF
JOHNSON, WILLIAM ARTHUR	COL	AL 4TH CAV (RODDY'S)
JOHNSON, WILLIS	JR 2LT	NC 8TH SENIOR RESERVES
JOHNSTON, ALBERT SIDNEY	GEN	AOT CMDR
JOHNSTON, ALEXANDER H	CAPT	TX 11TH INF, CO H
JOHNSTON, JAMES D	CMDR	RAM CSS TENNESSEE, CSN
JOHNSTON, JOSEPH E	GEN	ANV
JOHNSTON, PINCKNEY ALEXANDER REV	CHAPLAIN	MS 22ND INF, F&S
JOHNSTON, THOMAS HENRY	CAPT	VA 28TH INF, CO A
JOHNSTONE, FRANCIS WITHERS	CAPT	NC 25TH INF, CO E
JOINES, MAJOR F	1LT	NC 33RD INF, CO D
JONES, BENJAMIN RUSH JR	2LT	VA 64TH MTD INF, CO A
JONES, BENNETT COOPER	CAPT	SC 1ST INF, CO B
JONES, BURRELL MARION SR	COL	SC 22ND INF
JONES, CALEB BAKER	CAPT	TN 13TH INF, CO L
JONES, CHARLES H	CAPT	TN 7TH CAV (DUCKWORTH'S), CO F
JONES, CHARLES HENRY	CAPT	VA 57TH INF, CO C
JONES, CHARLES MELTON	1LT	GA 36TH INF, CO F
JONES, DUDLEY WATSON MD	ASST SURG	MS 36TH INF, CO K
JONES, FRANCIS MARION	JR 2LT	AL 23RD INF, CO E
JONES, GEORGE WASHINGTON	QM	AL 4TH INF (CONEUCH GUARDS), F&S
JONES, HENRY S	2LT	KY 10TH CAV (JOHNSON'S), CO E
JONES, ISAAC NEWTON	1LT	VA 3RD INF, CO I
JONES, J FRANKLIN	2LT	TX 5TH INF, CO K
JONES, J S	MAJ	SC 24TH INF, F&S
JONES, JACOB	2LT	VA 3RD INF, CO I
JONES, JAMES ALLEN THOMAS	1LT	NC 24TH INF, CO I
JONES, JAMES M	CAPT	NC 69TH MILITIA (ROCKINGHAM COUNTY)
JONES, JAMES W	3LT	MS 1ST INF (PATTON'S), CO B
JONES, JESSE N	CAPT	FL 2ND CAV, CO K
JONES, JOHN ABRAHAM	COL	GA 20TH INF, F&S
JONES, JOHN ALVIN	ADJ	GA 9TH INF, F&S
JONES, JOHN G	CAPT	KY 6TH INF, CO K
JONES, JOHN G	COL	NC 35TH INF, CO E
JONES, JOHN HENRY	2LT	AL 58TH INF, CO C
JONES, JOHN HENRY	CAPT	GA 3RD CAV (STATE GUARDS), CO H
JONES, JOHN M	1LT	TN 61ST INF, CO E
JONES, JOHN RANDOLPH MD	ASST SURG	CSA
JONES, LEWIS H MD	ASST SURG	CSA
JONES, MATTHEW DAVIS	2LT	TX 24TH/25TH CONSOLIDATED CAV, CO E
JONES, MILTON RAGAN	1LT	MS 16TH INF, CO C
JONES, RICHARD CHANNING	1LT	AL 44TH INF, CO C
JONES, ROBERT HARRIS	COL	GA 22ND INF
JONES, RUFUS LEAF	1LT	MS 29TH INF, CO I
JONES, RUFUS LOYD	1LT	AL 56TH PARTISAN RANGERS, CO G
JONES, S HENRY	CAPT	SC 1ST CAV, CO A
JONES, STARLING WARREN MD	SURG	AL 39TH INF, F&S
JONES, THOMAS BERRY	1LT	GA 35TH INF, CO H
JONES, THOMAS BURTON	1LT	KY 8TH MTD INF, CO A
JONES, THOMAS GOODE	1LT	CSA MG JOHN B GORDON - ADC
JONES, WALTER CLARENCE	1LT	VA 41ST INF, CO G
JONES, WILEY C	CAPT	AR 45TH CAV, CO H

JONES, WILLIAM B	2LT	FL 6TH INF, CO K
JONES, WILLIAM EDMONDSON	BRIG GEN	VA 7TH CAV "GRUMBLE"
JONES, WILLIAM MANNING	CAPT	SC 3RD RESERVES, CO H
JONES, WILLIAM SMITH	2LT	AR 2ND MTD RIFLES, CO I
JOPLING, GEORGE WASHINGTON	3LT	TX 14TH CAV, CO K
JORDAN, ALONZO B	CAPT	VA 3RD INF, CO B
JORDAN, G C MD	SURG	TN 4TH CAV
JORDAN, JAMES PINKNEY	CAPT	GA 57TH INF, CO G
JORDAN, MORTIMER H	CAPT	AL 43RD INF, CO G
JORDAN, ROBERT	CAPT	AR 15TH INF (JOHNSON'S), CO C
JORDAN, THOMAS	BRIG GEN	AOT - BRAXTON BRAGG & P G T BEAUREGARD - COS
JORDAN, TYLER CALHOUN	MAJ	VA SMITH'S (BEDFORD) L ARTY CO
JORDAN, WILLIAM TURNER	2LT	VA 3RD INF, CO F
JOYNER, JULIUS M	CAPT	MS 34TH INF, CO E
JUDD, DANIEL B JR	1LT	VA 97TH MILITIA, CO F
JUDKINS, JAMES HENRY JR	ADJ	AL 1ST CAV
JULIAN, ROBERT McCARNY	2LT	GA 21ST INF, CO E
JULIAN, THOMAS J	LT	AR 18TH INF, CO A
JUMPER, JOHN	LT COL	CSA 1ST SEMINOLE MTD, F&S
JUNKIN, ROBERT	CAPT	SC 1ST RIFLES (ORR'S), CO D
JUSTICE, HIRAM	CAPT	KY 10TH CAV, CO H
KAIGLER, E G	1LT	SC 1ST INF (HAGOOD'S), CO B
KARR, FREDERICK C	MAJ	MS 32ND INF, CO A
KAVANAUGH, HUBBARD HINDE	CHAPLAIN	KY 6TH MTD INF, F&S
KAY, JAMES HARRISON	2LT	MS 17TH INF, CO E
KEARNEY, SHEMUEL HAWKINS	1LT	NC 8TH BN CAV (PARTISAN RANGERS), CO C
KEARNS, ISAAC NEWTON	1LT	NC 38TH INF, CO H
KEELS, ISAAC	1LT	SC 9TH INF, CO C
KEETON, WILLIAM BASS	CAPT	AR 3RD CAV, CO K
KEFAUVER, GEORGE M	1LT	VA 54TH INF, CO I
KEFFER, CHARLES H	1LT	VA 14TH CAV, CO G
KEISLER, WADE	2LT	SC 15TH INF, CO I
KEISTER, HENRY JACKSON	CAPT	VA 4TH INF, CO L
KEITH, JAMES A	LT COL	NC 64TH INF, CO A
KEITH, JOSEPH HARDY	1LT	GA 55TH INF, CO F
KEITH, KOSCIUSZKO DEWITT	CAPT	TX 13TH VOLS, CO I
KELL, JOHN MCINTOSH	1LT	CSS RICHMOND
KELLER, JOHN L	CAPT	VA 34TH BN CAV (WITCHER'S NIGHTHAWKS), CO A
KELLEY, ALLEN	CAPT	GA 48TH INF, CO A
KELLEY, ESOM D	CAPT	AL 4TH CAV (RODDY'S), CO K
KELLEY, GEORGE W	2LT	GA 22ND INF, CO B
KELLEY, JAMES M	1LT	AL 10TH CAV, CO B
KELLY, JOSEPH	1LT	VA 29TH INF, CO A
KELLY, THOMAS BENTON	CAPT	AL HAZEL GREEN PRIVATE SCOUTS
KELLY, WILLIAM FOSTER	2LT	TN 17TH INF, CO I
KELTON, JOHN H	1LT	TN 39TH MTD INF, CO H
KEMP, ISAAC ROBERTS	2LT	LA 3RD CAV (WINGFIELD'S), CO A,K
KEMPER, DELAWARE	LT COL	VA 18TH BN H ARTY
KEMPER, JAMES LAWSON	MAJ GEN	VA 1ST BDE
KENAN, THOMAS S	COL	NC 43RD INF, CO A
KENDALL, WILLIAM SAMUEL	2LT	LA 8TH CAV, CO D
KENDRICK, BURRELL JONES	CAPT	GA 51ST INF, CO F

KENDRICK, GEORGE DRAYTON S	CAPT	VA 34TH BN CAV (WITCHER'S NIGHTHAWKS), CO I
KENDRICK, WILLIAM P	1LT	VA 34TH BN CAV (WITCHER'S NIGHTHAWKS), CO G
KENNARD, SAMUEL J	1LT	FL 1ST CAV, CO G
KENNEDY, DUNCAN CAMERON	CAPT	TN 52ND INF, CO G
KENNEDY, JAMES HERRING	CAPT	MS 23RD INF, CO E
KENNEDY, JOHN MULDROW	1LT	SC 19TH BN CAV, CO D
KENNEDY, JOHN THOMAS	LT COL	NC 16TH BN CAV, CO F
KENNEDY, JOSHUA	1LT	AL 8TH INF, CO H
KENNEDY, STEPHEN H	CAPT	GA 61ST INF, CO D
KENNEY, WILLIAM F	1LT	AR 23RD INF, CO H
KENNON, RICHARD WILLIAM HINES	CAPT	AL 3RD INF, CO L
KENT, JOSEPH FERDINAND	LT COL	VA 4TH INF - HOME GUARD
KENTON, CHARLES H	1LT	TX 17TH INF, CO B
KEOWN, JAMES LEVI	CAPT	MO 4TH INF (STATE GUARD), CO D
KERR, ROBERT WILLIAM	2LT	MS 44TH INF, CO G
KESLER, JEREMIAH M	CAPT	NC 33RD INF, CO C
KEVILL, THOMAS	CAPT	VA 41ST INF, CO E
KEY, JOHN C G	COL	TX 4TH INF, CO A
KEYSER, PETER JAMES JR	2LT	VA 3RD RESERVES, CO G
KIBLER, LANGDON CALVIN	2LT	SC HOLCOMBE'S LEGION INF, CO H
KIDD, REUBEN VAUGHN	1LT	AL 4TH INF (CONEUCH GUARDS), CO A
KIDD, SAMUEL ALEXANDER	1LT	MS 5TH INF, CO I
KIEROLF, SALEM EMANUEL	CAPT	TN 27TH INF, F&S
KILLEBREW, THOMAS LEROY	CAPT	TN 33RD INF, CO H
KILLEBREW, WILLIAM MARION	2LT	TN 5TH INF, CO E
KILLEN, HENRY ALEXANDER	1LT	AL 27TH INF, CO E
KILLIAN, DANIEL WILKINSON	CAPT	GA 52ND INF, CO E
KILPATRICK, WILLIAM H	2LT	MS 24TH INF, CO K
KIMBALL, ROLLIN HIBBARD	2LT	SC 10TH INF, F&S
KIMBROUGH, WILLIAM BRADLEY	CAPT	GA 21ST INF, CO A
KINCHLOE, ELIJAH B	2LT	TX 37TH CAV, CO K
KINDRED, ELISHA THOMAS	CAPT	TX 4TH INF, CO F
KING, ALEXANDER A	1LT	SC 3RD INF (LAURENS' & JAMES), CO A
KING, CHARLES T	BVT LT	GA 46TH INF (WEBSTER COUNTY INVINCIBLES), CO F
KING, GEORGE WASHINGTON	CAPT	AR BORLAND'S MILITIA, KING'S SCOUTS
KING, HENRY H	JR 2LT	AR 6TH INF, CO F
KING, JAMES M	CAPT	AR 2ND MTD RIFLES, CO C
KING, JAMES PLEASANT	COL	AR 35TH INF, CO G
KING, JESSE PALMER	3LT	GA 23RD INF, CO B
KING, JOHN RHODES	ACS	TX 1ST CAV (MCCULLOCH'S) CAV, F&S
KING, JOSEPH HORACE	COL	AL 9TH INF, F&S
KING, MADISON T	2LT	TX 2ND INF, CO C
KING, ROBERT NEWTON	CAPT	GA 3RD CAV, CO D
KING, RUFUS Y	CAPT	TX 8TH CAV, CO A
KING, THOMAS H	1LT	VA 24TH CAV, CO H
KING, THOMAS R	1LT	TN 23RD BN INF (NEWMAN'S), CO B
KING, WILLIAM THOMAS	CAPT	AL 44TH INF, CO D
KINNEY, DANIEL F	1LT	NC 7TH INF, CO F
KINZER, WILLIAM FRANCIS MARION	2LT	TN 6TH CAV (WHEELER'S), CO A
KIRBY, GEORGE L MD	SURG	NC 2ND INF, F&S
KIRK, ALGERNON SIDNEY	CAPT	MS 35TH INF, CO D
KIRK, JAMES HUEY	CAPT	SC 1ST INF, CO D

KIRK, STEPHEN DECATUR	CAPT	SC 16TH INF, CO 3
KIRKLAND, J M	2LT	SC 11TH RESERVES, CO L
KIRKLEY, JAMES ELLISON MD	ASST SURG	TX 19TH INF, F&S
KIRKLEY, JAMES SIMON	2LT	SC 26TH INF, CO F
KIRKMAN, GEORGE	1LT	NC 7TH SENIOR RESERVES, BOON'S CO
KISER, ABEDNEGO ABNER	2LT	VA 29TH INF, CO A
KITCHEN, SOLOMON GEORGE	COL	MO 7TH CAV
KITTRELL, ROBERT H	2LT	TN 2ND CAV, CO C
KLINCK, THEODORE KECKLEY	1LT	SC HAMPTON LEGION INF, CO A
KLINK, JOHN J JR	1LT	GA 3RD CAV, CO A
KLUTTS, GEORGE W	3LT	GA 44TH INF, CO C
KNIGHT, JOHN HUGHES JR	CAPT	VA 3RD CAV, CO K
KNIGHT, JOHN W	2LT	TN 31ST INF, CO A
KNIGHT, JOHN	CAPT	LA CRESCENT INF, CO H
KNIGHT, LEVI J	CAPT	GA 29TH INF, CO G
KNOX, JAMES ROBERT	1LT	GA 22ND INF, CO E
KNOX, OSCAR FITZALLEN	1LT	AL 1ST INF, CO E
KRONE, FREDERICK GUSTAVE	CAPT	TN ARTY CORPS (McCOWN'S), CO B
KUYKENDALL, JAMES WASHINGTON	1LT	GA 8TH BN INF, CO G
KYLE, FERGUS	CAPT	TX 8TH CAV, CO D
LABORDE, OSCAR WHITFIELD	1LT	SC 1ST ARTY, CO A
LACHLISON, JAMES JR	CAPT	GA 1ST INF (OLMSTEAD'S), CO H
LACKEY, WILLIAM A	CAPT	VA 14TH CAV, CO C
LACOUR, ROLLIN	2LT	LA 2ND CAV, CO G
LACY, JAMES HORACE	MAJ	CSA QM
LACY, JOHN ARCHIBALD FLEMING	CAPT	VA 44TH INF, CO B
LACY, WILLIAM SAMUEL	CAPT	VA 44TH INF, CO B
LADD, THOMAS MIFFLIN	CAPT	VA LADD'S GUARDS CO
LAKE, GABRIEL PERRY	CAPT	MS 2ND CAV, CO I
LAKE, JOHN L	1LT	VA 8TH INF, CO K
LAMAR, GAZAWAY BASIL JR	2LT	GA 1ST INF, CO F
LAMAR, JOHN BASIL	ADC	CSA - BG HOWELL COBB
LAMAR, LUCIUS QUINTAS CINCINNATUS	LT COL	MS 19TH INF, F&S
LAMAR, THOMAS GRESHAM	COL	SC 2ND ARTY, F&S
LAMB, JOHN CALHOUN	LT COL	NC 17TH INF, CO A
LAMBERSON, GEORGE W	2LT	AR 23RD INF, CO I
LAMPKIN, ALEXANDER WOODS	COL	AL 1ST MOBILE VOLS, CO A
LANCASTER, A L	CAPT	NC 4TH BN JUNIOR RESERVES, CO B
LANCASTER, BYRD	1LT	NC 3RD ARTY, CO F
LAND, AARON	1LT	GA 54TH INF, CO H
LANDERS, HENRY BAXTER	CAPT	AR 7TH INF, CO H
LANDRUM, JOHN GILL REV	CHAPLAIN	SC 13TH INF, F&S
LANDRUM, WILLIAM S	CAPT	KY 13TH CAV, CO G
LANE, JAMES HENRY	BRIG GEN	NC 1ST INF
LANE, JOHN RANDOLPH	COL	NC 26TH INF, CO G
LANE, WALTER PAYE	BRIG GEN	TX CAV, LANES BDE
LANFORD, JOHN BERRYMAN	BVT 2LT	AL 43RD INF, CO C
LANG, FELDER	JR 2LT	GA 4TH CAV, CO D
LANGFORD, PICKENS B	3LT	SC 3RD INF, CO E
LANGSTON, DAVID MASON HENRY	CAPT	SC 3RD INF, CO I
LANGSTON, MILES L	1LT	MO FREEMAN'S CAV, CO G
LANHAM, ROBERT GLOVER	CAPT	SC 6TH INF, CO D

LANKFORD, NATHAN ALEXANDER	2LT	MS 2ND BN CAV, CO A
LANN, HENRY JEROME BONAPART	CAPT	MS 43RD INF, CO L
LARISEY, JOHN EARLE	1LT	SC 5TH INF, CO C
LARKIN, W D	CAPT	MS 1ST BN STATE TROOPS, CO F
LAROSE, AUGUSTIN	CAPT	LA 8TH INF (BIENVILLE RIFLES), CO B
LASHLEY, THOMAS D	CAPT	MO 12TH INF, CO F
LATHAM, JOHN S	1LT	SC 2ND CAV, CO F
LATHAM, WESTON ALEXANDER	CAPT	GA BIBB COUNTY HOME GUARD
LATIMER, JAMES H	CAPT	GA 47TH INF, CO F
LATIMER, JOHN T	2LT	GA 55TH INF, CO K
LATIMER, JOSEPH G WHITE	CAPT	VA COURTNEY ARTY (HENRICO)
LATTA, HENRY CLAY	2LT	NC 46TH INF, CO E
LATTIMORE, THOMAS D	2LT	NC 34TH INF, CO F
LAUDERDALE, JAMES SHELBY	CAPT	TX 10TH INF, CO G
LAURENS, JOHN BAPTIST	CAPT	VA 41ST INF, CO E
LAW, EVANDER MCIVER	BRIG GEN	AL LAW'S BDE
LAWHON, WILLIAM HENRY HARRISON	CAPT	NC 48TH INF, CO D
LAWHORNE, HENRY CLAY	2LT	TN 4TH INF (NEELY'S), CO E
LAWLER, THOMAS JEFFERSON	2LT	CSA 10TH CAV, CO B
LAWRENCE, LEWIS COWPER JR	CAPT	NC 68TH INF - AAQM
LAWSON, JEFFERSON T	CAPT	VA 50TH INF, CO K
LAWTON, ALEXANDER ROBERT	BRIG GEN	ANV - QM GENERAL, R E LEE'S STAFF
LAWTON, RICHARD FURMAN	CAPT	GA 2ND CAV, F&S - ADJ
LAWTON, WILLIAM P	2LT	VA 3RD LOCAL DEFENSE INF, CO D
LAY, JOHN FITZHUGH	CAPT	VA 4TH CAV, CO E
LAY, JOHN M	CAPT	AR 47TH CAV, CO I
LEA, JAMES MUNROE	2LT	MS 22ND INF, CO E
LEACH, GEORGE THOMAS	1LT	NC 53RD INF, CO C
LEAPHART, GODFREY	MAJ	SC 2ND INF
LEATH, JAMES HILL	1LT	AL 19TH INF, CO G
LEATHERWOOD, ALBERT N	1LT	NC 39TH INF, CO E
LEDBETTER, ALEXANDER HAMILTON	1LT	MS 35TH INF, CO F
LEE, AARON	1LT	GA 26TH INF, CO G
LEE, AUGUSTUS JAMES	2LT	GA 42ND INF, CO E
LEE, BAKER P JR	MAJ	VA 32ND INF, F&S
LEE, BENJAMIN W	2LT	TX 22ND INF, CO H
LEE, DAVID AMAN	2LT	NC 20TH INF, CO H
LEE, EDWIN GRAY	BRIG GEN	ANV
LEE, ELIAS M C	2LT	GA 59TH INF, CO A
LEE, FITZHUGH	MAJ GEN	ANV CAV CORPS
LEE, GEORGE WASHINGTON	COL	GA 38TH INF, F&S
LEE, GEORGE WASHINGTON CUSTIS	MAJ GEN	PRESIDENT DAVIS - ADC
LEE, HUTSON	MAJ	CSA
LEE, JOHN MOSBY	MAJ	CSA AQM
LEE, JONATHAN R	2LT	VA 4TH INF, CO H,I
LEE, JOSEPH ANDREW LLOYD	REPRESENTATIVE	GA STATE REPRESENTATIVE, MUSCOGEE COUNTY
LEE, MOSES	3LT	TX 13TH CAV, CO G
LEE, PATRICK HENRY	CAPT	VA 5TH CAV (NANSEMOND CAV), CO G
LEE, ROBERT EDWARD JR	1LT	CSA - GEORGE WASHINGTON CUSTIS LEE - ADC
LEE, ROBERT EDWARD	GENERAL-IN-CHIEF	CSA
LEE, STEPHEN DILL	LT GEN	HOOD'S CORPS
LEE, SYDNEY SMITH JR	CAPT	CSN

LEE, WILEY	1LT	FL 1ST CAV, CO E
LEE, WILLIAM HENRY FITZHUGH	MAJ GEN	VA 9TH CAV
LEE, WILLIAM M	CAPT	AL 10TH INF, CO C
LEE, WILLIAM PETER FRANCIS	CAPT	VA 4TH INF, CO B
LEETH, JOSIAH DAMERON	2LT	TN 23RD BN INF (NEWMAN'S), CO B
LEGARDEUR, GUSTAVE JR	CAPT	LA L ARTY, LEGARDEUR'S CO (ORLEANS GUARD BTRY)
LEGG, LOVELL LANEL	1LT	TX 2ND INF, CO C
LEGGETT, ANDREW J	CAPT	MS 7TH INF, CO G
LEGRAND, THOMAS EDWARD	2LT	VA 2ND CAV, CO H
LEHEW, FRANCIS W	CAPT	VA 17TH INF, CO B
LEIGH, BENJAMIN WATKINS	CAPT	VA 1ST BN INF (IRISH BN), CO A
LEIGH, JOHN HENRY	2LT	NC 43RD INF, CO E
LEIGH, WILLIAM DRANE	LT COL	VA 29TH INF
LELAND, JOHN ADAMS	CAPT	SC MANIGUALT'S BN, CO C
LELAND, WILLIAM A MD	SURG	AL 41ST INF, F&S
LEMLEY, JACOB H	1LT	VA 51ST MILITIA, CO B
LEMON, JAMES LILE	CAPT	GA 18TH INF, CO A
LENNON, JAMES A	1LT	VA 27TH INF, CO B
LENNON, JOHN CALE	1LT	NC 51ST CAV, CO H
LEONARD, JAMES L	1LT	GA 36TH INF, CO E
LEOPOLD, ALEIX	CAPT	LA 1ST MILITIA, CHASSEURS A PIED, CO 2
LESESNE, CHARLES MD	ASST SURG	NC 18TH INF, CO K
LESLEY, JOHN THOMAS	MAJ	FL 4TH INF, CO K
LESLIE, SAM	COL	AR 45TH INF, F&S
LESTER, DANIEL	1LT	SC 1ST STATE TROOPS, CO E
LESTER, GEORGE H	CAPT	MS 22ND INF, CO K
LESTER, GRANVILLE B MD	ASST SURG/1LT	TN 8TH INF, CO K
LESTER, JAMES THOMAS	2LT	CSA 1ST INF, CO H
LESTER, WILLIAM WHARTON	AQM	CSA VA RICHMOND
LESUEUR, CHARLES M	LT COL	TX 4TH CAV, DFS
LETCHER, JOHN	GOV	VA GOVERNOR 1861-1864
LETTON, STODDARD FORREST	2LT	MO L ARTY, H M BLEDSOE'S CO
LEWIS, ABNER MCCOY	MAJ	GA 2ND INF, F&S
LEWIS, ANDREW JACKSON	2LT	TX MARTIN'S CAV (5TH PARTISAN RANGERS), CO C
LEWIS, CHARLES IRVINE	CAPT	VA 8TH CAV, CO I
LEWIS, DANIEL MILLS	2LT	FL 5TH INF, CO F
LEWIS, EDWARD TAYLOR	CAPT	LA 2ND CAV, CO G
LEWIS, G W	CAPT	AR 36TH INF, CO E
LEWIS, GRANVILLE REVERE MD	ASST SURG	CSA
LEWIS, HENRY CLAY	2LT	FL 6TH INF, CO F
LEWIS, JOSEPH HORACE	BRIG GEN	KY 1ST BDE
LEWIS, LEVI BRANSON	2LT	NC 75TH MILITIA (YADKIN COUNTY)
LEWIS, WILLIAM H T	1LT	VA 2ND INF, CO G
LEWIS, ZACARIAH W	3LT	GA 16TH MILITIA, 2ND CO (EMANUEL COUNTY BN)
LIDDELL, ST JOHN RICHARDSON	BRIG GEN	ATM
LIGON, HIRAM SKIDMORE	CAPT	NC 21ST INF, CO G
LIKENS, BERRY	JR 2LT	VA 34TH BN CAV (WITCHER'S NIGHTHAWKS), CO B
LIKENS, MARION	1LT	VA 34TH BN CAV (WITCHER'S NIGHTHAWKS), CO B
LILES, WILLIAM ALEXANDER	1LT	NC 14TH INF, CO C
LILLARD, WILLIAM WALLACE	CAPT	TN 5TH CAV (MCKENZIE'S), CO C
LILLEY , ROBERT DOAK	BRIG GEN	ANV - PEGRAM'S OLD BDE, EARLY'S CORP - CMDR
LINDLEY, JOHN BENSON	CAPT	GA 7TH INF, CO D

LINDSAY, DAVID HERNDON	CAPT	MO 9TH INF, CO H
LINDSAY, JOHNSON WILBORNE	2LT	CSA MEAD'S CAV, CO A
LINDSAY, LEWIS E	CAPT	AL 4TH INF (CONEUCH GUARDS), CO K
LINDSAY, RICHARD PRESTON	1LT	MO 3RD INF, CO F,D
LINDSAY, ROBERT H	ACS	KY 4TH INF, CO A
LINDSAY, THOMAS J	JR 2LT	LA 17TH INF, CO F
LINDSEY, CARLTON ALEXANDER	1LT	MS 5TH CAV, CO B
LINDSEY, JOHN GREEN	2LT	GA 29TH INF, CO C
LINEBERGER, JOHN FREDERICK	1LT	NC 49TH INF, CO H
LINER, WYATT V	2LT	GA 35TH INF, CO A
LINGLE, ADAM D	2LT	NC 58TH INF, CO K
LINKOUS, MILBOURN FLOYD	1LT	VA 16TH CAV, CO C
LINTHICUM, CHARLES FREDERICK	CHAPLAIN	VA 8TH INF, F&S
LINVILLE, RICHARD MCDOWELL	1LT	MS 23RD INF, CO A
LIPSCOMB, JOHN CALVIN	CAPT	TN 27TH INF, CO D
LIPSCOMB, THOMAS	LT COL	MS 6TH CAV, CO K
LITTLE, JOSEPH W	2LT	TX 11TH INF, CO A
LITTLE, LEWIS H	1LT	TX 32ND CAV, CO C
LITTLE , JOHN MORGAN	2LT	TX 11TH INF, CO A
LITTLEFIELD, ASAHEL	LT COL	GA 8TH INF BN
LITTLEFIELD, JAMES	1LT	AR 7TH INF, CO C
LITTON, ELISHUE VERMILLION	CAPT	VA 64TH MTD INF, CO G
LIVELY, WILSON	CAPT	VA 166TH MILITIA
LIVINGSTON, BARNETT	1LT	SC 20TH INF, CO D
LIVINGSTON, JAMES LARKIN	BVT 2LT	TN 7TH CAV (DUCKWORTH'S), CO M
LLEWELLYN, DAVID HERBERT MD	ASST SURG	CSN CSS ALABAMA
LOCKE, JAMES BENJAMIN	CAPT	MS 40TH INF, CO A
LOCKE, JESSEE CULP	2LT	MS 13TH INF, CO G
LOCKETT, ROBERT A	2LT	KY 10TH CAV (JOHNSON'S), CO A
LOCKETT, SAMUEL HENRY	MAJ	CSA - ENGINEERS (DEPT OF E LA, MS, & AL)
LOCKETT, THOMAS FRANCIS	CAPT	MO 10TH CAV
LOCKHART, ROBERT HENRY	2LT	TX 14TH INF (CLARK'S), CO K
LOGAN, ELLIS	CAPT	AL 13TH INF, CO H
LOGAN, GEORGE WASHINGTON	REPRESENTATIVE	CSA 2ND CONFEDERATE CONGRESS
LOGSDON, JAMES VAUGHN	1LT	TX 27TH CAV, CO L
LOKE, JAMES BENJAMIN	1LT	TN 40TH INF, CO A (WALKER'S)
LONG, HENYARD	CAPT	NC 18TH INF, CO C
LONG, JOHN E	1LT	SC 4TH INF, CO D
LONG, JONATHAN P	1LT	NC 62ND INF, CO I
LONG, SAMUEL ARETUS	2LT	NC 18TH INF, CO C
LONG, WILLIAM STATON	2LT	NC 1ST INF, CO A
LONG, WILLIAM	1LT	AL 1ST INF, CO G
LONGSTREET, JAMES	LT GEN	ANV CMDR, 1ST CORPS
LOONEY, ABRAHAM MCCLELLAN	MAJ	TN 1ST/27TH CONSOLIDATED INF
LOONEY, ROBERT FAIN	COL	TN 38TH INF (LOONEY'S), CO L
LOPER, FRANCIS B	CAPT	MS 37TH INF, CO H
LOPER, JOEL W	1LT	MS 5TH INF, CO A
LORD, JOHN	1LT	GA 57TH INF, CO K
LORING, WILLIAM WING	MAJ GEN	MS PACS COMDG FIRST ARMY CORPS
LOTT, JOEL	TAX COLLECTOR	GA COFFEE COUNTY
LOTT, THOMAS C	CAPT	GA 26TH INF, CO F
LOTT, WILLIAM H	2LT	TN 52ND INF, CO C

LOUDERMILK, JOHN	MAJ	GA 36TH INF, CO D
LOVE, JAMES HARRISON	CAPT	AR 7TH CAV, CO C
LOVE, JAMES ROBERT JR	LT COL	NC THOMAS' LEGION INF, F&S
LOVE, ROBERT CALVIN GRIER	CAPT	NC 87TH MILITIA, CO 5 (GASTON COUNTY)
LOVE, ROBERT G O	COL	NC 62ND INF, F&S
LOVE, SAMUEL T	MAJ	TN 27TH INF, CO K
LOVE, THOMAS R	CAPT	FL 8TH INF, CO B
LOVE , ROBERT CALVIN GRIER	CAPT	NC 87TH MILITIA, CO 5 (GASTON COUNTY)
LOVELACE, EDMOND J	2LT	NC 55TH INF, CO D
LOVELL, MANSFIELD	MAJ GEN	LA COMMANDER OF NEW ORLEANS
LOVINS, RANSOM J	2LT	VA 45TH BN INF, CO E
LOWE, ADEN	COL	MO 3RD INF (STATE GUARD), CO A
LOWE, STEPHEN R	2LT	GA 48TH INF, CO B
LOWRANCE, JOHN A	2LT	NC 56TH INF, CO K
LOWRANCE, WILLIAM LEE J	COL	NC 34TH INF, F&S
LOWREY, MARK PERRIN	BRIG GEN	MS 32ND INF
LOWRY, JAMES A	3LT	NC 48TH INF, CO A
LOWRY, JOHN J	1LT	TN 35TH INF, CO D
LOWRY, ROBERT GADDEN HAYNES	BRIG GEN	MS 6TH INF
LUBBOCK, FRANCIS RICHARD	COL	JEFFERSON DAVIS - ADC
LUBBOCK, THOMAS SALTUS	COL	TX 8TH CAV, F&S
LUCAS, CHARLES W	1LT	VA 11TH INF, CO F
LUCAS, ICHABOD MONROE	CAPT	TN 15TH CAV, CO B
LUCKETT, BENJAMIN GORDON	1LT	MS 48TH INF, CO H
LUGAR, WILLIAM BARNEY	1LT	VA 46TH INF, CO K
LUKE, DAVID PERRY	CAPT	GA 50TH INF, CO I
LUM, JESSE D JR	1LT	TX 25TH CAV, CO B
LUMLEY, JAMES W	2LT	GA 14TH CAV, CO F
LUMPKIN, SAMUEL PUETT	COL	GA 44TH INF, CO C
LUNDY, WILLIAM A	CAPT	VA 45TH INF, CO E
LURTY, WARREN S	CAPT	VA HORSE ARTY, LURTY'S CO
LUSE, WILLIAM HENRY	LT COL	MS 18TH INF, CO B
LUTHER, ANDREW ALLEN	2LT	NC 25TH INF, CO I
LUTTERLOH, JARVIS BUXTON	1LT	NC 56TH INF, CO E
LUTZ, LEVI	CAPT	VA 12TH CAV, CO K
LYLE, CHARLES JOSEPH	1LT	TN 60TH MTD INF, CO F
LYNCH, GIDEON MOON	2LT	SC 13TH BN INF, CO C
LYNDON, JESSE FRANKLIN	1LT	NC 63RD MILITIA (RANDOLPH COUNTY)
LYNHAM, WILLIAM J JR	CAPT	VA 1ST BN INF (IRISH BN), F&S AQM
LYNN, DAVID	CAPT	VA 19TH CAV, CO F
LYON, ELKANAH EDWARD	CAPT	NC 44TH INF, CO A
LYON, HYLAN BENTON	BRIG GEN	KY - GEN FORREST
LYON, JOHN	CAPT	SC 7TH INF, CO C
LYON, PATTERSON HAMPTON	2LT	GA 43RD INF, CO A
LYON, RICHARD	COL	AR 6TH INF, F&S
LYTLE, EPHRIAM FOSTER	LT COL	TN 45TH INF, CO D
LYTLE, FRANK H	1LT	TN 18TH INF, CO C
LYTLE, GEORGE W	CAPT	NC 49TH INF, CO A
LYTTON, JOHN F	1LT	VA 5TH INF (IMMORTAL 600), CO C
MABRY, CHARLES W	MAJ	GA 19TH INF, CO E
MABRY, CLOUGH H	CAPT	SC 7TH RESERVES, CO M
MABRY, HENCHE PARHAM JR	COL	TX 3RD CAV, F&S

MABRY, LEONARD S	1LT	NC 46TH INF, CO C
MACAULAY, ROBERT GRIER	1LT	NC 7TH INF, CO I
MacGREGOR, JOHN RIDOUT	2LT	VA 47TH INF, CO I
MACHEN, FRANCIS MARION	CAPT	AL 52ND INF, CO E
MACK, JOSEPH BINGHAM REV	CHAPLAIN	TN 55TH INF
MACK, YOUNG MILTON	CAPT	AR 8TH INF, CO H
MacLIN, WILLIAM E	1LT	TN 53RD INF, CO C
MacMAHON, F S MD	SURG	CSA - SHELLEY'S BDE, LORING'S DIV, STEWART'S CORPS
MACON, JACOB MICHAUX	CAPT	MS 19TH INF, CO A
MACON, JOHN	CAPT	TN 35TH INF, CO D
MADDEN, DEMOSTHENESE ROBERT MALCOLM	2LT	AL 60TH INF, CO E
MADDOX, JOSEPH JEFFERSON	1LT	GA 38TH INF, CO B
MADDOX, WILLIAM ALEXANDER	MAJ	LA 17TH INF, F&S
MADDUX, EMORY M	2LT	GA 44TH INF, CO B
MAFFETT, GEORGE CLINTON	LT	SC INF (HOLCOMBE'S LEGION), CO H
MAGEE, JOHN	1LT	MS 7TH INF, CO F
MAGEE, NEHEMIAH	REPRESENTATIVE	LA STATE REPRESENTATIVE, WASHINGTON PARISH
MAGEE, TURPIN DICKSON	MAJ	MS 46TH INF, CO B
MAGRATH, ANDREW GORDON	GOV	SC GOVERNOR 1864-1865
MAGRUDER, JOHN BANKHEAD	MAJ GEN	TX, NM, AZ CMDR DIST
MAGRUDER, WILLIAM THOMAS	CAPT	CSA - DAVIS' BDE, HETH'S DIV - AAG
MAHAFFEY, WILSON L	2LT	GA 57TH INF, CO K
MAHARRY, WILLIAM F MD	ASST SURG	AL 2ND CAV, CO D
MAHONE, JOHN JAMES	2LT	VA 19TH BN H ARTY, CO D
MAHONE, WILLIAM	MAJ GEN	VA 6TH INF
MAHOOD, FONTAINE WATTS	2LT	VA 24TH INF, CO G
MAKEMSON, JOHN	BVT 2LT	KY 4TH CAV, CO D
MALBONE, JAMES M	2LT	VA 6TH INF, CO B
MALCOLM, WILLIAM DAVID	CAPT	GA 42ND INF, CO G
MALLETT, CHARLES PETER	1LT	NC 3RD INF, CO C
MALLORY, STEPHEN RUSSELL	SECRETARY - NAVY	CSA - SECRETARY OF THE NAVY
MALONE, DANIEL	JUDGE	VA DINWIDDIE COUNTY, JUSTICE OF THE CHANCERY COURT
MALONE, GEORGE YEWELL	CAPT	AL 15TH INF, CO F
MALONE, JOHN THOMAS	2LT	MS 24TH INF, CO A
MALONE, MILES M	1LT	AL 16TH INF, CO B
MALONE, R D	1LT	TN 45TH INF, CO G
MANESS, ALEXANDER	CAPT	VA 21ST INF, CO D
MANGHAM, WILEY PAUL	2LT	AL 25TH INF, CO D
MANLEY, W B	1LT	TN 33RD INF, CO B
MANN, EMMETT JACKSON	1LT	VA 6TH INF, CO I
MANN, ROBERT N	CAPT	NC 35TH INF, CO F
MANN, WILLIAM H	MAJ	GA 54TH INF, F&S
MANNING, WILLIAM H	MAJ	LA 6TH INF, F&S
MANSON, JOSEPH RICHARD	CAPT	VA 12TH INF, CO I
MARCUS, MADISON A	CAPT	GA 15TH INF, CO I
MARIS, LEWIS	2LT	MO 3RD BN CAV, CO D
MARKS, CHARLES H	1LT	CSA 8TH BN INF (2ND FOREIGN BN)
MARKS, LEON DAWSON	COL	LA 27TH INF, F&S
MARKS, WASHINGTON	MAJ	LA 22ND INF, F&S
MARMADUKE, JOHN SAPPINGTON	MAJ GEN	ATM
MARMION, JAMES R	CAPT	TX 3RD INF, CO G

MARRINER, WILLIAM MCMAIN	CAPT	KY 1ST INF, CO H
MARRIOTT, JOSEPH G W	2LT	MD 1ST INF, CO E
MARSHALL, CHARLES A	LT COL	ANV, GENERAL LEE'S F&S - AAG
MARSHALL, CHARLES ALEXANDER	1LT	VA 2ND INF, CO I
MARSHALL, EDMOND	1LT	VA 45TH INF, CO I
MARSHALL, HUMPHREY	BRIG GEN	SW VA
MARSHALL, JAMES KEITH	COL	NC 52ND INF, F&S
MARSHALL, JOHN ALFRED	2LT	AL 2ND CAV, CO H
MARSHALL, JOHN FOSTER	COL	SC 1ST INF, F&S
MARSHALL, JOHN	COL	TX 4TH INF, F&S
MARSHALL, RICHARD SPENCER	CAPT	TN 37TH INF, CO G
MARSHALL, THOMAS JEFFERSON	CAPT	GA 6TH INF, CO E
MARSHALL, THOMAS	2LT	VA 12TH CAV, CO E
MARSHALL, THOMAS	LT COL	VA 7TH CAV (ASHBY'S), F&S
MARSHALL, WILLIAM ALEXANDER MD	SURG	MO 4TH CAV (BURBRIDGE'S)
MARSHBOURNE, SAMUEL WILLIAM	CAPT	GA 53RD INF, CO C
MARSHBOURNE, SAMUEL WILLIAM	CAPT	GA 53RD INF, CO C
MARSTON, JOSEPH	2LT	VA 35TH BN CAV, CO E
MARTIN, ANDERSON DUKE	1LT	MS 10TH CAV, CO C, K
MARTIN, BARTLETT YANCEY	1LT	NC 34TH INF, CO A
MARTIN, BENJAMIN CROCKETT	CAPT	SC 18TH INF, CO D
MARTIN, BENJAMIN F	CAPT	MS 3RD CAV, CO F
MARTIN, FRANCIS ROBERT	LT	MO 2ND INF, 8TH DIV (STATE GUARD), CO E
MARTIN, GILES SMITH	CAPT	VA 63RD INF, CO G & I
MARTIN, JAMES T	CAPT	MS 8TH INF, CO A
MARTIN, JOHN MARSHALL	COL	FL 9TH INF, F&S
MARTIN, ROBERT M	COL	KY 10TH CAV (MORGAN'S PARTISAN RANGERS)
MARTIN, SYLVESTER G	2LT	VA 19TH INF, CO K
MARTIN, VALENTINE T	2LT	GA 41ST INF, CO H
MARTIN, WILLIAM ALLEN	ENSIGN	GA 65TH INF, F&S
MARTIN, WILLIAM HARRISON	MAJ	TX 4TH INF, F&S
MARTIN, WILLIAM HOWDY	MAJ	TX 4TH INF, F&S
MARTIN, WILLIAM RICHARD	1LT	NC 21ST INF, CO H
MASON, ALEXANDER	CAPT	AR 2ND BN CAV (BARNETT'S), CO A
MASON, JOHN WILBURN	2LT	GA FAYETTE COUNTY MILITIA
MASON, JOHN NICHOLAS	2LT	GA 27TH INF, CO H
MASON, ROBERT	2LT	VA 34TH BN CAV (WITCHER'S NIGHTHAWKS), CO H
MASSIE, JOSIAH CAMILLIS	LT COL	TX 9TH INF (NICHOLS'), GFS
MASSIE, THOMAS B	LT COL	VA 12TH CAV, F&S
MASSINGILL, JOSEPH	1LT	SC 4TH INF, CO H
MAST, MILTON	CAPT	TX 11TH INF, CO A
MASTERSON, THOMAS	3LT	AL 10TH DIV, 4TH BRIG, CO C MILITIA
MASTIN, THOMAS B	LT	AL 53RD PARTISAN RANGERS, CO G
MATHENY, JOHN A	CAPT	TN 28TH INF, CO B
MATHENY, WILLIAM GRIMSLEY	LT COL	AR 21ST INF, CO B
MATHEWS, JAMES DAVIDSON	COL	GA 38TH INF, CO F&S
MATHEWS, JOHN SAMPSON	1LT	TN 5TH INF, CO H
MATHEWS, THOMAS PHILIP	CAPT	VA 18TH INF, CO H
MATHIS, WILLIAM J	1LT	TN 11TH INF, CO C - ADJ
MATLOCK, NICHOLAS GAINES	CAPT	MO PERKIN'S BN INF, CO B
MATTHEWS, CHARLES W	LT COL	GA 17TH INF (MUSCOGEE VOL), F&S
MATTHEWS, JAMES FISKE	CAPT	TX 8TH CAV (TERRY'S RANGERS), CO K

MATTISON, JOSEPH BENJAMIN	CAPT	MS 9TH INF, CO F
MAULDIN, JAMES ERVIN	CAPT	NC 83RD MILITIA (STANLEY COUNTY)
MAULDIN, JAMES HUGHDIA	1LT	MS 2ND CAV, CO A
MAULTSBY, SAMUEL WHITE	CAPT	NC 51ST INF, CO H
MAUPIN, SETH W	2LT	KY 11TH CAV, CO E
MAURY, DABNEY HERNDON	MAJ GEN	AOT - DEPT OF THE GULF
MAURY, MATTHEW FONTAINE	2LT	CSA 3RD ENGINEERS, CO F
MAURY, THOMAS FRANCIS MD	SURG/MAJ	VA 1ST INF (WILLIAMS RIFLES), F&S
MAXEY, SAMUEL BELL	BRIG GEN	TX 9TH INF
MAXEY, WILLIAM P	CAPT	MS MTD INF, MAXEY'S CO
MAXSON, GEORGE W	MAJ	KY 6TH MTD INF, CO B
MAXWELL, DAVID ELWELL	CAPT	FL 1ST CAV, CO D
MAXWELL, HARVEY LEWIS	1LT	TX BAYLOR'S CAV, CO H
MAY, JOHN S	LT	KY 6TH CAV, CO C
MAY, WILLIAM HENRY	1LT	AL 3RD INF, CO H
MAY, WILLIAM JASPER	1LT	GA 59TH INF, CO B
MAY, WILLIAM WOODSON	CAPT	TN 24TH INF, CO G
MAY, WILLIAM	CAPT	AL LEWIS' BN CAV, CO C
MAYATT, JOHN H	2LT	MO 9TH CAV, CO B
MAYER, SIMON	1LT	MS 9TH INF, CO D
MAYES, JUNIUS ALCEAUS MD	ASST SURG	CSA
MAYES, MACE ANDREW AUGUSTUS	CAPT	GA 9TH BN CAV, CO C
MAYES, WILLIAM HENRY	LT	CSA 1ST CHEROKEE MTD INF, CO G
MAYFIELD, JAMES JEFFERSON	CAPT	TN 38TH INF, CO G
MAYFIELD, THOMAS B	2LT	TX CRUMP'S CAV (1ST PARTISAN RANGERS), CO E
MAYNARD, JOHN	1LT	TN 27TH INF, CO F
MAYO, CLAUDIUS	JR 2LT	LA 18TH INF, CO B
MAYO, ROBERT FRANCIS MARION	BVT 2LT	MS 6TH INF (LOWRY RIFLES), CO D
MAYS, RUFUS A	CAPT	TN 6TH INF, CO C
MAYS, SAMUEL	CAPT	TN 50TH INF, CO G
McALEXANDER, EDWARD	COL	AL 27TH INF, F&S
McANALLY, JAMES KYLE	CAPT	TN 37TH INF, CO K
McARTHUR, JOHN STAFFORD	1LT	NC 3RD ARTY, CO E
McAULAY, ROBERT G	1LT	NC 7TH INF, CO I
McBLAIR, WILLIAM	CMDR	CSN CSS ATLANTA
McBRIDE, JAMES H	BRIG GEN	MO STATE GUARDS
McBRIDE, JOHN KARNS	1LT	AL 9TH INF, CO C
McBRYDE, MALCOLM HUGHES	CAPT	NC 3RD ARTY, CO E
McCALL, JOHN GOLDWIRE	CAPT	GA 50TH INF, CO K
McCALL, MOSES NATHANIEL JR	CAPT	GA 5TH CAV, CO F
McCAMPBELL, WILLIAM DANIEL	CAPT	VA 55TH INF, CO F
McCANN, JOSEPH RICHARD	MAJ	TN 9TH CAV, F&S
McCARDEL, ALFRED VINCENT	2LT	GA 29TH INF, CO F
McCARDELL, WILLIAM H	2LT	FL 4TH INF, CO G
McCARLEY, MOSES	LT COL	MS 23RD INF, CO G
McCARTY, KENDRICK	2LT	MS 8TH INF, CO F
McCAUGHAN, JAMES JEFFERSON	2LT	MS 37TH INF, CO G
McCAUGHAN, JOHN DAWSON	2LT	TX 6TH INF, CO C
McCAUGHAN, THOMAS JACKSON	2LT	MS 37TH INF, CO G
McCAULEY, DAVID M	2LT	NC 46TH MILITIA, CO 7 (ORANGE COUNTY)
McCAUSLAND, JOHN B	BRIG GEN	VA 36TH CAV
McCAY, ROBERT C	MAJ	MS 38TH CAV, CO B

McCLAIN, JOHN	LT	TN 3RD MTD INF (LILLARD'S), CO E
McCLARTY, CLINTON C	MAJ	CSA KY - ACS FOR BG JOHN C BRECKINRIDGE
McCLELLAN, CHRISTOPHER COLUMBUS	2LT	NC 7TH BN JUNIOR RESERVES, CO A
McCLESKEY, SAMUEL RHEA	3LT	GA 9TH CAV, CO C
McCLONEY, FRANCIS MARION	LT	AL 31ST INF, CO A
McCLUNG, HUGH L	CAPT	TN 26TH INF, CO F
McCLUNG, LUNDY M	ENSIGN	TX 10TH CAV, CO K
McCLURE, MATHEW T	2LT	VA 52ND INF, CO I - COMMISSARY
McCOLLUM, DUNCAN	1LT	MS 4TH CAV, CO A
McCOLLUM, LEVI	LT COL	TN 42ND INF, CO F
McCOMAS, WILLIAM WIRT	CAPT	VA ARTY (WISE LEGION)
McCOMBS, JAMES P MD	ASST SURG	NC 11TH INF, F&S (BETHEL'S)
McCONAHA, JOHN H	2LT	VA 34TH BN CAV (WITCHER'S NIGHTHAWKS), CO A
McCONNELL, GREEN DUKE	CAPT	AL 23RD INF, CO K
McCONNELL, HENRY M	CAPT	VA 48TH INF, CO E
McCONNELL, ISAAC	CAPT	CSA - AQM
McCORD, THOMAS KNICELY	CAPT	MS 4TH CAV, CO K
McCORKLE, HEZEKIAH	2LT	GA 37TH INF (PETTUS VOLUNTEERS), CO H
McCORKLE, WILLIAM ALEXANDER MD	SURG	TN 2ND CAV, CO E
McCORMIC, JAMES L	CAPT	NC 1ST BN H ARTY, CO D
McCORMICK, JOSEPH PLUNKET	POSTMASTER	LA BATON ROUGE POST OFFICE
McCOWN, JEROME B	CAPT	TX 5TH CAV, CO G
McCOWN, JOHN PORTER	MAJ GEN	CSA - ARMY OF THE WEST, 2ND DIV
McCOY, HENRY R	MAJ	AL 34TH INF, F&S
McCRAW, ALEXANDER CAMPBELL	2LT	VA 21ST INF, CO E
McCRAY, THOMAS HAMILTON	COL	AR 31ST INF, F&S
McCREARY, JAMES BENNETT	LT COL	KY 11TH CAV
McCRORY, FELIX GRUNDY	2LT	AR 2ND CAV, CO E
McCUISTION, JOHN GWINN	CAPT	MO 3RD INF, CO C
McCULLOCH, BENJAMIN	BRIG GEN	CSA - ARMY OF THE WEST, INDIAN TERRITORY
McCULLOCH, HENRY EUSTACE	BRIG GEN	TX 1ST MTD RIFLEMEN
McCULLOCH, ROBERT ALLEN	COL	MO 2ND CAV, PACS
McCULLOUGH, DANIEL ALEXANDER	2LT	AL 19TH INF, CO G
McCULLOUGH, JAMES L	CAPT	SC 16TH/24TH CONSOLIDATED INF, CO F
McCURRY, BENJAMIN C	LT COL	GA 22ND INF, F&S
McCUTCHEN, JOHN ALLEN REV	CHAPLAIN	AL 34TH INF, F&S
McCUTCHON, SAMUEL BUTLER	LT COL	LA 8TH CAV, F&S
McDANIEL, CHARLES ADDISON	COL	GA 41ST INF
McDANIEL, JOHN H	1LT	MO ROBERTSON'S STATE GUARD, CO 5
McDAVID, JAMES A	CAPT	SC 2ND RIFLES, CO F
McDAVID, PETER ACKER	1LT	SC 2ND RIFLES, CO L
McDAVID, RICHMOND M	2LT	CSA 15TH CAV, CO C
McDONALD, GEORGE WASHINGTON	CAPT	TN 17TH INF, CO K
McDONALD, JAMES REDDING	MAJ	NC 51ST INF, CO D
McDONALD, JAMES	LT COL	GA 61ST INF, F&S
McDONALD, JOHN CLAIBORNE	LT COL	VA 22ND INF, F&S
McDONALD, MARCUS LAFAYETTE	3LT	MS 6TH INF, CO K
McDONALD, MARTIN LUTHER	2LT	GA 34TH INF, CO H
McDONALD, THOMAS S	1LT	AL 13TH INF, CO H
McDOWELL, JAMES WILLIAM	1LT	VA 26TH BN INF, CO D
McDOWELL, RUSSELL DAVIS	CAPT	MS 7TH INF, CO C
McDOWELL, WILLIAM THOMAS	BVT 2LT	AL 51ST PARTISAN RANGERS, CO B

McDUFFIE, BENJAMIN FRANKLIN	2LT	GA 54TH INF, CO G
McDUFFIE, NEILL C	AQM	SC 21ST INF, CO L
McELROY, JACKSON CARROL	CAPT	MS 39TH INF, CO D
McENTIRE, JOHN CUNNINGHAM	2LT	GA 12TH CAV, CO B
McEWEN, JOHN BELL	CAPT	MS 4TH CAV, CO K
McFADYEN, ARCHIBALD	3LT	NC 5TH CAV, CO A
McFALL, JAMES M	ADJ	SC PALMETTO SHARPSHOOTERS, F&S
McFARLAIN, DAVID B	JR 2LT	VA 34TH BN CAV (WITCHER'S NIGHTHAWKS), CO I
McFARLAIN, JOHN A	MAJ	VA 34TH BN CAV (WITCHER'S NIGHTHAWKS), F&S
McFARLAND, HORATIO HARRIS	2LT	MO FREEMAN'S CAV, CO B
McFARLAND, JAMES	1LT	GA 15TH INF, CO B
McFARLAND, ROBERT IV	MAJ	TN 39TH INF, CO C
McFARLAND, ROBERT	CAPT	KY 2ND CAV (DUKE'S), CO G
McFARLIN, JAMES M	1LT	GA 46TH INF, CO A
McFARLIN, ROBERT M	1LT	GA 1ST RESERVE CAV BN, CO C
McFERRIN, JAMES A	1LT	TN 32ND INF, CO K
McGAHAGIN, JOSHUA LUCAS	CAPT	FL 1ST INF RESERVES, CO K
McGAVOCK, RANDALL W	LT COL	TN 10TH INF
McGEE, JOHN WESLEY	CAPT	GA 60TH INF, CO B
McGEE, WILLIAM III	1LT	LA 9TH INF, CO I
McGEHEE, GEORGE THOMAS	CAPT	MS 21ST INF, CO I
McGEHEE, JOHN L	CAPT	MS 7TH INF, CO C
McGEHEE, LUCIUS MIRABEAU	CAPT	AL 27TH INF, CO K
McGEHEE, SAMUEL M	1LT	AR 2ND INF BN, CO B - AQM
McGEHEE, SAMUEL M	MAJ	CSA - QM
McGEHEE, VALENTINE MERIWETHER	CAPT	AR 2ND INF, CO G
McGHEE, THOMAS JEFFERSON	1LT	CSA 1ST CHEROKEE MTD RIFLES, CO E
McGINNIS, IRA J	AQM	VA 34TH BN CAV (WITCHER'S NIGHTHAWKS), F&S
McGINNIS, NOBLE LAFAYETTE	LT COL	TX 2ND INF, HFS
McGOUGH, CHRISTOPHER COLUMBUS	2LT	GA 45TH INF, CO B
McGOVERN, PATRICK	CAPT	GA PHILLIP'S LEGION, CO F
McGOWAN, SAMUEL	BRIG GEN	SC MCGOWAN'S BDE
McGRAW, JAMES W	2LT	MS 23RD INF
McGUFFIN, SAMUEL JORDAN	2LT	AR 1ST MTD RIFLES, CO K
McGUIRE, HUNTER HOLMES MD	SURG	CSA II CORPS MEDICAL DIRECTOR
McGUIRE, JOHN W	JR 2LT	MO 3RD CAV, CO B
McHENRY, ELI BASS	LT	MO WOODS'S CAV, F&S - ADJ
McINTOSH, DANIEL N	COL	CSA 1ST CREEK MTD, F&S
McINTOSH, JOHN CHARLES	1LT	SC 9TH INF, CO G
McINTYRE, DAVID M	LT	NC 38TH INF, CO A - ADJ
McINTYRE, GEORGE ALEXANDER	CAPT	SC 1ST INF (McCREARY'S), CO E
McKAUGHAN, BARRON DEKALB	2LT	NC 2ND DETAILED MEN, CO E
McKAY, GILCHRIST	CAPT	TX 17TH CAV, CO K
McKAY, WILLIAM D	JR 2LT	MS 24TH INF, CO I
McKEE, JOHN V	CAPT	AL 47TH INF, CO G
McKENZIE, ARTHUR A	1LT	SC 5TH INF, CO H
McKENZIE, CARLTON J	2LT	GA 62ND CAV, CO C
McKENZIE, GEORGE WASHINGTON	COL	TN 5TH CAV, CO C
McKIM, RANDOLPH HARRISON REV	CHAPLAIN/CAPT	VA 2ND CAV, F&S
McKINLEY, WILLIAM	2LT	MS 7TH BN INF, CO A
McKINNEY, WILLIAM M	1LT	TN NEWSOM'S CAV, CO A
McKINNON, JOHN M	2LT	NC 3RD ARTY, CO E

McKNIGHT, CALEB	CAPT	TN 31ST INF, CO B
McKNIGHT, JOSEPH MADISON	1LT	TX 35TH CAV, CO C
McLAMB, MINSON	2LT	NC 46TH INF, CO I
McLAWS, WILLIAM RAYMOND	1LT	GA 1ST RESERVES (SYMONS'), CO I
McLEAN, JAMES DICKSON	1LT	NC 13TH L ARTY, CO B
McLELLAN, ALDEN	1LT	CSA
McLEMORE, JOSHUA	2LT	MS 37TH INF, CO I
McLEMORE, WILLIAM SUGARS	COL	TN 4TH CAV, CO F
McLENDON, JOSIAH DOUGLAS	2LT	AL 46TH INF, CO H
McLENDON, LEWIS MD	ASST SURG	AR 2ND INF, F&S
McLEOD, BELA B	2LT	LA 17TH INF, CO G
McLEOD, DANIEL	CAPT	AL 24TH INF, CO E
McLEOD, ROBERT YOUNG	LT	SC 19TH INF, CO E
McLEOD, WILLIAM LEON	CAPT	GA 38TH INF, CO C
McMAKIN, PEYTON LEE	2LT	KY 6TH CAV, CO A
McMANAWAY, JAMES MONROE	LT	VA 58TH INF, CO K
McMANUS, AMOS	CAPT	SC 2ND INF, CO H
McMASTER, FITZ WILLIAM	COL	SC 17TH INF, F&S
McMATH, JAMES HILLMAN	CAPT	AL 11TH INF, CO G
McMICHAEL, JAMES ROBERT	CAPT	GA 12TH INF, CO K
McMICHAEL, RUFUS W	CAPT	GA 14TH INF, CO I
McMILLAN, HUGH	2LT	AL 8TH CAV (HATCH'S), CO G
McMILLAN, THOMAS J	1LT	MS 2ND INF (QUINN'S), CO E
McMILLAN, WILLIAM WALLACE	CAPT	AL 17TH INF, CO H
McMILLIAN, LAWANCE PINKNEY	2LT	SC 1ST INF (HAGOOD'S), CO K,A
McMINN, WILLIAM J	MAJ	CSA - CHIEF QM
McMULLAN, JOHN GIBSON	CAPT	GA 9TH INF, CO A
McMULLEN, JAMES PARRAMORE	CAPT	FL PINELLAS INF.
McMULLEN, M J	MAJ	GA 22ND H ARTY BN
McMULLIN, JAMES JORDAN	2LT	MO 1ST CAV, CO G
McMURRAY, W J	2LT	TN 20TH INF, CO B
McMURTREY, ELISHA LAWLEY	CAPT	AR 2ND CAV, CO D
McNEER, WILLIAM RICHARDS REV	CHAPLAIN	VA 4TH INF, F&S
McNUTT, JACOB M	JR 2LT	MS 17TH INF, CO C
McQUIDDY , THOMAS JEFFERSON	MAJ	MO 3RD CAV BN, F&S
McRANEY, JOHN	1LT	MS 1ST BN CAV (STATE TROOPS), CO B
McSWANE, WILLIAM H	MAJ	TX 19TH BDE MILITIA BEAT #6
		(FREESTONE COUNTY, TX)
McSWINE, THOMAS	AQM	AR 26TH INF, CO C
McWHORTER, SAMUEL W	CAPT	MS 23RD INF, CO I
MEADE, RICHARD KIDDER JR	MAJ	CSA 1ST L ARTY - STAFF OFFICER FOR GENERALS
		JACKSON & TALIAFERRO
MEADOWS, ISAAC H	1LT	VA 34TH BN CAV (WITCHER'S NIGHTHAWKS), CO K
MEADOWS, RUFUS M	2LT	VA 34TH BN CAV (WITCHER'S NIGHTHAWKS), CO K
MEARS, ERWIN JASPER	1LT	MS 42ND INF, CO K
MEARS, GOLDSBOROUGH B	CAPT	MS 42ND INF, CO K
MEDEARIS, WILEY W MD	ASST SURG	TX 16TH INF
MEEK, A T	MAJ	AR 2ND INF, CO I
MEEK, JEFFERSON K	CAPT	MS 42ND INF, CO I
MEEK, LITTLETON C	2LT	MS 7TH CAV, CO K
MEETZE, HENRY A	AQM	SC 13TH INF, CO K
MEIERE, WILLIAM STACK MD	SURG	VA 42ND INF, F&S

MELCHERS, THEODORE WILHELM ANTON	CAPT	SC 1ST RIFLES (MILITIA)
MELLETT, FRANCIS MARION	LT COL	SC 4TH INF, CO I
MELTON, SAMUEL WYLE	LT COL	CSA - AAG
MELVIN, EPHRAIM P	CAPT	FL 11TH INF, CO K
MENEFEE, WILLIAM ADDISON JR	CAPT	VA 2ND CAV, CO B
MERCER, JOHN THOMAS	COL	GA 21ST INF, F&S
MERCHANT, BENJAMIN DYER	1LT	VA 4TH CAV, CO A
MERCHANT, CLAIBORNE WALKER	CAPT	TX 14TH CAV, CO H
MERCIER, JAMES NICHOLSON	CAPT	GA 22ND INF, CO F
MERRICK, EZRA CARN	LT GOV	SC SIGNER SECESSION CSA ATTORNEY
MERRITT, JAMES WESLEY	2LT	VA 34TH BN CAV (WITCHER'S NIGHTHAWKS), CO D
MERRITT, JOHN H	1LT	VA 48TH INF, CO B
MERRITT, REUBEN W. BENNETT	1LT	GA CAPT GARTRELL'S CAV; FORREST'S ESCORT
MERRITT, WILLIAM OWEN	2LT	GA 65TH INF, CO D, I
METHVIN, JOHN WOODARD	1LT	AR 27TH INF, CO A
METTS, JAMES ISAAC	CAPT	NC 3RD INF, CO G
MEWBORN, LEMUEL JOSHUA	CAPT	NC 20TH MILITIA (LENOIR COUNTY)
MICKLER, JOHN H	CAPT	SC 11TH INF, CO E
MICKLER, THOMAS M	CAPT	FL 10TH INF, CO D
MIDDLETON, ALEXIUS LLEWLYN MD	ASST SURG	TX 2ND INF, F&S
MIDDLETON, JOHN BOWEN	1LT	MS STOCKDALE'S BN CAV, CO A
MILAM, BENJAMIN F	1LT	AL 4TH CAV (RODDY'S), CO G
MILAM, DUDLEY	CAPT	AR GUNTER'S BN CAV, CO B
MILAM, THOMAS RICHARDSON	SURG	GEN NATHAN BEDFORD FORREST, F&S
MILES, DANIEL	2LT	GA 47TH INF, CO F
MILES, JOHN RHETT	1LT	TN L ARTY (MEMPHIS L BTRY), TOBIN'S CO
MILFORD, JOHN WILLIAM	2LT	GA 35TH INF, CO E
MILLARD, DAVID C MD	SURG	CSA
MILLEN, JOHN M	LT COL	GA 20TH CAV BN, F&S
MILLER, ANDREW K	JR 2LT	TN 7TH INF, CO D
MILLER, BENJAMIN FRANKLYN	2LT	TN 12TH CAV (GREEN'S), CO H
MILLER, JAMES SIDNEY	LT COL	NC 79TH MILITIA (IREDELL COUNTY)
MILLER, JOHN B	2LT	TX 13TH CAV, CO E
MILLER, JOHN Y	CAPT	AL 28TH INF, CO G
MILLER, JONATHAN B	1LT	NC 58TH INF, CO G
MILLER, JOSEPH C	1LT	NC 7TH INF, CO K
MILLER, JOSEPH LAWTON	CAPT	GA 54TH INF, CO D
MILLER, LEWIS	CAPT	TN 48TH INF (NIXON'S), CO G
MILLER, ROBERT HENRY	CAPT	VA 44TH INF, CO C
MILLER, WILLIAM ALEXANDER CARTWRIGHT	CAPT	GA 38TH INF, CO A
MILLER, WILLIAM FRANKLIN	1LT	TN 35TH INF, CO D
MILLER, WILLIAM JOHNSON	2LT	TN 45TH INF, CO D
MILLIKIN, RICHARD A	1LT	LA CONFEDERATE GUARDS MILITIA, CO A
MILLING, DAVID C	LT	SC 21ST INF, CO B
MILLS, COLUMBUS	SURG	NC 16TH INF, CO K
MILLS, JAMES W	CAPT	AL 43RD INF, CO D
MILLS, LUTHER RICE	2LT	VA 26TH INF, CO K
MILNER, ARNOLD J	1LT	GA 40TH INF, CO B
MILTON, JOHN	GOV	FL GOVERNOR 1861-1865
MIMS, AARON LEMUEL	CAPT	TN 5TH CAV (MCKENZIE'S), CO F
MINETREE, JOSEPH POWHATAN	LT COL	VA 41ST INF, F&S
MINGEA, HESLOP M	CAPT	VA 41ST BN CAV (WHITE'S), CO C

MINNIECE, WALTER RUSSELL MD	ASST SURG	MS 12TH CAV, F&S
MINTER, JOHN ABNER	COL	AL 54TH INF
MIRE , EVARISTE CAMILLE	CAPT	LA 18TH INF, CO E
MITCHAM, GEORGE THOMAS	2LT	CSA 8TH CAV (WADE'S), CO I
MITCHELL, EMANUEL H	CAPT	VA 46TH INF, CO A
MITCHELL, HARVEY	ASSESSOR	TX CONFEDERATE STATE TAXES (BRAZOS COUNTY)
MITCHELL, HENRY C	CAPT	GA 20TH INF, CO B
MITCHELL, HENRY LAURENS	CAPT	FL 4TH INF, CO K
MITCHELL, JAMES B	1LT	AL 34TH INF, CO B
MITCHELL, JAMES H	2LT	NC 23RD INF, CO E (PEE DEE GUARDS)
MITCHELL, JAMES	CAPT	SC 7TH INF, CO E
MITCHELL, MOSES	2LT	VA 34TH BN CAV (WITCHER'S NIGHTHAWKS), CO E
MITCHELL, PEYTON R	2LT	TX 8TH INF, CO F
MITCHELL, PHILLIP F	1LT	AL 6TH CAV, CO F, H
MITCHELL, ROBERT S	2LT	NC 22ND INF, CO G
MITCHELL, WILLIAM DIXON	COL	GA 29TH INF, CO I
MITCHELL, WILLIAM T	1LT	TN 3RD INF (CLACK'S), CO B
MIXON, JOHN MILES	2LT	SC 11TH INF, CO F
MIXSON, JOSIAH SETH	1LT	SC 1ST INF (HAGOOD'S), CO I
MOBLEY, STEPHEN D	CAPT	GA 32ND INF, CO H
MOFFAT, THOMAS BOSTON	CAPT	TN 47TH INF, CO A
MOFFETT, ROBERT FRANKLIN	LT	VA 8TH INF, CO K
MOFFITT, PATRICK GEORGE	JUDGE	TX GRIMES COUNTY - CHIEF JUSTICE
MOFFITT, WILLIAM D	CAPT	NC 44TH INF, CO H
MOLER, LEE HENRY	CAPT	VA 2ND INF, CO B
MOLLOHAN, WILLIAM HARRISON	CAPT	VA 9TH BN INF, CO B
MOLONEY, PATRICK K	CAPT	SC 1ST INF (HAGOOD'S), F&S - ADJ
MONCURE, EUSTACE CONWAY	2LT	VA 9TH CAV, CO B
MONCURE, JOHN CONWAY	CAPT	CSA
MONCURE, W PEYTON	2LT	VA 47TH INF, CO A
MONETTE, JAMES WILKINS	CAPT	AL 19TH INF, CO G
MONEY, MORGAN JONES	CAPT	AL 18TH BN INF, CO E
MONIN, JOSEPH NORRIS	2LT	TX 7TH INF, CO K
MONK, CLAUDIUS BUCHANAN	CAPT	NC 20TH INF, CO H
MONROE, FRANKLIN MARION	CAPT	SC CABELL'S BDE - ADC
MONROE, JOHN W	2LT	NC 18TH INF, CO K
MONTGOMERY, JAMES	CAPT	MO 8TH INF, CO I
MONTGOMERY, JOHN C	1LT	NC 44TH INF, CO F
MONTGOMERY, JOHN HENRY	ACTING COMMISSARY	SC 18TH INF, CO E
MONTGOMERY, JOSEPH PERRY MD	SURG	MS 24TH INF, F&S
MONTGOMERY, NORRIS	CAPT	VA BELLE ISLE PRISON COMMANDANT
MONTGOMERY, ROBERT CICERO	2LT	GA 9TH ARTY BN, CO D (GWINNETT ARTY)
MONTGOMERY, RUFUS F	2LT	GA 19TH INF, CO A
MONTGOMERY, VINCENT ALPHIUS	1LT	LA JEFF DAVIS INF, CO J
MONTGOMERY, WILLIAM A	CAPT	MS MONTGOMERY'S CO OF SCOUTS
MOODY, YOUNG MARSHALL	BRIG GEN	AL 43RD INF
MOONEY, ROBERT M	1LT	CSA DENEALE'S CHOCTAW WARRORS - ADJ
MOORE, ANDREW BARRY	GOV	AL GOVERNOR 1861
MOORE, ANDREW McNAIRY	CAPT	AL 40TH INF, CO K
MOORE, EDWARD	1LT	SC 5TH CAV, CO K
MOORE, ELIAS ROBERT	1LT	AL 18TH INF, CO K
MOORE, GEORGE C	1LT	TN 4TH CAV (MURRAY'S), CO D

MOORE, GEORGE WASHINGTON	1LT	TN 53RD INF, CO E
MOORE, HARDIN T	1LT	TX 6TH CAV, CO A
MOORE, HENRY DANNELLY REV	CHAPLAIN	AL 12TH INF
MOORE, JAMES LEWIS	CAPT	TN 23RD BN INF, CO E
MOORE, JAMES WRIGHT	2LT	NC 70TH MILITIA (ROCKINGHAM COUNTY)
MOORE, JOHN CALHOUN	2LT	AL 40TH INF, CO H
MOORE, JOHN MCCLUNG	2LT	AL 4TH CAV (RODDY's), CO F
MOORE, JOHN RANDOLPH	1LT	MS 32ND INF, CO A
MOORE, JOHN WILLIAM	CAPT	TX 9TH INF, CO E
MOORE, JOHN CREED	BRIG GEN	TX 2ND BDE, FORREST'S DIV
MOORE, JOSEPH LEIGH	2LT	AL 13TH INF, CO A
MOORE, ROBERT AUGUSTUS JR	3LT	MS 17TH INF (CONFEDERATE GUARDS), CO G
MOORE, ROGER WILLIAMS	MAJ	NC 3RD CAV, F&S
MOORE, SAMUEL LAFAYETTE	DELEGATE	GA SIGNER SECESSION ORDINANCE, DELEGATE BULLOCH COUNTY
MOORE, SAMUEL LEWIS	CAPT	GA 12TH MILITIA
MOORE, THOMAS H	1LT	TN 25TH INF, CO C
MOORE, THOMAS HARTWELL	1LT	TN 25TH INF, CO C
MOORE, THOMAS J	CHAPLAIN	KY 9TH CAV
MOORE, THOMAS JEFFERSON	2LT	FL 3RD INF, CO H
MOORE, THOMAS OVERTON	GOV	LA GOVERNOR 1862-1864
MOORE, WILLIAM E	CAPT	AR 25TH INF, CO E
MOORE, WILLIAM HENRY	COL	MS 43RD INF, F&S
MOOREHEAD, ROBERT MONROE	2LT	MS 3RD INF (STATE TROOPS), CO K
MOORMAN, GEORGE TRIPLETT	LT COL	MS 24TH CAV BN (MOORMAN'S)
MOORMAN, MARCELLUS NEWTON	MAJ	CSA BRAXTON'S ARTY BN
MOOSE, DAVID W	2LT	NC, 94TH MILITIA (ALEXANDER COUNTY)
MORECOCK, GEORGE WASHINGTON	2LT	VA 1ST BN INF, CO D
MOREHEAD, GEORGE W F	1LT	VA LOCAL DEFENSE (PULASKI), MOREHEAD'S CO
MORELAND, THOMAS A	1LT	KY 1ST INF, CO G
MORGAN, ALEXANDER GIBSON	MAJ	CSA - COMMISSARY OF SUBSISTENCE
MORGAN, HIRAM	CAPT	MS 33RD INF, CO B
MORGAN, JOHN H	CAPT	AR 12TH BN SHARPSHOOTERS, CO D
MORGAN, JOHN HENRY JR	CAPT	MS 34TH INF, CO F
MORGAN, JOHN HUNT	BRIG GEN	KY 2ND CAV
MORGAN, JOSEPH HARGROVE	MAJ	SC 5TH CAV, F&S
MORGAN, MARK	1LT	NC CUMBERLAND COUNTY BN, DETAILED MEN, CO A
MORGAN, ROBERT GREER	1LT	MS 34TH INF, CO F
MORGAN, THOMAS CALVIN	CAPT	SC 24TH INF, CO K
MORGAN, THOMAS JEFFERSON	COL	AR 8TH CAV, F&S
MORGAN, WILLIAM H	LT COL	MS 3RD INF (LIVE OAK RIFLES), CO B
MORING, JOEL JOSIAH	CAPT	GA MORING'S CO INF (EMANUEL TROOPS)
MORRILL, WILLIAM HENRY	CAPT	NC 27TH INF, CO E - ACS
MORRIS, BENJAMIN F	2LT	MS 27TH INF, CO H
MORRIS, BENJAMIN NARCISIS	LT COL	AL 29TH INF, CO G
MORRIS, BENJAMIN T	2LT	GA 38TH INF, CO C
MORRIS, CORNELIUS VAN CLEEF	1LT	AL 15TH INF, CO G - ACS
MORRIS, E T	CAPT	TX 34TH CAV, CO B
MORRIS, JAMES F	2LT	CSA 8TH CAV (WADE'S), CO A
MORRIS, JAMES PATRICK	CAPT	TX 30TH CAV, CO B
MORRIS, JAMES R	1LT	VA 16TH CAV, CO D
MORRIS, JOSEPH W	CAPT	VA 16TH CAV, CO D

MORRIS, NATHANIEL D	1LT	VA 4TH CAV, CO K
MORRIS, OSCEOLA RICHARD	1LT	TX 25TH CAV, CO H
MORRIS, REUBEN J	3LT	VA 13TH INF, CO C
MORRIS, WILLIAM F	1LT	GA 34TH INF, CO A
MORRIS, WILLIAM G BROWNLOW	CAPT	NC 64TH INF, CO B
MORRIS, WILLIAM MARSHALL	1LT	VA 46TH INF, CO G
MORRISON, ANGUS	CAPT	GA 1ST RESERVES (SYMONS'), CO E
MORRISON, HENRY MCGRADY	CAPT	TX 6TH CAV, CO I
MORRISON, HENRY RUFFNER	CAPT	VA 4TH INF, CO I
MORRISON, JOSEPH G	CAPT	NC 57TH INF, CO F
MORRISON, THOMAS JEFFERSON	2LT	VA 57TH INF, CO F
MORROW, SAMUEL PEDEN	1LT	AL 26TH INF, CO B
MORTON, JOHN WATSON JR	CAPT	TN L ARTY, MORTON'S CO - ORDINANCE OFFICER
MORTON, ROBERT	1LT	VA 19TH CAV, CO B
MOSBY, JOHN SINGLETON	COL	VA MOSBY'S CAV, F&S
MOSELEY, BENJAMIN F	CAPT	GA 26TH INF, CO H
MOSELEY, JOAB W	JR 1LT	SC 2ND ARTY, CO I
MOSELEY, WILLIAM HENRY	2LT	VA 3RD RESERVES, CO I (BOOKER'S)
MOSER, FRANKLIN M	1LT	AR 21ST INF, CO B
MOSER, ISRAEL	1LT	NC 7TH SENIOR RESERVES
MOSES, GUSTAVE A	1LT	LA 21ST INF (KENNEDY'S), CO D
MOSS, ANSON FREDRICK	CAPT	TX 12TH CAV, CO K
MOSS, H E	CAPT	TX 1ST INF, CO D
MOSS, J V	2LT	VA 32ND INF, CO E
MOSS, JACKSON CARROLL COFFEE	CAPT	AR 11TH INF (POE'S BN), CO E
MOSS, JOSEPH VALENTINE	CLERK	LA CALCASIEU PARISH CLERK OF DISTRICT COURT
MOSS, THOMAS OVERTON	1LT	VA 23RD INF, CO G
MOTLEY, B H	CAPT	VA L ARTY (PITTSYLVANIA), MOTLEY'S CO
MOUTON, JEAN JACQUES ALEXANDRE ALFRED	BRIG GEN	LA 18TH INF
MUCKENFUSS, ALLEN WESLEY	BVT 2LT	SC 1ST BN INF, CO B
MUDD, JOSEPH A MD	ASST SURG	CSA RICHMOND HOWARD'S GROVE HOSPITAL
MUIR, HEZEKIAH P	1LT	MO 12TH CAV, CO K
MULKENFUSS, ALLEN WESLEY	2LT	SC 27TH INF, CO B
MULL, PETER M	CAPT	NC 55TH INF, CO F
MULLENS, JAMES H	2LT	MO 3RD BN CAV, CO F
MULLIGAN, A B	CAPT	SC 5TH CAV, CO B
MULLIKIN, JAMES MONROE	1LT	SC 19TH INF, CO G
MULLINS, BENJAMIN BERRY	CAPT	KY 3RD BN MTD RIFLES, CO C
MULLINS, SPENCER A	1LT	VA 34TH BN CAV (WITCHER'S NIGHTHAWKS), CO D
MUNN, DANIEL	CAPT	NC 2ND ARTY, CO B
MUNSON, ROBERT A B	ASST SURG	VA 2ND INF, CO F
MURFEE, JAMES THOMAS	LT COL	AL 41ST INF, F&S
MURPHEY, FERDINAND EUGENE	SR 2LT	AR 1ST INF, CO F
MURPHEY, ROBERT HUNTLEY	LT COL	TN 30TH INF, F&S
MURPHY, DANIEL J	1LT	AR 4TH BTRY L ARTY (WEST'S)
MURPHY, JOHN J	MAJ	CSA - GEN POLKS STAFF - CHIEF OF SUBSISTENCE
MURPHY, JOHN SALMON	CAPT	VA 9TH CAV, CO C
MURRAH, PENDLETON	GOV	TX GOVERNOR 1863-1865
MURRAY, WILLIAM W	JR 2LT	MO 16TH INF, CO D
MURRELL, WILLIAM ESTES	CAPT	TN 41ST INF, CO G
MUSTAIN, RICHARD AVERY	CAPT	VA 53RD INF, CO G

MUSTAIN, SHERWOOD THOMAS	CAPT	VA 21ST INF, CO H
MYATT, JOHN H	2LT	MO 9TH CAV, CO B (ELLIOTT'S)
MYERS, HENRY	CAPT	MS 12TH INF (VICKSBURG SHARPSHOOTERS), CO E
MYERS, RUSSELL JAMES	2LT	AL 56TH PARTISAN RANGERS, CO H
MYNHIER, WILLIAM	MAJ	KY 5TH INF, CO A
MYRICK, RICHARD L	2LT	AL 22ND INF, CO K
NABORS, JAMES HALAWAY	2LT	AL 44TH INF, CO D
NAIL, JONATHAN	MAJ	CSA SHECOE'S CHICKASAW BN MTD VOLS, F&S
NANCE, JAMES DRAYTON	COL	SC 3RD INF, CO E
NANCE, JOHN BRADLEY	3LT	TN 41ST INF, CO B
NAPIER, NATHAN CAMPBELL	CAPT	GA 6TH CAV, CO K
NAPIER, THOMAS LEROY JR	LT COL	GA 8TH INF BN, FG
NASH, EDWIN ALBERT	LT COL	GA 4TH INF, CO C
NASH, JAMES NEWTON	1LT	TX WAUL'S LEGION, CO E
NASH, THOMAS	2LT	TX 5TH INF, CO E
NAVE, JESSE	2LT	MO 7TH INF, CO F
NEAL, JOSEPH GRAYSON	SR 2LT	NC 35TH INF, CO B
NEAL, REESE BOWEN	CAPT	GA 23RD INF, CO H
NEAL, THOMAS CHALMERS	1LT	NC 1ST JUNIOR RESERVES, CO E
NEALE, BENJAMIN MAYBERRY	CAPT	MO 5TH CAV, CO B
NEALY, JOHN HENRY	1LT	AR 20TH INF, CO B
NEELY, JAMES J	COL	TN 14TH CAV (NEELY'S), F&S
NEELY, JOHN S	2LT	NC 4TH SENIOR RESERVES, CO G
NEELY, RUFUS POLK	COL	TN 4TH INF (NEELY'S), F&S
NEFF, JACOB GARBER	CAPT	VA 7TH CAV, CO K
NEIGHBORS, JAMES	2LT	AL 20TH INF, CO I
NEILL, LAMBERT CLAYTON	CAPT	NC 62ND INF, CO E
NELMS, CHARLES G	LT COL	MS 22ND INF, CO F
NELMS, MATTHIAS M	CAPT	MS 2ND INF, CO I
NELSON, ANDREW BERNHARDT	1LT	AL 24TH INF, CO D
NELSON, JOSEPH HENRY	1LT	VA MOSBY'S CAV, CO A
NELSON, JOSEPH JOHNSON	CAPT	AR 19TH INF, CO I - ACS
NELSON, WILIAM CALVIN	2LT	SC HAMPTON LEGION INF, CO C
NESBITT, THOMAS	MAJ	CSA IG
NESBITT, WILLIAM HENRY	1LT	GA 34TH INF, CO K
NESMITH, SAMUEL PERRY	MAJ	AL 6TH INF, CO M
NETTLES, JOHN R	CAPT	SC 10TH INF, CO H
NETTLES, TIMOTHY DARGAN	1LT	TX L ARTY, 12TH FIELD BTRY (VAL VERDE)
NEWBERRY, COLUMBUS MADISON	2LT	GA 27TII INF, CO C
NEWBY, GENERAL NEPTHILIA MARION	CAPT	TN 35TH INF, CO A
NEWLAND, HUGH S	CAPT	TX BORDER'S CAV (ANDERSON'S) - ACTING QM
NEWMAN, BYRD S	1LT	TN 51ST INF, CO E
NEWMAN, GEORGE	1LT	AL 6TH CAV, CO E
NEWSOM, W B	1LT	AL 4TH CAV (RODDY'S), CO L
NEWTON, DAVID H	1LT	FL 11TH INF, F&S - ADJ
NEWTON, ELKANAH BAZALLEL	CAPT	AL 26TH INF, CO G
NEWTON, JOHN BROCKENBROUGH MD	SURG	VA 40TH INF, F&S
NEWTON, SAMUEL BARNETTE	2LT	NC 30TH INF, CO E
NEWTON, SAMUEL GALITZEN	LT COL	TX 3RD INF (LUCKETT), CO H
NICHOLS, FRANCIS REDDING TILLOU	BRIG GEN	LA 8TH CAV
NICHOLSON, JAMES A	LT	GA 11TH INF (WALTON'S), CO B
NIXON, ABNER	2LT	AL 13TH INF, CO E

NIXON, WILLIAM GREEN	1LT	NC 18TH INF, CO G
NOKES, WILLIAM NELSON	CAPT	MS 31ST INF, CO E
NOONAN, ROBERT C	LT	VA 21ST INF, CO B
NORES, JOHN ERNEST	2LT	LA WATSON'S ARTY BTRY
NORMAN, H T	CAPT	TN 1ST H ARTY, CO C
NORMAN, WILLIAM SANFORD	CAPT	GA 25TH INF, CO H
NORRIS, GEORGE WASHINGTON	2LT	AL 41ST INF, CO G
NORTH, HENRY A	CAPT	GA 1ST CAV, CO K
NORTHCUTT, SAMUEL HOUSTON	2LT	TN 1ST INF (TURNEY'S), CO A
NORTHROP, LUCIUS BELLINGER	BRIG GEN	CSA - COMMISSARY GEN
NORTHROP, WILLIAM HARRIS	CAPT	NC 3RD IN, CO F - AQM
NORTON, GEORGE HATLEY REV	CHAPLAIN	VA 17TH INF
NORTON, JAMES WASHINGTON	2LT	MS 34TH INF, CO A
NORTON, JAMES OGBURN	1LT	TN 32ND INF, CO K
NUNEZ, FELIX E	JR 2LT	LA 18TH/YELLOW JACKET BN CONSOLIDATED INF, CO D
NUNNALLY, MATTHEW TALBOT	CAPT	GA 11TH INF (WALTON'S), CO H
OAKES, PLEASANT JOHN	CAPT	TX 5TH CAV, CO A
OATES, JOHN R	1LT	TX 22ND INF, CO F (HUBBARD'S)
OATES, WILLIAM CALVIN	COL	AL 15TH INF, CO G
O'BRIANT, ALBERT	2LT	NC 50TH INF, CO A
O'CONNOR, JOSEPH S	JUDGE	TX DISTRICT JUDGE
ODEN, GEORGE WASHINGTON	CAPT	MS 35TH INF, CO B
ODEN, JOHN PINEY	CAPT	AL 10TH INF, CO K
OFFICER, JOHN HOLFORD	2LT	TN 43RD INF, CO A
OGDEN, EDMUND STRUDWICK	2LT	LA 1ST H ARTY, CO D
OGLESBY, DRURY PATRICK	1LT	GA 37TH INF, CO G
O'KEEFFE, LAWRENCE EUGENE	2LT	GA 17TH INF (MUSCOGEE), CO C
O'KELLEY, GEORGE WILBURG	1LT	GA 16TH INF (COBB'S LEGION), CO A
OLD, WILLIAM WHITEHURST	CAPT	VA 20TH H ARTY BN, F&S - AQM
OLDHAM, WILLIAM BISHOP	CAPT	TN 45TH INF, CO F
OLDHAM, WILLIAM PLEASANT	CAPT	NC 44TH INF, CO K
OLIVER, ANDREW JACKSON MD	SURG	TX 18TH INF, BFS
OLIVER, JOHN M	CAPT	VA 21ST INF, CO C (OLIVER GREYS)
OLIVIER, ALEXANDRE	LT	LA 7TH CAV - AACS
OLMSTEAD, CHARLES HART	COL	GA 1ST INF, F&S
OMOHUNDRO, JOHN WASHINGTON	2LT	VA 19TH BN H ARTY (ATKINSON'S), CO E
OMOHUNDRO, ORVILLE CALHOUN	2LT	VA 5TH CAV, CO E
O'NEAL, EDWARD ASBURY	BRIG GEN	AL 4TH INF (CONEUCH GUARDS)
O'NEIL, FRANKLIN AUGUSTAS	CAPT	MS 1ST BN SHARPSHOOTERS, CO D
OPIE, HIEROME LINDSAY	1LT	VA 20TH CAV - DRILLMASTER
ORR, JAMES LAWRENCE	COL	SC 1ST INF (ORR'S RIFLES), F&S
ORR, JOHN PRESTON	1LT	VA 64TH MTD INF, CO F
OSBORN, NATHANIEL LAFAYETTE	LT	GA 3RD BN INF, CO B
OSBORN, NELSON CAPERS	1LT	GA 9TH INF BN, CO B
OSBORNE, HENRY W	CAPT	VA 48TH INF, CO C
O'STEEN, JOHN RILEY	CAPT	GA 50TH INF, CO G
OUTLAW, BENJAMIN E	1LT	TN 14TH INF, CO E
OVERALL, WILLIAM J	2LT	TN 12TH CAV (GREEN'S), CO H
OVERSTREET, JOHN HENRY	1LT	VA 6TH INF, CO F
OVERTON, ABDON ALEXANDER MD	ASST SURG	TX 14TH CAV, DFS
OVERTON, THOMAS	CAPT	LA 1ST INF, CO B
OWEN, HENRY T	CAPT	VA 18TH INF, CO C

OWEN, JOHN JASPER	CAPT	GA 29TH INF, CO B
OWEN, M T	MAJ	SC 1ST CAV, F&S
OWEN, ROBERT A	MAJ	CSA POWER'S CAV, CO G
OWEN, THOMAS HOWENTON	COL	VA 3RD INF
OWEN, THOMAS M	LT	VA 16TH INF, CO E
OWEN, WILLIAM MILLER	LT COL	CSA MCINTOSH'S ARTY BN
OWENS, BERRY	CAPT	MO SEARCYS SHARPSHOOTERS BN, CO D
OWENS, JOHN T	1LT	SC 7TH INF, CO D
OWENS, JOSEPH T	CAPT	VA 26TH INF, CO D
OWENS, SQUIRE	LT	MO 2ND INF STATE GUARDS, CO E
OWINGS, ARCHIBALD CRESWELL	2LT	SC 14TH INF, CO E
OYLER, WILLIAM HENRY HARRISON	2LT	AR 8TH INF, CO A
PACE, ALFRED ELKINS	BRIG GEN	TX ST TROOPS BRIG # 14
PACE, WILLIAM H	2LT	GA 29TH BN CAV, CO E
PACK, JOHN	CAPT	TN 35TH INF, CO I
PAGE, HASKEW	1LT	AL 18TH INF, F&S - ADJ
PAGE, RICHARD CHANNING MOORE	CAPT	VA L ARTY, MONTGOMERY'S CO
PAGE, RICHARD LUCIEN	BRIG GEN	AL FT MORGAN, MOBILE
PAGE, WILLIAM W	1LT	KY 6TH MTD INF, CO F
PAINTER, SIDNEY CROCKETT	2LT	VA 29TH INF, CO B
PAINTER, WILLIAM PINCKNEY	1LT	MS 15TH INF, CO F
PALMER, ORREN ALSTON	2LT	NC 3RD CAV, CO E
PANKEY, PETER BRANCH	LT	VA 21ST INF, CO E
PANNILL, JOSEPH BLACKWELL	CAPT	VA 1ST BN RESERVES, CO F
PARDUE, THOMAS JAMES	1LT	NC 33RD INF, CO D
PARIS, WILLIAM HENRY	CAPT	GA 42ND INF, CO C
PARISH, SAMUEL MATTHEW	1LT	NC DETAIL DEPT, CONSCRIPT OFFICE
PARK, FRANK	CAPT	AL 15TH INF, CO I
PARK, JAMES FLETCHER	CAPT	GA 64TH INF, CO F
PARK, ROBERT EMORY	LT	AL 12TH INF
PARKER, DURANT A	AQM	NC 28TH INF, CO D
PARKER, GEORGE THOMAS	CAPT	NC 5TH INF, CO H
PARKER, JAMES BERTRAM	2LT	GA 3RD RESERVES, CO C
PARKER, JOSEPH J	LT	NC 1ST INF, CO A
PARKER, MUMFORD S	CAPT	NC 83RD MILITIA (STANLY COUNTY)
PARKER, NATHAN	MAJ	KY 4TH CAV, F&S
PARKER, WILLIAM BALLARD	2LT	TN 25TH INF, CO C
PARKER, WILLIAM FLETCHER	CAPT	NC 16TH BN CAV, CO C
PARKER, WILLIAM WATTS	CAPT	VA PARKER'S L ARTY CO
PARKS, JAMES M	CAPT	TN 16TH INF, CO H
PARKS, WILLIAM WOODRUFF	CAPT	TX 19TH CAV, CO A
PARR, JAMES S	CAPT	GA 3RD INF, CO K
PARR, LEWIS JARREL	LT COL	GA 38TH INF, F&S
PARRAMORE, JAMES H	CAPT	TX 8TH CAV (TERRY'S RANGERS), CO I
PARRISH, ISAAC WHITAKER	CAPT	AL 20TH INF, CO F
PARRISH, JOEL JACKSON	1LT	GA 29TH INF, CO G, K
PARRISH, WILLIAM KNIGHT	CAPT	NC 6TH INF, CO B
PARROTT, JAMES W	MAJ	MO 8TH CAV, F&S
PARROTT, JOSIAH RHOTON	MAJ	CSA QM BG WILLIAM T. WOFFORD'S BDE
PARSONS, HOMER LEE MD	SURG	AR 18TH INF, F&S
PARSONS, JOB WARD	CAPT	VA 18TH CAV, CO A
PARSONS, LEMUEL HALL	JR 2LT	TX 6TH BN CAV, CO A

PARTEE, DANIEL MASON	1LT	AR 27TH INF, CO G
PARTIN, CHARLES P	MAJ	MS 36TH INF, CO C
PARTIN, WILLIAM	1LT	GA 61ST INF, CO B
PATE, HENRY CLAY	COL	VA 5TH CAV, CO D
PATRICK, FREDERICK F	1LT	NC 32ND INF, CO A
PATRICK, GEORGE A	CAPT	SC 5TH INF, CO B
PATRICK, WILLIAM	MAJ	VA 11TH CAV, F&S
PATTERSON, EDMUND DeWITT	1LT	AL 9TH INF, CO D
PATTERSON, ROBERT DONNELL	2LT	NC 27TH INF, CO G
PATTERSON, WILLIAM HENRY	1LT	VA 37TH BN CAV, CO C
PATTON, ALEXANDER EDGAR	CAPT	TN 1ST INF (TURNEY'S), CO A
PATTON, GEORGE SMITH	COL	VA 22ND INF, CO H
PATTON, JASON OTIS	2LT	AL 12TH INF, CO I
PATTON, MOSES MONTRAVILLE	1LT	GA 11TH BN STATE GUARDS, CO D
PATTON, THOMAS W	CAPT	NC 60TH INF, CO C
PAUL, D'ARCY W	1LT	VA 12TH INF, CO K
PAULK, SAMUEL	2LT	AR MTD STATE TROOPS, ABRAHAM'S CO
PAXTON, ELISHA FRANKLIN	BRIG GEN	STONEWALL BRIGADE
PAXTON, JAMES	2LT	MO 11TH INF, CO A
PAXTON, WILLIAM GALLATIN	ADJ	MS 1ST CAV, F&S
PAYNE, FIELDING F	LT	VA 8TH INF, CO B
PAYNE, THOMAS W	2LT	VA 57TH INF, CO I
PAYNE, WILLIAM HENRY FITZHUGH	BRIG GEN	VA 4TH CAV
PAYNE, WILLIAM K	CAPT	TX 13TH CAV (BURNETT'S), CO E
PAYNE, WILLIAM RILEY	1LT	NC 39TH INF, CO G
PEACE, ABNER DAVID	CAPT	NC 23RD INF, CO E (PEE DEE GUARDS)
PEARCE, FURNEY P	2LT	NC 24TH INF, CO K (POPLAR SPRING GRAYS)
PEARCE, JAMES FURMAN MD	SURG	SC 8TH INF, F&S
PEARCE, JAMES WASHINGTON	2LT	FL 9TH INF, CO E
PEARCE, JOHN BRYANT	1LT	AL 31ST INF (HALES)
PEARSON, JOHN WILLIAM	CAPT	FL 9TH INF, CO B
PEAY, GORDON NEILL	COL	CSA - ADC
PECK, PEMBROKE PEMBERTON	SR 2LT	VA 26TH INF, CO F
PECK, WILLIAM RAINE	BRIG GEN	LA 9TH INF
PECK, WILLIAM SMITH	LT	LA 3RD CAV (HARRISON'S), CO H
PEDDY, GEORGE WASHINGTON MD	SURG	GA 56TH INF, CO K
PEDEN, DAVID D	CAPT	GA 12TH INF, CO D
PEDEN, ROBERT M	1LT	MS 5TH INF, CO I
PEDRICK, THOMAS	JR 2LT	FL 1ST CAV, CO I, A
PEEBLES, WILLIAM HUBBARD	COL	GA 44TH INF, F&S
PEEK, LEONARD WEST	CAPT	NC 64TH INF, CO D
PEEK, OSCAR FITZALAN	CAPT	FL 11TH, CO G
PEELER, JOSEPH REV	CHAPLAIN/CAPT	TN 3RD MTD INF (LILLARDS)
PEEPLES, WILLIAM BRISBANE	CAPT	SC 3RD CAV, CO K
PEERY, TERRY H C	CAPT	TN 27TH INF, CO C
PEGRAM, JOHN	BRIG GEN	CSA - ANV
PEGRAM, THOMAS HOWARD REV	CHAPLAIN/CAPT	NC 68TH INF
PELHAM, JOHN	LT COL	VA STUART'S HORSE ARTY
PELL, JAMES A	LT COL	CSA 1ST CAV, CO B
PEMBERTON, JOHN CLIFFORD	LT GEN	MS, COMMANDER AT VICKSBURG
PENDER, WILLIAM DORSEY	MAJ GEN	ANV - DIV CMDR, 3RD CORPS
PENDLETON, A "SANDIE" SWIFT	LT COL	CSA ANV II CORPS, CHIEF OF STAFF

PENDLETON, ELDRIDGE HOWARD	1LT	TX 16TH CAV, CO E
PENDLETON, JOHN STROTHER MD	ASST SURG	VA 45TH BN INF, F&S
PENDLETON, JOSEPH HENRY	MAJ	VA 23RD INF
PENDLETON, WILLIAM NELSON	BRIG GEN	ANV CHIEF OF ARTY
PENN, GRANVILLE	CAPT	VA 42ND INF, CO H
PENNINGTON, ABRAHAM ANDERSON	LT COL	AR 23RD INF, CO H
PEPPER, DANIEL GILBERT	ACS	MS 39TH INF, CO I
PERCIVAL, WILLIAM F	CAPT	SC AIKEN MTD INF (PERCIVAL'S)
PERKINS, JOHN NICHOLAS PRYOR GRAVES		1LT GA 1ST CAV, F&S - ADJ
PERRIN, JAMES MIDDLETON	COL	SC 1ST INF (ORR'S RIFLES), CO B
PERRY, CLINTON	2LT	TX 1ST INF, CO E
PERRY, FRANCIS	CAPT	VA 23RD BN INF, CO C
PERRY, JAMES EBENEZER	1LT	VA 129TH MILITIA
PERRY, LEIGHTON MAYNARD	CAPT	FL 2ND INF, CO L
PERRY, MADISON S	GOV	FL GOVERNOR 1861
PERRY, THOMAS WATKINS	1LT	AL 39TH INF, CO E
PERRY, WILLIAM FLAKE	BRIG GEN	AL 44TH INF
PERSONS, WILLIAM PINKNEY	1LT	GA 32ND INF, CO A
PETERKIN, J A	CAPT	SC 20TH INF, CO L
PETERMANN, PETER	JR 2LT	FL, 2ND CAV, CO B
PETERSON, EVERETTE	2LT	NC 5TH CAV, CO C
PETTIGREW, JAMES JOHNSTON	BRIG GEN	SC 12TH INF
PETTUS, JOHN J	GOV	MS GOVERNOR 1861-1863
PETTWAY, JOHN ROBERT	3LT	MS 18TH INF, CO I
PETTY, ELIJAH PARSONS	CAPT	TX 17TH INF, CO F
PETTYJOHN, ANDREW JACKSON	2LT	TN 20TH CAV, CO E
PEYTON, C MD	SURG/CAPT	AR 18TH INF, F&S
PEYTON, THOMAS WEST	1LT	LA 11TH INF, CO F
PFOHL, WILLIAM JACOB	MAJ	NC 21ST INF, CO D
PHILLIP, CHARLES VICTOR	2LT	AL 56TH PARTISAN RANGERS, CO F
PHILLIPPI, ALEXANDER	1LT	VA 29TH INF, CO B
PHILLIPS, ALONZO LAFAYETTE	2LT	VA 15TH INF (ASHLAND GRAYS), CO D
PHILLIPS, JAMES ELDRED	1LT	VA 12TH INF, CO G
PHILLIPS, JAMES JASPER	COL	VA 9TH INF, F&S
PHILLIPS, JEFFERSON CURLE	COL	VA 13TH CAV, F&S
PHILLIPS, NATHAN GONO REV	CHAPLAIN	AL 43RD INF
PHILLIPS, SAMUEL GROVER	CAPT	AR HARRELL'S BN CAV, CO B
PHINNEY, JAMES MONROE	CAPT	SC 6TH INF, CO G
PICKENS, FRANCIS WILKINSON	GOV	SC GOVERNOR 1860-1862
PICKERING, ALFRED SAMUEL	MAJ	AL 20TH INF, CO A
PICKETT, CHARLES FRANCIS	MAJ	CSA PICKETT'S DIV - AAG
PICKETT, GEORGE BIBLE	LT COL	TX 15TH CAV, CO B
PICKETT, GEORGE EDWARD	MAJ GEN	ANV
PICKETT, GEORGE WASHINGTON JR	2LT	TN 1ST INF (TURNEY'S), CO H
PICKETT, MALACHI THOMAS JR	2LT	GA 19TH INF, CO H
PICKLE, FRANK S	CAPT	MS 37TH INF, CO D
PIERCE, ALBERT J	CAPT	CSA - ACS
PIERCE, FURNEY P	2LT	NC 24TH INF, CO K (POPLAR SPRING GRAYS)
PIERSON, DAVID	LT COL	LA 3RD INF, CO C
PIGFORD, TIMOTHY SAMUEL	2LT	MS 6TH CAV, CO G
PIKE, ALBERT	BRIG GEN	INDIAN TERRITORY COMMANDER
PIKE, THOMAS J	2LT	AL 10TH INF, CO K

PILGRIM, THOMAS J	CAPT	GA 43RD INF, CO E
PILLOW, GIDEON JOHNSON	BRIG GEN	AOT VOLUNTEER & CONSCRIPTION BUREAU
PINCKNEY, BARTHOLOMEW GAILLARD	CAPT	SC 2ND SHARPSHOOTERS BN, CO B
PINKERTON, ALFRED H	2LT	NC 29TH INF, CO H
PIRKLE, JOHN L	CAPT	GA 4TH CAV (STATE GUARDS), PIRKLE'S CO
PITTMAN, ALFRED BUCKNER	1LT	CSA ENGINEERS
PITTMAN, WILLIAM NELSON	CAPT	MS 3RD BN INF, CO D
PITTS, AQUILLA BEDFORD	1LT	NC 121ST MILITIA (FORSYTH COUNTY)
PLASTER, GEORGE EMORY	CAPT	VA 6TH CAV, CO H
PLEASANTS, JOHN FIELDING	1LT	TX 27TH CAV, CO C
PLEASANTS, JOHN	2LT	NC 117TH MILITIA (JOHNSTON COUNTY)
PLEASANTS, WILLIAM HENRY	2LT	NC 47TH INF, CO G
PLEMMONS, JOHN SEABORN	1LT	GA 11TH INF (WALTON'S), CO D
PLOWDEN, EDGAR NELSON	CAPT	SC 21ST INF, CO C
PLUNKETT, O C	2LT	SC 14TH INF, CO H
POAG, ALONZO WALKER	1LT	SC 12TH INF, CO H
POARCH, SAMPSON D	1LT	GA 6TH CAV, CO L
POE, JAMES T	MAJ	AR 11TH INF (POE'S BN), CO A
POINDEXTER, JOHN A	COL	MO 5TH STATE GUARDS
POINDEXTER, PARKE JR	CAPT	VA 14TH INF, CO I
POLK, GEORGE	CAPT	MS POLK RANGERS CAV
POLK, JAMES MONROE	CAPT	TX RECRUITING OFFICER HOOD'S BDE
POLK, LEONIDAS C	LT GEN	AOT CMDR
POLK, LEONIDAS L	1LT	NC 43RD INF, CO I
POLK, MARSHALL TATE	CAPT	TN ARTILLERY CORPS, CO G (POLK'S BATTERY, L ARTY)
PONDER, WILLIAM A	2LT	LA 12TH INF (JACKSON'S SHARPSHOOTERS), CO M
PONS, FRANCIS JOSEPH	CAPT	FL 1ST CAV, CO D
POOLE, GREEN P	CAPT	SC 4TH INF, CO F
POORE, ROBERT HENRY	MAJ	VA 14TH INF, F&S
POPE, ELI M	2LT	NC 81ST MILITIA (ANSON COUNTY)
POPE, JAMES WILLIAM	2LT	GA 57TH INF, CO B
POPE, NATHANIEL WELLS	CAPT	LA 1ST CAV, CO B
POPLIN, STEPHEN HENRY	3LT	NC 38TH INF, CO B
PORTER, EDWARD ETHELL	CAPT	TN 2ND INF (WALKER'S), CO E
PORTER, FRED M	1LT	AL 15TH INF, CO K
PORTER, HENRY J	2LT	GA 1ST INF
PORTER, JOHN GAY	CAPT	GA 24TH INF, CO K
PORTER, JOHN L	2LT	MO 9TH CAV (STATE GUARD), CO B
PORTER, JOSEPH BARTLETT	2LT	AR 1ST MTD RIFLES, CO C,B
PORTER, PLEASANT	2LT	CSA 2ND CREEK MTD VOLS, CO A
PORTER, WILLIAM NICOLUS	CAPT	CSA 14TH CAV, CO I
POSEY, CARNOT	BRIG GEN	ANV POSEYS BDE, ANDERSONS DIV
POSEY, JOHN WESLEY	1LT	TX MORGAN'S CAV, CO A
POSEY, WILLIAM KIMZEY	CAPT	MS 2ND CAV, CO B
POTEAT, JOHN MILES	ADJ	NC 1ST INF, F&S
POTTER, FRANCIS WHITFORD	SURG/CAPT	NC 50TH INF, F&S
POTTER, WILLIAM C	1LT	TN 16TH INF, CO A
POU, LEWIS ALEXANDER	CAPT	AL 6TH INF, CO G
POULTON, JOHN FRANCIS REV	CHAPLAIN	VA 38TH INF, F&S
POWE, JAMES HARRINGTON	CAPT	SC 1ST SC INF (BUTLER'S)
POWELL, ALBERT ADDISON MD	ASST SURG	CSA
POWELL, ALBERT THEODORE	1LT	VA 3RD CAV, CO C

POWELL, CHARLES STEVENS	1LT	NC 24TH INF, CO E
POWELL, EDWARD B	CAPT	SC 1ST STATE TROOPS, CO H
POWELL, EDWARD F	2LT	VA 11TH CAV, CO K
POWELL, GEORGE GREEN	1LT	MS 8TH INF, CO K
POWELL, JOHN JEFFERSON	1LT	GA 7TH INF, CO E
POWELL, JOHN RICHARD	1LT	NC 3RD BN L ARTY, CO C
POWELL, JOHN	CAPT	MS 33RD INF, CO B
POWELL, THOMAS JEFFERSON	1LT	SC 15TH INF, CO B
POWELL, WILLIAM H H	1LT	VA 36TH CAV, CO D
POWELL, WILLIAM FRANCIS SPAIGHT	CAPT	GA COBB'S LEGION, CO F
POWER, WILLIAM CARR	CHAPLAIN	NC 14TH INF, F&S
POWERS, LEMUEL	DETECTIVE	CONFEDERATE SECRET SERVICE
POWERS, LEWIS E	LT	NC 21ST INF, CO A
PRATHER, JOHN S	LT COL	CSA 8TH CAV (WADE'S), CO B
PRATT, JOHN L	LT	NC 21ST INF, CO K
PRATT, RICHARD HOPKINS	CAPT	AL 20TH INF, CO D
PRESNELL, URIAH	CAPT	NC 63RD MILITIA (RANDOLPH COUNTY)
PRESSLER, CHARLES WILLIAM	CAPT	TX 4TH INF, CO C
PRICE, ALFRED C	CAPT	AL 4TH INF (CONEUCH GUARDS), CO C
PRICE, DUDLEY CLANTON	2LT	AR GORDON'S CAV, CO D
PRICE, HENRY MANORE	CAPT	VA 19TH H ARTY BN, CO G
PRICE, JONATHON M JR	JR 2LT	MS 38TH CAV, CO E
PRICE, PRESTON GANO	1LT	TN 11TH INF, CO D, B
PRICE, STERLING	MAJ GEN	MO STATE GUARDS
PRICE, WILLIAM CECIL	MAJ	CSA
PRIEST, JAMES	2LT	TX 17TH INF, CO B
PRILLAMAN, CHRISTIAN SNIDOW	1LT	VA 57TH INF, CO B
PRINCE, SAMUEL	CAPT	MS 8TH INF, CO K - ASM
PRINCE, WILLIAM L	2LT	SC 10TH INF, CO C
PRINGLE, FRANK M	SR 2LT	MS 20TH CAV
PRINTUP, DANIEL SCHERMERHORN	MAJ	GA 55TH INF, F&S
PRITCHARD, CALVIN	1LT	NC 32ND INF, CO G
PROCTOR, GEORGE A	AQM	AR 6TH INF, CO H
PROCTOR, S L	CAPT	AR 15TH INF (JOHNSON'S), CO A
PROFFITT, WILLIAM W	LT COL	NC 58TH INF, CO C
PROPST, WILLIAM	1LT	NC 57TH INF, CO F
PROUDFOOT, JOHN ROBINSON	CAPT	TX 25TH CAV, CO H
PRUDEN, WILLIAM DOSSEY JR	1LT	NC 1ST JUNIOR RESERVES, CO K
PRUITT, RICHARD WASHINGTON	LT	AL 34TH INF, CO K
PRUITT, WILLIS CRAYTON	1LT	SC 20TH INF, CO E
PRYOR, ROGER ATKINSON	BRIG GEN	VA 3RD INF
PRYOR, SHEPHERD GREEN	CAPT	GA 12TH INF, CO A
PRYOR, WILLIAM HAMLIN	CAPT	VA 3RD INF, CO C
PUCKETT, HENRY DOUGLAS	2LT	VA 42ND INF, CO I
PUCKETT, WILLIAM B C	MAJ	GA PHILLIPS LEGION, F&S
PUGH, ANDREW JACKSON	2LT	TN 9TH BN CAV (GANTT'S), CO E
PUGH, JAMES LAWRENCE	REPRESENTATIVE	AL 1ST & 2ND CONFEDERATE CONGRESS
PULLEY, JAMES ASHTON	2LT	VA 14TH INF, CO K
PULLEY, WILLIAM CASSIUS	2LT	AR 8TH CAV, CO G
PURCELL, JAMES R	1LT	VA 49TH INF, CO A
PURIFOY, JOHN WESLEY	CAPT	AL 44TH INF, CO C
PURNELL, JOSEPH BENSON MD	ASST SURG 2LT	MS 23RD INF, CO B

PURVIANCE, ANTHAIRES	3LT	MS 18TH INF, CO G
PURVIS, JAMES M	1LT	MS 6TH INF (LOWRY RIFLES), CO D
PYRTLE, LEWIS W	1LT	VA 32ND BN CAV, CO B
QUARLES, CLARENCE	1LT	CSA - ADC
QUARLES, JOHN	1LT	MS 5TH INF, CO D
QUATTLEBAUM, JOAB	CAPT	SC 9TH INF, CO F
QUATTLEBAUM, PAUL	DELEGATE	SC SIGNER SECESSION ORDINANCE, DELEGATE LEXINGTON COUNTY
QUATTLEBAUM, WALTER	MAJ	SC 2ND INF, CO G
QUIMBY, MATHEW S	CAPT	VA 30TH INF, CO A
QUIN, WILLIAM MONROE	MAJ	MS 39TH INF, F&S
QUINN, PATRICK	1LT	LA IRISH MILITIA (BEAUREGARD GUARDS), CO 3
QUINN, SILVANUS JACKSON	CAPT	MS 13TH INF, CO A
RADER, LEWIS FRANKLIN	1LT	TN 61ST MTD INF, CO B
RADFORD, RICHARD CARLTON WALKER	COL	VA 2ND CAV, F&S
RAGLAND, EVAN JAMES	1LT	VA 53RD INF, CO A
RAGLAND, STILES A	CAPT	AR 26TH INF, CO B,F
RAGON, ELI E	CAPT	AR 62ND MILITIA, CO A
RAINBOLT, FRANCIS MARION	2LT	TX 4TH CAV, CO H
RAINEY, E F	LT	TN 11TH CAV, CO C
RAINS, GEORGE W	COL	GA 1ST INF (AUGUSTA LOCAL TROOPS)
RAINWATER, ELI D	JP	TN JEFFERSON COUNTY
RAKER, DAVID MICHAEL	CAPT	MO 16TH INF, CO D
RAMAGE, JAMES THOMAS HENDERSON	BVT 2LT	MS 1ST INF, CO I
RAMSAY, ABIEZER FRANKLIN	CAPT	MS 3RD INF (LIVE OAK RIFLES), CO A
RAMSEUR, STEPHEN DODSON	MAJ GEN	NC 5TH INF
RAMSEY, JOHN TAYLOR	2LT	AL 58TH INF, CO D
RAMSEY, WILLIAM HENRY	LT COL	VA 57TH INF, CO E
RAND, PARKER NATHANIEL GREEN	CAPT	AL 11TH CAV, CO H
RANDAL, HORACE	COL	TX 28TH INF, F&S
RANDALL, CHARLES WESLEY	2LT	SC 19TH INF, CO K
RANDALL, H I	SR 1LT	GA 9TH BN ARTY, CO B
RANDALL, PUTMAN PALIAH	2LT	MS 9TH CAV, CO B
RANDLE, EDMUND TROUP	CAPT	AL 3RD INF, CO D
RANDLE, JOHN WESSLY	2LT	NC 28TH INF, CO D
RANDOLPH, GEORGE WYTHE	BRIG GEN	CSA; SECRETARY OF WAR
RANDOLPH, WILLIAM W	CAPT	TN 9TH INF, CO K
RANGELEY, JAMES HENRY	2LT	VA 50TH INF, CO K
RANKIN, THOMAS JESSE	SR 2LT	MS 7TH INF, CO F
RANKIN, WILLIAM JAMES	CAPT	MS 7TH INF, CO F
RANKIN, WILLIAM RUFUS	MAJ	NC 37TH INF, CO H
RANSOM, ROBERT JR	MAJ GEN	ANV
RAPER, BLUFORD	CAPT	AL MORELAND'S CAV, CO E
RASBERRY, MANSELL W	CAPT	GA 2ND BDE STATE TROOPS
RATCHFORD, JAMES WYLIE	MAJ	CSA LEE CORPS - AAG
RATCLIFFE, WILLIAM C	3LT	AR 6TH INF, CO A
RATLIFF, JOHN S	CAPT	KY 10TH CAV (DIAMOND'S), CO I
RATLIFF, ROBERT	2LT	VA 34TH BN CAV (WITCHER'S NIGHTHAWKS), CO G
RATLIFF, SPARREL	CAPT	VA 21ST BN INF, CO F
RATLIFF, WILLIAM T	CAPT	MS 1ST L ARTY (WITHERS), CO A
RAULERSON, JOHN G	1LT	FL 5TH INF, CO B
RAWLES, BENJAMIN F	2LT	MS 7TH BN INF, CO B

RAXSDALE, FRANCIS MARION	MAJ	LA 16TH INF, CO E
RAY, BUCKNER	2LT	NC 6TH SENIOR RESERVES, CO K
RAY, I PHILLIP	2LT	TN 19TH INF, CO H
RAY, JAMES MOORE	1LT	NC 64TH INF, CO A
RAY, WILLIAM BLUE	CAPT	MS 30TH INF, CO K
RAY, WILLIAM HENRY	CAPT	MS 28TH CAV, CO A
RAYBURN, JOHN QUINCY	1LT	MS 36TH INF, CO D
RAYBURN, WILLIAM CLARK ADAM	LT	MS 22ND INF, CO K
REA, JOHN CURTIS	CAPT	AR 27TH INF, CO A
READ, ALPHEUS LA FAYETTE	CAPT	GA 22ND BN CAV (STATE GUARDS), CO C
READ, EDMUND STRUDWICK	CAPT	VA 26TH BN INF (EDGAR'S), CO B
READ, ISAAC HENRY	2LT	TN 7TH CAV (DUCKWORTH'S), CO D
READ, STEPHEN PETTUS	CAPT	VA 14TH INF, CO F (CHAMBLISS GRAYS)
READY, SAMUEL LEWIS	2LT	SC 22ND INF, CO A
REAGAN, JOHN HENNINGER	POSTMASTER GENERAL CSA	
REASOR, DANIEL SHEFFEY	2LT	VA 64TH MTD INF, CO A
REAUX, JEAN	1LT	LA FRENCH VOL BN
RECTOR, CLAIBORNE	CAPT	TX CIBOLO GUARDS L INF (STATE TROOPS)
RECTOR, HENRY MASSEY	GOV	AR GOVERNOR 1861-1862
RED, ALSON	1LT	MS 8TH INF, CO B
REDD, MARCUS L F	CAPT	NC 3RD INF, CO E
REDDICK, SAMUEL CLARKE	1LT	FL 2ND CAV, CO C
REDDING, DANIEL SEARCY	CAPT	GA 45TH INF, CO D
REDDY, RICHARD WALTER	CAPT	SC 21ST INF, CO G
REDWINE, JAMES O	CAPT	GA 30TH INF, CO H
REDWINE, WILLIAM PARKS	CAPT	GA 10TH INF (FAYETTE RIFLE GRAYS), CO I
REDWINE, WILLIAM PINCKNEY	2LT	NC 65TH MILITIA (DAVIDSON COUNTY)
REED, CHILTON ALLEN	LT	KY 2ND CAV, CO C
REED, JAMES WILLIAM	CAPT	SC 14TH BN CAV, CO D
REED, JOHN BALUS	3LT	MS 41ST INF, CO B
REED, SAMUEL T	CAPT	SC 2ND ARTY, CO B
REEDER, SAMUEL N	1LT	AR 18TH INF, CO G
REEVE, JOHN J	MAJ	CSA STEVENSON'S STAFF - AAG
REEVES, DAVID POINDEXTER	1LT	TN 28TH INF, CO C
REICH, CORNELIUS	1LT	TX 4TH INF, CO D
REID, ALEXANDER HUDSON	CAPT	GA 66TH INF, CO F
REID, RICHARD WALKER	CAPT	CSA - ACS
REID, ROBERT ALEXANDER	2LT	TN 29TH INF, CO B
REILLY, JAMES	MAJ	NC 1ST ARTY, CO D
REILLY, PETER	1LT	GA 1ST INF, CO B
REMINGTON, BENJAMIN F	CAPT	KY 2ND CAV (DUKE'S), CO E
RENICK, ROBERT F	1LT	MO 4TH INF, CO H
RENO, JOSEPH LOUIS	1LT	LA 12TH INF (JACKSON'S SHARPSHOOTERS), CO H
REPASS, WILLIAM GORDON	CAPT	VA 51ST INF, CO F
REYNES, CHARLES E	1LT	LA 22ND INF
REYNOLDS, JAMES MARION	2LT	GA 1ST CAV, CO C
REYNOLDS, JOHN HASKEW	LT	NC 60TH INF, CO F
REYNOLDS, WILLIAM SAXBY	CAPT	MS 1ST CAV RESERVES, CO A
RHEA, JAMES DAVID	CAPT	TN 3RD INF, CO G
RHEA, MATTHEW JR	1LT	TN 13TH INF, CO A
RHOADES, MARCUS MORTON	ADJ	MO 9TH INF, CO G
RHODES, LEWIS D	2LT	MS 6TH INF, CO I

RHYNE, ADAM MARION	2LT	NC 42ND INF, CO K
RICE, DAVID HOLMAN	1LT	SC 17TH INF, CO H
RICE, HIRAM A	1LT	KY 5TH MTD INF, CO D
RICE, SAMUEL	1LT	VA 27TH INF, CO H
RICE, ULYSSES A	CAPT	GA 48TH INF, CO G
RICE, WILLIAM B	BVT 2LT	TN 24TH INF, CO E
RICE, WILLIAM G	LT COL	SC 3RD BN INF, F&S
RICH, SOLOMON HILL	CAPT	GA LEDFORD'S MILITIA CAV, CO B
RICH, WILLIAM WOFFORD	LT COL	GA PHILLIPS LEGION, CO B
RICHARDSON, CORNELIUS JUDSON	CAPT	NC 1ST JUNIOR RESERVES, CO D
RICHARDSON, GEORGE WASHINGTON	1LT	MS 6TH INF, CO A
RICHARDSON, JOHN MANLY	CAPT	SC 22ND INF, CO H
RICHARDSON, JOHN SMYTHE	ADJ	SC 23RD INF, F&S
RICHARDSON, JOHN WILLIAM	CAPT	TX 18TH INF, CO A
RICHARDSON, WILLIAM CHAPMAN WASHINGTON	2LT	MS 41ST INF, CO L
RICHARDSON, WILLIAM CURRIN	MAJ	TN 53RD INF, CO A
RICHARDSON, WILLIAM RASMUS	ADJ	NC 38TH MILITIA, F&S (WAKE COUNTY)
RICKS, DANIEL L	1LT	GA 32ND INF, CO G
RIDDLE, JAMES A	1LT	SC 3RD BN INF, CO E
RIDDLE, JOHN M	2LT	KY 11TH CAV, CO D
RIERSON, JOHN W	MAJ	NC 53RD INF, CO G
RIFE, GORDON W	CAPT	VA 22ND CAV, CO B
RIGGINS, A D	BVT 2LT	GA 28TH INF, CO E
RIGGS, ARTHUR PERRY	CAPT	VA PLEASANTS CO MILITIA
RIGGS, JAMES MONROE	LT COL	AR 27TH INF, F&S
RILEY, AMOS CAMDEN	COL	MO 1ST INF, F&S
RINGER, W J	CAPT	GA 37TH MILITIA, CO C
RINKER, ISRAEL PUTMAN	CAPT	VA 12TH CAV, CO K
RION, JAMES HENRY	LT COL	SC 7TH INF BN, CO B
RISHER, JOSEPH KOGER	CAPT	SC 24TH INF, CO E
RITCHIE, ISAAC	LT	VA 7TH CAV (ASHBY'S), CO B
RITTENBERRY, NATHANIEL B	BVT 2LT	TN 3RD INF (CLACK'S), CO I
RIVES, GEORGE STITH	1LT	VA 13TH CAV, CO K
ROACH, JOHN R	CAPT	NC 44TH INF, CO I
ROANE, ARCHIBALD THOMAS	1LT	MS 17TH INF (MAGNOLIA GUARDS), CO K
ROANE, THOMAS RUSK	2LT	NC 39TH INF, CO B
ROANE, THOMAS W	SURG	TN 51ST INF, F&S
ROBARTS, EDGAR	2LT	FL 2ND INF, CO G
ROBB, EDWARD L	1LT	TX 4TH CAV, CO K
ROBBINS, BENJAMIN WELLS	3LT	LA 28TH INF (GRAY'S), CO G
ROBERTS, ABISHAI WOODWARD	2LT	LA 4TH INF, CO C
ROBERTS, ARTHUR L	CAPT	FL 1ST CAV, CO A
ROBERTS, BRIGHT J	CAPT	TN 31ST INF, CO A
ROBERTS, GREENBERRY	1LT	KY 2ND CAV (DUKE'S), CO A
ROBERTS, HENRY	CAPT	MS 24TH INF, CO A
ROBERTS, JAMES ADDISON	1LT	MS 20TH INF, CO B
ROBERTS, JEREMIAH L	1LT	MS 41ST MS, CO L
ROBERTS, JOHN ANDERSON	CAPT	NC 34TH INF, CO H
ROBERTS, JOHN CLARKE	2LT	TX 14TH CAV, CO F
ROBERTS, JOHN HENRY	CAPT	KY 1ST CAV (BUTLER'S)
ROBERTS, JOHN IVERSON	1LT	MS 30TH INF, CO D
ROBERTS, JOHN TODD	MAJ	CSA QM

ROBERTS, MOSES OLIVER	1LT	MO 5TH CAV (STATE GUARD), CO B
ROBERTS, OBA E	CAPT	TX 11TH INF, CO K
ROBERTS, ORAN MILO	COL	TX 11TH INF, F&S
ROBERTS, ST FRANCIS CALLAWAY	CAPT	VA 5TH INF, CO F
ROBERTS, WILLIAM PAUL	BRIG GEN	NC 59TH INF
ROBERTSON, CHARLES SEVIER	LT COL	CSA 1ST CAV, CO G
ROBERTSON, EDWARD SHEPHERD	LT	VA 57TH INF, CO D
ROBERTSON, JAMES WESLEY	2LT	TN 2ND INF, CO K
ROBERTSON, JOHN A	1LT	AL 45TH INF, CO I
ROBERTSON, JOHN D	CAPT	CSA CHIEF OF ORDINANCE
ROBERTSON, SLEDGE M	CAPT	AL 37TH INF, CO G
ROBESON, JOHN H	CAPT	NC 29TH INF, CO H
ROBINS, JOSIAH	MAJ	AL 3RD CAV, CO C
ROBINSON, ADAM	2LT	GA 24TH INF, CO F
ROBINSON, ALEXANDER	CAPT	VA 29TH INF, CO C
ROBINSON, BENJAMIN MCCAIN	1LT	AL 63RD INF, CO G
ROBINSON, JAMES H	3LT	AL 32ND INF, CO D
ROBINSON, JOHN M	CAPT	CSA ENGINEERS
ROBISON, WILLIAM FISHER REV	CHAPLAIN	GA 15TH INF, CO K
ROCKWELL, HENRY CLAY	QM	NC 51ST INF, CO H
ROCKWELL, WILLIAM SPENCER	LT COL	GA 1ST INF, F&S
RODDY , JAMES ALEXANDER	2LT	AR 21ST INF, CO F
RODES, ROBERT EMMET	MAJ GEN	CSA
ROGERS, ANSEL	1LT	NC 39TH INF, CO A
ROGERS, BENJAMIN FRANKLIN	1LT	GA 2ND INF, CO D
ROGERS, CALVIN	2LT	NC 4TH SENIOR RESERVES, CO I
ROGERS, CHRISTOPHER COLUMBUS	COL	NC 112TH MILITIA (HAYWOOD COUNTY)
ROGERS, DAVID W	2LT	MS 32ND INF, CO A
ROGERS, FRANKLIN L	1LT	NC 15TH INF, CO B
ROGERS, GEORGE	CAPT	AL 18TH BN INF, CO C
ROGERS, HENRY A III	LT COL	NC 13TH INF, CO D
ROGERS, HENRY A	MAJ	TN 9TH INF, CO I
ROGERS, HIRAM CYRUS	CAPT	NC 29TH INF, CO E
ROGERS, JASON	1LT	NC 119TH MILITIA (UNION COUNTY)
ROGERS, JOHN HENDERSON	CAPT	AL 27TH INF, CO B
ROGERS, JOHN W	2LT	KY 2ND INF, CO C
ROGERS, LIEUEN MORGAN	MAJ	TX 3RD CAV (STATE TROOPS)
ROGERS, ROBERT WOODING	CAPT	MO 5TH INF - IG
ROGERS, WILLIAM EARLTON	MAJ	MS 23RD INF
ROGERS, WILLIAM J	CAPT	GA 26TH INF, CO C
ROHMER, FRANCOIS JEAN BAPTISTE MD	SURG	CSA AL MEDICAL LABORATORY, MOBILE
ROLLINGS, J C	1LT	SC 12TH INF, CO I
ROLLINS, JOHN MARTIN	2LT	MS 14TH INF, CO G
ROOF, SAMUEL MARTIN	CAPT	SC 20TH INF, CO H
ROPER, BENJAMIN	CAPT	SC 7TH INF, CO I
ROSBOROUGH, DAVID DECATUR	CAPT	TX 17TH INF, F&S - AQM
ROSEMAN, DANIEL FREDERICK	CAPT	NC 38TH INF, CO F
ROSHONG, JOHN JACOB	LT	GA 19TH INF, CO A
ROSS, EGBERT A	MAJ	NC 11TH INF, CO A
ROSS, HUGH W	MAJ	GA 11TH ARTY BN, CO A
ROSSER, THOMAS LAFAYETTE	MAJ GEN	ANV CAV DIV CMDR
ROSTEET, MIGUEL JUAN JR	1LT	TX RAGSDALE'S BN CAV, CO A

ROTAN, JAMES EDWARD	2LT	TN 16TH INF, CO K
ROTHROCK, GUSTAVUS M	LT	TN 10TH/11TH CONSOLIDATED CAV, CO E
ROUGHTON, GEORGE WASHINGTON	1LT	GA 49TH INF, CO C
ROUNTREE, LEONIDAS C	MAJ	TX 35TH CAV, F&S
ROUNTREE, THOMAS JEFFERSON	2LT	TX 5TH CAV (PARTISAN RANGERS), CO C, I
ROWE, ACHILLES	1LT	VA 26TH INF, CO F
ROWE, DAVID PINKNEY	MAJ	NC 12TH INF, CO A
ROWELL, EZEKIEL HUMPHREY	CAPT	AL 12TH INF, CO K
ROWLAND, JAMES R	1LT	VA 52ND MILITIA, CO B
ROWLAND, RANSOM PINKNEY	2LT	TN 35TH INF, CO A
ROWLES, WILFORD GRAYSON	1LT	VA 57TH INF, CO D
ROWSEY, WASHINGTON F	1LT	TN 52ND INF, CO H
ROYAL, STEPHEN A	BVT 2LT	GA 48TH INF, CO B
ROYALL, EDWARD MANLY MD	ASST SURG	VA 18TH L ARTY BN, F&S
ROYCROFT, ANSON COLUMBUS	2LT	AL 41ST INF, CO A
ROYSTER, THOMAS W	LT	MO 12TH CAV, CO E
RUCKER, EDMOND WINCHESTER	MAJ	TN 16TH CAV BN (NEAL'S)
RUCKER, URIAH S L	2LT	SC 1ST INF, CO B
RUCKER, VALENTINE H	2LT	VA 2ND CAV, CO E
RUCKER, W P	CAPT	TN 20TH INF, CO D
RUCKER, WOOSTER B	2LT	VA 58TH INF, CO H
RUDDER, JONATHON M	2LT	AL 37TH INF, CO F
RUDICIL, ROBERT YOUNG MD	SURG	GA 6TH CAV, F&S
RUDOLPH, WILLIAM H	1LT	TN 49TH INF, CO F
RUDULPH, JOHN BARRATT	MAJ	CSA 10TH CAV, CO D
RUFFIN, J E	1LT	TN 50TH INF, CO E
RUFFIN, THOMAS	LT COL	NC 1ST CAV, CO H
RUGELEY, EDWARD SALMON	CAPT	TX 35TH CAV, CO D
RUGGLES, DANIEL	BRIG GEN	CSA - COMMISSARY GENERAL OF PRISONERS
RUSH, BENJAMIN ANDREW	1LT	AL MACON COUNTY HOME GUARD, PARK'S CO
RUSH, NOAH	CAPT	NC 38TH INF, CO H
RUSHING, FRANCIS MARION	1LT	AL BARBIERE'S BN CAV, BROWN'S CO
RUSS, CHARLES D	2LT	NC 8TH INF, CO C
RUSS, THOMAS JEFFERSON	1LT	FL 4TH INF, CO H
RUSSELL, DAVID MARION	CAPT	SC PALMETTO SHARPSHOOTERS, CO B
RUSSELL, JOHN R	CAPT	GA 52ND INF, CO I
RUSSELL, JOSEPH OLIVER	1LT	GA CAPT RUSSELL'S COMPANY CAV
RUSSI, DAVID II	1LT	TX 3RD INF, CO H
RUST, ALBERT	BRIG GEN	CSA ATM; PROVISIONAL CONGRESS
RUST, JAMES A	CAPT	TN CSA AQM
RUTHERFORD, WILLIAM WILLIAMSON	CAPT	MS 2ND CAV, CO A
RUXTON, ROBERT	CAPT	MO ACS
RYALS, HENRY J	MAJ	NC 50TH INF, CO D
RYAN, ELIJAH F	2LT	AL 12TH INF, CO H
RYAN, GEORGE WASHINGTON	CAPT	MS 8TH INF, CO G
RYAN, ISAAC	2LT	LA 10TH INF (YELLOW JACKETS), CO K
RYAN, JOHN J	COL	SC 11TH RESERVES
SADLER, JAMES OVERTON	CAPT	AR 1ST MTD RIFLES, CO C
SALES, JOHN THEOPILUS	2LT	NC 60TH INF, CO K
SALLEY, ALEXANDER SAMUEL MD	SURG	SC 20TH INF, F&S
SALLEY, DONALD DECATUR	2LT	SC 11TH RESERVES, CO G
SALMON, JOHN M	3LT	TX CHISUM'S CAV, CO D

SALYER, LOGAN HENRY NEAL	LT COL	VA 50TH INF, F&S
SAMFORD, THOMAS PRESTON	1LT	TX 1ST INF, CO M
SAMUEL, PHILIP JR	1LT	VA 30TH INF, CO E
SANDERS, CHARLES W	CAPT	SC 6TH INF, CO E
SANDERS, EDWARD JOHN	1LT	KY 4TH CAV, CO C
SANDERS, JOHN CALDWELL CALHOUN	BRIG GEN	AL 11TH INF
SANDERS, JOHN H	1LT	MS 33RD INF, CO A
SANDERS, JOHN J	2LT	TN 49TH INF, CO D
SANDERS, THOMAS LEMNEL	2LT	MO SCHNABEL'S BN CAV, CO F
SANDIDGE, JOHN MILTON	MAJ	CSA - CHIEF OF ORDINANCE
SANDS, ROBERT M	LT COL	AL 3RD INF, CO A
SANFORD, JOHN WILLIAM A	COL	AL 60TH INF, F&S
SAPP, BENJAMIN HARRISON	CAPT	AL 29TH INF, CO F
SAPP, NEWELL WESLEY	LT	NC 9TH BN SHARPSHOOTERS, CO B
SAPPINGTON, JAMES A T	CAPT	AL 50TH INF, CO A
SAPPINGTON, JOSEPH H	1LT	FL 1ST CAV, CO F
SARVER, WILLIAM T	2LT	VA 8TH CAV, CO G
SASSER, BOAZ W	2LT	NC 35TH INF, CO I
SASSER, HENRY JR	LT	GA 54TH INF, CO D
SATTERFIELD, REUBEN W	CAPT	GA 7TH INF, CO B
SAUCIER, JOHN	CAPT	MS 3RD INF, CO F
SAUNDERS, ROBERT CHANCELLOR	CAPT	VA 11TH INF, CO B
SAUNDERS, WILLIAM MONROE	CAPT	VA 30TH INF, CO H
SAVAGE, ALEXANDER	LT COL	VA 13TH CAV, CO I
SAVAGE, SOUTHEY LYTTLETON	3LT	VA 3RD CAV, CO F
SAYERS, DAVID G	CAPT	VA 34TH BN CAV (WITCHER'S NIGHTHAWKS), CO C
SCAIFE, HAZEL FURMAN	1LT	SC MCBETH'S L ARTY, JETER'S CO
SCAIFE, WILLIAM L MD	ASST SURG	TX 9TH INF, F&S
SCALES, JAMES ROBERT	CAPT	VA 54TH INF, CO H
SCALES, THOMAS H	3LT	KY 10TH CAV (MORGAN'S PARTISAN RANGERS), CO I
SCALLY, JOHN N	CAPT	MS 32ND INF, CO E
SCARBOROUGH, HANFORD AUGUSTUS	LT	SC 23RD INF, CO K
SCARBROUGH, WILLIAM MILES	SURG	SC 14TH INF, F&S
SCELLEN, JOHN D	1LT	VA 9TH INF, CO D
SCHALLER, FRANK EMIL	COL	MS 22ND INF, F&S
SCHEARER, GEORGE MARTIN E	2LT	MD 1ST INF, CO A
SCHEIHAGAN, THEODORE H	CAPT	TX 3RD INF, CO G
SCHERMERHORN, JOHN POOL II	2LT	VA 10TH CAV, CO I
SCHLATRE, GERVAIS	MAJ	LA 1ST CAV, F&S
SCHLEICHER, GUSTAV	CAPT	CSA ENGINEERS
SCHOOLING, JOHN R	2LT	KY 6TH CAV, CO F
SCHWING, WILLIAM FRANCIS	CAPT	MS 19TH INF, CO D
SCOGGINS, JOHN	CAPT	GA L ARTY (GRIFFIN L ARTY), SCOGGIN'S BTRY
SCOTT, AZARIAH FRANCIS	JP	VA GLOUCESTER
SCOTT, CALVIN	2LT	NC 28TH INF, CO G
SCOTT, EMMETT D B	2LT	LA 1ST CAV, CO K
SCOTT, FREDERIC ROBERT	MAJ	CSA COMMISSARY OF SUBSISTENCE
SCOTT, GEORGE WALTON	LT	GA 2ND INF, CO K
SCOTT, J D	1LT	TN 51ST CONSOLIDATED INF, CO E
SCOTT, JAMES N	CAPT	TX MORGAN'S CAV, CO G
SCOTT, WILLIAM BIBB	1LT	CSA - ADJ
SCOTT, WILLIAM THOMAS	SR 2LT	LA CONSOLIDATED CRESCENT INF, CO F

SCOTT, WINFREY BOND	MAJ	LA 19TH INF, F&S
SCRUGGS, MARSHALL L	2LT	MO 3RD BN CAV, CO A
SEAGRAVES, REUBEN FRANKLIN	1LT	AR 45TH INF, CO G
SEAL, DANIEL JR	JR 2LT	MO 1ST CAV, CO E
SEALE, ELIAS THOMPSON	MAJ	TX 13TH CAV, CO G
SEALE, JAMES A	CAPT	AL 7TH CAV, CO E
SEARCY (SIRCY), JAMES S	2LT	TN 55TH (McKOIN'S), DILLEHAYS CO
SEARLES, JAMES M	1LT	LA MILES' LEGION, CO G
SEAWRIGHT, JOHN NEWTON	1LT	SC 4TH BN RESERVES, CO B
SEAWRIGHT, WILLIAM ROBERT	CAPT	GA 1ST CAV, CO D
SEAY, JOHN W JR	1LT	GA 60TH INF, CO A
SEAY, RIAL B	CAPT	SC 5TH INF, CO C
SEGARS, DOVE	CAPT	SC 7TH BN INF (ENFIELD RIFLES), CO A, F
SELF, DAVID WASHINGTON	MAJ	LA 17TH INF, F&S
SELLERS, JOHN	CAPT	NC 56TH MILITIA (BRUNSWICK COUNTY)
SELLERS, SAMUEL ANDREW	CAPT	AL 13TH INF, CO A
SELLERS, WILLIAM HARVEY	LT COL	CSA GEN HOOD'S BDE - AAG
SELMAN, WILLIAM W	CAPT	AL 14TH INF (JACKSON'S AVENGERS), CO H
SELPH, COLIN MCREA	CAPT	CSA - AAG
SELVIDGE, WILLIAM R	CAPT	AR 11TH/17TH CONSOLIDATED INF, CO E
SEMMES, PAUL JONES	BRIG GEN	GA 2ND INF
SEMMES, RAPHAEL	ADM/BRIG GEN	CSN CSS ALABAMA/CSA
SENN, RUFUS D	CAPT	SC POST GUARD AT COLUMBIA, SC
SENTER, CALVIN HALBERT	CAPT	VA 51ST INF, CO I
SENTER, WILLIAM H	1LT	NC 8TH SENIOR RESERVES
SESSIONS, DANIEL ABSALOM JOSHUA	CAPT	GA 51ST INF, CO B
SETTLE, THOMAS BATTLE	CAPT	GA 31ST INF (CROWDERS), CO D
SEVIER, T F	LT COL	TN 1ST INF (FIELD'S), CO A
SEXTON, ELBERT GREEN	CAPT	TN 50TH INF, CO H
SEYMOUR, ISAAC GURDON	COL	LA 6TH IRISH INF, F&S
SHACKLETT, HENRY R	CAPT	TN NIXON'S CAV - AQM
SHAFER, CARLTON	2LT	CSA DRILLMASTER
SHANNON, ALEX M	CAPT	TX 8TH CAV, CO C
SHANNON, DENMAN WILLIAM	LT COL	TX 5TH CAV, CFS
SHANNON, THOMAS JR	2LT	NC 8TH INF, CO F
SHARKEY, ALLEN NEWMAN	2LT	MS 1ST L ARTY, CO A
SHARP, ALEXANDER B	MAJ	MO 2ND CAV
SHARP, JACOB H	BRIG GEN	MS 5TH INF
SHARP, ROBERT CHARLES	CAPT	SC 1ST STATE TROOPS, CO F
SHARP, SAMUEL	MAJ	TN 31ST INF, F&S
SHARPE, MATTHEW	1LT	GA 20TH BN CAV, CO F
SHARPE, SILAS ALEXANDER	COL	NC 79TH MILITIA, F&S (IREDELL COUNTY)
SHAVER, ROBERT GLEN	COL	AR 7TH INF, F&S
SHAVER, W B	1LT	AL 40TH INF, CO I
SHAW, HENRY MARCHMORE	COL	NC 8TH INF, F&S
SHAW, WILLIAM A	LT COL	TN 49TH INF, F&S
SHAW, WILLIAM PINCKNEY	2LT	NC 4TH CAV, CO D
SHAW, WILLIAM NELSON	PASSED MIDSHIPMAN	CSN
SHEARIN, JESSE THOMAS	2LT	TN 42ND INF, CO D
SHEFFIELD, JAMES LAWRENCE	COL	AL 48TH INF, F&S
SHEFFIELD, PLINEY	LT COL	GA 50TH INF, CO K
SHEHAN, JAMES DECATUR	1LT	GA 12TH CAV, CO I

SHEID, HENRY S	LT COL	TN 44TH INF, CO C
SHELBURNE, WILLIAM JAMES	2LT	VA 54TH INF, CO F
SHELBY, ISAAC III	CAPT	MS 28TH CAV, CO E
SHELBY, JOSEPH ORVILLE	BRIG GEN	MO CAV IRON BDE
SHELBY, WILLIAM ALEXANDER	ASST SURG	CSA CONFEDERATE TROOPS
SHELBY, WILLIAM HOUSTON	CAPT	AL 31ST INF (HALES), CO C & G
SHELLMAN, WILLIAM FEAY	1LT	GA 8TH INF, CO B - ADJ
SHELTON, EDWARD O	CAPT	TN 51TH INF, CO A
SHELTON, ELI JENWAY	CAPT	TX 9TH INF, CO A
SHELTON, JOHN ELLIOTT	2LT	GA 3RD BN SHARPSHOOTERS, CO E
SHEPARD, EDWARD P	LT	VA 25TH BN INF, CO C
SHEPARD, JOSEPH CHRISTOPHER	ASST SURG	NC 3RD CAV, CO A
SHEPHERD, SAMUEL NELSON	1LT	NC 37TH INF, CO F
SHERAM, EDWARD M	2LT	GA 45TH INF, CO D
SHERARD, WILLIAM YANCEY	1LT	SC 2ND RIFLES, CO F
SHERMAN, SIDNEY	GEN	TX PORT OF GALVESTON - COMMANDANT
SHERMAN, WILLIAM HENRY	ASST SURG	MS 9TH, 10TH, & 44TH MS, F&S
SHERRARD, JOHN BROOME	MAJ	VA 13TH INF, CO K
SHERRILL, GILBERT M	CAPT	NC 32ND INF, CO D, E
SHERRILL, SIDNEY ELAM	CAPT	TN 51ST CONSOLIDATED INF, CO G
SHEWMAKE, VIRGIL P	BVT 2LT	GA 3RD INF, CO A
SHIBLEY, WILLIAM HENRY HARRISON	2LT	AR 35TH INF, CO G
SHIELDS, JOHN HOWARD	2LT	TN 54TH INF, CO H
SHIELDS, WILLIAM A	1LT	GA 8TH INF, CO B
SHIRAH, JAMES	1LT	GA 27TH INF, CO F
SHIRLEY, JOHN JASPER	1LT	SC 20TH INF, CO E
SHIRLEY, JOSEPH W	2LT	KY 3RD BN MTD RIFLES, CO E
SHIVER, JOHN MASON	1LT	GA 4TH INF, CO K
SHIVERS, JAMES ALDOLPHUS	1LT	GA 5TH INF, CO D
SHOFNER, BEDFORD DAVIS	CAPT	TN 22ND INF (FREEMAN'S), CO E
SHOLL, EDWARD HENRY MD	ASST SURG/CAPT	TN 3RD CAV (FORREST'S)
SHORT, ANDREW JACKSON	1LT	MS 12TH INF, CO H
SHORTER, JOHN GILL	GOV	AL GOVERNOR 1861-1863
SHOTWELL, R H	LT COL	MS 35TH INF, CO K
SHOWALTER, DANIEL	LT COL	TX 4TH CAV, F&S
SHULER, MICHAEL	CAPT	VA 33RD INF, CO H
SHULL, DANIEL	CAPT	VA 136TH MILITIA, CO H
SHUMATE, JAMES JASPER	CAPT	SC 3RD BN INF (LAUREN'S), CO C
SHUMATE, SAMUEL GEORGE	CAPT	VA 37TH INF, CO E
SIBLEY, HENRY HOPKINS	BRIG GEN	NM
SICELUFF, ALPHEUS EDWIN	2LT	NC 42ND INF, CO A
SIFFORD, AARON	1LT	NC 88TH MILITIA, CO B (LINCOLN COUNTY)
SIKES, JOSIAH PEYTON RANDOLPH	JUDGE	GA TATTNALL COUNTY JUDGE, ORDINARY PROBATE
SIKES, NATHANIEL	LT	GA 25TH INF, CO D
SILER, JULIUS THOMAS	CAPT	NC 6TH CAV, CO A, E
SILVER, SAMUEL MARION	LT COL	NC 58TH INF, F&S
SIMMONS, JAMES ED	CAPT	MS 33RD INF, CO A
SIMMONS, JAMES M MD	ASST SURG/CAPT	MS 31ST INF, F&S
SIMMONS, R T M	JR 2LT	AL 40TH INF, CO K
SIMMONS, THOMAS JEFFERSON	1LT	LA 3RD CAV (WINGFIELD'S), CO A
SIMMONS, WILLIAM CLIFFORD	LT	SC 11TH INF, CO B
SIMMS, PARIS LINDSEY	JP	TN LAWRENCE COUNTY

SIMONTON, ABSALOM KNOX	MAJ	NC 4TH INF, CO A
SIMONTON, CHARLES B	CAPT	TN 9TH INF, CO C
SIMPSON, JOHN RICHARD	CAPT	AL 3RD INF, CO B
SIMPSON, PETER RINE	CAPT	MO 7TH DIV STATE GUARDS, CO D
SIMPSON, SAMUEL R	AQM	TN 30TH INF, F&S
SIMPSON, WILLIAM DUNLAP	LT COL	SC 14TH INF, F&S
SIMS, THOMAS W	MAJ	GA 53RD INF, CO B
SIMS, WILLIAM S	CAPT	AL 33RD INF, CO H
SIMS, WILLIAM VANNA	CAPT	TN 31ST INF, CO I
SINCLAIR, FLETCHER CLARK	2LT	MS 13TH INF, CO C
SINCLAIR, HENRY STUART	1LT	VA 32ND INF, CO I
SINEATH, FREDERICK R M	2LT	SC 11TH INF, CO C
SINGELTARY, GEORGE EDMOND BADGER		COL NC 27TH INF, CO H
SINGELTARY, RICHARD WILLIAMS	COL	NC 27TH INF, CO H
SINGELTARY, THOMAS CHAPEAU	COL	NC 44TH INF, F&S
SINGLETON, JOHN WHITE	1LT	SC 4TH INF, CO H
SIRMANS, BENJAMIN	DELEGATE	GA SIGNER SECESSION ORDINANCE,
		DELEGATE CLINCH COUNTY
SIRMANS, EZEKEIL J	1LT	GA 4TH CAV, CO I
SISK, WILLIAM S	CAPT	GA 16TH INF (COBB'S LEGION), CO E
SISSON, WILLIAM A	1LT	MS 19TH INF, CO B
SIZEMORE, JAMES MARION	ENSIGN	GA 1107TH MILITIA DISTRICT
SKELTON, JOHN H H	MAJ	GA 16TH INF, CO C
SKELTON, SILAS JACKSON	2LT	VA 23RD INF, CO C
SKINNER, SEABORN J	2LT	AL 22ND INF, CO I
SKINNER, URIAH L	CAPT	GA 48TH INF, CO D
SLACK, WILLIAM YARNELL	BRIG GEN	MO 2ND BDE STATE GUARD
SLADE, JAMES JEREMIAH	2LT	GA 10TH INF, CO A
SLADE, SIMON D	1LT	GA 2ND STATE LINE
SLATER, ROBERT B	CAPT	GA 1209TH MILITIA (BULLOCH COUNTY)
SLAUGHTER, CHRISTOPHER COLUMBUS	LT	TX RANGERS
SLAUGHTER, JOHN T MD	SURG/LT COL	GA 56TH INF
SLAUGHTER, WILLIAM		
RHADAMANTHUS MONTGOMERY	SR 2LT	AL 6TH INF, CO L
SLAYDON, JOHN THOMAS	2LT	VA 57TH INF, CO F
SLAYTON, JAMES RABUN MD	ASST SURG	CSA SEMPLES BTRY
SLEDGE, MORFLEET RUFFIN	1LT	MS 28TH CAV, CO F
SLEDGE, SHIRLEY JR	CAPT	GA 2ND CAV, CO H
SLEMP, CAMPBELL BASCOM	COL	VA 64TH MTD INF, F&S
SLIGH, JOHN HILARY	2LT	SC 20TH INF, CO F
SLIGH, THOMAS WESLEY	1LT	SC 7TH BN INF (ENFIELD RIFLES), CO G
SLOAN, DANIEL	1LT	FL 1ST SPECIAL BN CAV, CO B
SLOAN, JAMES HENRY	CAPT	NC 57TH INF, CO A
SLOAN, JAMES FOWLER	CAPT	SC HOLCOMBE LEGION INF, CO B
SLOAN, JOSEPH BERRY	1LT	SC 1ST IN, CO D
SMALL, EZEKIEL PICKENS	2LT	MS 8TH INF, CO D
SMITH, ADOLPHUS CORNELIUS MD	SURG	CSA VA WAYSIDE HOSPITAL, LYNCHBURG
SMITH, ALEXANDER D	COL	SC 26TH INF, F&S
SMITH, ALLEN DELONIA MD	SURG/MAJ	GA 62ND CAV
SMITH, ANDREW PICKENS REV	CHAPLAIN	SC 2ND INF, F&S
SMITH, ARCHIBALD C	CAPT	FL 5TH CAV, CO B
SMITH, BENJAMIN SYLVIUS GOSPERO	1LT	FL 6TH INF, CO C

SMITH, CALVIN MORGAN	1LT	TN 39TH MTD INF, CO D
SMITH, CHARLES THOMAS	QM	VA 59TH INF, F&S
SMITH, DAVID D	1LT	TN 17TH INF, CO K
SMITH, EDMOND M	2LT	FL 1ST CAV, CO E
SMITH, EDMUND KIRBY	GEN	ATM CMDR
SMITH, EUGENE ROBINETTE	CAPT	TN 25TH INF, CO B
SMITH, FREDERICK F	MAJ	VA 17TH CAV, F&S
SMITH, GEORGE R	1LT	GA 18TH INF, CO H
SMITH, HENRY JOHN MD	SURG/MAJ	GA 15TH MILITIA DISTRICT
SMITH, J FLETCHER	CAPT	KY 9TH CAV, CO G
SMITH, JAMES BELL	CAPT	GA 61ST INF, CO H
SMITH, JAMES DICKSON MD	SURG	CSA
SMITH, JAMES M	2LT	SC 24TH INF, CO A
SMITH, JEREMIAH	2LT	SC 9TH BN INF (SMITH'S), CO A
SMITH, JOHN F	2LT	SC 10TH INF, CO L
SMITH, JOHN HOLMES	CAPT	VA 11TH INF, CO G
SMITH, JOHN L	CAPT	NC 72ND MILITIA, CO E (STOKES COUNTY)
SMITH, JOHN ANDERSON	LT COL	TN 36TH INF, F&S
SMITH, JOHN RUFUS	MAJ	TX WAUL'S LEGION, CO B
SMITH, JONATHAN NORTHROP	BVT 2LT	GA 3RD INF, CO E
SMITH, JOSEPH L	1LT	VA 34TH BN CAV (WITCHER'S NIGHTHAWKS), CO I
SMITH, MILTON	CAPT	NC 2ND BN INF, CO A, B
SMITH, ROBERT MARION	1LT	SC 3RD INF, CO K
SMITH, ROBERT S	2LT	SC 6TH INF, CO K
SMITH, SAMUEL FARROW	CAPT	SC 13TH INF, CO I
SMITH, SAMUEL WEBB	CAPT	AR 3RD INF, CO I
SMITH, SHELDON PERKINS	REPRESENTATIVE	GA STATE REPRESENTATIVE, TOOMBS COUNTY
SMITH, THOMAS B	2LT	TN 42ND INF, CO H
SMITH, THOMAS BENTON	BRIG GEN	TN 20TH INF
SMITH, THOMAS ROBERSON	CAPT	MS 42ND INF, CO G
SMITH, WILLIAM ALEXANDER	2LT	VA 50TH INF, CO I
SMITH, WILLIAM BEATY	CAPT	SC PALMETTO SHARPSHOOTERS, CO G
SMITH, WILLIAM GOOCH	CAPT	TN 25TH INF, CO C
SMITH, WILLIAM PUGH	REPRESENTATIVE	GA STATE REPRESENTATIVE, HALL COUNTY
SMITH, WILLIAM RANKIN	2LT	TX 6TH CAV, CO C
SMITH, WILLIAM	CAPT	KY 13TH CAV, CO I
SMITH, WILLIAM	GOV	VA GOVERNOR 1864-1865
SMYTH, JAMES S	CAPT	MS PARTISAN RANGERS, SMYTH'S CO
SNAPP, JAMES PHAGAN	MAJ	TN 61ST MTD INF
SNAPP, LANDON K	2LT	TN 61ST MTD INF, CO E
SNEAD, CHARLES GOODALL	CAPT	VA L ARTY (FLUVANNA), SNEAD'S CO
SNEAD, EDWARD DUDLEY	CAPT	NC 5TH INF, CO C
SNODGRASS, CHARLES EDWARD	MAJ	CSA GEN R S EWELL - CHIEF QM
SNODGRASS, DAVID WHITFIELD	CAPT	TX 27TH CAV, CO D
SNODGRASS, WILLIAM NEWTON MD	SURG	CSA
SNOW, CHARLES FRANKLIN	1LT	VA 40TH INF, CO A
SNOW, WILLIAM T	CAPT	TN 1ST CAV, CO B
SNOWDEN, ROBERT BOGERDAS	LT COL	TN 25TH INF, F&S
SNOWDEN, SAMUEL JAMES	CAPT	SC 4TH CAV, CO I
SNYDER, PETER	LT COL	AR 7TH INF, CO A
SOLOMON, RICHARD ALEXANDER JR	JR 2LT	FL 5TH BN CAV, CO I
SOMERS, WILLIAM DAVIDSON MD	ASST SURG/CAPT	CSA

SONDLEY, JOHN RICHARD	1LT	SC 2ND CAV, CO H
SORRELLS, JAMES WARREN	1LT	AR GORDON'S CAV, CO I
SOUTH, WILLIAM TYLER BARRY	CAPT	KY 5TH MTD INF, CO B
SOUTHERLAND, JAMES	1LT	NC 12TH INF, CO C
SOUTHWORTH, CLINTON JAMES	2LT	VA L ARTY (FREDERICKSBURG ARTY), POLLOCK'S CO
SOWELL, GEORGE N	CAPT	AL 29TH INF, CO I
SOWERS, PHILLIP WADE	1LT	NC 65TH MILITIA (DAVIDSON COUNTY)
SPANGLER, A LEMUEL	CAPT	VA 10TH INF, CO A
SPANGLER, ABRAHAM	COL	VA 33RD INF, CO F
SPANN, RANSOM D	CAPT	CSA - AAG
SPARKS, JAMES E	CAPT	AR 23RD INF, CO H
SPARKS, JAMES MARTIN	1LT	GA 40TH INF, CO A
SPARKS, JOHN WESLEY	CAPT	KY 5TH MTD INF, CO C,K
SPEAKS, WILLIAM TATE JR	2LT	SC 19TH BN INF, CO A
SPEARS, CHRISTOPHER COLUMBUS	2LT	TN 19TH INF, CO K
SPEARS, EDWARD FORD	CAPT	KY 2ND MTD INF, CO G
SPEER, ALEXANDER M	MAJ	GA 46TH INF, F&S
SPEER, ALEXANDER	CAPT	MS 3RD CAV, CO A
SPEER, WILLIAM HENRY ASBURY	COL	NC 28TH INF, CO I
SPEIR, JAMES H	ASST SURG	GA 23RD INF, F&S
SPENCE, JEREMIAH	CAPT	VA 54TH INF, CO G
SPENCER, JONATHAN EATON	CAPT	TN 44TH CONSOLIDATED INF, CO K
SPENGLER, ABRAM	COL	VA 33RD INF, CO F
SPENGLER, ADAM LEMUEL	CAPT	VA 10TH INF, CO A
SPICER, RICHARD MONTGOMERY	CAPT	VA 49TH INF, CO K
SPINDLE, SAMUEL JEROME	1LT	VA 12TH CAV, CO G - ADJ
SPINK, JAMES W	1LT	KY 1ST CAV, CO F
SPINKS, WILLIAM L	1LT	MS 14TH INF, CO H
SPIVEY, DAVID WESLEY	CAPT	NC 24TH INF, CO K (POPLAR SPRING GRAYS)
SPIVEY, JOHN A	SHERIFF	GA, COFFEE COUNTY
SPOTTSWOOD, WILLIAM ELLIOTT	2LT	AL WARD'S L ARTY BTRY
SPRAGGINS, ELIAS C	1LT	AL 4TH INF (CONEUCH GUARDS), CO I
SPRIGG, JOHN SMITH	CAPT	VA 19TH CAV, CO B
SPURLOCK, HURSTON H	CAPT	VA 16TH CAV, CO E
SPURLOCK, JOHN L	LT COL	TN 35TH INF, CO D
SQUIRE, NEWTON	2LT	TX 1ST FIELD BTRY L ARTY, EDGAR'S CO
SQUIRES, CHARLES WINDER	CAPT	LA WASHINGTON BN ARTY, CO 1
ST JOHN, ANDREW FULTON	CAPT	VA 48TH INF, CO A
ST JOHN, CHARLES J	1LT	TN 19TH INF, CO C
ST JOHN, ISAAC MUNROE	BRIG GEN	CSA COMMISSARY GENERAL
ST PAUL, HENRY H	MAJ	LA 7TH INF, CO A
STACK, MICHAEL EDWARD	1LT	LA IRISH MILITIA, CO 6
STACKPOLE, ELLIS MERRILL	CAPT	CSA GEN R M GANO'S BDE, QM
STACY, JOHN CALVIN	2LT	TN 23RD BN INF, CO E
STAFFORD, LEROY AUGUSTUS	BRIG GEN	LA 2ND BDE
STAGG, LOUIS	CAPT	LA 16TH INF, CO K
STAKES, EDWARD THOMAS	MAJ	VA 40TH INF, CO A
STALLINGS, DANIEL STANLEY	1LT	TN 23RD INF, CO F
STALLINGS, JAMES EARNEST	JR 2LT	GA 41ST INF, CO A
STALNAKER, HARRISON H	1LT	VA 62ND MTD INF, CO E
STAMPER, HIRAM H	CAPT	KY 13TH CAV, CO A
STAMPER, ISAAC JONES	2LT	TN 43RD INF, CO F

STAMPS, ISAAC DAVIS	CAPT	MS 21ST INF (HURRICANE RIFLES), CO E
STANDEFER, MORDECAI HOUSTON	1LT	TX 15TH INF, CO C
STANDIFER, THOMAS CUNNINGHAM	LT COL	LA 12TH INF (JACKSON'S SHARPSHOOTERS), CO B
STANFORD, THOMAS JEFFERSON	CAPT	MS L ARTY, STANFORD'S CO
STANLEY, EDWARD ROWELL	2LT	AL 11TH CAV, CO H
STANLEY, JOHN BUNN	CAPT	NC 20TH INF, CO D
STANLEY, THOMAS EDWARD	ACS	SC 21ST INF, F&S
STANLEY, WILLIAM JASPER	CAPT	NC 20TH INF, CO D
STANLEY, WILLIAM Y	CAPT	KY 6TH MTD INF, CO G
STANSBURY, SMITH	MAJ	CSA ARTY
STAPLER, JOHN A	LT	AL 49TH INF, CO D
STAPLETON, JAMES FRANKLIN	2LT	GA 46TH INF, CO F
STAPLETON, JAMES	COL	GA 2ND STATE LINE
STARKE, PETER BURWELL	BRIG GEN	MS 28TH CAV
STARR, JOSEPH BLAKE	LT COL	NC 13TH L ARTY, CO B
STARR, SILAS HENRY JR	2LT	GA 3RD INF, CO H
STEARNS, THOMAS GREEN JR	1LT	GA 43RD INF, CO C
STEELE, ARCHIBALD	CAPT	MS 6TH INF, CO G
STEFFEY, BENJAMIN M	1LT	KY 6TH MTD INF, CO C
STELL, ALBERT J	3LT	AR 33RD INF, CO C
STENNIS, ADAM TURNER	ADJ	MS 5TH INF, F&S
STEPHENS, ALEXANDER HAMILTON	VICE PRES	CSA
STEPHENS, GEORGE W	CAPT	TN 4TH CAV, CO C
STEPHENS, JOHN ALEXANDER	2LT	GA 1ST REGULARS, CO G,I
STEPHENS, JOHN	2LT	GA 52ND INF, CO E
STEPHENS, M D L	COL	MS 31ST INF, F&S
STERLING, BENJAMIN FRANKLIN	CAPT	TX WAUL'S LEGION, CO F
STEVENS, BENJAMIN	CAPT	MS 9TH CAV, CO D
STEVENS, HUBBARD WALLACE	1LT	GA 28TH BN SIEGE ARTY, CO B
STEVENS, THOMAS	2LT	MS 1ST CAV, CO F
STEVENS, WALTER HUSTED	BRIG GEN	ANV - CHIEF ENGR
STEVENSON, JOHN PHILLIP	CAPT	TX 4TH CAV, CO I
STEWART, ALEXANDER PETER	LT GEN	POLK'S CORPS
STEWART, ARCHIE W	LT	AL 20TH INF, CO H
STEWART, ASA ALEXANDER	CAPT	FL 9TH INF, CO E
STEWART, DAVID FINNEY MD	SURG	TX 10TH INF, F&S
STEWART, ELAM CRAWFORD	3LT	NC 48TH INF, CO I
STEWART, EUGENE GOLDING	1LT	GA 2ND INF, CO G
STEWART, GOAH WATSON	CAPT	MO 1ST/4TH CONSOLIDATED INF, CO H, G
STEWART, HUGH MENART	CAPT	MO 6TH CAV (JACKSON'S), CO A
STEWART, JAMES E	CAPT	TN 19TH/20TH CONSOLIDATED CAV, CO H
STEWART, JAMES M	1LT	AR 30TH INF, CO a
STEWART, JAMES MADISON	MAJ	SC 22ND INF, CO G
STEWART, JOHN PURVIS	1LT	VA 30TH INF, CO I
STEWART, JOHN THOMAS	CAPT	VA 55TH INF, CO J
STEWART, JONATHAN CLAY	CAPT	FL 8TH INF, CO G
STEWART, JOSEPH ALEXANDER	CAPT	GA 18TH INF, CO B
STEWART, WILLIAM PATTERSON	CAPT	MS 10TH INF, CO K
STIGLER, JAMES M	MAJ	MS 1ST SHARPSHOOTERS BN, F&S
STILTNER, MILBURN JACKSON	1LT	KY 10TH CAV (DIAMOND'S), CO I
STINSON, DAVID WASHINGTON	LT	VA 56TH INF, CO D
STINSON, JACK BRYANT MD	SURG	AL 23RD BN SHARPSHOOTERS

STINSON, JOHN	CAPT	MS 5TH INF, CO C
STOCKS, JOHN THOMAS	CAPT	GA 17TH BN INF (STATE GUARDS)
STOCKSTILL, DAVID WARDEN	3LT	MS 3RD INF (LIVE OAK RIFLES), CO G
STOCKTON, WILLIAM TENNENT	LT COL	FL 1ST CAV, F&S
STOKER, RICHARD JAMES	2LT	MS 30TH INF, CO C
STOKES, BURRELL T	1LT	FL 1ST CAV, CO I
STOKES, MONTFORD SYDNEY	COL	NC 1ST INF, F&S
STOKES, THOMAS J	CAPT	MS 11TH INF, CO F
STOKES, WILLIAM	COL	SC 4TH CAV
STONE, BARTON WARREN JR	COL	TX 6TH CAV, F&S
STONE, JOHN D REV	CHAPLAIN/2LT	AL 4TH CAV (RODDY'S), CO K
STONE, JOHN F	1LT	SC 18TH INF, CO D
STONE, LEFTWICH H	1LT	AR 5TH INF
STONE, P W	ADJ	TN ALLISON'S SQUADRON CAV
STONE, SARDINE GRAHAM	1LT	CSS FLORIDA, CSN
STOREY, LEONIDAS JEFFERSON	1LT	TX 26TH CAV, CO B
STOUGH, ROBERT W	2LT	AL 4TH BN HILLIARD'S LEGION ARTY, CO A
STOVALL, ABSOLEM ROUSSEAU	1LT	MS 1ST INF, CO C
STOVALL, ALVIN D	BVT 2LT	GA 64TH INF, CO K
STOVALL, DAVID MCGOWAN	CAPT	TX 25TH CAV, CO C
STOVALL, MARCELLUS AUGUSTUS	BRIG GEN	GA 3RD ARTY
STOWE, HUBERT DELAMBERT	CAPT	CSA - COMMISSARY OF SUBSISTENCE
STOWE, WILLIAM ALEXANDER	COL	NC 16TH INF, CO M
STRADLEY, JOHN RYLAND	CAPT	TN 59TH MTD INF, CO E
STRAHAN, WILLIAM L	3LT	MS STOCKDALE'S BN CAV, CO A,B
STRAHL, OTHO FRENCH	BRIG GEN	TN 4TH INF
STRAIT, G LAFAYETTE	CAPT	SC 6TH INF, CO A
STRANGE, JOHN BOWIE	LT COL	VA 19TH INF, CO F&S
STRANGE, THOMAS C	1LT	FL 3RD INF, CO K - ADJ
STRATTON, JOHN W C	CAPT	TN 59TH INF, CO G
STRATTON, JOHN WILLIAM	MAJ	VA 34TH BN CAV (WITCHER'S NIGHTHAWKS), F&S
STREET, SOLOMON G	MAJ	TN 15TH CONSOLIDATED CAV
STRICKLAND, CHARLTON HINES	CAPT	GA 3RD BN SHARPSHOOTERS, CO C
STROTHER, WILLIAM H JR	2LT	NC 40TH MILITIA (FRANKLIN COUNTY)
STUART, JAMES EWELL BROWN	MAJ GEN	ANV CAV CORPS
STUBBS, FRANK PETER	CAPT	LA 2ND INF, CO C
STUBBS, JOHN T	CAPT	AL 1ST INF, CO C
STUMP, GEORGE WASHINGTON	CAPT	VA 18TH CAV, CO B
STYRON, WALLACE SYLVESTER	CAPT	NC 18TH MILITIA (CARTERET COUNTY)
STYRON, WILLIAM D	JR 1LT	NC 2ND ARTY, CO G
SUBER, CHRISTIAN HENRY	MAJ	SC 14TH INF, F&S - QM
SUGGS, JOHN	2LT	GA 65TH INF, CO K
SUITS, JOHN	3LT	NC 7TH SENIOR RESERVES
SULLINS, DAVID	MAJ	TN 19TH INF - QM & CHAPLAIN
SULLIVAN, CHARLES LEE JR	JR 2LT	TN 12TH CAV, CO C
SULLIVAN, DANIEL ASBURY	1LT	GA 65TH INF, CO G
SULLIVAN, J MIMS	1LT	SC 6TH CAV, CO A
SULLIVAN, JOHN SCALLY	CAPT	KY 6TH MTD INF, CO B
SUMMER, JOHN C	CAPT	SC 3RD INF, CO H
SUMMERS, JOHN S	2LT	NC 49TH INF, CO E
SUMMERS, JOHN CALHOUN	LT COL	VA 60TH INF, CO A
SUMNER, JOHN C	2LT	GA 53RD INF, CO D

SUMNER, NELSON N	2LT	NC 1ST BN JUNIOR RESERVES, CO A
SURRAT, RICHARD L	CAPT	NC 6TH SENIOR RESERVES, CO F
SUTPHIN, JAMES S	CAPT	VA 14TH INF, CO K
SUTTON, LEWIS BOND	2LT	NC 4TH CAV, CO F
SUTTON, WILLIAM	CAPT	NC 3RD ARTY, CO A
SWAIM, COLUMBUS FRANKLIN	1LT	NC 2ND BN INF, CO G
SWAIM, JOSEPH SPURGEON	1LT	NC 2ND BN INF, CO G
SWAIN, RICHARD D	2LT	LA 5TH INF, CO E
SWANGO, HENRY CHAPMAN	CAPT	KY 5TH MTD INF, CO I
SWANN, WILLIAM JAMES	2LT	TN 35TH INF, CO G
SWEENEY, JAMES T	CAPT	VA 34TH BN CAV (WITCHER'S NIGHTHAWKS), CO K
SWINFORD, JOHN A	JR 2LT	GA 36TH INF, CO E
SWITTENBERG, JOHN CALVIN	CAPT	MS 16TH INF, CO H
SWOR, WILLIAM C	LT COL	TN 5TH INF
SWYGERT, EMANUEL ZEDDO	1LT	SC 15TH INF, CO C
SWYGERT, GEORGE SAMUEL	CAPT	SC 3RD INF, CO H
SYDNOR, THOMAS WHITE	1LT	VA 4TH CAV, CO G
SYKES, EDWARD TURNER	CAPT	MS 10TH INF, CO K
SYKES, WILLIAM E	1LT	MS 43RD INF, F&S - ADJ
SYPERT, LEONIDAS ARMSTEAD	LT COL	KY SYPERT'S CAV
TABOR, JOHN WASHINGTON	MAJ	TX 17TH INF, F&S
TALBERT, BARTLEY MARTIN	CAPT	SC 7TH INF, CO K
TALBOT, ISHAM STROTHER MD	ASST SURG	CSA
TALIAFERRO, ALEXANDER GALT	COL	VA 23RD INF, F&S
TALIAFERRO, THOMAS DORSEY	LT COL	TX 20TH CAV
TALIAFERRO, WILLIAM W	2LT	VA 52ND MILITIA, CO B
TALLY, SIDNEY J	1LT	NC 44TH INF, CO E
TANNEHILL, BENJAMIN WILLIAM	1LT	MO 1ST CAV, CO B
TANSILL, ROBERT	COL	CSA - IG
TARPLEY, MATTHEW COLEMAN	2LT	GA 63RD INF, CO G
TATE, A J	2LT	TN 45TH INF, CO F
TATE, JAMES R	LT	NC 16TH INF, CO D
TATOM, ABNER CURRAN	2LT	MS 11TH CONSOLIDATED CAV, CO H
TATOM, JONATHAN S	CAPT	MS 36TH INF, CO D
TATUM, JOHN ABE	1LT	VA 42ND INF, CO H
TATUM, ROBERT HALEY	REPRESENTATIVE	GA STATE FROM DADE COUNTY
TAVENNER, WILLIAM C	LT COL	VA 17TH CAV BN, F&S
TAYLOR, BENJAMIN WALTER MD	SURG	SC INF (HAMPTON'S LEGION), F&S
TAYLOR, BYRON LUDWELL	1LT	TX 4TH CAV, CO F
TAYLOR, CHARLES COLEMAN	2LT	VA 15TH INF (ASHLAND GRAYS), CO E
TAYLOR, CHARLES DOWNING	1LT	AR 21ST INF, CO H
TAYLOR, DAVID C	2LT	TN 28TH CONSOLIDATED INF, CO I
TAYLOR, HILLARY	CAPT	NC 58TH INF
TAYLOR, JAMES MADISON	1LT	NC 62ND INF, CO F
TAYLOR, N C	CAPT	TN 21ST, CO H
TAYLOR, RICHARD	LT GEN	LA 9TH INF
TAYLOR, ROBERT H	COL	TX 22ND CAV, CO F&S
TAYLOR, ROBERT HUDSON	CAPT	MS 7TH CAV, CO K
TAYLOR, SAMUEL WOOD	2LT	LA 17TH INF, CO C
TAYLOR, THOMAS S	1LT	AL 6TH INF, CO G
TAYLOR, TILMON	2LT	NC 18TH MILITIA (CARTERET COUNTY)
TAYLOR, WALLACE	1LT	NC 18TH MILITIA (CARTERET COUNTY)

TAYLOR, WALTER H	LT COL	CSA - AAG
TAYLOR, WILLIAM FORD	2LT	TN 1ST INF (TURNEY'S), CO E
TAYLOR, WILLIAM HENRY MD	SURG	VA 19TH INF, CO F&S
TAYLOR, WILLIAM HENRY	COL	MS 12TH INF, CO A
TEAFF, WILLIAM J	1LT	AR 27TH INF, CO K
TEAGARDEN, OSWIN	PURCHASING AGENT	CSA
TEASLEY, ALFRED J	2LT	GA 15TH INF, CO I
TEASLEY, JOHN HENRY H	1LT	GA 38TH INF, CO F
TEBBS, WILLOUGHBY W	CAPT	VA 2ND CAV, CO K
TEMPLE, CHRISTOPHER COLUMBUS	2LT	MS 3RD INF (LIVE OAK RIFLES), CO K
TENNEY, SAMUEL FISHER	1LT	CSA ORDINANCE OFFICER
TERRAL, JAMES STEPHENS JR	LT COL	MS 7TH INF BN, CO F&S
TERRY, LAMPKIN STRAUGHN	MAJ	MS 15TH INF, CO A
TERRY, NATHAN B	1LT	VA 51ST INF, CO H
TERRY, WILLIAM	BRIG GEN	VA 4TH INF
TEW, CHARLES H	CAPT	LA 1ST INF, ACF
THARP, SIMEON A	1LT	GA 4TH INF, CO C
THAXTON, HENRY J C	2LT	GA 14TH INF, CO I
THEOBALD, GRIFF P	CAPT	CSA - AQM
THIGPEN, ABRAM H	2LT	LA CONSOLIDATED CRESCENT INF, CO B
THOMAS, EDWARD S	ENSIGN	VA 61ST INF, CO D
THOMAS, GEORGE W	1LT	VA 42ND INF, CO E
THOMAS, JAMES JACKSON JR	1LT	NC 47TH INF, CO F - AQM
THOMAS, JOHN ALEXANDER WILLIAM	CAPT	SC 21ST INF, CO F
THOMAS, JOHN PEYRE	MAJ	SC CORPS OF CADETS, CO B
THOMAS, LEWIS M	2LT	AR 15TH INF (JOHNSON'S), CO A
THOMAS, LOVICK PIERCE	LT COL	GA 42ND INF, CO A
THOMAS, RIDLEY BROWN	2LT	TX BAYLOR'S CAV, CO G
THOMAS, WILLIAM DAVID	1LT	GA 45TH INF, CO I
THOMAS, WILLIAM E	CAPT	MS 3RD INF, CO D
THOMASSON, WILLIAM B	CAPT	GA 41ST, CO I
THOMPSON, BENJAMIN FRANKLIN	3LT	VA 64TH MTD INF, CO G
THOMPSON, BENJAMIN VANDIVER	2LT	SC 16TH INF, CO E
THOMPSON, HENRY BRADFORD	CAPT	AL 51ST PARTISAN RANGERS, CO B
THOMPSON, HUGH SMITH	CAPT	SC STATE CADETS BN (CITADEL), CO A
THOMPSON, JAMES T S MD	ASST SURG/JR 2LT	TN 3RD INF
THOMPSON, MERIWETHER JEFF	BRIG GEN	MO STATE GUARD
THOMPSON, PARHAM	1LT	MS POWERS' CAV, CO K,B
THOMPSON, PHILLIP B	COL	CSA
THOMPSON, PRESTON	LT COL	KY 5TH CAV, F&S
THOMPSON, ROBERT W	2LT	TX BOURLAND'S CAV, CO A
THOMPSON, SAMUEL W	2LT	VA 16TH CAV, CO I
THOMPSON, THOMAS	COL	SC 2ND INF, CO A
THOMPSON, WILLIAM ALBERT	2LT	NC 23RD INF, CO B
THOMPSON, WILLIAM FLINT	CAPT	TX 17TH CONSOLIDATED DSMTD CAV, CO C
THOMPSON, WILLIAM	MAJ	AR 15TH INF, F&S
THOMSON, JAMES MATTHEW	ASST SURG	CONFEDERATE TROOPS
THOMSON, JOHN HOUSEAL	CAPT	SC 1ST INF (HAGOOD'S), CO E
THORINGTON, JACK	LT COL	AL 1ST BN HILLIARD'S LEGION
THORNHILL, NEWEL	JUDGE	GA WORTH COUNTY, INFERIOR COURT
THORNTON, DOZIER	1LT	AL 15TH INF, CO D
THORNTON, JAMES T	LT COL	GA 3RD CAV, CO E

THORNTON, WILLIAM M	2LT	MS 3RD CAV, CO I
THOROUGHMAN, THOMAS H	LT COL	MO 5TH DIV STATE GUARDS
THORPE, JOHN HOUSTON	CAPT	NC 47TH INF, CO A
THORPE, PATRICK HENRY	CAPT	KY 1ST INF, CO H
THORPE, SPENCER ROANE	2LT	KY 2ND CAV (DUKE'S), CO A
THRAILKILL, JOHN	CAPT	MO 1ST CAV, CO F
THRASHER, DAVID HUGHEY	CAPT	TN 38TH INF, CO K
THRIFT, GEORGE NATHANIEL	2LT	VA 7TH INF, CO A
THROCKMORTON, JOHN ARIS	CAPT	VA 6TH CAV, CO F
THURMAN, WILLIAM PLEASANT MD	ASST SURG	VA L ARTY (BEDFORD), J.D. SMITH'S CO
TICKELL, YANCEY	CAPT	NC 48TH MILITIA (ALAMANCE COUNTY)
TIDWELL, FRANKLIN FULTON	CAPT	TN 11TH INF, CO K
TILGHMAN, LLOYD	BRIG GEN	KY 3RD INF
TILGHMAN, OSWALD	SR 2LT	TN L ARTY, WELLER'S CO
TILLMAN, ANDREW JACKSON	2LT	MS 1ST INF (COPIAH'S), CO B
TILLMAN, BASIL MANLEY	CAPT	TN 52ND INF, CO C
TILLMAN, ELIJAH	2LT	GA 50TH INF, CO H
TILLMAN, FRANCIS C	CAPT	GA 46TH INF, CO C
TILLMAN, ISAIAH HAMILTON	2LT	GA 26TH INF, CO H
TILLMAN, JAMES D	COL	TN 41ST INF, CO F
TILLMAN, LEONIDAS H	CAPT	MS 39TH INF, CO E
TIMBERLAKE, WILLIAM P	CAPT	TN 27TH INF, CO D
TIMMONS, JOHN MORGAN	DELEGATE	SC SIGNER SECESSION ORDINANCE, DELEGATE DARLINGTON COUNTY
TINSLEY, PEMBROKE SOMERSET	LT	TN HAMILTON'S BN CAV, CO A
TIPPINS, PHILIP GLENN	CAPT	GA 47TH INF, CO G
TIPTON, ROBERT J	1LT	TN 19TH INF, CO B
TIPTON, WILLIAM LAWRENCE	CAPT	VA 29TH INF, CO D
TOBIN, WILLIAM GERARD	CAPT	TX 1ST CAV, CO D
TODD, ALEXANDER H	1LT	CSA - BRIG GEN HELM'S - ADC
TODD, CHARLES HENRY	SURG	VA 13TH INF, F&S
TODD, DAVID LOWE MD	ASST SURG	CSA
TODD, JOSEPH WARREN	1LT	NC 1ST CAV, CO D
TODD, WILLIAM HOCKER	CAPT	MO SEARCY'S BN SHARPSHOOTERS, CO E
TOLAR, WILLIAM J	CAPT	SC 10TH INF, CO B
TOLBERT, JAMES H	MAJ	TN 28TH CONSOLIDATED INF
TOMBERLIN, JOHN W	BVT 2LT	GA 49TH INF, CO E
TOMLINSON, AUGUSTUS AUSTERE	CAPT	TX 12TH INF, CO E
TOMLINSON, JONAS	2LT	GA 29TH INF, CO K
TOMLINSON, JOSEPH	1LT	GA 50TH INF, CO G
TOMLINSON, ROBERT REESE	CAPT	SC 26TH INF, CO H
TOOMBS, ROBERT AUGUSTUS	BRIG GEN	CSA ANV; SEC OF STATE
TOOTHMAN, DAVIS	1LT	VA 31ST INF, CO A
TOOTLE, COLUMBUS	2LT	GA 47TH INF, CO G
TOOTLE, JEREMIAH HAMILTON	2LT	GA 47TH INF, CO G
TOPP, ROBERT CARUTHERS	CAPT	MS 13TH INF, CO H
TORREY, ROBERT DOUGALD	2LT	MS 2ND BN INF (STATE TROOPS), CO F
TOULMIN, HARRY THEOPHILUS	COL	AL 22ND INF, CO H
TOWERS, JOHN REED	COL	GA 8TH INF, CO E
TOWNS, J RANDOLPH	CAPT	GA 62ND CAV, CO A
TOWNS, WILLIAM JEFFERSON	2LT	TX 1ST INF, CO M
TOWNSEND, THOMAS SHELLEY	1LT	TX 7TH INF, CO E

TOXEY, CALEB MD	ASST SURG	AL 19TH INF, F&S
TRACY, G B	1LT	TN 48TH INF, CO K
TRAVIS, AMOS CAMPBELL WHITFIELD MD		ASST SURG GA 8TH INF, CO G
TRAVIS, MARK BUTLER	BVT 2LT	AL 4TH INF (CONEUCH GUARDS), CO E
TRAWEEK, LAFAYETTE WASHINGTON	2LT	AL 17TH INF, CO C
TREVILLIAN, CHARLES B	1LT	VA 4TH CAV, CO F
TREZEVANT, JOHN TIMOTHY	MAJ	SC CHARLESTON ARSENAL BN
TRIBBLE, ABRAM KILBY	CAPT	SC 9TH RESERVES, CO F
TRIGG, BINGHAM JOHN	LT COL	MO MCBRIDE'S BDE
TRIMBLE, EDWIN	CAPT	KY 10TH CAV (MORGAN'S PARTISAN RANGERS), CO A
TRIMBLE, ISAAC RIDGEWAY	MAJ GEN	VA CMDR OF VALLEY DIST, SHENANDOAH VALLEY
TRIMBLE, JOHN A	CAPT	AR 30TH INF, CO E
TRIMMIER, THEODORE GILLARD	LT COL	AL 41ST INF, CO A
TRIPLETT, MARSHALL	MAJ	VA MOSBY'S CAV, F&S
TRIPLETT, THOMAS H	CAPT	VA 18TH CAV, CO G
TRIPPE, TURNER HUNT	1LT	GA 10TH BN CAV (BARTON COUNTY HOME GUARDS), CO D
TROGDON, JOHN RANDOLPH	1LT	NC 63RD MILITIA (RANDOLPH COUNTY)
TROLINGER, JAMES THOMAS	1LT	VA 7TH BN INF (LOCAL DEFENSE), CO C
TROTTER, THOMAS B JR	2LT	NC 1ST INF, CO C
TROTTER, TILLMAN RICHARD MD	SURG	MS 15TH INF, F&S
TROUT, ERASMUS STRIBLING	CAPT	VA 52ND INF, CO H
TROUT, HENRY S	2LT	VA 28TH INF, CO I
TRUDEAU, JAMES DEBERTY	BRIG GEN	LA LEGION
TRUESDALE, J ERASMUS	CAPT	SC 2ND INF, CO G
TRUSSELL, JOHN F H	2LT	MS 37TH INF, CO I
TRUSSELL, JOHN W	1LT	GA 32ND INF, CO B
TUCK , WILLIAM MUNFORD	2LT	VA 3RD INF, CO K
TUCKER, FRANCIS MARION	CAPT	SC 18TH INF, CO E
TUCKER, GEORGE LIVINGSTON	2LT	TN 5TH BN CAV (McCLELLAN'S), CO A
TUCKER, GEORGE W	2LT	VA 36TH INF, CO C
TUCKER, JOHN B	CAPT	MS 28TH CAV, CO H
TUCKER, JOHN M	CAPT	VA 41ST INF, CO B
TUCKER, JOHN	1LT	GA 50TH INF, CO H
TUCKER, NERIA	CAPT	AL 45TH INF, CO F
TUCKER, WILLIAM FEIMSTER	BRIG GEN	MS 41ST INF
TUCKER, WILLIAM H	ASST SURG	CSA
TUPPER, TULLIUS CICERO	MAJ GEN	MS STATE TROOPS
TURBIVILLE, WILSON D	CAPT	FL 1ST INF RESERVES, CO E
TURK, A L	CAPT	VA BALDWIN'S MTD INF (HOME GUARDS)
TURK, JAMES A	1LT	KY 3RD MTD INF, CO D
TURK, JOHN MILTON	2LT	AL 5TH BN, CO B
TURK, JOHN NEWTON	CAPT	GA 24TH INF, CO A
TURK, RANDOLPH	CAPT	CSA QM
TURK, THOMAS A	AQM	CSA
TURLEY, PATTERSON D	2LT	VA 62ND MTD INF, CO B
TURMAN, GEORGE HYLTON	CAPT	VA 54TH INF, CO G
TURNAGE, WILLIAM GEORGE	CAPT	AR 8TH INF, CO E
TURNBO, JAMES COFFEY	2LT	AR 14TH INF, CO C
TURNER, CHESLEY SR	2LT	TN 1ST BN INF (COLM'S), CO C
TURNER, HENRY BLOUNT	MAJ	AL 29TH INF, CO A
TURNER, ISAAC NEWTON MORELAND	CAPT	TX 5TH INF, CO K

TURNER, JAMES McNEILL	CAPT	NC 2ND CAV, CO B
TURNER, JESSE C	2LT	FL 9TH INF, CO D
TURNER, JOHN WILLIAM	1LT	VA 10TH BN H ARTY, CO C
TURNER, SMITH SPENGLER	1LT	VA 17TH INF, CO B
TURNER, STERLING TALLEY	CAPT	TN 43RD INF, CO F
TURNER, THOMAS JEFFERSON	CAPT	VA 38TH INF, CO A
TURNER, THOMAS W	LT	MO 2ND CAV, CO G
TURNER, WILLIAM HIRAM	CAPT	VA L ARTY, TURNER'S CO
TURNER, WILLIAM IREDELL	MAJ	FL 8TH INF, CO K
TURNEY, JOHN FLETCHER	1LT	AL FENNEL'S MORGAN RANGERS
TURNEY, PETER	COL	TN 1ST INF (TURNEY'S)
TURPIN, WILLIAM HANCE	2LT	GA 12TH INF, CO A
TUTEN, REDDING ROBERSON	1LT	NC 4TH INF, CO I
TUTEN, THOMAS ATKINS ELLERSON	2LT	NC 40TH INF, CO I
TUTTLE, MILLS VIRONA	2LT	NC 21ST INF, CO G
TUTTLE, ROMULUS MORRISON	CAPT	NC 26TH INF, CO F
TWIGGS, JOHN DAVID	LT COL	SC 1ST CAV, CO C
TWOMEY, MORRIS DAVID	2LT	TN 48TH INF, CO I
TYLER, AUGUSTUS	CAPT	AR 21ST INF, CO D
TYLER, HENRY ASHBURN	CAPT	KY 12TH CAV, CO A
TYLER, JOHN	REPRESENTATIVE	CONFEDERATE CONGRESS, VIRGINIA
TYLER, ROBERT	2LT	CSA GEN JOHN HUNT MORGAN'S ADC
TYNES, A J	CAPT	CSA - COMMISSARY OF SUBSISTENCE
UNDERWOOD, WILLIAM R	2LT	MO 4TH CAV, CO K
URQUHART, CHARLES FOX JR	CAPT	VA 3RD INF, CO D
UTLEY, JAMES ALLEN	2LT	TN 10TH CAV, CO K
UTZ, JAMES MORGAN	MAJ	MO 9TH INF, CO G
VADEN, WALTER PENDLETON	1LT	AR 12TH INF, CO H
VAN BRACKLE, ISRAEL E	1LT	GA 7TH CAV, CO K
VAN CLEAVE, WILLIAM B	CAPT	TN 46TH INF, CO G
VAN DOREN, EARL	MAJ GEN	AOT CAV CMDR
VAN HOOSE, GEORGE W	CAPT	AR 17TH INF (GRIFFITH'S), CO D
VAN NESS, GEORGE H C	CAPT	AL 2ND INF, CO A
VAN ZANDT, ISAAC AVERY	1LT	GA 52ND INF, CO H
VAN ZANDT, KHLEBER MILLER	MAJ	TX 7TH INF, DFS
VANCE, JOHN D	CAPT	MS 14TH BN L ARTY, CO A
VANCE, WILLIAM D	1LT	SC 16TH INF, CO E
VANCE, ZEBULON BAIRD	COL	NC 26TH INF, F&S
VANDIVIERE, HOUSTON SOLOMON	LT COL	GA 52ND INF, F&S
VAUGHAN, ALFRED JEFFERSON JR	BRIG GEN	TN 13TH INF
VAUGHAN, HUGH REES	CAPT	MS 18TH INF, CO B
VAUGHAN, JAMES W	1LT	GA 61ST INF, CO E
VAUGHAN, SAMUEL WATKINS MD	SURG/MAJ	AR 37TH INF, CO A
VAUGHN, THOMAS HOWELL	CAPT	GA 31ST INF, CO D
VAUGHN, THOMAS HOWELL	1LT	CSA 1ST CHOCTAW AND CHICKASAW MTD RIFLES, CO K
VEAL, WILLIAM G	CAPT	TX 12TH CAV (PARSON'S), CO F
VENABLE, CHARLES SCOTT	LT COL	CSA - AAG
VENABLE, SANFORD	1LT	GA 8TH BN INF, CO A
VERNON, THOMAS GAINES II	2LT	TX 23RD CAV, CO E
VIA, ELIJAH DEHART	1LT	VA 51ST INF, CO H
VINCENT, WILLIAM GERMAIN	COL	LA 2ND CAV, F&S
VINING, FRANCIS J	1LT	GA 2ND SHARPSHOOTERS, CO B

VINSON, SAMUEL SPERRY	1LT	VA 8TH CAV, CO K
VIOSCA, JOAQIUN JOSEPH LOUIS	CAPT	LA MILITIA ORLEANS GUARDS, CO H
VLECK, ABRAM VAN	2LT	TN STEUBEN ARTY, MARSHALL'S CO
VON BORCKE, HEROS	MAJ	CSA - AAG
VON ROEDER, LUDGWIG AUGUST	1LT	TX 4TH CAV, CO C
WADDEY, JOHN H	2LT	TN 32ND INF, CO D
WADE, HENRY W	CAPT	TX 6TH CAV, CO B
WADE, JAMES ANDREW	CAPT	CSA
WADE, JOHN JESSE	LT COL	VA 54TH INF, CO E
WADE, JOHN T S	ASST ADJ	CSA
WAKEFIELD, GEORGE NATHANIEL	2LT	TX 10TH INF, CO I
WALDEN, WESTLEY D	CAPT	AL 2ND BN HILLIARD'S LEGION, CO B
WALDRON, MATTHIAS H	1LT	VA 34TH BN CAV (WITCHER'S NIGHTHAWKS), CO D
WALDROP, WILLIAM CARROLL	1LT	MS 41ST INF, CO F
WALKER, BENJAMIN FRANKLIN	2LT	GA 42ND INF, CO K
WALKER, DAVID	COL	JAG FOR GENERAL STERLING PRICE
WALKER, GEORGE HAMILTON MD	SURG	LA 1ST H ARTY, F&S
WALKER, JAMES ARTHUR	2LT	GA 12TH INF, CO B
WALKER, JAMES MADISON	COL	MS 10TH INF, F&S
WALKER, JAMES VANCE	1LT	TN 3RD MTD INF (LILLIARD'S), CO G
WALKER, JOHN GEORGE	MAJ GEN	TX WALKER'S DIV
WALKER, JOHN STEWART	MAJ	VA 15TH INF, CO B
WALKER, JOSHUA	2LT	GA 49TH INF, CO A
WALKER, LEGARE' JONES	1LT	SC 7TH CAV, CO B
WALKER, LEVI H	1LT	NC 6TH INF, CO H
WALKER, NATHANIEL SADLER MD	ASST SURG	GA 44TH INF, F&S
WALKER, ROBERT DOWNIE	CAPT	GA 1ST INF, CO K
WALKER, THOMAS FOWLER	1LT	VA 36TH INF, CO G
WALKER, WILLIAM A	CAPT	NC 68TH MILITIA (GUILFORD COUNTY)
WALKER, WILLIAM E	2LT	GA CAV, ALLEN'S CO
WALKER, WILLIAM HENRY TALBOT	MAJ GEN	AOT HQ
WALKUP, SAMUEL H	COL	NC 48TH INF, F&S
WALL, IVERSON JEFFERSON	1LT	LA 9TH BN INF, CO C
WALL, JAMES A	2LT	MS 36TH INF, CO I
WALLACE, ALFRED LEONARD	2LT	TX WELLS' CAV, CO F
WALLACE, HUGH	2LT	KY 3RD MTD INF, CO K
WALLACE, JAMES ADAMS	CAPT	TX 2ND INF (STATE TROOPS), CO G
WALLACE, WILLIAM H	1LT	TX 13TH BDE MILITIA, CASKEY'S CO, (HENDERSON COUNTY)
WALLING, JESSE	1LT	TN 16TH INF, CO E
WALSH, THOMAS V	CAPT	SC HOLCOMBE LEGION CAV BN , CO A
WALSTON, DAVID P	CAPT	KY 7TH MTD INF, CO D
WALSTON, WILLIAM PERKINS	JR 2LT	NC 32ND INF, CO H
WALTERS, WILLIAM HENRY HARRISON	CAPT	GA 18TH INF, CO H
WALTHALL, EDWARD CARY	LT COL	MS 15TH INF, CO H
WALTON, DAVID HARRISON	CAPT	VA 33RD INF, CO K
WAMPLER, JOHN MORRIS	CAPT	VA 8TH INF, CO H
WARD, GEORGE T	COL	FL 2ND INF, F&S
WARD, HARRISON CLAY	CAPT	VA 49TH INF, CO C
WARD, JAMES PINCKNEY	1LT	MS 37TH INF (YANCY GUARDS), CO G
WARD, JOHN JAMES	CAPT	AL LT ARTY, WARD'S BATTERY
WARD, JOHN MD	SURG/MAJ	CSA

WARD, RICHARD WILLIAMS	1LT	NC 3RD INF, CO H
WARD, ROBERT F	1LT	MS 42ND INF, CO B
WARD, WILLIAM THOMAS	CAPT	MS 8TH INF, CO C
WARD, WILLIAM WALKER	COL	TN 9TH CAV
WARDLAW, ANDREW BOWIE	MAJ	CSA MCGOWANS BDE
WARDLAW, FRANCIS HUGH	DELEGATE	SC SIGNER SECESSION ORDINANCE, DELEGATE EDGEFIELD COUNTY
WARE, EDMOND MACON	CAPT	VA 5TH CONSOLIDATED CAV, CO E
WARFIELD, BURTON	1LT	TN 6TH TN CAV, CO A
WARREN, HERBERT CHARLES	1LT	CSA BDE ORDINANCE OFFICER
WARREN, THOMAS ABNER	SURG	GA 4TH RESERVES, F&S
WASDEN, JOSEPH A	COL	GA 22ND INF
WASHINGTON, JAMES H R	REPRESENTATIVE	GA STATE REPRESENTATIVE
WASHINGTON, JOHN AUGUSTINE	LT COL	CSA GEN ROBERT E LEE - ADC
WATERS, JAMES A	1LT	GA 50TH INF, CO A
WATERS, JAMES H	CAPT	VA 5TH INF, CO L - ACS
WATERS, M S MD	ASST SURG	TN 6TH CAV, F&S
WATIE, STAND	BRIG GEN	CSA CHEROKEE MTD RIFLES
WATKINS, ANDERSON	LT COL	AR 8TH INF, F&S
WATKINS, HENRY W	1LT	TN 7TH CAV (DUCKWORTH'S), CO A
WATKINS, JOHN N	1LT	KY 10TH CAV (DIAMOND'S), CO F
WATKINS, WILLIAM H H	2LT	AL 43RD INF, CO B
WATSON, BURTON	1LT	GA 40TH INF, CO G
WATSON, LARKIN D	CAPT	GA 6TH INF, CO D
WATSON, ORASMUS ALLEN	CAPT	SC 3RD INF (LAURENS' & JAMES), CO B
WATSON, SAMUEL C	2LT	NC 33RD INF, CO F
WATT, GEORGE	1LT	VA 1ST STATE RESERVES, CO D
WATTS, FREDERICK JULIUS	CLERK	TX ANDERSON COUNTY 1864
WATTS, JAMES W	COL	VA 2ND CAV, CO A
WATTS, LEWIS FRANKLIN	CAPT	VA 22ND INF, CO F
WATTS, THOMAS H	COL	AL 17TH INF
WATTS, THOMAS H	GOV	AL GOVERNOR 1863-1865
WATTS, WILLIAM HENRY	CAPT	NC 7TH SENIOR RESERVES
WEAKLEY, SAMUEL MORFORD	1LT	TN 20TH INF, CO E,G
WEAR, JAMES HAYWOOD	CAPT	AL 4TH CAV (RODDY'S), CO A
WEATHERLY, COLIN MCRAE	ADJ	SC 8TH INF, F&S
WEAVER, ROBERT POTTS	ADJ	AR 40TH MTD INF
WEAVER, WILLIAM MCLEOD	1LT	MS 1ST INF, CO H (JOHNSTON'S)
WEBB, CHANNCEY ORIN	2LT	LA CONSOLIDATED CRESCENT INF, CO C,E
WEBB, DAVID C	1LT	AL 19TH INF, CO D
WEBB, ENOCH A	CAPT	KY 13TH CAV, CO D
WEBB, ISAAC	1LT	VA 63RD INF, CO G,I
WEBB, JOHN G	MAJ	GA 9TH INF, CO D
WEBB, JUNIUS Y	CAPT	LA WEBB'S CO CAV
WEBB, LEONIDAS A	CAPT	VA 34TH BN CAV (WITCHER'S NIGHTHAWKS), CO G
WEBB, ROBERT FULTON	COL	NC 6TH INF, CO B
WEBB , JAMES K POLK	CAPT	TN 16TH INF, CO E
WEEDEN, JOHN DAVID	LT COL	AL 49TH INF, F&S
WEEKLEY, GEORGE	2LT	TX 2ND INF, CO I
WEEKS, ELBERT MARION	LT	TX CRUMP'S CAV (LANES'S), CO E
WEINGES, SAMUEL H	2LT	FL 3RD INF, CO F
WEIR, JAMES ADAM	1LT	AR 8TH BN INF, CO C

WELCH, ASHLEY STEWARD	2LT	KY 2ND CAV (DUKE'S), CO E
WELCH, JOHN WESTLEY	1LT	TN 2ND CAV (BIFFLE'S), CO C
WELLMAN, LABAN T	1LT	VA 34TH BN CAV (WITCHER'S NIGHTHAWKS), CO B
WELLONS, CHARLES MARMADUKE	CAPT	TN 22ND INF, CO B
WELLS, DAVID BONY	1LT	GA 46TH INF, CO H
WELLS, HENRY W	2LT	NC 52ND INF, CO G
WELLS, JAMES D	CAPT	NC 52ND INF, CO G
WELLS, JOHN B	1LT	MD 2ND BN CAV, CO A
WELLS, JOSEPH M	COL	MS 23RD INF, F&S
WELLS, SAMUEL A	CAPT	AR 15TH INF (JOSEY'S), CO A
WELLS, WILLIAM GREEN	CAPT	KY 10TH CAV, WELLS' CO
WENTWORTH, JAMES HAMILTON	2LT	FL 5TH INF, CO D
WEST, GEORGE III	CAPT	BRIG GEN JOHN H VILLEPIQUE @ FT PILLOW, TN - ADC
WEST, HANDY H	2LT	NC 20TH INF, CO H
WEST, HEZEKIAH REV	CHAPLAIN	NC THOMAS' LEGION INF, F&S
WEST, MARTIN SPARKS	JR 2LT	TX 3RD INF, CO E
WEST, R L	1LT	KY 9TH CAV, CO D
WESTBROOK, JOSEPH WARREN	2LT	MS 4TH INF, CO B
WESTMORELAND, SILAS	CAPT	NC 21ST INF, CO G
WEYMOUTH, JOHN EDWARD	1LT	VA 18TH INF, CO E
WHALEY, CALEB A	CAPT	GA 2ND CAV, CO H
WHALEY, DAVID M	MAJ	TX 5TH INF, CO C
WHARTON, JOHN JAMES	1LT	CSA GEN JUBAL A EARLY - ADC
WHARTON, RUFUS W	MAJ	NC 67TH INF
WHATLEY, GEORGE CROGHAN	CAPT	AL 10TH INF, CO G
WHEARY, WILLIAM H	CAPT	VA HOOD'S BN RESERVES, CO B
WHEAT, CHATHAM ROBERDEAU	MAJ	LA 1ST SPECIAL INF BN (WHEAT'S), F&S
WHEELER, BURDIN	1LT	TN 4TH CAV, CO A
WHEELER, JOSEPH	MAJ GEN	AOT CAV CMDR
WHELESS, JOHN FRANK	CAPT	TN 1ST INF, CO C
WHERRY, BENJAMIN CHAPIN JR	1LT	VA 1ST BN INF (IRISH BN), CO ABD
WHIDDEN, JOHN W	CAPT	FL 7TH INF, CO E
WHILDEN, JOHN M	MAJ	SC 23RD INF, CO B
WHILDEN, LOUIS A	CAPT	SC 5TH CAV, CO E
WHISENANT, JACOB WILLIAM	CAPT	AL 2ND CAV, CO A
WHITAKER, CARY	CAPT	NC 43RD INF, CO D
WHITE, BENTON	LT	VA 60TH INF, CO I
WHITE, CHARLES ALEXANDER	CAPT	NC 67TH INF, CO E
WHITE, EDWARD	CAPT	CSA GEN CLINGMAN'S BDE - AG
WHITE, ELIJAH VIERS	LT COL	VA 35TH CAV BN, F&S
WHITE, HENRY S	2LT	VA 34TH BN CAV (WITCHER'S NIGHTHAWKS), CO B
WHITE, JAMES EDWARD	CAPT	SC 9TH INF, (1ST) CO F (REPUBLICAN BLUES)
WHITE, JAMES MARION	1LT	TN 32ND INF, CO C
WHITE, JAMES	CAPT	AL 41ST INF, CO G
WHITE, JOHN FLETCHER	LT COL	TN 5TH CAV (McKENZIE'S), CO A
WHITE, JOHN	COMMISSIONER	STATE OF NORTH CAROLINA
WHITE, JOHN R	COL	TN 53RD INF, CO I
WHITE, JOSEPH C	1LT	NC 4TH INF, CO C
WHITE, ROBERT ADAM	1LT	NC 28TH INF, CO B
WHITE, ROBERT	MAJ	CSA (MO) PRICE'S BDE
WHITE, SAMUEL GORE MD	SURG	GA COBB'S LEGION

WHITE, WALTER S	1LT	AL 22ND INF, CO G
WHITE, WILLIAM PARKER	COL	GA 7TH CAV, F&S
WHITEHEAD, JAMES WYATT	2LT	VA 53RD INF, CO I
WHITEHEAD, THOMAS	MAJ	VA 2ND CAV, CO E
WHITEHURST, JOHN J	2LT	VA 20TH BN H ARTY
WHITESIDE, SAMUEL ALLISON	CAPT	TN 48TH INF, CO B
WHITFIELD, JOHN WILKINS	BRIG GEN	TX CAV
WHITFIELD, THOMAS JEFFERSON	CAPT	TN 42ND INF, CO H
WHITING, HENRY CLAY	CAPT	CSA - AQM
WHITLEY, WILLIAM	2LT	TX 1ST INF
WHITMAN, JAMES P	ADJ	VA 16TH CAV
WHITMORE, SAMUEL P	LT	VA L ARTY (LOUDON ARTY), ROGER'S CO
WHITNER, JOHN CHARLES	MAJ	CSA COMMISARY OF SUBSISTNCE
WHITSON, JAMES M	COL	NC 8TH INF, CO B
WHITTEN, DANIEL McKNEEL	ENSIGN	MS 17TH INF, CO H
WHITTHORNE, SAMUEL HOUSTON	1LT	TN 23RD INF, CO D
WHITTHORNE, WASHINGTON CURRAN	ADJ GEN	TN
WHITTLE, LEWIS NEALE	COL	GA 8TH BN CAV (STATE GUARDS), CO A
WHYTE, GEORGE W	2LT	TN 27TH INF, CO D
WICKHAM, WILLIAM CARTER	COL	VA 4TH CAV, CO G
WICKLIFFE, CHARLES	COL	KY 7TH MTD INF, F&S
WIDGEON, JOHN T	1LT	VA 41ST INF, CO F
WIER, JAMES HARVEY	2LT	AL 40TH INF, CO B
WIGFALL, LOUIS TREZEVANT	BRIG GEN	TX BRIGADE
WIGGINS, JACKSON C	2LT	GA 38TH INF, CO K
WIGGINS, OCTAVIOUS A	1LT	NC 37TH INF, CO E
WIGGS, JAMES ALPHAEUS	AQM	TN 4TH INF, F&S
WILBOURN, MADISON WALLACE	CAPT	MS 1ST INF, CO E
WILCOX, CADMUS MARCELLUS	MAJ GEN	CSA WILCOX'S DIV
WILEY, WILLIAM M	CAPT	NC 68TH MILITIA CAV, CO S (GUILFORD COUNTY)
WILKERSON, SIMEON C	CAPT	AL 18TH INF, CO E
WILKES, JAMES SESSUMS	1LT	AR 32ND INF, CO A
WILKINSON, HENRY THOMAS	1LT	VA 22ND BN INF, CO E
WILKINSON, JAMES RICHARD	2LT	SC 26TH INF, CO C
WILKINSON, JOSEPH BIDDLE	1LT	TN 3RD MTD INF (LILLARD'S), CO E
WILKINSON, TILDEN J	CAPT	MO 5TH CAV, CO G
WILLIAMS, ABRAHAM ENGLISH MD	SURG	SC 11TH INF, F&S
WILLIAMS, C K	2LT	SC 17TH INF, CO F
WILLIAMS, DAVID	CAPT	NC 3RD INF, CO K
WILLIAMS, GEORGE F	2LT	AR 4TH BN INF, CO E
WILLIAMS, HAZAEL JOSEPH	LT COL	VA 5TH INF, CO D
WILLIAMS, ISAAC	2LT	NC 28TH INF, CO E
WILLIAMS, J F C	1LT	GA 31ST INF, CO H
WILLIAMS, J LOUIS	CAPT	VA 34TH BN CAV (WITCHER'S NIGHTHAWKS), CO H
WILLIAMS, JACOB CALVIN	2LT	NC 31ST INF, CO C
WILLIAMS, JAMES BERRY	CAPT	NC 20TH INF, CO C
WILLIAMS, JAMES L	CAPT	AL 31ST INF, CO H
WILLIAMS, JAMES M	2LT	TN 29TH INF, CO D
WILLIAMS, JEREMIAH H J	MAJ	AL 9TH INF, F&S
WILLIAMS, JOHN CULPEPPER	1LT	NC 119TH MILITIA (UNION COUNTY)
WILLIAMS, JOHN DRUMGHOULE SR	1LT	CSA GEN MAXEY'S ESCORT
WILLIAMS, JOHN H	CAPT	CSA

WILLIAMS, JOHN MADISON	2LT	VA 36TH INF, CO H
WILLIAMS, JOHN R	2LT	GA 10TH BN INF, CO C
WILLIAMS, JOHN SIDDLE	CAPT	MO 12TH CAV, 8TH DIV (STATE GUARDS), CO C
WILLIAMS, JOHN STUART	BRIG GEN	TN EAST
WILLIAMS, JOHN T	CAPT	KY 2ND MTD RIFLES, CO A
WILLIAMS, JOHN THOMAS	LT	VA 1ST ARTY, CO E
WILLIAMS, JOSEPH HENRY	2LT	VA 12TH INF, CO K
WILLIAMS, LEVI BRANSON	2LT	NC 5TH CAV, CO E
WILLIAMS, LEWIS B JR	LT COL	VA 7TH INF, F&S
WILLIAMS, LUCIUS L	CAPT	GA 49TH INF, CO B
WILLIAMS, PRICE JR	CAPT	AL 1ST BN CADETS, CO A - (PELHAM - MOBILE)
WILLIAMS, ROBERT THOMAS	1LT	TX 4TH CAV (SIBLEY'S), CO E
WILLIAMS, ROLAND SAMPSON	1LT	NC 13TH INF, CO I
WILLIAMS, THOMAS GREENFIELD	2LT	TN 20TH INF, CO B
WILLIAMS, THOMAS HERBERT	BVT 2LT	SC 16TH INF, CO I (PALMETTO SHARPSHOOTERS)
WILLIAMS, THOMAS JEFFERSON JR	SHERIFF	LA DESOTO PARRISH
WILLIAMS, THOMAS L	CAPT	TN 16TH BN CAV (NEAL'S), CO E
WILLIAMS, WILEY J	LT COL	GA 49TH INF, CO B
WILLIAMS, WILLIAM WILEY	CAPT	GA 47TH INF, CO C
WILLIAMS, WILSON H	CAPT	NC 55TH INF, CO I
WILLIAMSON, BAILEY PEYTON	1LT	NC 2ND BN INF, CO C
WILLIAMSON, GEORGE MACWILLIE	1LT	LA 1ST SPECIAL INF BN (RIGHTOR'S), CO D
WILLIAMSON, HENRY EDMUND	CAPT	MS 17TH INF, CO D
WILLIAMSON, JOHN H	2LT	SC 26TH INF, CO K
WILLIAMSON, KENNETH MCDONALD	MAJ	NC 53RD MILITIA, F&S (CUMBERLAND COUNTY)
WILLIAMSON, ROBERT D	1LT	TN 31ST INF, CO F
WILLIAMSON, SAMUEL T	2LT	AL 23RD BN SHARPSHOOTERS, CO G
WILLIAMSON, THOMAS HOOMES	LT COL	CSA - ENGINEERS
WILLIAMSON, THOMAS JEFFERSON	CAPT	AL 19TH INF, CO E
WILLINGHAM, ALFRED JACKSON MD	ASST SURG/CAPT	TX 4TH CAV, F&S
WILLINGHAM, STERLING ANDREW JACKSON		1LT TX 4TH CAV, CO G (ARIZONA BDE)
WILLIS, ABRAM BARNES	CAPT	MS 6TH INF, CO G
WILLIS, EDWARD JEFFERSON	CAPT	VA 15TH INF, CO A
WILLIS, JAMES T	CAPT	KY 4TH CAV, CO G
WILLIS, PRIESTLY EARL	CAPT	GA 22ND INF, CO I
WILLIS, THEODORE GUSTAVUS ADOLPHUS		AQM TX 12TH CAV, CO F
WILLIS, WORDEN P	CAPT	MO 1ST NORTHEAST CAV, CO D
WILLMON, JOSIAH	1LT	AR 4TH INF, CO K
WILMETH, JOSEPH BRISON	2LT	TX 6TH CAV, CO D
WILMOT, DANIEL HICKS	CAPT	GA 17TH INF, CO A
WILSON, ANDREW N	COL	TN 21ST CAV
WILSON, BRYCE A	ADJ	AL 16TH INF, F&S
WILSON, DIONYSIUS A	2LT	SC 2ND RIFLES, CO A
WILSON, JAMES P	1LT	KY 4TH INF, CO B
WILSON, JOHN P	MAJ	VA 5TH INF BN, CO F&S
WILSON, JOHN R	CAPT	GA 48TH INF, F&S - ACS
WILSON, JOHN ROPER	1LT	AL 4TH INF (CONEUCH GUARDS), CO C
WILSON, JOHN T	2LT	AL 10TH INF, CO C
WILSON, JOHN	CAPT	VA 34TH BN CAV (WITCHER'S NIGHTHAWKS), CO B
WILSON, JOSEPH RUGGLES MD	ASST SURG	CSA - AAS
WILSON, MARTIN VAN BUREN	3LT	TN 1ST BN CAV (MCNAIRY'S), CO E
WILSON, NAPOLEAN BONAPARTE	LT	MS 7TH INF, CO K

WILSON, SAMUEL BOONE	CAPT	TN 45TH INF, CO A
WILSON, STEPHEN ALFRED	CAPT	GA 47TH INF, CO I
WILSON, WILLIAM A	2LT	NC 27TH INF, CO F
WILSON, WILLIAM HAMPTON	CAPT	MS 2ND INF, CO D
WILSON, WILLIAM PEYTON REV	CHAPLAIN	AR 16TH INF, CO I
WILSON, WILLIAM THOMAS	2LT	VA CAPT DONALD'S LIGHT ARTY
WIMBERLEY, JOHN THOMAS	CAPT	GA 29TH CAV BN, CO B
WIMBERLY, WILLIAM H	1LT	TN 43RD INF, CO A
WIMER, JOHN M	LT COL	MO 4TH CAV (BURBRIDGE'S), CO D
WINDERS, MARSHALL B	CAPT	NC 26TH MILITIA (DUPLIN COUNTY)
WINFREE, CHRISTOPHER VALENTINE	CAPT	VA 11TH INF, CO E
WINGARD, JOB FRANKLIN	2LT	SC 14TH BN CAV, CO C
WINGO, ROBERT SQUIRE	1LT	VA 37TH BN CAV, CO K
WINGO, WILLIAM ANDERSON	2LT	TX 9TH CAV, CO B
WINHAM, EDWARD L	1LT	TN 2ND INF, CO C
WINKLER, PEYTON HERBERT	2LT	TN 30TH INF, CO G
WINN, ABIAL	CAPT	GA 1ST BN CAV, WINN'S CO
WINN, WALTER E	CAPT	CSA
WINSTON, BURTON H	2LT	NC 55TH INF, CO I
WINSTON, FRANK VELLIUS	CAPT	VA 13TH INF, CO D
WINSTON, JAMES EDWARD	CAPT	TX BAIRD'S CAV, CO F
WINSTON, WILLIAM BENJAMIN	1LT	TN 7TH CAV (DUCKWORTH'S), CO C
WINTER, JOHN	2LT	GA 48TH INF, CO I
WINTER, THOMAS H	1LT	SC 2ND CAV, CO D
WINTERS, JAMES WASHINGTON JR	ENROLLING OFFICER	TX 29TH BDE STATE MILITIA
WIRZ, HEINRICH (HENRY) HARTMANN	CAPT	CSA - COMMANDANT CAMP SUMTER PRISON ANDERSONVILLE - AG
WISE, HENRY ALEXANDER	BRIG GEN	ANV WISE LEGION
WISE, LAWRENCE W	3LT	SC 7TH INF, CO F
WISE, WILLIAM FRANKLIN	1LT	NC 88TH MILITIA, CO H (LINCOLN COUNTY)
WISEMAN, JOHN N	2LT	VA 36TH INF, CO F
WISEMAN, MARTIN DAVENPORT	CAPT	NC 58TH INF, CO A
WISEMAN, W	1LT	KY 11TH CAV, CO D
WISEMAN, WILLIAM H	1LT	NC 58TH INF, CO A
WISEMAN, WILLIAM HENDERSON	CAPT	TN 43RD INF, CO G
WISHART, WELLINGTON	2LT	NC 46TH INF, CO A
WITCHER, VINCENT ADDISON	LT COL	VA 34TH BN CAV (WITCHER'S NIGHTHAWKS), F&S
WITCHER, WILLIAM JAMES	CAPT	AR 34TH INF, CO D
WITHERS, EMILE QUARLES	2LT	MS 3RD CAV, CO E
WITHERS, JOHN MCCLELLAN	3LT	TN 6TH INF, CO G
WITHERSPOON, JAMES F	1LT	KY 5TH CAV, CO H
WITHERSPOON, MILES RANKIN	2LT	NC 89TH MILITIA, CO A (CATAWBA COUNTY)
WITT, ASA A	COL	VA 49TH INF
WITT, HORACE HITCHCOCK	MAJ	GA 7TH INF, CO B
WITT, WADE HAMPTON	CAPT	TX 18TH CAV, CO B
WITTEN, WILLIAM HENRY HARRISON	2LT	VA 16TH CAV, CO F
WITTY, WILLIAM HERBERT	CAPT	MS 30TH INF, CO C
WOFFORD, JEREMIAH	LT	SC 9TH RESERVES, CO I
WOFFORD, JOSEPH LEWELLYN MD	MAJ	SC 13TH INF, CO E
WOFFORD, WILLIAM TATUM	BRIG GEN	GA 18TH INF
WOLFE, CALVIN COLUMBUS	CAPT	AR 1ST CAV (MONROE'S), CO L
WOLFE, JAMES D	1LT	SC HOLCOMBE'S LEGION BN CAV, CO B

WOLFE, UDOLPHO	QM	TX 6TH INF, CO F&S
WOLFF, FRANCIS A	CAPT	MS 3RD BN INF, CO F
WOLTZ, FERDINAND LEWIS	2LT	VA LOCAL DEFENSE, BURKS' REGT
WOMACK, JAMES T	CAPT	TN 16TH INF, CO E
WOMBLE, JAMES M	1LT	AL 10TH CAV, CO L
WOOD, EASON BLUE	CAPT	AL 34TH INF, CO B
WOOD, JAMES H	COL	NC 4TH INF, CO B
WOOD, JOEL GILMORE	CAPT	AR 8TH BN INF, CO E
WOOD, JOHN TAYLOR	CAPT/COL	CSN/CSA - ADC
WOOD, LAWRENCE B	CAPT	TX 28TH CAV (RANDAL'S), CO M
WOOD, MIRABEAU DALLAS	2LT	FL 6TH INF, CO K
WOOD, MOSES	2LT	SC 15TH INF, CO F
WOOD, STERLING ALEXANDER MARTIN	BRIG GEN	AL 7TH INF
WOOD, THOMAS FANNING MD	ASST SURG	NC 3RD INF, F&S
WOOD, WILLIAM MORISON	CADET	VMI
WOOD, WILLIAM NATHANIEL	2LT	VA 19TH INF, CO A
WOOD, WILLIAM	1LT	AL 24TH INF, CO K
WOODARD, THOMAS WILLIAM	MAJ	SC 6TH INF, F&S
WOODBURN, JOHN D	ENSIGN	NC 26TH INF, CO K
WOODHOUSE, VIRGINIUS GUSTAVIUS MD	SURG	MS 24TH INF, F&S
WOODRUFF, ANDREW BARRY	CAPT	SC HOLCOMBE LEGION INF, CO E
WOODRUM, RICHARD	MAJ	VA 26TH INF BN, F&S
WOODRUM, WILLIAM T JR	BVT 2LT	VA HERBIG'S INF, LYNEMAN'S CO
WOODS, PETER CAVANAUGH	COL	TX 36TH CAV, CO AFS
WOODS, R H	CAPT	GA 53RD INF, CO G
WOODS, SAMUEL ROBERT	MAJ	MO STATE GUARD, 6TH DIV, 1ST CAV
WOODWARD, BENJAMIN WEBB	3LT	NC 64TH INF, CO A
WOODWARD, JOSEPH C	1LT	AL 40TH INF, CO E
WOOLFOLK, JOHN W	1LT	VA 6TH CAV, CO I,G
WOOLFOLK, JOHN WASHINGTON	MAJ	GA 55TH MILITIA (HOUSTON COUNTY)
WOOLFOLK, RICHARD OSCAR	1LT	MO 2ND INF, CO C
WOOTEN, EDWARD W	2LT	NC 3RD ARTY, CO K
WOOTEN, JOHN BARCLIFF	1LT	NC 67TH INF, CO H
WOOTEN, THOMAS DUDLEY MD	SURG/MAJ	CSA - CHIEF SURGEON
WOOTEN, THOMAS JONES	MAJ	NC 18TH INF, CO K
WOOTERS, JOHN HENRY	CAPT	TX 1ST INF, CO I
WORD, JOHN COLLINS MD	ASST SURG	TN 7TH CAV (DUCKWORTH'S), CO A
WORD, JOHN COLLINS MD	ASST SURG	TN 7TH CAV (DUCKWORTH'S), CO A
WORK, PHILLIP ALEXANDER	LT COL	TX 1ST INF, F&S
WORKMAN, LEANDER W	2LT	VA 34TH BN CAV (WITCHER'S NIGHTHAWKS), CO A
WORKMAN, WILLIAM H R	2LT	SC 7TH INF, CO B
WORLEY, AMBROSE	JR 2LT	GA 23RD INF, CO E
WORLEY, THOMAS F	3LT	NC 27TH INF, CO D
WORSHAM, ROBERT D	LT	GA 12TH INF (DAVIS RIFLES), CO C
WORSHAM, THOMAS R	CAPT	KY 5TH MTD INF, CO E
WORTHAM, R BEVERLY	SR 2LT	VA HORSE ARTY, JACKSON'S CO
WORTHINGTON, JAMES	1LT	TN 16TH INF, CO I
WORTHINGTON, SAMUEL HENRY	2LT	FL 9TH INF, CO A
WOTRING, JOHN H	2LT	VA 33RD INF, CO D
WRIGHT, AMBROSE RANSOM	MAJ GEN	ANV
WRIGHT, ANDREW W	2LT	VA 26TH INF, CO A
WRIGHT, AUGUSTUS ROMALDUS	COL	GA 38TH INF

WRIGHT, GEORGE M	ADJ	AR WRIGHT'S CAV, F&S
WRIGHT, JAMES C	CAPT	AR 34TH INF, CO E
WRIGHT, JAMES TYRIE	CAPT	MO 11TH CAV, CO C
WRIGHT, LEROY CLAY	1LT	TX BENAVIDES CAV
WRIGHT, MARCUS JOSEPH	BRIG GEN	TN 108TH MILITIA
WRIGHT, ORREN B	2LT	TN ALLISON'S SQUADRON CAV, CO C
WRIGHT, SAMUEL CARSON	CAPT	NC 60TH INF, CO E
WRIGHT, THOMAS COOPER	CAPT	TX MCCORD'S FRONTIER CAV, CO I
WRIGHT, WILLIAM RANKIN	CAPT	MO 3RD BN CAV, CO E
WRIGHT, WILLIAM W	CAPT	NC 28TH INF, CO H
WYANT, JAMES CHARLES	CAPT	VA 56TH INF, CO H
WYATT, JOSEPH BENJAMIN	JR 2LT	FL 2ND INF, CO F
WYATT, WILLIAM JOSEPH	SR 2LT	TX 36TH CAV, CO A
WYMAN, BENJAMIN F	CAPT	SC 11TH INF, CO F
WYNN, OBADIAH	CAPT	GA 7TH INF (COWETA GUARDS), CO A
WYNN, THOMAS J	2LT	VA 34TH BN CAV (WITCHER'S NIGHTHAWKS), CO C
WYNN, WILLIAM T	CAPT	VA 59TH INF, CO B
WYNNE, THOMAS ELIJAH	MAJ	GA 24TH INF, F&S
YANCEY, DALTON HUGER	CAPT	AL 7TH CAV, CO K
YANCEY, JAMES M	1LT	AL 11TH CAV, CO I,K
YANCEY, JOSEPH S	1LT	VA 14TH INF, CO G
YANCEY, THOMAS B	2LT	AR 1ST INF, CO B
YANDLE, MILAS M	2LT	NC 35TH INF, CO F
YARBROUGH, FRANKLIN	1LT	AL 60TH INF, CO K
YARBROUGH, JAMES GUINN	2LT	AL 34TH INF, CO A
YARD, NAHOR B	COL	TX 1ST INF
YARNALL, MORDECAI	1LT	VA 27TH INF, CO G
YATES, ROBERT ELLIOTT VALENTINE	CAPT	MS 41ST INF, CO D
YEATMAN, ALBERT ALLMAND	CAPT	VA 11TH INF, CO K
YEATMAN, HENRY C	LT COL	AOT - ADC IN GEN POLK'S CORPS AOT
YEATTS, JOHN RICHARD	CAPT	VA 46TH INF, CO C
YELVERTON, WYATT E	1LT	NC 2ND INF, CO D
YERGER, WILLIAM GWIN	2LT	MS 18TH INF, CO K
YONGE, CHANDLER COX	MAJ	CSA - FL STATE CONTROLLING QM
YOPP, THOMAS MCCALL	CAPT	GA 14TH INF, CO H
YORK, LARKIN BLAKE	2LT	GA FLOYD LEGION (STATE GUARDS), CO G
YORK, WILLIAM THOMAS	CAPT	GA 1ST CAV, F&S
YOST, JOHN IV	CAPT	VA 34TH BN CAV (WITCHER'S NIGHTHAWKS), CO E
YOUMANS, JAMES PEEPLES	1LT	SC 3RD CAV, CO E
YOUNG, ALEXANDER FRANKLIN	2LT	SC 14TH INF, CO G
YOUNG, HENRY EDWARD	MAJ	CSA - AAG
YOUNG, HENRY	2LT	TX 30TH CAV, CO H
YOUNG, JAMES BENNETT	LT	AL 35TH INF, CO I
YOUNG, JAMES H	CAPT	AL 4TH INF (CONEUCH GUARDS), CO K
YOUNG, JAMES LOUIS	1LT	MO 15TH CAV, CO I
YOUNG, JAMES MADISON	1LT	CSA 1ST CAV, CO E
YOUNG, JOHN ALBERT	LT COL	NC 4TH INF
YOUNG, JOHN MADISON	1LT	TN 25TH INF, CO F
YOUNG, JOHN SIMPSON	1LT	MS 1ST L ARTY, CO L
YOUNG, JOHN W	CAPT	VA 20TH CAV, CO E
YOUNG, L GEORGE	2LT	GA 49TH INF, CO F
YOUNG, LOT DUDLEY	1LT	KY 4TH MTD INF, CO H

MILITARY ORDER OF THE STARS AND BARS

YOUNG, PIERCE MANNING BUTLER	MAJ GEN	SC INF (HAMPTON'S LEGION)
YOUNG, ROBERT ALLEN	1LT	TN 16TH INF, CO K
YOUNG, THOMAS ERSKIN	CAPT	MS 43RD INF, CO I
YOUNG, W R	1LT	NC 32ND INF, CO L
YOUNG, WILLIAM HENRY	2LT	AR 2ND CAV, CO G
YOUNGBLOOD, JOHN WILLIAM	CAPT	CSA SIGNAL CORPS
ZABLE, DAVID	LT COL	LA 14TH INF, F&S
ZIGLAR, COLEMAN BARNES	1LT	NC 21ST INF, CO K
ZIMMERMAN, GEORGE RUFUS	CAPT	MO 4TH INF, CO B
ZIMMERMANN, J F	2LT	LA 4TH MILITIA EUROPEAN BDE, CO D
ZOLLICOFFER, FELIX KIRK	BRIG GEN	GA 3RD MILITIA BRIGADE